WHO NEED

Does Greek matter? To whom and why? This interdisciplinary study focuses on moments when passionate conflicts about Greek and Greekness have erupted in both the modern and the ancient worlds. It looks at the Renaissance, when men were burned at the stake over biblical Greek, at violent Victorian rows over national culture and the schooling of a country, at the shocking performances of modernist opera – and it also examines the ancient world and its ideas of what it means to be Greek, especially in the first and second centuries CE. The book sheds fresh light on how the ancient and modern worlds interrelate, and how fantasies and deals, struggles and conflicts have come together under the name of Greece. As a contribution to theatre studies, Renaissance and Victorian cultural history, and to the understanding of ancient writing, this book takes reception studies in an exciting new direction.

SIMON GOLDHILL is Reader in Greek Literature and Culture at the University of Cambridge and a Fellow of King's College. He has also held Visiting Professorships at Stanford University and the University of Michigan. He is the author of numerous books, including *Reading Greek Tragedy* (1986), *The Poet's Voice* (1991), *Aeschylus: The Oresteia* (1992) and *Foucault's Virginity* (1995), and has most recently edited *Being Greek Under Rome: Cultural Identity in the Second Sophistic* (2001).

WHO NEEDS GREEK?

Contests in the Cultural History of Hellenism

SIMON GOLDHILL

Reader in Greek Literature and Culture, University of Cambridge and Fellow of King's College

CAMBRIDGE
UNIVERSITY PRESS

PUBLISHED BY THE PRESS SYNDICATE OF THE UNIVERSITY OF CAMBRIDGE
The Pitt Building, Trumpington Street, Cambridge, United Kingdom

CAMBRIDGE UNIVERSITY PRESS
The Edinburgh Building, Cambridge CB2 2RU, UK
40 West 20th Street, New York, NY 10011-4211, USA
477 Williamstown Road, Port Melbourne, VIC 3207, Australia
Ruiz de Alarcón 13, 28014 Madrid, Spain
Dock House, The Waterfront, Cape Town 8001, South Africa

http://www.cambridge.org

First published 2002

Printed in the United Kingdom at the University Press, Cambridge

Typeface Baskerville Monotype 11 /12.5 pt.   *System* LaTeX 2ε [TB]

A catalogue record for this book is available from the British Library

Library of Congress Cataloguing in Publication data
Goldhill, Simon.
Who needs Greek? Contests in the cultural history of Hellenism / Simon Goldhill.
p.   cm.
Includes bibliographical references and index.
ISBN 0 521 81228 3 (hardback) – ISBN 0 521 01176 0 (paperback)
1. Greek language – Study and teaching – History.   2. Civilization, Modern – Greek
influences.   3. Greece – Civilization.   4. Hellenism.   I. Title.
PA231 .G65 2002
303.48′24038 – dc21
2002043593

ISBN 0 521 81228 3 hardback
ISBN 0 521 01176 0 paperback

Contents

Illustrations

Abbreviations

CPW   *Matthew Arnold. Collected Prose Works*, ed. R. Super, 12 vols., Ann Arbor

CWW   *Richard Wagner's Prose Works*, trans. W. Ellis, 8 vols., London (1892–9)

CWE   *Collected Works of Erasmus*, Toronto (1976–)

CWM   *Yale Edition of the Complete Works of St Thomas More*, New Haven (1963–)

EE   *Erasmi Epistolae*, ed. P. S. Allen, 12 vols., Oxford (1906–58)

OL   *Orbis Litterarum*

GQ   *German Quarterly*

MLR   *Modern Language Review*

DVLG   *Deutsche Vierteljahrschrift für Literaturwissenschaft und Geistesgeschichte*

All other abbreviations as in *L'Année philologique*

Introduction: shaking the foundations

During the siege of Jerusalem in 65 BCE, the Jews inside the walls let down baskets with money in them to buy animals, so that they could complete the regular Passover sacrifices at the Temple. 'An old man, learned in Greek wisdom, spoke with the besiegers in Greek: "As long as they continue the Temple service, they will never surrender." When the next basket came, the money was taken, but a pig was put in it. Half way up, the pig's claws dug into the wall, and the whole land of Israel shook for 400 parasangs about. "Cursed be a man who rears pigs; cursed be a man who teaches his son Greek wisdom"', cry the Jews.[1]

What the pig is to Jewish ritual, it would seem, Greek wisdom is to intellectual and social life.

It is tempting to let this story stand as a kind of epigraph to the following chapters. But such a knowing silence would play false to the tradition of the Talmud, which never fails to add commentary to commentary (to commentary), and it would also run counter to my own nature as a scholar and teacher (which may be lured by the poetical but can't resist the exegetical). Resonances need sounding out . . . Indeed, the Talmudic passage continues with a question (of course). Is speaking Greek the same thing as learning Greek wisdom? Not necessarily. And what of Rabbi Gamaliel, did not his school have 500 pupils learning Talmud and 500 pupils learning Greek wisdom? But that was 'because they had close associations with the government'. And there, pregnantly, the discussion ends. The man who teaches Greek wisdom is cursed, yet Rabbi Gamaliel can teach it parallel to the Bible itself, because of the requirements of dealing with the authorities. The slide from aggressive cursing to necessary accommodation tellingly traces the lures and threats of Hellenization in the culture wars of ancient Palestine.

[1] Babylonian Talmud: *Sotah* 49b.

I

What this Talmudic passage knows is that Greek is *foundational*. Greek wisdom, learning Greek, means an absorption not only of a linguistic resource but also of a cultural paradigm. The threat of Greek is that it will inveigle its way into your culture, it will destroy the foundations, an enemy within that will bring the walls tumbling down. This image of the *danger* of Greek to a cultural identity will be central to this volume: in my story too, Greek books lead to death and murder, to cultural crisis, to social, religious and intellectual mayhem.

The narrative context of the Talmudic anecdote is especially pointed therefore. The story is told in a sequence of stories leading up to the destruction of the Temple, that is, the cataclysmic loss of the defining centre of Jewish ritual practice. Rabbinic Judaism, with its insistence on the centrality of Talmudic and Biblical study, constitutes the forced redirection of Judaism, with all the inevitable conflicts, confusions and and changing claims of cultural affiliation that follow such an upheaval, such a political disenfranchisement. This story, then, is not only part of an ideologically laden, retrospective construction of that history, but it is also *performative*. It is designed to have an effect in a social and polemical context. Its telling is an *act* of boundary reinforcement. There is in the Talmud a fiercely explicit (and fearful) set of injunctions about the risks of imitating dominant Greek and Roman cultures, injunctions that build on the Pentateuch's proclamations of separateness, chosenness, and holiness to enforce a social and intellectual exclusion from the norms and practices of Empire. Yet this is coupled with a more insidious invasion of the text of the Talmud by Greek and Roman words, by Greek and Roman ways of thought, and by a recognition of the institutional structures of the Empire, and by a life in the architecture of Empire. The tension between the desire for integrity and the necessity of engagement produces a string of fascinating stories, which struggle, like this Talmudic passage does, to control the conflicting impulses of cultural negotiation, often through the uneasy projection of an image of secure exclusiveness.[2]

The performative value of this story is highlighted sharply by a very different account of the event by the historian Josephus, who had been a general of the Jews, but who, as an honoured hostage and finally representative of the Roman conquerors, wrote a history of the war first in Aramaic and then in Greek (a political and cultural position that makes *his* version far from transparent). Josephus explains that the besieged in Jerusalem offered large amounts of money to their fellow countrymen

---

[2] For discussion and bibliography, see Schwartz (2001a) and generally Schwartz (2001b).

outside the walls for the animals for the Passover sacrifices. The Jews outside agreed, but then reneged, merely stealing the money as it came down in the baskets. God, comments the historian, punished their breach of trust and their impiety with an instant crop failure. The story here is one of religious corruption and mistrust between Jews during a civil war, and Josephus happily calculates that the impious made no profit because of the increased price of wheat. The pig and the Greek (and all the politics of accommodation with authority) *structure* the Rabbis' tale, but have no place in Josephus.[3]

What interests me most in the Talmudic story, however – and what makes it an excellent introduction to this book – is the strange passions of its extreme formulation: a world shaken by a pig's foot. The end of the story is the violent destruction of a community (with all the freight of such an image for ancient and modern Jews), but the rhetoric of the story focuses on the necessity of fearing the apparently small causes of destruction. It demands from you not an epic battle (no Iliadic siege, no Vergilian sack) but rather a heroic *caring*: a caring about what you read and study. The displacement of military violence onto the power of Greek words aims to make cultural resistance a matter of life and death.

Who Needs Greek? is about such climaxes of passionate caring about Greek – it is about critical moments when cultural identity has become inextricably linked with an idea of Greek and Greek becomes a bitterly contested area of social and intellectual activity; it is about highly charged scenes where obsession, fantasy and projection lead to wild commitments and to bizarre declarations which now seem barely comprehensible. By '[the idea of] Greek' I mean not only the Greek language, though that is often the key battleground, but the whole ideological and symbolic value of Greek culture – Greekness itself. The slippage between an ideal image of a past society and the language in which its literature is enshrined is constantly at work in the debates I will be tracing.

It should be clear from the outset, then, that this is not a history of classical scholarship (for all that classical scholarship has its fair share of the obsessive, wild and the bizarre). Nor is it a history of the 'reception' of Greek texts in the West – there are no lists here of who read what or of the ancient sources of modern literature. Nor is it a history of education, nor a plea for a place for Greek in the modern curriculum. (It will end with some remarks about the consequences of forgetting

[3] *Jewish Antiquities* XIV 25–8.

about Greek, but these comments will not be framed explicitly in terms of educational policy.) The question of the title will not be answered with a conservative nostalgia for a lost world when Classics formed the basis of all education ('we all need Greek'); nor with the foolish blinkers of the contemporary presentism that makes a barely considered idea of 'relevance' the criterion of educational and cultural value ('no one needs Greek').

The following chapters put together authors and histories that do not usually appear between the same covers and consequently, more than many books, this volume needs to explain the structure of its argument with some care and to justify both its selectiveness and its narrative strategy. Here is how the chapters unfold. I begin with the story of the *resistance* to Greek in the Renaissance. The triumph of classical learning is, of course, a defining narrative of the move out of medieval darkness into the splendour of modern Europe (though medieval scholars don't usually put it in those terms), and makes an obvious point of departure: the Renaissance is when the need for Greek is (re)discovered in the West. Less familiar, however, is the fierce and persistent opposition to Greek study, epitomized by the extraordinary claim of John Standish who told his congregation in London in around 1520 that 'Learning Greek is Heresy' – in a period, note, where 'heresy' not merely had its full religious import, but also constituted a charge which could lead to trial and death. How could a Christian religious leader – Standish was a Doctor of Divinity and an authority in the Church – declare that to learn the language in which the Gospels were written was such an act of religious error that it deserved the death penalty? What made Oxford men break up Greek classes? What led a scholar to be burnt at the stake for mistranslating two words of Plato?

My first chapter attempts to answer these questions by exploring the polemics about studying Greek that surrounded the central intellectual figure of this turbulent period of reform, Desiderius Erasmus of Rotterdam. Erasmus was a tireless promoter of Greek as the route to a true understanding of early Christianity (as well as the ancient Greek world itself), but his work was perceived as an outrageous challenge to the authority of the established Church, and particularly to the authority of the Latin Bible, the so-called Vulgate. His hugely influential new educational methods threatened vested institutional interests. His delight in the humour and sarcastic wit which he found in ancient texts, disturbed the self-image of the dignitaries of the Church. The resistance to Greek – to Erasmus' Greek – became a heady conflict through the bloody development of the Reformation, where politics, theology, and cultural and educational control overlapped, often with great intellectual and physical violence. Promoting and resisting Greek was fully and dramatically a mainstay in the exercise of power in society. A burning issue . . .

The starting point of this volume is with Erasmus not merely to correct the way in which the Renaissance is so often described as the re-discovery of Greek *without* taking account of the resistance to the new learning. Rather and above all, my concern is with what such resistance indicates. The very widest concerns of politics and power, religion and the soul are at stake in the battle over knowing Greek. It is a moment that fully embodies 'a passionate caring' about Greek – a life-and-death matter, both in this world and the next.

One of Erasmus' favourite writers was the satirist, Lucian, who wrote in Greek in the second century CE. Erasmus first came to prominence in Europe through the translations of Lucian he made with Sir Thomas More (and which remained bestsellers for many years). Erasmus' most celebrated and most polemical work is *Praise of Folly*, a satirical text that was explicitly understood – loved and reviled – as 'Lucianic'. Erasmus made Lucian central to new and trendy Greek studies. Yet – or perhaps because of this – the Catholic Church placed Lucian on the Index of banned books in the sixteenth century. Martin Luther detested and reviled him too. Lucian was an author who acted as a lightning-rod for the controversies of the Reformation. Lucian summed up the value of Greek for Erasmus: yet Lucian was a Syrian. He made his way in the Roman Empire as a Greek-speaking orator. This exemplary Greek had to *learn* how to be Greek. My second chapter, 'Becoming Greek, with Lucian' looks first (and at greatest length) at how Lucian represents himself as a learned Greek (in both senses of 'learned'). How can you become (culturally, educationally, linguistically) Greek? Lucian writes extensively and very funnily about the signs of Greek culture, and he satirizes with brilliant wit the desire to possess culture and to fit in. Lucian shows how even in the ancient world there is a recognition that 'Greekness' is a constructed quality, crossed by fantasy, projection and desire. Being Greek is a real *performance*.

Towards the end of the nineteenth century, however, Lucian's reputation underwent an extraordinary change. Particularly in Germany, and particularly as German nationalism burgeoned, Lucian became viewed as the paradigm of a false, imitative, unreliable Greekness. The reasons for this are complex but necessarily involve the wholesale re-evaluation of the Greek writing of the Roman Empire (the so-called Second Sophistic). The writers of the Second Sophistic in the second century CE found their inspiration, their literary models, their very language in the works of classical Athens of the fifth and fourth centuries BCE: the Second Sophistic is often termed a 'revival' of (ancient) Greek learning. Romanticism's privileging of originality, sincerity, authenticity and emotional grandeur consequently found it easy to dismiss Second Sophistic prose as derivative, insincere, and, simply, second-rate. Lucian's love of role-playing, sarcasm, irony and masks was declared to be not merely the sign and symptom of a thorough-going cultural degeneracy (second-hand culture), but also and more specifically, a *racially* marked characteristic. Lucian became the exemplar not of Greekness (as he had been for Erasmus: clarity, purity, intelligence) but of the East, and, worse, of 'mixed race' origins (corruption, insincerity, flattery). By 1941, he could be dismissed (quite falsely and quite remarkably) as 'the Jew'. 'Greekness', then, is what Lucian sets at stake and in play – and the modern era has made his Greekness part of religious conflict and of a murderous nationalist politics. In this way, Lucian epitomizes two of the major concerns of this book; first, how learning Greek and studying the Greek past play an integral part in fashioning a cultural identity – even in the ancient world; second, how the figures of the Greek past undergo drastic and far-reaching re-evaluation – and how this re-evaluation in turn plays an integral role in readers' self-fashioning. Lucian, in particular, demonstrates a specific and significant shift in the comprehension of ancient Greece between the Renaissance and the eighteenth century, on the one hand, and the post-Enlightenment world of late nineteenth-century society, on the other – culminating finally in the self-consciously deconstructive modernism of the twentieth century. Lucian is, in short, a yardstick for the construction of cultural tradition.

The third chapter, 'Blood from the shadows: Strauss' disgusting, degenerate *Elektra*', goes to the heart of this modernist engagement with things Greek, and specifically with the very acme of classicism, Sophocles. This chapter focuses on the first performance of Strauss' opera *Elektra* in London in 1910, which caused a storm of controversy. The *Elektra* is chosen not just because of the huge importance of its cultural impact, but in particular because it so vividly encapsulates a modernist assault on Victorian classicism. It epitomizes the rupture between the nineteenth-century ideological appropriations of classical Greece and the deliberately shocking, violent reworkings of modernism. In a debate riven with the new concerns of nationalism, psychoanalysis and anthropology, the responses to this opera show the full force of the crisis in modern Hellenism (in which Lucian too was being rethought). This is a case where Greek culture and its ideals, far more than the Greek language, are being set at stake. The libretto was by Hugo von Hofmannsthal from his own play, which had been an immense scandal and success in German-speaking theatres a few years earlier. Hofmannsthal's modernist poetics and Strauss' modernist music took the most 'pious' of classical authors and offered a version full of blood and violence and sexual perversion. The responses to this shocking play in Germany and to the horrifying opera in England, Germany and America reveal the deep investment of different national cultures in ideals of Greek value. Fierce debates about Greekness rapidly turned into vitriolic arguments about Germanness and Englishness. Again, what a struggle about Greekness encapsulates is the passionate commitments of political and cultural self-definition. Dress, music, poetry, education, party politics, governmental agendas, set-design, all become part of a growing war of national identity. Greek theatre, in the years leading up to the first world war, became thus (as Aeschylus might put it), 'a contest about everything'.

In the nineteenth century, however, for all the privilege of Greek in Victorian intellectual self-representations, and for all that 'Victorian Greece' offered a looming target for Hofmannsthal's modernism, the place of Greece in Victorian cultural life and educational institutions was itself deeply contested. Where the third chapter treats a production whose circumstances reveal the intellectual and socio-political turmoil in which the re-evaluation of Lucian took place, the fourth and longest chapter, 'Who knows Greek?', takes a step back from 1910 to consider one fundamental and constitutive element of the conflict over Greek theatre, namely, the question of what it means to say in the nineteenth century 'I know Greek', and how this cues a long-running argument about what the need for Greek is. This chapter looks at the construction of the Victorian Hellenism against which Hofmannsthal was rebelling – and finds a far more complex and contested picture than modernism's dismissiveness would lead us to believe. I start from the Romantic Hellenism of the early years of the century (and the fight for Greek independence), and trace an argument that brews throughout the century about the place of Greek in the education system and what the *point* of knowing Greek might be. This is never merely a question of linguistic competence or training. Rather a host of political, cultural and personal politics making 'knowing Greek' a very complex idea indeed, as it is debated in parliament, in the lecture halls of America, in the common-rooms of

Cambridge colleges. The increasing professionalization of the study of classics, coupled with increasing attacks on the validity of studying Greek from the disciplines of science and English, constantly make the discussion of Greek a heated row about the most general values and direction of society. Between leading politicians, major poets, cutting-edge academics, intellectual superstars, 'the Greek question' becomes a national and international debate.

In particular, in the different sections of the chapter, I look at three different moments in time and three different types of argument about knowing Greek. First, with the scandalous prose of Thomas De Quincey and the classicizing verse of Keats, I look at the literary re-workings of knowing Greek in the first quarter of the century. Second, through the politician Robert Lowe and the writer and educationalist, Matthew Arnold, I explore the political and educational arguments about the role of Greek in the curriculum and in culture, from the middle of the century on in England and America. Third, from the last part of the century, I investigate arguments within academia about knowing Greek, especially through a row between two leading Cambridge dons, Walter Headlam and A. W. Verrall. It is a chapter that travels from Shelley emoting in front of the newly displayed Elgin Marbles to Headlam, self-marginalized and cocooned in his rooms in Cambridge – a catalogue of men, ring-fencing the privilege of Greek from female eyes. The story of 'knowing Greek' is also the story of the building of scholarly and institutional walls around Greek knowledge.

What, then, is the *value* of Greek culture? This general question, which underlies so many of the debates of the fourth chapter, takes on a further specific form in the fifth and final chapter, where my primary subject is Plutarch, an author who for many centuries epitomized the value of classical learning. Plutarch, who lived in the first century, in the first years of the dominance of Greece by the Roman Empire, is himself in the business of trying to construct a new sense of Greekness, a new model of how to be Greek, when the old ways of military and political heroism are no longer available. Plutarch is part of an ongoing re-invention of Greekness. Both in his lives of the military and political heroes of the past and in his encyclopedic collection of treatises on subject after subject, from science to religion to history, he brings the whole world under the gaze and appropriative comprehension of Greek wisdom. Everything is subject to the knowing Greek's understanding, and the knowing Greek expresses his cultural identity in and through such activity. What's more, as with Lucian, the evaluation of Plutarch underwent a sea-change in the later nineteenth century. Once regarded as the exemplary repository of ancient knowledge (on the one hand) and the inspiration of revolution (on the other), Plutarch becomes the touchstone of the outdated and the boring, the incoherent and unimportant collector of other peoples' knowledge. He becomes dismissed by academics and increasingly ignored by readers. What has been lost in forgetting Plutarch's value? More than any other writer from the ancient world, Plutarch's status has veered from one of the greats of culture to an almost wholly silenced figure. My interest is not just in the construction of Greekness in Plutarch, nor just in the different values placed on Plutarch in the modern period, but rather on the process itself of what I shall call 'cultural forgetting'. What are the forces that led Plutarch to fall so far so suddenly in the cultural expectations of the West? How did we forget Plutarch?

Each chapter of the book, then, treats a critical, cultural *conflict* about Greek and Greekness: opposition to learning Greek, hostility to representations of Greek, drastic redrafting of the value of a previously privileged idea of Greek. Each of these conflicts is passionate because it concerns the construction of a cultural (religious, national, intellectual) identity. This in itself provides one thematic continuity for the volume. The question 'Who Needs Greek?' announces the arena of these battles.

That is the basic story line, then. It should be immediately obvious that that the book makes no attempt to give an exhaustive treatment of the passion for Greek even in nineteenth-century England (let alone the modern West): that would be an impossibly huge undertaking. The cases that my argument focuses on are *examples*, examples which seem to me to be especially important and particularly telling. I am well aware that other exciting areas have been (temporarily) silenced. A full history of the passionate battles over Greek(ness) would certainly have to include the emancipation of modern Greece (with its fights over *katherevousa* and *dimotiki*, formal, 'pure' Greek, and 'the people's Greek'), seventeenth-century political theory (Hobbes' Thucydides, the rows over 'belles lettres' and so forth), and eighteenth-century political revolutions (leading into Romantic Hellenism and the emancipation of Greece). And more besides. But examples do not have to be arbitrary. In offering my account, the selection of material is based on three criteria. First, each of these battles represents a major juncture in cultural history – events whose fall-out is extensive and long-lasting, involving actors of outstanding importance in Western culture, and writings whose impact is still being felt. They each matter, and can be shown to have mattered widely. Yet each chapter is also concerned with cultural re-evaluation and with cultural memory and forgetting. Each chapter is about how what matters in Greekness changes and can be forgotten. What makes an event an event? What gives it its significance and impact? How does the constant reworking of the past inform the present? Despite the historical importance of each of the areas I treat, none, I think, is (yet) 'fashionable' in current cultural history. Contemporary forgetting of these intense conflicts over Greek partly motivates my project to recover them – and is in itself a telling example of the historical processes I am discussing. Like so many stories, this is also a tale of how passion flares and fades – and what this means for cultural history.

Second, this selection of subjects brings into play a considerable range of materials and disciplines from many different levels and areas of cultural production: theology and newspaper reports, opera and cartoons, music and politicians' speeches, painting and educational polemics, photographs and novels, biography and poetry, drama and dinner-table talk, clothes and racist theory . . . Such an interdisciplinary approach is absolutely necessary if the question 'what makes an event an event?' is to be answered with any depth. There is a polemical agenda here too. I want to move critical discussion away from too exclusive a focus on texts and on tracing 'literary influence' and 'literary sources' towards considering what texts (images, music) *do* in society. Students of 'the classical tradition' all too often ignore how an engagement with Greek *matters* (socially, politically, intellectually). This is a story not just of books and readers, but of how cultural battles are fought out.

This leads to my third point. Each of these battles over Greek also leads into some of the most pressing and complex general problems of understanding cultural identity. The first chapter on Erasmus must be seen within the Reformation's murderous arguments about the word of God and the truth of the past. Lucian's self-presentation speaks to a fascination with the construction of the self in society and how the signs of culture function. Strauss' opera raises the question of how theatrical performance is framed by a national culture (and a culture of nationalism). The politicians who argue about Greek are explicitly debating the role of education and models of social good in the modern nation state. The criticism of Plutarch sets at stake the value of knowledge and of heroic action. What is more, in each case the idea of 'Greece' is formulated specifically through a sense of another culture: in Lucian's case, 'Greece' is triangulated via Syria and Rome; in Plutarch's via Rome and, to a lesser degree, Egypt; for Erasmus, Greece is conceptualized in relation to Christendom, or the New Jerusalem; for Strauss and Hofmannsthal, it is Germany and Austria; and for the scholars and politicians of chapter four, it is England and Germany that is at stake. Each chapter's subject has been chosen precisely because it is *paradigmatic* of the different ways that caring about Greek opens into the widest social and political concerns.

It should also be obvious from my summary of chapters that this book does not offer a chronological or teleological account ('the triumph and tragedy of Greek studies'). This strategy is not mere whimsy, nor just the product of the partiality of my examples. Rather, it is an integral part of my argument and emphasizes in particular one overriding point about historical narrative. There have always been writers, ancient and modern, who have thought there is an essence of Greekness. That there is evident and wholesale disagreement about what such an essence is, makes it easy enough, these days, to concede that the idea of Greekness is differently constructed by different writers in different eras (including in ancient Greece). But that cautious relativism has far-reaching implications for contemporary historians, who cannot help finding their own reconstructions of those differences becoming *part* of the history being related. Erasmus and the Nazi theologian do not – cannot – have the same Lucian, but that very recognition, that juxtaposition of Erasmus and the Nazi, is part of *my* rhetorical and ideological organization of the past. Just as your critical comprehension is all the time working on this paragraph. You and I are active participants – players – in the debate over 'Who Needs Greek?' (and not just the umpire or judge). Trying to recognize one's own engaged self-positioning in the present, one's stake in the past, and the shifting models of Greekness in the past and present means that the historian is placed, as it were, between two mirrors, in a play of multiple reflections. Especially on a topic like 'cultural identity', the historian's narration has to go back and forth between present and past, like a weaver's shuttle, to make up a picture. It needs to be *sinuous*. Hence the lack of a straightforward, chronological account. I wouldn't be a literary critic if I weren't a fool for narrative: but I am deeply suspicious of any history that either wholly ignores its own jaggedness and mess, or totally represses the self-implicating activity of story telling.

I am not the first to adopt a non-linear chronological narrative in response to the foundational difficulties of history writing or story telling; but it makes me a little nervous too, I confess. (Self-awareness always has its costs.) Modern academic reading habits and library policies and catalogue requirements all encourage an author to write on a single period and a closely delimited topic: why not a book on nineteenth-century

classics, or a book on Greek writing in the Roman empire, or a book
on the Renaissance rediscovery of Greek? My wager is that resisting the
limitations of such institutional exigencies, putting together interrelated
topics otherwise kept apart, seriously working with the dynamics of past
and present in history writing, will produce enough insights, enough
intellectual stimulation to outweigh any disconcerting bumpiness in
the journey. It is not just that new collocations reveal new meanings
(as Aristotle says of metaphor): rather this narrative strategy is my
attempt to write in the space between the mirrors of past and present.

What links these five paradigmatic conflicts about Greek, then, is
not just that they are each hugely significant cultural moments, nor
just that they are each viewed through the lens of an interdisciplinary
methodology. What links them also is an argument about how cultural
traditions function and the sort of history we should write about them.
It is to the current debate about cultural identity and the value of the
past that this book is addressed. But my agenda is also intended to wave
a flag more specifically in the direction of students of what is usually
called 'the classical tradition' and 'reception studies'. I hope that the
focus on an extended range of cultural activity, and the insistence on
the critical junctures of cultural history, will be programmatic for further
work. I want to broaden the questions to be asked in contemporary
understandings of how ancient and modern texts interact, and to offer a
more *dynamic* account of how the classical and the modern interpenetrate.

Finally, a word on scholarship: although a lot of reading over many
years has gone into the production of this book, the footnotes contain
the barest possible acknowledgment of my scholarly debts, along with
the necessary references to sources. Although the book is polemical in
form and content, I have avoided almost all *ad hominem* infighting on
scholarly issues. Scholars will be able to follow up the implicit screams
via the footnotes. I have translated all non-English texts, modern and
ancient: where texts are difficult to find or contested or where specific
linguistic points are necessary, I have put brief quotations in the footnotes.
Where possible, I have tried to give references to modern facsimiles or re-
printings of material sometimes difficult to source in original editions. In
general, however, the footnotes are not intended to distract from reading
the main body of the book.

I can, however, here with greatest pleasure offer my heartfelt thanks to
the friends and scholars who have cheerfully answered specific questions
and read chapters and provided so much necessary support: Stephen

Alford, Hadassah Brooks-Morgan, Stefan Collini, Tim Duff, Pat Easterling, Jas Elsner, Ian Patterson, Michael Reeve, Tim Whitmarsh, Froma Zeitlin, and David Konstan (who read the whole first draft). And, especially for reading and discussing each and every chapter as it progressed, my friends John Henderson and Miriam Leonard. Intellectual communities matter. I have been lucky to have the support not only of those individuals mentioned but also of the Classics Faculty of Cambridge University and the Fellows of King's College, Cambridge, not least during the wonderfully long sabbatical which made the writing of this book possible.

CHAPTER ONE

Learning Greek is heresy! Resisting Erasmus

I

Why should you care about Erasmus?

Let me make a case, as best I can. First of all – and this is not a joking matter – he invented the academic, at least for the modern West. I don't mean the scholarly bore, the trivial questioner, the man – yes, this one usually is a man – who has no connection with the Real World of power and politics. And I am certainly not talking about the job of university lecturer. No, I mean *your* fantasy of what *you* might be doing by reading and writing or teaching. The intellectual whose pursuit of truth changes the way that the world is perceived. The writer whose contribution does not merely mark a massive shift in the cultural and intellectual world but *creates* it. The teacher whose teaching dominates a culture and whose values are passed across the generations. The very grandest fantasy one could share.

Erasmus was the first and greatest international intellectual super-star of the modern West. During the violent invention of Protestantism, Erasmus was accused of being a founding father of that passionate revolution and of rejecting its basic tenets – by different sides in the Reformation. He was instrumental in the complete overhaul of the education system, particularly in England, and his works still made up the basic tools of the schoolroom centuries later. By law, his paraphrases of the Gospels were placed in every parish church in the kingdom, 'next to the Bible', and every cleric below the level of Doctor of Divinity was required to own his own copy of that work. His words were placed in all those mouths and minds. The writer he translated first, however, and always loved was put on the Index of banned books by the Catholic Church and became a byword for cynical blasphemy. Yet he dedicated

The following footnotes contain mainly references for passages cited, major academic debts, and some further reading on detailed points. They are the barest minimum, and need not be consulted while reading the text.

his most controversial religious volume – the first Greek edition of the Gospels – to the Pope and received a letter of praise in reply. He wrote letter after self-promoting letter, many hundreds of which were collected and published in book form in his lifetime, constructing an image of an international brotherhood of scholars so strongly that a scholar's name and standing could be denigrated simply by the rhetorical question, 'Where is his letter from Erasmus?' By any conventional standard, Erasmus matters. If all the name Erasmus evokes is a vague image of a pious humanist, that would be really missing the boat. He was an ambivalent, provocative, polemical figure who divided and dominated European intellectual life. He was profoundly instrumental in the construction of conflicts still being waged today. We are all his heirs.

But I have another concern, which some might think a touch parochial. I care about Erasmus because he made learning Greek sexy. That is, important, politically charged, socially relevant, and trendy. He has become, I confess, a major figure in *my* fantasy.

Erasmus had a Mission with Greek. He wrote repeatedly about learning Greek and tirelessly performed his role of demanding, cajoling, teaching, stimulating knowledge of Greek in cities across Europe, often in the face not just of apathy but of organized and extended opposition. This is a story with a Hero for a classicist like me. He made learning Greek a myth of his own coming to be, and made it a requirement of those who wanted to follow him into his version of an intellectual calling. 'How is your Greek progressing?', he kept nagging bishops, theologians, politicians, students. It is with missionary pride that he writes from from Calais to Reuchlin, the distinguished German scholar of Hebrew in Stuttgart, that Colet – the founder of St Paul's School in London – 'old man as he is, is learning Greek'.[1] And adds, 'The Bishop of Rochester has made good progress.' And he encourages Reuchlin also to send a letter to Colet to gee him up in the enterprise. The shared international enterprise. There were many major issues which demanded Erasmus' attention and engagement, of course, but learning Greek was not just an adjunct to his religion or his scholarly agenda, nor was it a byproduct of his university training. Studying Greek was integral and essential to Erasmus' sense of self and to the project that was his life.

Now at some point every discussion of Erasmus has to rehearse that (auto)biographical project. There are biographies aplenty, of course,

---

[1] *EE* 1: 330–1 [*ep* 457], 27 August 1516. For the state of Greek studies in England, see Tilley (1938).

many of which are fascinating historical documents in themselves.[2] (His illegitimate birth, his leaving his first monastery because the conversation was sterile, his choosing his own first name, I will leave to the novel – though I admit that in view of the story of translation I am about to tell, I do find it at very least intriguing that the name he chose for himself, 'Desiderius', is – with self-conscious wit – the Latin translation of what his name 'Erasmus' would mean in Greek, 'desired', 'desirable', 'love(ly)'.[3] This is also a story of desire, inevitably, and change. 'Thou art translated . . .' How could a self-chosen name not be *telling*?) But it is the Letters that make all the difference to what gets said about Erasmus. Some of his letters are formal introductions to his books – dedicatory epistles. Some are apologias – statements of defence – for his life and work. There are numerous letters of recommendation, of encouragement, of commentary on his work and relationships and the politics of religious controversy. Every work of Erasmus is surrounded by the filagree of self-representation, carefully preserved, circulated and edited by generations of scholars, starting with Erasmus himself. Reading Erasmus is continuously to watch him addressing 'you . . .', telling 'you' how to read and live. The celebrated and remarkable twelve volume edition of *Erasmi Epistolae* by P. S. Allen is crowding my desk as I write this, constantly offering from its six thousand pages another gloss to any comment on Erasmus' work and biography. Erasmus' *life* – as he and others re-tell it – was important, politically charged, socially relevant, trendy: in part, it is because learning Greek is such an important thread in Erasmus' self-told life that it becomes such a hot topic.

But not only because of that. The excitement and passion of Erasmus' discovery of Greek doesn't lead simply to a desire to promote its pursuit among his friends, as if Greek were a brilliant new game or technology. Rather, knowledge of the Greek language provides a seminal link between Erasmus' scholarly activity and his hugely influential role in the increasingly bitter and vitriolic politics of the Reformation.[4] This is a story where knowing how to translate Greek – or *whether* you should translate Greek – becomes a life and death conflict about religious affiliation. It is the way in which studying Greek becomes intertwined with

---

[2] From Erasmus' own *Compendium Vitae* (1524) and Rhenanus (1540) (both translated usefully in Olin ed. (1975)) to Huizinga (1952), Bainton (1969), Tracy (1972), Halkin (1993); Tracy (1996).

[3] See Rhenanus (1540), [Olin ed. (1975) 53] for the self-recognition of the meaning of 'Erasmus'/ἐράσμ[ι]ος.

[4] For general intellectual background to Erasmian polemics, see Kristeller (1961); Nauert (1973); Shuger (1994); Tracy (1980); Rummel (1992) and Nelson (2001), each with further bibliographies.

sixteenth-century politics, theology and cultural change that makes it mean so much. A matter of your eternal soul. Thomas More (I can't avoid those conflicts even by not calling him either 'Sir' or 'Saint'...), Erasmus' close friend, who translated the witty blasphemer Lucian along with Erasmus, died on the scaffold with a calm witticism on his lips – and it makes sense to see that life's journey as a coherent intellectual narrative, a consistent commitment to an ideal and a practice.[5] The combination of integrity and humour, commitment and wit, passion and learning, mean that these friends have continued to be embraced as heroes of the intellect. Our stars of the Renaissance. The study of Greek is integral to this founding story of a new Europe, a new sense of the person.

II

I am going to begin my account of this engagment with Greek and with religious and cultural politics through the study of Greek at the point where Lisa Jardine begins her fine study of Erasmus' self-construction through his writing, namely, with a picture and a story.[6] The picture is the famous portrait of Erasmus painted by Quentin Metsys in 1517 (the year after Erasmus was writing to Reuchlin about Colet's Greek studies) when Erasmus was fifty-one. It is reproduced here as plate 1. It may be pretty familiar, but that makes it hard to look (again) at its detail with enough care. Its power – and polemics – will take some teasing out. The story is the briefest of anecdotes about the painting from a letter to Thomas More in the same year, which provides also a vivid vignette of why one might not want to experience sixteenth-century medical practice. But I think it is Erasmus' wry self-recognition of his own Folly that has led biographers to love to re-tell this story. And so will I.

Erasmus and his close friend, Peter Gilles, paid to have their portraits painted in a diptych by Metsys to send as a present to their mutual dear friend in London, Thomas More. Gilles fell rather seriously ill and the project was delayed. Erasmus writes to More the following report: 'I myself was in excellent health, but somehow the physician took it into his head to tell me to take some pills to purge my bile, and the advice he foolishly gave me I even more foolishly agreed to take. My portrait had

---

5 As does especially Fox (1982). See also Duncan (1979) 52–76, and the extensive biographical tradition from William Roper (1557) and Harpsfield (1557) to Chambers (1935), Reynolds (1953) Marius (1984) and Ackroyd (1998). Monti (1997) rehearses the hagiographic tradition more obviously than most.
6 Jardine (1993).

1. Portrait of Erasmus, by Quentin Metsys

already begun, but after taking the medicine, when I went back to the painter, he said it was not the same face; and so the painting has been put off several days until I become somewhat more cheerful [*alacrior*].'[7]

You can see how seductive Erasmus' self-portrait can be. Wise after the event, writing to his intimate friend and partner in irony, the great scholar lets us see himself, apparently unbuttoned, foolishly following foolish advice. The foibles of the patient's dealings with his doctor are sharply etched because we – Thomas More and you and I – know that

---

[7] *EE* 2: 576 [*ep* 584], 30 May 1517.

the man who stupidly swallows the bile-reduction pills is the celebrated
arbiter of biblical authorities, the counsellor to Christian princes – and
the author of the scandalous book, *The Praise of* – precisely – *Folly*. His
face – though not, finally, his portrait – reveals his discomfiture. This self-
deprecating anecdote was published a bare two years after the painting
was finished in one of the many collections of Erasmus' letters published
in his lifetime, and it was widely circulated. We readers are being invited
to overhear the engaging private exchange of these famous friends. From
the beginning, then, the portrait of Erasmus which Metsys painted is
surrounded – framed – by Erasmus' self-portrait in words. So, it should
be appreciated that the little story also lets us glimpse the collusion of
painter and sitter. Erasmus must present the right face to his friends and
to the public, and the painter directs him towards a somewhat more
cheerful, less bilious expression. His best side. As ever with realism, the
construction of image is all.

The Metsys portrait has indeed become an icon of the sixteenth
century. It would be hard for us now to picture Erasmus without it, so
many times has it been reproduced. (Like the later Holbein and Dürer
portraits, which Metsys already has influenced.)[8] Concentrated, austere,
taut-faced, with a faint smile ('somewhat more cheerful'), the dark scholar
writes intently in his study, surrounded by his books and the candlewick
trimmer (or scissors) hanging from the shelf. Four of the books are inscribed with titles, and each is a volume written by Erasmus – defining
the scholar in and by his works. Even the candlewick trimmers may have
a symbolic significance, representing the editorial projects of Erasmus,
'trimming the wick of scriptures so that their light shines out strongly and
brightly'.[9] It is a picture designed to project a very particular image of
Erasmus. Thomas More is its recipient, of course, and ideal viewer. But as
the published letters show, you and I, the wider public, are never far away.
It is so well known and so authoritative an image by now that it is hard to
imagine its power to shock or outrage. But even as a private gift, a gesture
of complicity shared between friends, this remains a provocative picture,
which takes a strikingly bold stance on the significance of Erasmus and
his works. This portrait is designed to be, as they say, in your face.

I want to try to explain how this picture of a scholar and his books
could be so charged. The portrait is modelled, as many scholars state,
on the contemporary iconography of St Jerome in *his* study.[10] And the

---

[8] Hayum (1985); Gerlo (1969).   [9] Jardine (1993) 75.

[10] E.g. Jardine (1993); Gerlo (1969); Rice (1988), each with further bibliography.

light source which illumines the face of Erasmus and the pages on which
he writes, also picks out a book on the shelf. You can read clearly on it
'HIERONYMUS', that is, JEROME. The iconography and the book are both
keys that open a route to the heart of Erasmus' self-image. Lisa Jardine,
with particular flair, has explored the significance of this highlighted text
and Erasmus' iconographic affiliation to the saint. It is a fascinating story
of intellectual formation.

Erasmus had published his edition of Jerome's Letters in 1516, with
a life of Jerome by way of introduction. It was a work he had been
planning for years, and he takes great pains to point out to you what
a massive task it has been to complete. 'I had worked myself to death
that Jerome might live . . . it cost Jerome less to write his works than it
has cost me to restore and explain them.'[11] As early as 1500, he wrote
to James Batt that he needed money desperately to buy the collected
works of Jerome (and some clothes and Greek books) in order to write a
commentary on the saint's texts.[12] He lectured on Jerome in Cambridge
during his formative stay there.[13] Jerome is a constant reference point
for Erasmus over nearly forty years of study. He leads every list of heroes
of the Church for Erasmus, and is brought forward as an authority to
win argument after argument. He was the one figure writing in Latin
who could match or even better his beloved Greeks. As he wrote to Pope
Leo X, 'I saw that St Jerome was so completely the first among Latin
theologians that we might call him the one person worthy of that name.
What a fund in him of Roman eloquence, what skill in languages, what a
knowledge of antiquity and of all history, what a retentive memory, what
a perfect familiarity with mystic literature, above all, what zeal, what a
wonderful inspiration of divine breath! He is the one person who at the
same time delights by his eloquence, teaches by his erudition, and ravishes
by his holiness.'[14] So how should a saint be praised to the Pope, these
days? The smelly, painful, lonely, sufferings of a Simon Stylites are far
from the linguistically gifted, scholarly theologian of Erasmus' imagining.
(Is this the first time a saint has been lauded for his faculty of retentive
memory?) When Jerome goes to the desert, it was, as Erasmus tells it, to
're-read his entire library' and systematically to collect references and

---

[11] *EE* 2: 88 [*ep* 335], 21 May 1515, to Pope Leo X; see also 2: 76, 77 [*ep* 334], 15 May 1515, to
Domenico Grimani, for the same expressions.
[12] *EE* 1: 321 [*ep* 138], 11 December 1500, to James Batt.
[13] Thompson and Porter (1963) 38–43 (with, in particular, *EE* 1: 570 [*ep* 296], 8 July 1514, to
Servatius Rogerius).
[14] *EE* 2: 86 [*ep* 335], 21 May 1515, to Pope Leo X.

citations for later use.[15] More sabbatical than mortification. It is Jerome's eloquence and erudition that lead even his ravishing holiness. He is a good . . . historian. 'Jerome is Erasmus' hero and model', as Olin puts it succinctly, but 'the portrait he has given us is that of the ideal Christian humanist'.[16]

The Church itself, when it declared Jerome one of the four Fathers and Doctors of the Church back in 1295, had glowingly declared that 'their flowing discourse, fed by streams of heavenly grace, solves scriptural problems, unties knots, explains obscurities, and resolves doubts'.[17] But the dominant strand of medieval representations had a suffering penitent at its heart. Eugene Rice sums it up excellently: 'so holy was he that he remained a virgin until his death at ninety-six, traditional exaggerations of both his age and his continence. He drank no wine and ate no meat or fish. Indeed, he scarcely allowed even the words "meat" and "fish" to pass his lips, but lived entirely on uncooked fruit, greens and roots. He wore a hairshirt under rags, slept on the bare ground, whipped himself three times a day until the blood flowed . . . and patiently endured every imaginable abstinence, temptation and mortification.'[18] There were even groups of ascetic penitents, who particularly followed that example of flagellation and fasting, called 'Hieronymites'. It is against this that Erasmus is writing his life of Jerome. Here's how he puts his portrait to the leading churchman Warham (who as Archbishop of Canterbury led the Ashford inquisition in Kent which burnt five men at the stake in 1511[19]):

Was there ever an individual expert in so many languages? Who ever achieved such familiarity with history, geography, and antiquities? Who ever became so equally and completely at home in all literature, both sacred and profane? If you look to his memory, never was there an author, ancient or modern, who was not at his immediate disposal.[20]

Geography, history, languages and classical literature, coupled (again) with a good memory, make Jerome a classy patron saint of academia

---

[15] See Rice (1985) for balanced account of sources on Jerome in the desert.

[16] Olin (1979) 321.

[17] Papal decree, 20 September 1295, by Boniface VIII: *Corpus Iuris Canonici Lib vi Decretalium*, III tit. xxii, cap. I: *Eorum etiam foecunda facundia, coelestis irrigui gratia influente, scripturarum aenigmata reserat, solvit nodos, obscura dilucidat, dubiaque declarat.*

[18] Rice (1985) 50.

[19] Hughes (1956) 128: forty-six arrested, forty-one recanted, five burnt at the stake.

[20] *EE* 2: 215 [*ep* 396], 1 April 1516, to William Warham: the whole letter, the dedication of the volumes of Jerome, is an extended *laudatio* of the saint.

(or perhaps the core curriculum). Indeed, not only does Erasmus find an ideal Christian humanist in Jerome, but also, as he tells the story of Jerome's life, stripping away, as he claims, the fantastic tales of naive hagiography, Erasmus himself becomes disconcertingly overlapped with the figure he is describing. In a bizarre version of the 'imitation of saints' recommended by Augustine and others, Erasmus' scholarly struggles are Jerome's, Jerome's lifework his. In Erasmus' portrait, Jerome and Erasmus look a lot alike. Metsys' portrait of Erasmus, in depicting Erasmus as Jerome, is following a fundamental strategy of Erasmus' own self-representation – or as Jardine would put it, his self-construction.

Erasmus' identification with Jerome is not just because of the saint's academic powers. In a while, I will be discussing how vitriolically Erasmus was attacked for his passion for secular studies, and in particular the study of ancient Greece and Rome. The one story about St Jerome that everyone knew was the one about his dream. Jerome dreamt he appeared before the tribunal of Heaven, where the grim figure of Christ the Judge demanded he identify himself. 'I am a Christian', he declared. 'You lie', retorted the Judge, 'You are a Ciceronian, not a Christian. For where your treasure is, there will your heart be also.' And Jerome was flogged, and 'tormented by the flame of conscience', until he tearfully declared, 'Lord, if ever I again possess secular books or read them, I have denied you.'[21] Attempts to explain this dream as figurative, or to limit its purchase to 'excessive study of Cicero', or Cicero's philosophical texts, foundered on what Erasmus recognized as the story's simple and annoyingly powerful message. 'This is the story which everyone remembers, even those who have never read a word that Jerome has written. Jerome, they say, was flogged because he read Cicero.'[22] In this way, Jerome himself could be turned as an example against Erasmus and his mission. Although the authority, sanctity and scholarship of Jerome were privileged appropriations of Erasmus' self-fashioning, there lurked in Jerome's most famous self-description a more threatening image. To study Jerome required a knowledge of the classics, which Jerome himself seemed to ban. Jerome may be 'reborn in Erasmus',[23] but Erasmus could only try to explain away Jerome's famous tearful promise to give up the classics – or brazen

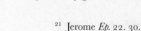

---

[21] Jerome *Ep.* 22. 30.

[22] Erasmus' commentary on Jerome's *Ep.* 22, in *CWE* 61. Jardine (1993) 65–9 points out the importance of Valla's earlier celebration of Jerome in his defence of classical literature.

[23] A phrase taken from Jardine (1993) 68. I have learnt a great deal from Jardine and Rice in particular throughout this discussion of Jerome. The great Italian humanist, Lorenzo Valla, is an important intermediary here also. Erasmus read Valla – who both praised Jerome and wrote *Annotationes* to the New Testament.

it out: 'I would rather be whipped with Jerome than fêted in the company of those who are so frightened by Jerome's ideas that they scrupulously avoid good literature.'[24] As Jardine puts it beautifully: 'At the heart of the Jerome edition – the opus Erasmus produced at the zenith of his international career – and on the threshold of his self-formation as an icon of scholar-piety – is the fusion or perhaps confusion of secular and sacred attention.'[25]

Erasmus had actually learnt Greek precisely in order to rescue his hero and model: 'I would rather be mad with Jerome than as wise as you like with the crowd of modern theologians', he writes in 1501, 'Moreover, I am struggling with a laborious task which one might call the work of Phaethon: to make it my role to restore the books of Jerome which in part have been ruined by those half-educated fellows, and in part obscured or mangled or mutilated or certainly falsified and full of monstrosities because of ignorance of classical matters and of Greek literature ... I see that Greek must be my first priority of study. I have decided to learn some months with a Greek teacher, a real Greek, or rather doubly Greek, since he is always hungry and teaches for a large fee!'[26] The desire to learn Greek (which doesn't stop the standard Latin jokes about hungry and money-grabbing Greeks) is in service of his aim of restoring Jerome to the world as 'prince of theologians'.

Knowledge of Greek, however, will turn out also to be the means by which his own standing as theologian is achieved and contested – primarily because of his edition of the Greek Bible. This celebrated and scandalous edition – which I will come to very shortly – was inevitably seen by many as an attack on Jerome, because he was traditionally regarded as the author of the Vulgate, the standard Latin version of the Bible, whose text Erasmus freely criticized and emended. Erasmus denied that Jerome wrote the Vulgate (he was not the first to do so; and it is clear that on any scholarly argument Jerome cannot be its author[27]; but even the Council of Trent could not bring itself to make such a bold declaration against tradition.[28]) Thus Erasmus found himself once again going into battle both for himself and for his version of Jerome.

---

[24] *Hieronymi Stridensis Vita* [Ferguson (1933)] 178.   [25] Jardine (1993) 74.

[26] *EE* I. 353 [*ep* 149], 16 ? March 1501, to Antony of Bergen; the whole letter extols Greek learning.

[27] Lefèvre d'Étaples and Paul of Middleburg had already denied Jerome was the translator. See Rice (1985) 178–87; Schwartz (1965) for a general background; Bentley (1983) 113–93 for Erasmus' biblical philology. Particularly important for Erasmus was his (re)discovery of Valla's *Adnotationes* to the New Testament. See also the works cited below n. 31.

[28] Indeed it defended the Vulgate as authentic precisely because it was hallowed by the long tradition of use in the Church. For everything you might want to know (and more) about the Council of Trent, see Jedin (1961), especially, for our purposes here, vol. II, 52–98.

So learning Greek, studying Jerome, and becoming a polemical theologian, fighting over Jerome, are interwoven ventures that stretch throughout Erasmus' life. When Metsys paints Erasmus in his study in the iconographic pose of Jerome in his study, and highlights the text of Jerome on which Erasmus had spent so many years' effort, he is marking out not merely a fundamental strand of Erasmus' own self-fashioning, but also the site on which Erasmus' polemics have been waged. The image of intently gazing sage with his book also signifies the intricate and extended intellectual journey of the sitter and the strongly contested struggles along the way.

III

The second most brightly lit book on the shelves of Metsys' portrait, shaded by an unnamed volume leaning over it, but with its title directly facing the viewer, is marked 'NOVUM TESTAMENT', 'The New Testament', truncated of its last syllable in Latin. Erasmus' most celebrated contribution to theological debate was his edition of the New Testament. The outline of the story is simply told; the fallout complex and compelling.

Erasmus' Greek studies led him back to the texts of the Gospels, written originally in Greek, of course. They were, he recognized, in rather poor Greek, especially when judged by the standard of the classical masterpieces of Athens or by the assiduous imitators of those classical masterpieces in the second century CE such as Lucian or Philostratus. So, he set out to produce a critical edition of the Greek text, with a facing Latin translation. Not only did he find many places where he thought he needed to correct, tidy up, or emend the Greek manuscripts, but also he produced his Latin translation directly from the Greek text afresh – and thus offered a Bible that was outrageously different from the Vulgate, the Latin text, which was ascribed to Jerome, and used every day in every church in Europe. The Vulgate was hallowed by tradition (and eventually by the Council of Trent, which declared in 1546, with dizzying theological assertiveness, that this Latin translation of the Greek text was 'authentic' (not 'good' or 'reliable' but '*authentic*'), and that 'nobody dare or presume to reject it under any pretext'[29]), and it was the basis of all theological discussion from basic sermon to the debates of university Divines. Indeed, the whole edifice of Medieval theology, and, consequently, the social order that depended on the structure and

---

[29] That a translation is declared 'authentic' should give pause: it certainly outraged the Reformers. For a rather apologetic discussion of *authentia*, see Sutcliffe (1948).

authority of the Church relied on the status of the Vulgate. It was this text to which Erasmus offered a corrective. The outrage and scandal which arose, came about – not unreasonably – not just because of a question of wording but because of what was at stake in the Word of the Vulgate: social and moral order itself.

The first edition of the *Novum Testamentum* was rushed through the press in 1516.[30] It was lousy with misprints and other typesetters' errors, and the notes were often perfunctory. It caused none the less a considerable stir. Erasmus was sufficiently upset by the printing fiasco – for which he was upbraided by scholars of the exalted status of Budé, the leading classicist of his generation – that he rushed to plague-ridden Basel to produce a second edition personally and as soon as possible. The second edition early in 1519 pulled no punches. Egged on by his friends and supporters, Erasmus added new and even more radical suggestions, and defended them with more strident polemical scholarship. They weren't the sort of changes in translation that might slip by missed. A whole and crucial sentence of Paul's *Letter to John 1*, now known as the 'Comma Johanneum' [1 John 5:7], he failed to find in any Greek manuscript – so he deleted it from his text.[31] (We will see a particularly bloody fallout from this later.) For centuries the Gospel of John had begun *In principio erat verbum*, 'In the beginning was the Word' (as the usual translation has it). Now Erasmus printed *In principio erat sermo*, 'In the beginning was the speech/conversation.' Pugnacious, arresting, an opening designed to shock the reader into reaction.

So what's with *sermo*? The scholarship, first: Erasmus' notes on this passage reveal that Cyprian, the Church Father, used *sermo* whenever he cites this verse. Tertullian, the second- /third-century theologian, who also uses it, notes that *sermo* is the 'customary' reading. Augustine knew two textual traditions, both *sermo* and *verbum*. (Erasmus – though not his opponents – is less than exhaustive in his pursuit of countercases, however.) Why is *sermo* Erasmus' choice? *Sermo* implies, as *verbum* does not, a sense of dialogue, which, apart from the humanist love of dialogue, has a particular theological point. This sense of dialogue or address 'is essential

[30] This first edition was called *Novum Instrumentum*. All subsequent editions were entitled *Novum Testamentum*. 'Rushed through rather than published', is Erasmus' own well-known description of the process.

[31] See de Jonge (1980); Bentley (1983); Margolin (1990) for another test-case. De Jonge believes (against most) that Erasmus did not mean to edit the Greek text of the New Testament in a critical manner. His rhetoric of criticism may be different when he treats the New Testament (rather than Seneca, say), but the deletion of the *Comma* on grounds of manuscript authority is hard not to see as an act of 'textual criticism'.

to logos as the second person of the Trinity',[32] whereas '*verbum* . . . if not
so intended originally' came 'to support . . . christological and trinitarian
speculation'[33] of a scholastic type which Erasmus found hard to allow.
More shakily, Erasmus adds that *sermo* is a masculine noun and thus better represents the gender of Christ than a neuter noun (e.g. *verbum*), and
that *sermo* has a softer – *mollius* – sound than *verbum*. Even these dodgier
arguments, however, articulate what is at stake in this issue of translation:
not just capturing the Greek, but also how the perfection of divinely inspired language expresses the world perfectly. God's language. 'Softness'
is not just a phonological but a theological gloss. Although Erasmus does
express a further preference for *oratio* (a third translation: 'In the beginning was the Address'),[34] *sermo* has ancient authority and is 'more apt',
'more correct', 'more perfect'.[35] Theologically and semantically, *sermo*
thus is in all ways a better translation of the Greek *logos* than *verbum*,
argues Erasmus.

And argue he had to. Any disingenuousness he may have maintained
about this being simply a point of linguistic accuracy or intellectual
enquiry was rapidly dispelled. The *Novum Testamentum* was praised by
many and the second edition came with a letter of support from the Pope;
but it caused an extraordinary outburst of protest across Europe, and
years of bitter, often violent argument. The translation was proclaimed
an attack on the foundation of the Church and its traditions; the turn back
to the original language of the Gospels was rejected as threatening: for
the authority of the Vulgate was the very grounding of social and moral
understanding. Learning Greek became such an icon in the religious
wars that it could be declared that Greek was 'the fount of all evil',[36]
and to know Greek was a 'heresy'![37] The Preface of St Jerome's edition
of the Bible had worried precisely that 'Which man, be he educated or
uneducated, when he picks up the book and sees that what he is used
to read is different from the saliva he once drank, will not immediately
burst into cry and call me heretic and sacrilegious because I dare to add,

---

[32] Jarrott (1964) 36–7.
[33] Boyle (1977) 30 – a full and excellent study of the implications of the choice of *sermo*. See also
   Rummel (1989).
[34] Erasmus *Annotationum in Evangelium Joannis* 1: 2, cited and discussed by Boyle (1977) 33–57.
[35] Adjectives lifted from *Apologia de 'In principio erat sermo'*.
[36] The view of Baechem, cited by Rummel (1989) 139.
[37] Erasmus *Antibarbari*, *CWE* 23: 32; *EE* 4: 400–411 [*ep* 1167] to Lorenzo Campeggio is a full-scale
   description of the escalation of insult into attacks of heresy. So common becomes this attack
   that it is parodied in the anonymous farce, *Le Farce des Théologastres* (C. Longeon ed. [Geneva,
   1989] 493–5), cited by Rummel (1992) 723: 'He who speaks Greek is suspect of heresy.' Bentley
   (1983) finds a further root to the slur in the fact that the Greeks were schismatics.

change, correct something in the old texts?'[38] Ironically enough, it was Erasmus who prompted exactly the reaction his master anticipated. So, how were the battle-lines drawn up?

Erasmus' mission to have all educated people learn Greek worked at a personal and institutional level. I have already mentioned the network of letters which trace Erasmus continuing the work of Grocyn, Linacre, Latimer and Lily, by promoting Greek and by making the story of a struggle to learn Greek a fundamental myth of initiation into the Erasmian circle. No Greek, no title of scholar. 'In no learning are we anything without Greek',[39] he writes, 'all scholarship is blind without Greek learning'[40]; 'I affirm that with slight qualification the whole of attainable knowledge lies enclosed within the literary monuments of ancient Greece. This great inheritance I will compare to a limpid spring of undefiled water; it behoves all who are thirsty to drink and be restored.'[41] (The adaptation of the Gospels' language of thirst and fulfilment to Greek texts is the most shocking debt here.) As Latimer replies to Erasmus: 'You show a remarkable desire to promote Greek learning.'[42] The word for 'desire' there, 'desyderium', puns on Erasmus' name, Desiderius. Erasmus' own name becomes synonymous with his project of promoting Greek. His example was followed to the letter. Philip Melanchthon, giving his inaugural lecture in 1518, encourages his students in Wittenburg: 'Greek learning is especially necessary', 'Just give some extra hours to the Greeks', and – his professorial slogan – 'Embrace the Greeks!'[43]

This growing network of powerful friends – 'a vast mutual admiration society'[44] – is integral to any picture of humanism at work. Yet it had lasting and influential institutional effects. Colet's St Paul's School was paradigmatic in its statutes and lesson plans in requiring Greek – and deeply influential on (even) Wolsey's self-promoting programme of

---

[38] *Praefatio in Evangelio*: '*Quis enim doctus pariter vel indoctus, cum in manus volumen adsumpserit et a saliva quam semel inhibit viderit discrepare quod lectitat, non statim erumpat in vocem, me falsarium me clamans esse sacrilegum, qui audeam aliquid in veteribus libris addere, mutare, corrigere?'*

[39] *EE* 1: 406 [*ep*.181] to John Colet, December 1504.

[40] *EE* 6: 403 [*ep*. 1744] to Simon Pistorius, September 1526.

[41] *de rat. stud. CWE* 24: 669 (though I have cited the translation of Woodward, taken from Baldwin (1944) 80). This is a trope of much humanist writing. The return to the source(s), *ad fontem/ad fontes*. Interestingly, Valla [*Opera* 1.341: ed. E. Garin, 2 vols. (Turin, 1962)] defending himself in reply to Poggio Bracciolini already asks, 'Why then did I compare the Latin stream with the Greek fount?' For the importance of Valla to Erasmus, see e.g. Bentley (1983). The attack on the humanist project can be seen as early as the beginning of the fifteenth century, Hunt (1940).

[42] *EE* 2: 440 [*ep*. 520], from William Latimer, 30 January 1517.

[43] Keen (1988) 54, 54, 56.   [44] Mason (1959) 28.

establishing educational institutions.[45] Indeed, most, if not all schools
in England by the 1540s specified by statute that Latin and Greek were
the only languages to be *spoken* by the schoolchildren, 'whatever they are
doing in earnest or in play'.[46](As Erasmus wrote to Gilles advising him
about his son: 'even now let him absorb the seeds of Greek and Latin and
greet his father with charming prattle in two languages'.)[47] The State
became intimately involved with all aspects of the education system to an
increasing degree throughout the sixteenth century. Sir Thomas Smith
(whom we will meet later arguing over the pronunciation of Greek),
Ascham (Elizabeth's Greek tutor) and other politicians became closely
involved in the founding of schools, the redistribution of land after the
Chantries Act, and the establishment of County Commissions to oversee
educational provision.[48] One result of the mêlée of conflicting purposes
and patronage was the development through the 1540s of an 'authorized
uniformity' in education; and 'in the treatise *de ratione studii* ["On the
system of education"] by Erasmus is the fundamental philosophy of
the grammar schools in England'.[49] The Erasmian (or, more broadly,
Humanist) turn to Greek and the classics, supported by its educated and
committed administrators, continued to inform the shifting institutional
strategies and practices of school education well into the seventeenth
century and beyond.

It was at university level, however, where the re-invention of Greek
learning caused more trouble, not least because of the vested interests of
the ranks of theologians and scholars continuing the medieval tradition
based on Aquinas and the scholastic debates (in Latin). Erasmus can tell
the story in the mode of triumphal progression to his friend, Bullock, a
Fellow of Queens' College, Cambridge:

Thirty years ago nothing was taught in the University of Cambridge except
Alexander, the Parva Logicalia, as they call it, and those old sayings of Aristotle

---

[45] Baldwin (1944) is fundamental for material, and there is excellent analysis in Simon (1966) (with
discussion of the influence of St Paul's 124–62), McConica (1965) and Grafton and Jardine
(1984), and the still highly influential Bolgar (1954) 265–379.

[46] This phrase is taken from the statutes of Canterbury School written in 1541. 'This rule of speaking,
always Latin or Greek, is universal in grammar schools of the time, however well or ill it may
have been observed', Baldwin (1944) 333.

[47] *EE* 3: 146 [*ep.* 715], to Peter Gilles, November 1517, a letter of consolation for the death of Gilles'
father.

[48] See in particular Simon (1966) for this picture of 'profound change, not only in teaching but
in structure and in relations with the Government' (McConica (1965) 76). McConica (1965)
and Bolgar (1954) are good on the politics here; Grafton and Jardine (1984) on the coal-face of
teaching.

[49] Baldwin (1944) 179; 94.

and the questions of Scotus [the scholastic curriculum] . . . then arrived knowledge of Greek; then all those authors whose very names were unknown in the old days even to the brahmins of philosophy, Iarcas-like enthroned. And what, pray, was the effect of all of this on your University? Why it flourished to such a tune that it can challenge the first universities of the age . . . [50]

Erasmus, with an aggressive self-display, is *performing* the alienating change of scholarly focus by expecting the reader to understand his reference to the 'brahmins of philosophy, Iarcas-like enthroned'. Iarcas is an Indian sage met in Philostratus' *Life Of Apollonius of Tyana*, a second-century CE text, also referred to by St Jerome, and thus discussed by Erasmus in his edition of the letters.[51] Erasmus' slur demands your engagement in his intellectual ways, travelling back through Jerome to the Greeks. Such persuasive triumphalism is often rehearsed in a rather lazy way as the story of the Renaissance's attractive emergence from the greyness of Medieval Theology. But that developmental tale hides the compulsive conflicts that dogged Erasmus' mission for twenty years and more.

In the same letter from which I have just quoted, Erasmus tells us of another rather different reaction in Cambridge to his Greekified Bible studies and his new edition of the Gospels:

I have heard from trustworthy witnesses that you have one college, steeped in theology, whose members are regular Areopagites and who are said to have provided by solemn resolution that no man bring the said volume [the *Novum Testamentum*] by horse, boat, wagon, or porter within the curteledge of said college. I ask you, my learned friend, should one laugh or cry? How their zeal has led them astray![52]

This local attack on the leader of the humanists was pronounced by Richard Pace ('the typical humanist, the representative of what was thought to be daring and new in the early years of the sixteenth century'[53]) to be 'devoid of theology, indeed barely human' – expressions he puts tellingly in Greek. But true to his role model, he still 'laughed out loud' when he heard of the pompous college decree.[54]

---

[50] *EE* 2: 328 [*ep*. 456], to Henry Bullock, August 1516.
[51] Jerome *Ep* 53.1, with Erasmus' note *ad loc*: *CWE* 61: (text) 208; (commentary) 220.
[52] *EE* 2: 321 [*ep*. 456], to Henry Bullock, August 1516.
[53] Mason (1959) 33.
[54] *EE* 3: 39 [*ep*. 619], from Richard Pace. '*Istud collegium tu* θεολογικώτατον *vocas; sed ego ne* θεολόγον *quidem, immo vix* ἀνθρώπινον *iudico.*', '*Effusissimum mihi risum movit* . . . '. Rummel (1992) 716–17 has a nice discussion of the rhetoric of animal abuse in these discussions.

More damaging attacks on the *Novum Testamentum* came from all sides. Erasmus bitterly writes to Cardinal Wolsey – seeking support from the powerful, as ever – how even (especially?) those who haven't read his work 'traduce him to the populace with querulous shouting' and how 'someone' – a barely disguised John Standish, a Fransiscan Doctor of Divinity in London whom Erasmus particularly loathed – in a public meeting (in fact, the Sermon at St Paul's Cross) attacked his use of *sermo* for *verbum*. 'As if John had written in Latin!', Erasmus explodes, 'As if Cyprian, Hilary, Jerome and lots of others had not before me called the Son of God sermo instead of verbum! As if sermo isn't a better translation of the Greek word logos than verbum!'[55] To Cardinal Campeggio – enlisting further ecclesiastical power-brokers – he stridently recalls that 'they keep shouting in a quarrelsome way "Keep your children from Greek learning! That's where heresies are born! Don't touch the books of that man or that . . . the one who emends the Gospel of John!" '[56]

The attacks of Standish in London (and Egmondanus in Brussels, and Maier in Germany, and Lefèvre in France and Stunica in Spain and . . . [57]) prompted Erasmus to publish a brief but pungent pamphlet, 'Apologia for "In principio erat sermo" ', which he rewrote at greater and greater length in response to the continuing criticism of his work. In particular, Edward Lee, future Archbishop of York, wrote a detailed rebuttal of Erasmus' scholarly aims and practices (based on the first edition with its many mistakes). This involved a long and highly involved exchange between the two men and their supporters.[58] Lee, unlike Standish, was a scholarly figure who published a volume entitled 'annotationes ad annotationes Erasmi' ('Annotations on the Annotations of Erasmus'). Erasmus tried to get a look at this book pre-publication; he then quoted evidence from it in his own second edition, without attribution; then he denounced it. The row became a cause célèbre. Scornful letters were published (in collected books too; More, Lupset, other heavy hitters); poems, including

[55] *EE* 4: 158 [*ep.* 1060], to Cardinal Wolsey. See for the report of an extended exchange, *EE* 4: 309–18 [*ep* 1126] to Hermann Busch, 31 July 1520 – where Standish calls Erasmus *Graeculus iste*, 'that Greekling'. .

[56] *EE* 4: 182–3 [*ep.* 1062] to Lorenzo Campegio, 5 February 1520 [1519]. The preface to the *Paraphrasis ad Ephesios*, which also contains an extended defence of 'good learning'.

[57] Usefully collected and explored in Rummel (1989); on Stunica see also Bentley (1983) 197–219; on the theology of Standish see Hughes (1956) I: 152–5. For More's support of Erasmus see the *Letter to Dorp, Letter to Lee, Letter to Oxford,* and *Letter to a Monk,* collected in *CWM* xv. See now also Saladin (2000).

[58] See Rummel (1989) 94–120; and Coogan (1992).

a whole book making fun of Lee's name.[59] Perhaps the most extraordinary episode, however, concerns the display of Lee's book in a Minorite library. Three days after it went on display, users of the library complained of a foul smell. It was traced to Lee's book which was found to have been smeared by someone with human shit. Erasmus – one of those to recall the story not without pleasure some years later – is still quick to add that he doesn't know who did it. Erasmus' lack of regret at such theological guerilla tactics is matched by the anonymous composers of two poems which offer epigrammatic encomia to the man who smeared shit on the pages of Lee (as Nesen writes delightedly to Lupset, sending him the poems[60]). The classical paradigm here – always necessary – is Catullus' famous invective of a rival's historical prose as 'cacata carta', 'pages for wiping shit.'[61] Thomas More, a few years on, less than saintly: 'Luther has nothing in his mouth but privies, filth and dung . . . Mad friarlet and privy-minded rascal with his ragings and ravings, with his filth and dung, shitting and beshitted.'[62] One reader of Lee seems to have literalized this language of abuse in a gesture of theological disgust – to the pleasure of the supporters of Erasmus.

Such escalation of verbal violence (and its turning into more physical abuse) fuelled the fires of the Reformation. We should remember where this is all heading. Look at the following dialogue of inquisition recorded between the Fransiscan friar Cornelius Adrian and an Anabaptist called Hermann van Flekwyk [Flehwijt], who died at the stake on 10 June 1569:

Inquisitor: 'You have sucked at the poisoned breast of Erasmus . . . But St John says: 'There are three that bear record in heaven, the Father, the Word and the Holy Spirit, and these three are one.'

---

[59] *In Ed. Leum quorundam e sodalitate literaria Erphurdiensi Erasmici nominis studiorum epigrammata* (Erfurt, 1520); *Epistolae aliquot eruditorum* . . . (Antwerp, 1520). The humour of the Humanists is here repeatedly placed in service of the aggressive attack on Lee: 'how I laughed when I read . . .' is a topos of the letters, instantiated in the epigrams' spiteful wit. Other books of polemical letters also circulated, including even forged letters (*Epistolae obscurorum virorum* . . . – to which by the third edition even Hutten contributed a forgery), also full of often scurrilous and lewd humour.

[60] Nesen in *Epistolae aliquot eruditorum* . . . (Antwerp: Hillen 1520); Rummel (1989) 113 says that Nesen 'quotes an epigram': I have been unable to trace such a quotation in Nesen's letters, unless his comment that 'all that remains is to find another temple to keep the volume in, where it can be preserved with a liquid a long way from cedar-sap' is taken as the content of the epigrams. (Books were preserved with what is called *succum cedri*.) Nesen tells the story with the qualification that the Minorites themselves are beyond reproach, but with great pleasure in the details; see the recollection of Erasmus *EE* 8: 92–3 [*ep.* 2126] March 1529, to Valdes.

[61] Catullus 36.   [62] *Responsio ad Lutheram* (*CWM* v. i. 683).

Anabaptist: I have heard that Erasmus in his *Annotationes* upon that phrase shows that this text is not in the Greek original.[63]

Erasmus' textual criticism has become a martyr's shield in a murderous drama. Something to kill and die for. The omission of the 'Comma Johanneum' leads to the stake. I don't know if this is still within any scholar's *grandest* fantasies of intellectual importance.

In the years following the publication of Erasmus' Bible up until 1559, twenty-five academics and students from Cambridge, Erasmus' alma mater, were burnt at the stake for heresy, many pursued by the agents of More.[64] Many others went into exile.[65] Greek studies also opened the way for vernacular translations of the Bible (crucial to the development of a language of Protestantism, especially in Luther's Germany) and thus to further violent response from the authorities. Thomas More proposed, indeed demanded the burning of Tyndale's English version, not just because it was in English but because its choice of vocabulary constituted a Protestant attack on the Catholic Church:[66] to take one specific and pointed example, More bitterly objected on theological grounds to the use of 'love' rather than 'charity' to translate the Latin *caritas*, since 'love' implied 'faith', whereas 'charity' implied 'good deeds',[67] and this privileging of 'faith' over action and ritual was a Protestant tenet. (Irony is not quite the term for such violence over *those* words.) Though 'nearly all the first makers of English Protestantism suffered violent death',[68] the Cambridge reformers in particular were instrumental in the developments towards the religious settlement of 1559, which formally established Protestantism as the religion of England. The tutors of both Edward VI and of Elizabeth I, first Protestant monarchs, were Cambridge men, who were closely bonded through their shared commitment to learning Greek and to Protestant theory.[69] They taught the

---

[63] Wallace (1850) 2: 272–80 for a full account. The Anabaptist denies any influence from Erasmus earlier in the dialogue.

[64] Following the list of Rupp (1949) 195–209.

[65] On Marian exiles, see Porter (1958) (with list 91–8) and Garrett (1966) with fuller census 61–349.

[66] A partial account in Daniell (1994), especially 83–151; see also Rupp (1949); Fox (1982) 147–66; Marc'hadour and Lawler (1981). Tyndale, when he writes to More, also appeals to the history of Greek learning to form a bond with him: 'Remember ye not how within this thirty year and far less, and yet dureth until this day, the old barking curs, Dun's disciples and like draff called Scotists, the children of darkness, raged in every pulpit against Greek, Latin and Hebrew' (Walter (1850) 75–6.). The three languages are, of course, often cited together as a trio.

[67] Marc'hadour and Lawler (1981) especially 512–16. See *CWM* VI; *CWM* VIII – the immense length of these responses of More show the importance of Tyndale's threat. Ackroyd (1998) 299 calls it 'The most important dialogue within English religious discourse, perhaps of any age.'

[68] Rupp (1949) 196. [69] Hudson (1980).

Prince and Princess how to write and read Greek and, with it, theology. Greek knowledge and religious reform *did* go hand in hand, as the opponents of Greek had feared. The authority of the Catholic Church *was* undermined. The Cambridge Reformers met in an inn, the White Horse, opposite King's, which was known, because of their presence, as 'Germany', or 'Little Germany'.[70] (The church nearby, St Edward's, where the Reformers also spoke, still boasts on the sign by its gate that it was 'the cradle of the English Reformation'.) The pub was convenient because members of King's, Queens' and St John's could 'enter in on the backside'.[71] It was raided, but the Reformers had been tipped off from London and escaped. So, this lovingly preserved and retold story of revolution would have it, from earnest and precarious conversation in the pub to control of the State. (A model for so many future cells.) As John Foxe, with uncustomary understatement, recalls the beginning of religious war during those nights at the inn: 'At this time, much trouble began to ensue.'[72]

These horrifyingly violent consequences of theological difference may make you less willing to smile with Johannes Jäger's little satiric drama, 'Theologists in Council', set in 1520. Here's a fragment:

> Professor Duplicious: And even if they recommend it a hundred times I *won't* learn Greek and Hebrew. I can hardly read the Psalter – and now they want us to read these fantasies.
>
> Ed Lee: I never approved of that new fashion, and those new doctors, Jerome, Augustine, Athanasius. . . . [But] My Greek is progressing and I want to study Greek still further so that I may traduce Erasmus before the bishops, the Pope and the cardinals . . . [73]

It's hard to tell if such lumpy jokes on the 'newness' of Jerome, the malice of Lee, and the lazy ignorance of the anti-humanist divine were bitingly funny when first published. The play's conclusion, however, should still have an uneasy edge. It ends with a solemn decree banning 'these new doctrines which have emerged by the counsel of the Devil'. They must not be spoken of or written about 'even in private letters'. The attempt to silence the learning of Greek and its perceived threat to the religious establishment was indeed repeatedly enacted. Other cases of such authoritarian attempts to muzzle new questions or criticism are not hard to summon up. It is still disconcerting, however, to trace this

---

[70] Foxe (1837–41) v. 414–5 calls it simply 'Germany'; modern scholars, including the detailed account of Porter (1959), 'Little Germany'.
[71] Foxe (1837–41) v. 415.   [72] *Ibid.*   [73] Rummel (1993) 57–8.

trajectory from the passions of textual scholarship to burning books and burning people . . .

This story might seem rather more congenial. John Frith, at great personal risk to himself, returned incognito from exile (an exile necessary because of his Protestant views and support of Tyndale: he had been released into exile from the fish cellar of Cardinal College, Oxford, where he had been imprisoned for six months; two of his five fellow prisoners died). At Reading, probably at the instigation of the intelligence network of Thomas More, he was arrested as 'a rogue and a vagabond' – perhaps his disguise was too good – and he was put in the stocks. From where he spotted and was spotted by Leonard Cox, a local schoolmaster, who had been at Cambridge (and who was a friend of Erasmus and who translated not only Greek religious works into Latin but also one of Erasmus' paraphrases into English). From the stocks, Frith – as befits a scholar of Eton and King's – delivered an extempore Latin lament on his condition, before quoting in Greek 'Homer's verses from the first book of the *Iliad*.' Cox was won over and arranged for Frith's escape. This is, in all senses, a story about identification. The ragged man in the stocks could proclaim who he was – not just his class and education but his religious and political affiliations – by speaking Greek. And it had a persuasive effect, a hold over Cox. If we recall here Aristophanes' *Thesmophoriazusae*, a play where Euripides arranges the escape of his disreputable relative from the stocks partly through a series of quotations of his own 'escape' plays, there are all sorts of possible echoes here to be enjoyed. But Frith's escape was temporary (and the end is far from comic). He was burnt at the stake aged only thirty, after a disagreement about the doctrine of transubstantiation with John Fisher.[74]

Let us turn our eyes back, however, from these later scenes of murderous and holy violence to the foundational theological polemics of the word. John Maier of Eck – by now Professor of Theology at Ingolstadt – was a keen critic of the *Novum Testamentum*, as he was also active in opposition to Luther and other reformists. In 1518, he wrote to Erasmus. The letter is critical, and despite protestations of respect, relations with Erasmus were never cordial again (and Zasius, a supporter of Erasmus, published a rebuttal of Eck (as he is known) in 1519). Eck's letter shows in an exemplary manner the threat that learning Greek – and textual criticism based on Greek learning – posed to authority. 'Listen,

---

[74] Clebsch (1964) tells this story (100–101) (as does Foxe, of course, and the *DNB*), with discussion of Frith's thought (99–136): Clebsch calls Frith, rather too grandly, 'the Melanchthon of the English Reformation' (78).

dear Erasmus', he writes, 'Do you really think that any Christian will patiently endure being told that the Evangelists in their Gospels made mistakes? If the authority of the Holy Scriptures at this point is shaky, can any other passage be free from the suspicion of error?'[75] Eck stresses the destabilizing implications of Erasmus' recognition that the Gospel writers often used words oddly and that their Greek is not classical. If the Gospels' language could be questioned, changed, emended, what price the Word of God? So Eck defends the Greek of the Gospels – with divine support: 'What Christian does not know or could be ignorant if he wished to be that the Apostles knew divers kinds of tongues by the Holy Spirit . . . It was not from Greeks but from the Holy Spirit that they learnt their Greek.' [76] The Gospel writers had even better teachers than Erasmus. This is not just a question of prose composition marks, but of the perfection of divine utterance. The authority of the text, crucial to the authority of the Church, derives from the Holy Spirit itself. If the Evangelists were taught by the Holy Spirit, their texts have the authority of the divine, and any subsequent human attempt to question their Greek usage must be a mad arrogance.

Erasmus takes on this argument with a battery of sarcasm, scholarship and strident self-justification. 'If you maintain that the Greek which we see in the Apostolic Epistles is a gift from Heaven', he demands, 'from where comes all the clumsiness of language, not to say barbarism, which we cannot attempt to conceal?'[77] Why should God teach bad Greek? As he writes with a studied casualness in one of his defences against Lee: 'It is known that the Apostles wrote Greek, but not very correctly . . .'[78] And as ever Jerome carries the standard:

How can it be that Jerome in so many places is not afraid to charge Paul with imperfect knowledge of Greek? He also writes that Luke knew more Greek than Hebrew, because he came from Antioch; and, on the other hand, that Paul had a better command of his national language than he had of Greek. Similarly in the Letter to the Corinthians he wanted his Titus with him because he was more experienced in the language when it came to the interpretation of classical Greek.[79]

The authorities of the early Church already questioned each other's knowledge of Greek or confessed weakness in it. So how could repeating

[75] *EE* 3: 210 (*ep.* 769), 2 February 1518, from John Maier.
[76] *Ibid.*   [77] *EE* 3: 332 (*ep.* 844), 15 May 1518, to John Eck.
[78] *EE* 3: 314 (*ep.* 843), 7 May 1518, to Martin Lypsius, a point by point, and very long refutation of Lee's criticisms.
[79] *EE* 3: 332 (*ep.* 844), 15 May 1518, to John Eck. See also *EE* 3. 315 (*ep.* 843), 7 May 1518, to Martin Lypsius.

such criticisms be held against Erasmus? And the general point: 'Perhaps you regard a good knowledge of Greek and Hebrew of little moment. All philosophy and all theology in those days belonged to the Greeks.'[80] Without Greek, there is no hope of understanding the early Church. The foundations of the Church are not challenged by learning Greek: the foundations of the Church are Greek.

It might have have been wondered why I have not yet talked much formally about Latin study (unless it has been put down to the bias of a passionate Hellenist). Latin, however, does provide a crucial frame and contrast for my story of Greek studies. On the one hand, Latin was – of course – the language of education (and thus the educated) throughout the Middle Ages and remained so until 'the triumph of the vernacular' in the seventeenth century.[81] Most of the debates about Greek I have been looking at are written in Latin. Latin can pass for the norm, the unmarked language of elite exchange. On the other hand, a fixation on 'good' Latin – that is, Latin based on ancient and classical sources – is one of the defining characteristics of the Humanists,[82] and battles over the correct level of Ciceronian imitation,[83] or an acceptably 'high' style of Latin prose, recur throughout the first half of the fifteenth century. Erasmus, in Latin, reviles his Latin-writing opponents for 'not knowing Latin': 'Go Learn Latin!'; his opponents mocked his pretentious and difficult style. His satiric dialogue, the *Ciceronianus*, about excessive commitment to 'Ciceronianism', caused a brief flurry of resentful and deeply unironic response.[84] Latin – in an unqualified form – could function as an uncontested necessity of learning: the Vulgate was in Latin; Christianity was preached in Latin. Yet it could become a charged symbol of contestation, and, in its classical – difficult – style, a badge of belonging.

Hebrew, always sullied by its connection with the resolutely unconverted Jews, paralleled Greek as an instrument of challenge, especially in the wake of Reuchlin, and the scandal that his support of Hebrew learning prompted.[85] (Erasmus supported Reuchlin, but worried too that Hebrew study might have a bad effect in keeping the people away from all things Jewish.) There was the chance of learning Hebrew at Cambridge by the middle of the fifteenth century, and increasingly so in

[80] *EE* 3: 336 (*ep.* 844), 15 May 1518, to John Eck.
[81] 'The Triumph of the Vernacular' is a chapter title in Simon (1966). See also Waquet (2000).
[82] Kristeller (1961), most influentially.
[83] For bibliography on Ciceronianism see Tunberg (1997) 14 n.3, to which can be added Lloyd-Jones (1995).
[84] See for texts and background Scott (1910). For theological implications, see Hoffmann (1994).
[85] See Schwartz (1965) 61–91 for Reuchlin's contribution.

continental universities, despite counter movements to have all Hebrew books burnt.[86] Paradigmatic of the tensions around Hebrew study is the famous story of Buxtorf, the great Swiss Hebraicist, who was invited in 1619 by Abraham Braunschweig to his son's circumcision. Buxtorf took the opportunity to lecture the Jewish guests on embracing Christianity (he tells his friend, Waser, in a letter), but when the story came out, outrage was such that the Basel city Council, after considering exile for all the participants, fined Braunschweig the huge sum of 400 *Reichstaler* and fined Buxtorf 100 *Reichstaler*. Even attending a Jewish ritual – by a man whose description of Jewish life [*Juden Schule*] was the standard account for Christians into the eighteenth century – was just too provocative.[87] As with Greek, Hebrew opened access to the original words of the Bible, and was argued to be a necessary theological tool; but, as with Greek, it was also perceived as a threat and a danger – with the constant added nastiness of a slide into virulent anti-Jewish polemic.

The move to the vernacular (so often represented in a triumphalist historical mode as a return to the language of the people, to natural expression, to scripture for all) began as a shocking and aggressive and elite Reformist challenge, which was made possible by the destabilization of the Latin of Christianity by the re-evaluation of Greek and Hebrew. One of the corrollaries of the rediscovery of Greek was a change in how Latin could be looked at. The educational slogan of 'The Three Languages' projects an easy or natural connection between the classical tongues of Greek, Hebrew and Latin which belies its ideological purchase. Indeed, there is a grander history which runs through and well beyond the concerns of this chapter. This fascinating story traces first the political moment of the foundation of institutions dedicated to the study of 'the three languages'; second, the influence of such institutions on the whole education system; and, finally, the eventual privileged position of Latin and Greek in an otherwise vernacular educational system.[88] The threat of Greek, which Erasmus and Eck debate, is a threat which has profound and long-lasting intellectual *and institutional* implications.

The general argument of Erasmus and Eck was repeated in various forms and with increasing details and technical purchase in numerous exchanges. When the Humanists unearthed a Papal Decree from the

---

86 On the development of Hebrew study in the Tudor period, see Lloyd Jones (1983).

87 On Buxtorf, and the development of Hebrew after the Tudors, see Burnett (1996), who has extensive further bibliography. On the story of the circumcision, Burnett (1996) 50–3.

88 I have learnt in particular from Baldwin (1944); Bolgar (1954); McConica (1965); Simon (1966); Grafton and Jardine (1988), each with further bibliography. On Louvain in particular see Vocht (1951–5).

Council of Vienne of 1312, which established three chairs in ancient languages at Oxford (and which thus might provide the greatest Church authority for their own study of ancient languages), Franz Titelmans retorted that the decree intended that foreign languages should be learnt solely to take the Church's mission into foreign countries, and to translate foreign works safely into Latin for Christian circulation – and not to change Latin texts.[89] Neither side of the debate apparently noticed that the decree specified chairs in Chaldaean, Hebrew and Arabic and had nothing to do with learning Greek at all! The atmosphere of tension is palpable. Peter Shad, known as Mosellanus, writes from Leipzig in 1519 and gives a nice sense of the infighting:

the worthless fellows on the other side who are sworn foes to all liberal studies and especially to Greek (which I teach here publicly . . . as best I can and with all my heart) are always telling the crowd of inexperienced young men that, however much one ought to learn Greek (a concession I have won with difficulty after all these conflicts) yet it cannot be learnt from a German . . . If a man has time and money to waste in any case, he ought to seek his knowledge of Greek from Italians and Greeks. In this strain, these clever fellows go on croaking and try to dissuade the young from attending lectures in Greek . . . They declaim with great temerity against Greek studies.[90]

Mosellanus now in his first major university appointment, was the son of peasants who had had a real struggle to obtain his education. His opposition to scholasticism brought him many enemies, led by the vituperative and tenacious Jacques Masson, called Latomus – though also the important support of the Duke of Saxony.[91] It is Mosellanus who is taunted with his lack of letters from Erasmus. 'Stress of work' brought him to an early death aged only thirty-one. His embattled tale of Greek teaching at Leipzig is written to win over Erasmus, and it rehearses tellingly a version of Erasmus' own struggles. A report from the front line of Erasmus' mission.

Erasmus indeed replied with a parallel story about how trendy lectures at Oxford were interrupted by the barracking hooliganism of the conservatives. 'At Oxford, where a young man of more than common learning

[89] Titelmanus, F. *Collationes quinque super epistolam ad Romanos beati Pauli Apostoli . . .* (Antwerp, 1529): '*non enim . . . de scripturam emendatione . . . sed tantum de infidelium conversione, ordinatur*'; '*libros de linguis ipsis in Latinum fideliter transferentes*'. Useful discussion in Coogan (1992) 40ff.
[90] *EE* 3: 468–9 [*ep.* 911], 6 January 1519. 'Croaking' is κρώζοντες.
[91] An account in Rummel (1989) 57–76. See Masson's *de trium linguarum et studii theologici ratione* (1519) for his attack on learning languages as a bar to traditional theology.

was publicly teaching Greek with some success, some barbarian or other in a public sermon began to inveigh against Greek studies with many and great falsehoods.'[92] In this case, however, the King himself intervenes, and makes a declaration that 'those who wished should be able to study Greek'. (More's closeness to the King is plausibly thought significant in this high-level intervention.) And Erasmus goes on to add a second story of a theologian who preached before the King and declaimed against Greek study. Thomas More defended Greek studies so brilliantly that the theologian was quite crushed and, in a desperate attempt to shift position and salvage something from the wreckage of his humiliation, he stated 'I am not so much against Greek, because Greek is derived from Hebrew.'[93] This linguistic and theological desperation reduces the King to amazement at the man's stupidity, and he is promptly banned from preaching at court ever again. Erasmus is happy to swap tales of embattled supporters of Greek and even happier to record the royal support More has brought to bear and the series of public triumphs over opposition. Learning Greek is a cause which has reached the throne itself – and will continue to engage the major figures of power in the English state for the next fifty years.

Emblematic of the continued opposition to Greek study is an extraordinary club at Oxford. These confessed opponents of Greek studies called themselves 'The Trojans' (who else to oppose the Greeks?).

Their senior sage christened himself Priam; others called themselves Hector, Paris and so forth. The idea, whether as a joke or a piece of anti-Greek academic politics, is to pour ridicule on those devoted to the study of Greek. And I hear that things have come to such a pass that no-one can admit in public or in private that he enjoys Greek without being subjected to the jeers of these ludicrous 'Trojans' who think that Greek is a joke for the simple reason that they don't know what good literature is . . . [94]

That's Thomas More berating the academics of Oxford. He sees clearly enough how the Trojans might be thought funny or trivial, but he goes on to express outrage that one of the Trojans had actually preached that all classical literature should be discarded. (As late as 1579, Thomas Stockwood preached the Sermon at St Paul's Cross on that theme: 'I would have no other Authors read in Schooles, but only the

---

[92] *EE* 3: 546–7 [*ep.* 948], 22 April 1519; to Peter Mosellanus.
[93] *EE* 3: 547 [*ep.* 948], 22 April 1519; to Peter Mosellanus.
[94] Rogers (1961) 96. See also the *Letter to a Monk* in *CWM* xv, for further lengthy defence of humanist study; also, more particularly, *Letter to Dorp* and *Letter to Lee* in the same volume.

Scriptures.'[95]) So More turns his open letter to Oxford academics to a passionate appeal on behalf of humanist learning and Greek above all. The Trojans had called Greeks 'heretics', and Greek teachers 'chief devils', and pupils of Greek 'lesser devils' ('or more modestly and face-tiously as he thought "little devils"'[96]) – which prompts More to rehearse at length the tropes of how necessary Greek is for all true scholarship and theology. He even – back then – taunts Oxford with its competition with the Other place ('which you have always outshone'): in Cambridge, even those who don't study Greek make voluntary contributions to the Greek Professor's salary![97]

As ever with More, however, one shouldn't let the charm of his nar-rative and the elegance of his prose conceal his steely manipulation of power. He writes from the side of the King, and ends by reminding Oxford that the 'favour of Our Illustrious Prince' will be bestowed only if 'these stupid factions' are stopped. Like Athena, More is coming from the supreme power to make a significant intervention on behalf of the Greeks against the Trojans. But he is also more than usually prescient. The first sixty years of the sixteenth century are a period of extraor-dinary development for Oxford (and Cambridge) with the foundation of new colleges, redistribution of wealth and property, the redrafting of statutes and purposes – a series of struggles which not only involved the highest levels of power in the land, but also placed the construction of the university at the centre of the political and religious conflicts of the time. Henry VIII dissolved the monasteries and for a while it was feared he might treat the universities in a similar way. The universi-ties did finally come under the authority of the crown (and not only the royal foundations like Trinity, Cambridge, or Wolsey's Christchurch [Cardinal College]). 'The favour of Our Illustrious Prince' made and destroyed not merely individual careers, but also institutional structures for Oxford and Cambridge. By bringing the Greek row into the orbit of the throne, More is articulating – and manipulating – the lines of power that tightly enmeshed academic interchange with the authority of the crown, in a way which highlights again how readily the study of Greek is intertwined with the major political, theological and cultural revolutions of the time.

Back in the Fens, John Skelton, Poet Laureate of Henry VIII, when he was a Prince, whom Erasmus had once dutifully termed 'the one light

---

[95] John Stockwood 'A Very Fruitful Sermon Preeched at Paules Cross the tenth of May Last' (1579).
[96] Rogers ed. (1961) 100.   [97] Rogers ed. (1961) 101.

and glory of British letters',[98] was also not quite up with this modernist, Hellenist, movement. From the sidelines,[99] he dyspeptically satirizes the university's Greekness in his poem, 'Speke, Parrot' (of 1521):

> *In Academia* Parrot dare no problem keep
>> For *Graece fari* so occupieth the chair
> That *Latinum fari* may fall to rest and sleep
>> And *syllogisari* was drowned at Stourbridge fair;
>> Trivials and quadrivials so sore they now impair
> That Parrot the popinjay hath pity to behold
> How the rest of good learning is roufled up and trolled.[100]

The curriculum of scholasticism, its 'problems', its syllogisms (*syllogisari*), the seven liberal arts (the 'trivials and quadrivials'), even speaking Latin (*Latinum fari*) – summed up as 'the rest of good learning' – have all been sunk in the carnival topsy-turvy of the fair on Stourbridge Common. Now all instead is *Graece fari*, 'Greek speaking', 'Greek talk' – something which Skelton himself, it seems, had not learnt. Lily thus writes a nasty little poetic squib back at Skelton which ends up *doctrinam nec habes, nec es poeta*, 'You've got no learning and you are no poet.'[101] None of which stops Skelton with a typical satiric double-whammy also complaining that the Greek scholars don't know Greek well enough to get a horse a bundle ['bottle'] of hay:

> But our Greeks their Greek so well have applied
> That they cannot say in Greek, riding by the way,
> How, hosteler, fetch my horse a bottle of hay![102]

---

[98] *EE* 1: 241 [*ep.* 104] Autumn, 1499, to Prince Henry.

[99] For Skelton's precarious position see Walker (1988), especially 1–123.

[100] I have updated the spellings of this poem for ease of modern reading. Scattergood's standard edition – of what is a very difficult text – reads here:

> In *Achademia* Parrot dare no probleme kepe
>> For *Greci fari* so occupyeth the chayre,
> That *Latinum fari* may fall to reste and slepe,
>> And *silogisari* was drowned at Sturbrydge Fayre;
>> Tryvals and quatryvals so sore now appayre,
> That Parrot the popagay hath pytye to beholde
> How the rest of good lernyng is roufled up and trold.

[101] British Library Ms Harley 540 f57ᵛ. Not a very distinguished squib.

[102] Scattergood ed. (1983):

> But our Grekis theyr Greke so well have applyed
> That they cannot say in Greke, rydynge by the way,
> How, hosteler, fetche my hors a botell of hay!

The new Greek also invades the erotic scene of Skelton's verse, as in a more bizarre, picaresque moment, Parrot meets Galathea (don't ask):

> *Galathea*
> Now kus me Parrot, kus me, kus, kus,kus!
> God's blessing light on thy little sweet mus!
>   *Vita et anima*
>   *Zoe ke psiche*
> *Concumbunt Graece. Non est hic sermo pudicus*[103]

Galathea's desire to be kissed ('kus me') by the Parrot's beak ('mus') turns into a Latin ejaculation of pleasure, *vita et anima*, 'Oh life and soul', or, more precisely, a Latin ejaculation of pleasure followed by a (poorly) transliterated Greek version of the same phrase (*zoe kai psyche* = 'Oh life and soul'), which is itself a quotation from Juvenal's satire (in Latin, though Juvenal's text has the words in Greek letters) on how pretentious Roman women cry out in Greek during sexual pleasure.[104] (Greek 'has fingers', *digitos habet...*) Juvenal's joke against Roman women being polluted by Greekling mannerisms is replayed by Skelton with a further twist of knowing opposition to 'new' languages. Greek is the tongue to have sex (with a parrot) in ... and for you to have in your mouth (with whatever comprehension) while reading this poem. You always get the nastiest things in your mouth when you read satire like this. So the scene continues (in Latin, with two further quotations purloined from Juvenal): 'They lie down together in Greek. It is not a clean language.'[105] Juvenal had said that Greek is 'not a clean language for an old woman'. In Skelton's bad-tempered and foul-mouthed view, the problem with Greek is just that it's a filthy language.

This story of culture wars over Greek has been long enough – though it would have been much longer if I had put together all the relevant

---

[103] Scattergood ed. (1983) (who also points out the especially difficult textual problems throughout the Galathea episode, which is simply omitted from some (bowdlerized) modern texts):

> *Galatea*
> Now kusse me Parrot, kus me, kus, kus, kus!
> Goddes blissyng lyght on thy lyttel swete musse!
>   *Vita et anima*
>   *Zoe ke psiche*
> *Concumbunt Grece. Non est hic sermo pudicus*

[104] Juvenal 6. 195.

[105] Juvenal 6. 191, 194. There is more of a similar nature on Greek in this poem of Skelton's. For Skelton's role in the politics of the 1520s see Walker (1988) (with further bibliography), who sees the issue of Greek in this poem too restrictedly as an issue of the syllabus at St Paul's School (63–5).

letters and treatises written by Erasmus and his supporters and opponents, since the import of his role for the religious wars of the Reformation was repeatedly asserted, contested, and overlaid with competing
claims. The more intricate details of theological interaction have been
well traced elsewhere (in exhaustive detail, as we say) and there are hundreds of pages of Latin infighting to be read. But it should be clear
from what I have offered, I hope, just how intense and multiform the
debate over the place of Greek in theology and learning was – how
learning Greek became emblematic in the story you told of yourself.
Erasmus' *Novum Testamentum* proved to be the touchpaper to an already
simmering conflict about whether Greek was necessary for true study
of the Bible. The argument erupted into bitter and long-running rows;
spilled over into satire, drama, poetry, sermons, letters; led to claques
interrupting lectures, violent academic hooliganism, institutional conflict and change, and, all in all, became an icon in the religious conflict
which set at stake each person's commitment to faith, his idea of how
Christianity should be viewed and practised. The extreme arguments
that declared Greek, the language of the Gospels, to be the source of
heresy fed into the extremism of the Reformation's violence. The *Novum
Testamentum*'s engagement with Greek learning was perceived to raise a
question about the authority of the Church, the values of tradition – a
Christian's sense of his own place in the history of his religion. A sense
of self. Its *newness* was indeed a threat to many. And was fought over,
again and again, across Europe. The book on the top shelf of Erasmus'
study, then, its title facing you, was painted during the first year after
the publication of the first edition, as the protests are beginning to swell,
and Erasmus is preparing the second, more radical edition. The portrait
is painted at this crucial cusp of Erasmus' career. It makes a statement
about what Erasmus stands for. It marks his fame, his scandal. It would
also look very different and even more provocative if you looked at it
in 1520 or 1525, with the increasing disquiet around the second edition and the following turmoil of Reformation. Different again in 1559.
The history of the reading and contesting of the *Novum Testamentum*
continues to overlay this image with layers of significance. The picture of this book on the top shelf highlights why you should care about
Erasmus.

IV

There are two further books in Metsys' picture whose titles are written
in, and like Jerome and the *Novum Testamentum*, they are linked. They

might be linked in the economy of the image by both being shaded, and pushed back at an angle. They are certainly linked in Erasmus' intellectual history. On top of Jerome is a volume of Lucian – and his name is blazoned in Greek letters ΛΟΥΚΙΑΝΟΣ. From my discussion so far, the symbolic charge of the Greek letters and of the Greekness of the author should be evident. The Greek letters require the viewer's learning Greek to be read, and enacts the insider/outsider network which Erasmus' corrspondence continually constructs. (His personal letters are studded with Greek words in Greek type, once he has mastered the language.) This typography is striking here also, however, because it was for a Latin version of Lucian that Erasmus first came to prominence. Together with Thomas More, he translated more than thirty of Lucian's works from Greek into Latin, and they really put Lucian on the reading list. It was the first translation of Lucian of any scope and the first to achieve wide circulation. It was an immensely popular and influential enterprise that went through more than thirty editions in Erasmus' lifetime (many more than, say, *Utopia*). From Lucian, Erasmus also developed a dialogue form that was instantiated in his *Colloquies*, a collection of often humorous contemporary exchanges in Latin, which became the set reading for generations of schoolboys in order to learn Latin, the language of education. But what makes Erasmus' identification with Lucian much more than a paragraph in the history of translation and reception of a Greek author was the scandal and success of what is still Erasmus' best-known book, *Praise of Folly*, which was immediately praised and scorned by its readers specifically as a Lucianic piece. On the top shelf, above the *Novum Testamentum*, at the back to the right you can make out the letters HOR, which is a mistaken overpainting of MOR – that is, MOR[IAE ENCOMIUM], the *Praise of Folly*. Together, the text of Lucian and the *Praise of Folly* tell another remarkable story of Erasmus' engagement with Greek.

Lucian, first, who is going to be one of the heroes of this book. Now, it is rather difficult to produce a simply coherent picture of Lucian's importance to the culture of the sixteenth century.[106] On the one hand, Lucian in Greek and in Latin translation played an increasingly important role in the education system, as did Erasmus' Lucianic dialogues, particularly in England. The numbers of editions of Lucian's works across Europe suggest that he remained one of the most widely read ancient authors.

[106] For good starts, see Thompson (1937); Robinson (1979); Duncan (1979); Mattioli (1980); Mayer (1984); Lauvergnat-Gagnière (1988); Förster (1886) is an important early treatment, as is Caccia (1907). See also Marsh (1998).

On the other hand, particularly amid the cultural and theological conflicts I have been tracing, Lucian was often violently rejected. The word
'Lucianical', or 'Lucianiste' (in France), could be thrown about as a mor-
tal insult.[107] Lucian was reviled as an atheist, a scoffer of religion, and his
satires were perceived as violently disruptive of social order and authority. In 1549 some of his most worrying texts were placed on the Index
of banned books by the Catholic Church; in 1590 the whole corpus
of Lucian was placed on the Index by the Vatican. It was at the same
time required reading for those beginning their Greek studies in English
schools and universities (and in many places across Europe) and justified
as valuable preparation for reading the Gospels. In the 1430s, his works
could be 'fittingly dedicated to a Pope' (as did Lapo di Castiglionchio
to Eugenius).[108] In the 1530s, he could be declared 'the most vicious of
men'.[109] One of his little pieces stimulated a whole tradition of grand
and trivial art works and accompanying literary discussion, namely, his
description of the figure of 'Calumny', painted by Apelles (a subject which
has a certain historical irony).[110] Yet Vives, a friend of Erasmus, could
describe a Lucianic rhetoric of wit as 'slander, tauntings, the insinuations
of the basest suspicions, inversions of what is true, and the attempt to
do evil from a good purpose and to do good from an evil motive'.[111]
Or as Zwinger put it with even more direct hostility, in his brief work
on Lucian: 'bitterness leads him to transgress . . . one thinks of him as
motivated . . . by pathological ill-will'.[112] This continuing doubleness offers something of a paradox (to use the term of Lauvergnat-Gagnière) – a
paradox not so much because there is a multiform or polarized reaction to
his writing, but more because the institutional normalization of his texts
and the controversy over his scandalous atheism seem to have progressed
hand in hand. How did this remarkable state of affairs come about?

When it came to learning the basics of the Greek language, Lucian
was the man. Thomas Linacre sums it up simply enough at the beginning
of the century, within his patently humanist agenda: 'The true learning
you seek is acknowledged by all to be enshrined in the wisdom of the
Greeks. Your toil will become light and amusing and your progress sure,

---

[107] See especially Duncan (1979); Lauvergnat-Gagnière (1988). For further seventeenth–eighteenth
century shifts see Bury (1994).
[108] Robinson (1979) 84.
[109] Dolet, S. *Dialogus de Ciceroniana imitatione* . . . (1535), on which see Scott (1910) 63–93; Lloyd-Jones
(1995).
[110] Massing (1990).   [111] Watson (1913) 185.
[112] Zwinger's essay *de vita et scriptis Luciani narratio* in Cousin's 1563 edition of Lucian. Zwinger notes
the different views of Vives and Erasmus on Lucian.

if only you will read a little Lucian every day.'[113] A daily dose of Lucian, then, for what Erasmus praises as his 'purity' and 'elegance' of his Greek. Despite occasional remarks like Thomas Becon's declaration in 1560 that such a 'wicked and ungodly' author should be banned from the school curriculum,[114] Lucian was used to teach children from grammar schools across the country, right up to Edward VI himself, whose Cambridge educated Tutor, Sir John Cheke, had no difficulty in starting the King on Lucian before moving on to the more pressing Xenophon, Demosthenes and the New Testament.[115] (The future King's Greek prose exercises can still be read, if you are attracted by the romance of such Realia.) The continued availability of texts and the dominance of a standardized curriculum brought, as ever, a certain conservatism. The choice of Lucian by the early humanists, who pioneered Greek teaching, had thus its own momentum. Lucian for beginners continued into the nineteenth century.

But Lucian is funny, irreverent and in places not merely scurrilous but also mildly dismissive of a new cult group called 'Christians'. There was consequently a range of responses to the content of Lucian, which often attached itself to stylistic commentary, and often went well beyond it. So Thomas Elyot, in his book of political philosophy, *The Governor*, famously if somewhat ponderously declared, 'It is better that a childe should never reade any part of Luciane than all of Luciane.'[116] Pirckheimer and others questioned the value of Lucian as an educational text. Even Erasmus' correspondents, writing to the master, found it difficult not to see malice in 'that rascal Lucian'.[117] But it was Luther, the driving force of the Reformation, with the full weight of his authority, who 'first charged the name of Lucian with a purely negative connotation in a text which proved to be widely circulated'.[118] 'Lucian' became a slogan to reject the enemies of the passionate seriousness of the Reformation and Counter-Reformation. Both the Reformers and the Catholic Church by the last quarter of the century had made Lucian an anathema.

This development of hostility has two closely interrelated strands. First, the evaluation of the moral value of Lucian's satire underwent a sea change. Erasmus defended Lucian at length, and provides us with

---

[113] A letter to John Claymond, cited by Allen (1934) 153 (with a nice discussion of some elements of Greek at Oxford).

[114] Cited in Baldwin (1944) 109.

[115] See Hudson (1980) and Strype (1821). On Strype, see Cargill-Thompson (1980) 192–201.

[116] T. Elyot *The Book named The Governor* ed. Lehmberg, S.E. (London, 1962) 30.

[117] *EE* I: 505 [*ep.* 254] from Jerome Aleander, February 1512: *tuus nebulo Lucianus*. He adds *ipse* κόλαξ τε καί κόραξ *erat*, 'he was himself both flatterer and chatterer'.

[118] Lauvergnat-Gagnière (1988) 135.

a template of the vocabulary of praise: Lucian, he declared, 'shows amazing artistry and finesse in his wide-ranging criticisms, turning up his nose at the whole world, rubbing the salt of his wit into every pore and always ready with a nasty crack on any topic that crosses his path . . . He has so many good qualities: a graceful style, a sure imaginative touch, pleasant humour, biting shrewdness, teasing allusiveness. He has a way of mixing gravity with his nonsense and nonsense with his gravity, of laughing and telling the truth at the same time . . . And the result is, for profit and pleasure combined, I know of no stage comedy, or satire, which can be compared with this man's dialogues.'[119] The stylistic claims which justify the use of Lucian as a teaching text, inevitably move into an area of moral didacticism. Erasmus may begin with 'artistry' and 'finesse' and emphasize Lucian's 'graceful style', but it is locating his 'gravity' and 'profit' which underlies his defence. The wit and style of Lucian is – must be – in service to a moral message, which, in its uncovering of hypocrisy, can be assimilated to Christ's teaching. Peter Mosellanus puts the general case with exemplary clarity: 'It is a waste of time to try to present moral instruction in a direct form, as it will be so unpalatable that none of it will take effect. You must put it into pretty language, attractive and amusing, just as Christ found it advisable to express his philosophy through parable and allegory.'[120] Mosellanus' attempt persuasively to link the secular pleasures of Lucian to the agenda of a religious education is paradigmatic.

The attack on Lucian's moral worth began from his negative remarks about Christians – he is one of the ancient enemies of God; expanded to his satire on conventional religion – a mocker of the forms of worship; and concluded with a standard picture of him as the Atheist *par excellence*. This was coupled with a claim that his humour was indiscriminate and contained a psychological bitterness which scoffed at everything. To follow Lucian was to open yourself to the charge – in the grim words of the grim Scaliger – 'you have jeered at our religious orders', 'you hate supremely the human race'.[121] Far from offering a moralist's critique of hypocrisy, Lucian became increasingly portrayed as a malicious mocker, without belief and opposed to belief. The moral value of satire was wiped out by the policemen of theology.

[119] *EE* 1: 425–6 [*ep.* 193] June 1506, to Christopher Urswick. This is the preface to *Gallus* included in *Luciani Opuscula* of 1506.
[120] The dedicatory epistle to his translation of Lucian's 'The Downward Journey', [Κατάπλους] quoted and discussed also by Robinson (1979) 96.
[121] Scaliger *Oratio de M.T. Cicerone contra Desiderium Erasmium* (1531), quoted by Duncan (1979) 79. On Scaliger's conflict with Erasmus, see Scott (1910) 42–63.

Central to this sea change – my second strand – is the fear of laughter itself. Erasmus in his letter to Hutten[122] constructs a celebrated image of More as man of 'little tricks and japes' (which for us inevitably now looks forward to his jesting ascent of the scaffold): 'from boyhood he took such delight in joking that it could appear to be the whole object of his existence, though he balked at scurrility and never cared to be abusive'. Laughter – the right sort of laughter, of course, neither filthy nor abusive – is an integral element of humanist dialogue. 'His enjoyment of sharp intelligent repartee continues even now.' (It would make me feel like a spoilsport to recall the book-burning, heretic-hounding, abuser of Luther here, though it would help emphasize the partiality of Erasmus' profoundly influential picture.) And More's pleasure in badinage has, of course, its classical precedent: 'It also explains his special fondness for Lucian.' Indeed, More embodies a fully Lucianic ideal: 'You could call him another Democritus' (as Pace, ever willing, proudly does, at length[123]). Democritus, the acerbic, cynic wit, is one of the few philosophers to be treated with encomium rather than satire by Lucian. The erudite and sharp joking of friends makes up a privileged element in Erasmus' self-fashioning of the image of humanists at work. 'Lusus', 'play(fulness)' is the watchword.[124]

Religion, however, was no laughing matter, especially in 'the overheated religious atmosphere of the mid-century'.[125] Tyndale, reversing Erasmus' praise, accused More of 'jesting out the truth'[126]– mocking what really counts. Lucian was regularly accused of laughing indiscriminately at everything held dear by Christians. His laughter was disruptive, insidious, malicious and led to the undermining of authority. 'In Elizabethan England, "Lucianical" had become a term of abuse with devilish undertones.'[127] Lucian's grin had no place in Luther's world. The seriousness and passion of the Reformation with its heavy emphasis on faith as the only salvation found the satirical giggles of the Greek satirist profoundly enraging.

---

[122] *EE* 4: 12–23 [*ep.* 999] 23 July 1519, to Ulrich Hutten. For his exchanges with Hutten see Klawiter (1977).

[123] Manley and Silvester eds. (1967) 104–5: '*de illo autem Democrito loquor, qui omnes res humanas risit, quem non modo diligentissime est imitatus, verum etiam una syllaba superavit. Nam ut ille humana omnia ridenda censuit, ita hic deridenda*'.

[124] Excellent discussion in Duncan (1979).   [125] Robinson (1979) 98.

[126] *An Answer unto Sir Thomas More's Dialogue* (1530), in *The Works of the English Reformers*, ed. T. Russell, (London, 1831), 202.

[127] Duncan (1979) 78.

Yet the laugh still has its ripples, its legacies. The threat of this laughter was exactly what drew Rabelais to Lucian and Erasmus – and provoked Rabelais' outraged critics in turn. Rabelais, with adjectives purloined from the earlier debate was marked out as 'facétieux, mordant, utile-doux, raillard, second Epicure, gausseur ou gaudisseur, Lucian françois', 'jesting, biting, pleasure-monger, scoffer, second Epicurus, mocker or joyster, French Lucian'.[128] 'Lucianisme' enjoyed a long and turbulent tradition in France in particular,[129] a tradition marked out by Voltaire who wrote an emblematic dialogue – of course a dialogue – between Rabelais, Erasmus and Lucian. Gibbon, continuing the fiction more primly – I don't think he is being ironic – wrote, 'I have sometimes thought of writing a dialogue of the dead in which Lucian, Erasmus and Voltaire should mutually acknowledge the danger of exposing an old superstition to the contempt of the blind and fantastic multitude.'[130] That danger was indeed already willingly acknowledged by Erasmus (who publicly declared his biblical scholarshp in particular not to be for the rude masses[131]). But the irruption of laughter cannot be cancelled.

If Erasmus portrayed Lucian as a 'suave, versatile, festive wit, potentially Christian' in moral aim, none the less he became increasingly represented as a 'godless intellect, inherently Satanic',[132] whose laughter hated mankind. An author to be banned. In the middle of Metsys' portrait is Lucian in Greek type, inevitably linked to his first and most influential translator. Metsys' picture – again – represents a provocative and contentious story about cultural capital, and Erasmus' fiercely contested pursuit of it.

V

It was not his translations of Lucian which locked Erasmus into international fame and controversy, however – for all that by the date of Metsys' painting the very word 'Lucian', especially in Greek letters, could evoke the passions of that controversy. Rather, it was the *Praise of Folly* which made the connection between Lucian and Erasmus inevitable

---

[128] De la Porte, cited by Lauvergnat-Gagnière (1988) 235.

[129] See especially Lauvergnat-Gagnière (1988).

[130] Gibbon (1994) 214. Gay (1970) 3 begins his dialogues with Lucian saying 'It was good of Gibbon to bring us together by thinking of us in the same sentence.'

[131] Though I am not the first to point out he had earlier hoped through his work to bring Scripture to all...

[132] Both quotations from Duncan (1979) 83.

and scandalous, and drew Erasmus into religious battles in a blaze of publicity. The story is very well known in outline, in part, as usual, because of Erasmus' own brilliantly engaging version of events. The *Moriae Encomium* ['Praise of Folly'], was written, he tells us, without his books, in a few days relaxing time at More's house, at More's instigation. The plot was worked out, he says, riding his horse on the journey from Italy to England. He worries that the resultant satiric trifles may seem too airy for a theologian and too biting for a Christian – a good come-on for a preface, this: what you are about to receive is . . . ; but he finds support for his sharpness in the ancients, especially Lucian, and, inevitably, 'divine Jerome' who 'had fun [*lusit*] in many genres more freely and bitingly'.[133] Sacred and secular precedent, then. The punning joke on More's name in the title is explicitly made by Erasmus in his preface, but it isn't just an ironic jibe ('my mate, Mr Folly'). For the preface's loving story of composition and the model of sophisticated and ironic prose instantiated in the *Moriae Encomium* also project (and praise) a genuine humanist ideal: the friends, the wit, the sharp intellectual exchange. . . . The ironic praise of Folly also contains an encomium of humanist *lusus*. The invitation to participate in the sophisticated pleasure of More and Erasmus is part of the persuasive power of the combination of the dedication letter and the text. It can draw you into a shared, if sharply challenging circle.

The image of satiric squib between friends has remained a basic part of the book's fame, despite its huge printed circulation. If it is printing – in the simple technological sense – that makes possible the extraordinary circulation of his *Paraphrases* to every parish church in the kingdom and thus the continuation of an Erasmian influence, it is printing also that creates the possibility of the construction of the image of Erasmus, the image which makes him the first international intellectual superstar. A crucial factor in the construction of that image is the very wide circulation of a myth of intimacy. What it meant to know (of) Erasmus, to understand how you came to be holding his book, how he came to write it, is irrevocably altered by the new potentialities of mass printing, and Erasmus' brilliant deployment of those potentialities.

The *Moriae Encomium* begins as a lighthearted fantasy, which develops into a full-scale ironic oration in praise of folly – delivered by the figure of Folly herself as orator – but it ends with a statement of a Christian ideal of an ecstatic engagement, piety's mad inversion of the normal,

---

[133] *EE* I: 461 [*ep.* 222], 9 June 1511, to Thomas More: the preface to the *Moriae Encomium*.

instantiated in religious practice.[134] Its banter and more aggressive attacks on contemporary theologians, coupled with a mockery of conventional religious practice and the principles of scholasticism, provoked
an instant and hostile response particularly from those theologians who
felt that they were its victims, notably the Faculty at Louvain. I suppose
that if a pious Christian were to read casually that Christ and his fol-
lowers were called Sileni – that is, priapic, ugly, vinous, elderly leaders
of the satyrs, to whom the disreputable Alcibiades in Plato's *Symposium*
likened Socrates; or that St Paul confesses he speaks as a fool; or even that
Christ was 'something of a fool himself'; and if to those not self-evidently
pious remarks is added a barrage of jokes about the triviality and silli-
ness of the most dignified theologians, it is not too hard to imagine why
the conservative establishment responded with a certain distaste to the
Moriae Encomium. Not least because it was quickly and hugely popular,
with thirty-six Latin editions in Erasmus' lifetime, as well as translations
into French, German and even Czechoslovakian.

The text of the *Moriae Encomium*, I am afraid to say (with my classicist hat proudly on), is difficult. It was re-written in more than one
of the early editions with several lengthy sections added to it, as well
as many minor corrections. It should be read in a critical edition, I'd
say, because Erasmus' shifts of focus and sense, largely in response to
critical responses, are fascinating. Its theology has provoked lengthy and
sometimes brilliant exposition (although Erasmus disingenuously tried to
claim that its stance was just the same as the *Enchiridion Militis Christiani*,
his *Manual* (or *Flick-Knife* as one scholar translates it!) *Of a Christian Soldier*,
a laborious and conventional instruction kit for piety, which worried
no one).[135] The jokes of the *Moriae Encomium*, unfortunately, all too
often need explaining these days too, as much as its theology. One typically snide moment – one of my favourites – is when he calls Aquinas
ἀριστοτελικώτατος, 'most Aristotelian'. Aquinas couldn't read Aristotle
in Greek and had limited access to the Aristotelian corpus (which is one
reason the humanists had to be snooty about the master of scholastic
theology). So calling him 'most Aristotelian' in Greek, in Greek letters,
neatly spears Aquinas – and any other Greekless readers.[136] One can
see how this book – over many pages – could well annoy those it was

---

[134] See Screech (1980); Gordon (1990); Thompson (1973).
[135] O'Donnell (1981) xiv calls it 'repetitive . . . and flawed' – and notes it went through more than
   fifty editions. For a more sympathetic reading, see McConica (1966) 17–43; Grafton and Jardine
   (1988) 142–9.
[136] See Miller (1978) on the use of Greek proverbs to alienating effect.

destined to annoy (and I am even more (self-)conscious why explaining jokes is a bad idea).

So, what I am going to do here, then, is to make just two brief, relevant points, where clearly we could spend a lot of time on its very rich critical tradition. The first is this. Erasmus' book with its 'serio-comic art' was undoubtedly an event in the cultural shifts of the early sixteenth century, but by its own appropriation of Lucian, and, indeed, its adaptation of Lucianic strategies, it had the effect of enforcing a connection between the study of Greek and that cultural revolution. The threat of Greek studies was sharply felt by its opponents because a Lucianic work, based on Greek studies, could be so damagingly, insidiously, invidiously successful. The *Moriae Encomium* was the work whose success proved the damaging threat of Greek-led cleverness. Maarten Dorp, a young theologian at Louvain, was encouraged by the senior faculty there to write an attack on Erasmus, and he received a long – and now famous – letter in reply, in which Erasmus laid out his principles of study and defended both the *Novum Testamentum* and the *Moriae Encomium*.[137] In it, he wishes that anyone who wants to be called a theologian would stop all the back-biting and sniping: 'Instead of behaving like this, tearing each other to pieces and then being torn themselves, wasting their time and everyone else's, how much better it would be if they would learn Greek or Hebrew or Latin, at least!'[138] Dorp, continuing the exchange, replied that Jews didn't know Greek, and the Greeks didn't know Latin, so this exaggerated demand to know three languages was quite unnecessary. Dorp set the tone and agenda for a long series of opponents, although his own disagreements with Erasmus gradually dissipated to such a degree that Dorp finally confesses, 'Oh that I had been so fortunate as to be allowed to learn Greek; nor do I believe that one should listen to those who think Greek is of little value in the exegesis of the New Testament.'[139] But, significantly, both Erasmus and his opponents recognized that the study of Greek had become a fundamental sign and symptom of desired or deprecated cultural change.

---

[137] For Dorp's Letter see *EE* 2: 10–16 [*ep*. 304] Louvain, September 1514; for Erasmus' reply see *EE* 2: 90–114 [*ep*. 337], May 1515. This is extensively discussed in the works already cited, see e.g. Rummel (1989) 1–13 with further bibliography 192 n.11. For a full discussion of Dorp's works and life, see de Vocht (1934) 61–408, with Moringus' *Vita* (257–348), and discussion of row with Erasmus 139–59.

[138] *EE* 2: 106 [*ep*. 337], May 1515. He hopes rather *in scriptarum campo sine nostro dolore ludere. Ludere* is a marked term there. See also *EE* 4: 158 ll. 29–30 [*ep*. 1060] for the same phrase.

[139] *[Graecam] linguam utinam tam fortunatus fuissem ut licuisset discere*, cited by Rummel (1989) 11/196 n.47. Dorp changed his position more than once: Erasmus (*EE* 3: 59 [*ep*. 637, 28 August 1517 to Peter Gilles]) exasperated calls him 'quavis muliere inconstantior', 'more unreliable than a woman'.

The second point follows on directly. Because of the Lucianic strategies of Erasmus' satire, the figures of Lucian and Erasmus were constantly overlapped. Martin Luther wrote: 'On my deathbed I shall forbid my sons to read Erasmus' *Colloquies*. He is much worse than Lucian, mocking all things under the guise of holiness.'[140] Stephen Dolet (not such a name as Luther to conjure with) stated: 'Erasmus, whose custom it is to attack everybody... emulates Lucian.'[141] Scaliger: 'Let us say also Lucian for Erasmus. That name would be appropriate for you; since you have imitated him in the style of his History, have followed his despicable method of criticism...'[142] And so on.

I do not know if we are meant to see in Erasmus' smile in the Metsys portrait any of his penchant for savage mockery, or if we are to catch a gleam in his eye, but it is not only Jerome who informs the picture of the scholar in his study. The *Moriae Encomium* is on the top shelf by the *Novum Testamentum*, Lucian in Greek letters is on Jerome. This stack of books interleaves two linked engagements of Erasmus with the study of Greek, and allows us to see both Jerome and Lucian as figures who provide crucial models for Erasmus' representation. These four books ask the viewer to see the significance of Erasmus – a contentious history, a scandalous subject. They identify the sitter. As More, the recipient of the picture, noted in his verse poem of thanks, 'If the figure does not tell you who he is, the inscribed books will teach you: they are famous all over the world.'[143] The fine copy of the picture in the Corsini Gallery at Rome – once thought to be the original – does not have these inscribed titles, and the difference that blankness creates, is surely immense. The generic scholarly books have none of the bite, the testimony of debate, that the inscriptions so forcefully proclaim. The books tell you

---

[140] Luther (1908) 136. 'Stinking of Lucian' is another choice expression of Luther's.

[141] Stephen Dolet *Dialogus de Ciceroniana imitatione* (1535) – on which see Scott (1910) 63–93, and the more sophisticated Lloyd-Jones (1995) and (1999), and in general Hoffmann (1994). Amusingly, Scaliger was immensely annoyed at what he saw as Dolet's unacknowledged imitation of *his* dialogue about imitation (Scott [1910] 81–3) – his hatred, less amusingly, lasted long and bitterly (Christie [1899] 215–17). On Dolet's life, see Christie (1899); and on Dolet's execution – ostensibly for a translation of a line of Plato in a 'heretical' manner – see Christie (1899), and Wallace (1850) 2: 1–3, where his name is precisely something to conjure with: as he went to the stake, he declared *non dolet ipse Dolet, sed pia turba dolet* ['Dolet himself does not grieve, but the congregation of the pious grieves']. The more than usually well-versed Lieutenant replied: *non pia turba dolet, sed dolet ipse Dolet* ['The congregation of the pious does not grieve, but Dolet himself grieves']. (This story does not appear until 1622, according to Christie (1899), in Severt *L'Anti-Martyrologie* (Lyon, 1622) 475.) Erasmus offers a different pun [*EE* 11: 333 [*ep.* 3127], 6 June 1536, to Melanchthon: '...*Doletum, pene dixeram Oletum*' ['...Dolet, I almost said Mr. Shit'].

[142] *Oratio pro M.T. Cicerone contra Desiderium Erasmium* (1531), quoted by Duncan (1979) 79.

[143] *EE* 3: 106–7 [*ep.* 684] 7 October 1517, from Thomas More: *quanquam is qui sit, vt taceret ipse,/ inscripti poterant docere libri/ toto qui celebres leguntur orbe.*

more than a name. They say: this is what Erasmus means and why you should care.

VI

There is more, yet. The open book on Erasmus' desk shows you words 'which are written in a close imitation of Erasmus' own hand', and which record the beginning of his *Paraphrase of St Paul's Epistle to the Romans*. (Erasmus' name along with *Paul*'s, then, another twist in the representation of fame in this panel.) Like the letters, the image of intimate immediacy is carefully articulated in this snapshot of composition. He is in the process of writing another of his books, making the holy texts more available to all by those paraphrases, and the careful reader might just spot the next word emerging. The scholar and teacher is at work, preparing, as *you* can see. And there is perhaps a viewer within the artwork. For, in the other portrait of the diptych, we can turn to observe the pupil, Peter Gilles – this is plate 2 – looking out of the frame towards Erasmus writing. Gilles is also in his study (or is it *their* study?). He is surrounded by Latin books – Seneca, Plutarch (with a Greek title overwritten), Quintus Curtius, Suetonius, and the *Education of a Christian Prince*, its title given by a single word of Greek. Seneca, Plutarch, Suetonius, and Quintus Curtius were all edited by Erasmus. *The Education of a Christian Prince* is, of course, a didactic work by Erasmus, one of his attempts to dominate the (theory of) education market. The pupil of Erasmus – as Gilles describes himself – is surrounded by the Master's instructive texts (and may be assumed to know what Greek means). What is more, Gilles is pointing – with his finger firmly placed on the cover – to an ornately decorated volume. On the Longford version of the portrait, which I am convinced by Campbell is the original, the book is inscribed with ANTIBARBARI ['Against the Barbarians'].[144] This is one of the earliest works of Erasmus, a dialogue in support of classical studies – the Greek against the Barbarians. *Antibarbari* was not published until 1520, however, and so scholars say that the inscription may be a later addition (all the inscriptions in the painting have been painted over).[145] Or it may indicate, between More and Metsys and Gilles and now you (and me), the insider knowledge of the written but not yet published manuscript. Gilles – whose hands and face are illumined by an offstage light source as are Erasmus' – is holding a letter addressed to himself, which is

---

[144] Campbell *et al.* (1978); see also Gerlo (1969), Phillips (1975).
[145] I am reliant here on Campbell *et al.* (1978).

2. Portrait of Peter Gilles, by Quentin Metsys

'most readily interpreted as a letter from Erasmus'.[146] (He wrote so many.)
All here points, as Jardine teaches in particular, to the expression of a
pupil.[147] In a copy of Gilles' portrait in Antwerp (which has sometimes
been thought to be the original), the book is inscribed with a fragmentary

---

[146] Jardine (1993) 33.　　　[147] Jardine (1993) esp. 27–39.

inscription which is identified as 'Querela pacis', which would identify it as a miscellaneous volume of Erasmus' work, in press at the time of the painting.[148] A different insider knowledge. In each case, Gilles points knowingly to a text of his teacher which is about to be published. So when Gilles, unlike Erasmus, stares out of the frame, it is perhaps towards his teacher, book and letter to hand. The diptych's representation of two friends is also a hierarchical picture of teacher and pupil. You, the viewer – like More – can read this.

The potency of the teaching of Erasmus which this diptych embodies, was felt throughout the century and beyond: the *Paraphrases* in the churches; the *Colloquies* in the schools; the theological works in the universities. But to my mind what's most surprising is another less well-known afterlife. Its background is the continued premium on Greek teaching, and its integral link with England's turning to Protestantism. Roger Ascham and Sir John Cheke come from Cambridge to teach Edward VI and Elizabeth I, and Ascham's letters (along with those of other courtiers) have played a formative role in our image of Elizabeth as the Queen: the Queen who could read Greek; the learned woman; the hearer of speeches and plays, the giver of orations.[149] Ascham's commitment to an Erasmean model of self-formation (and his own obsession with reading Greek and Demosthenes in particular) contribute hugely to this portrait of the Queen. (My point, I should emphasize, isn't that she didn't read Greek, nor, more snootily, that she wasn't as good at it as all those courtiers' anecdotes have to claim. It is rather that the very construction of this image depends to a significant degree on a privileged inherited model: knowing Greek, how you learnt Greek, was an established story, shared by its many tellers. It is also important that her example led some other privileged women to study Greek, in a way which will find parallels later with some remarkable Victorian intellectual women's attempts to break through the gendered boundaries of education.) The narrative I want to tell is certainly part of the build up to the Religious Settlement of 1559. In this most important of political processes, 'Cambridge men . . . were utilized almost exclusively' in the negotiations.[150] They formed a hugely influential group of courtiers around the throne and their leader, William Cecil. How were they linked? 'A common enthusiasm for classical studies, Protestant doctrine, and a reformed pronunciation of Greek had drawn

[148] See Jardine (1993) 34–5, for bibliography and discussion.
[149] Important discussion with bibliography in Hudson (1980). On Smith see also Dewar (1964).
[150] Hudson (1980) 40.

them together.'[151] It will be appreciated from the previous pages how this particular bunch of students, growing up in the final years of Erasmus' life, could bond around a zeal for classical study and the lure of theological reformation. But what about the pronunciation of Greek? It is this that I want to follow up.

Erasmus had published a treatise on the subject of how to pronounce Greek some years before in 1528. Around the beginning of the 1540s, this treatise became part of a heated debate in Cambridge. Sir John Cheke, one of the most popular teachers in the University (we are told), and his pupil, Sir Thomas Smith, began to introduce the new – Erasmian – pronunciation in their lectures from about 1535. At first, as with the lectures on Greek in Oxford nearly thirty years earlier, they were interrupted by students who came to laugh and jeer. Eventually individuals, and then small groups, began to be persuaded by the new, strange-sounding Greek. (Erasmus himself in the treatise imagined such little bands: 'Nor was I content with this [re-reading all of Demosthenes, Herodotus, Plutarch, Homer and Lucian together]. I formed a select dining club of phil-hellenes. The rules were that anyone who lapsed from Greek at dinner should pay a fine . . . ')[152] In 1542, however, Stephen Gardiner, the Chancellor of the University, acted. He banned this new-fangled Erasmian pronunciation. He passed a university regulation which threatened any scholar found speaking it with the loss of his scholarship. Any ordinary student would be punished with public flogging. Gardiner was clear why he acted in this way: 'I will withstand fancies', he declared, 'even in pronunciation, and fight with the enemy of quiet at the first entry'. Gardiner is opposed to anything that stands against propriety and leads to disorder; 'quiet' must be maintained. So, he states, the new pronunciation 'would encourage presumption and insubordinateness on the part of younger scholars to the older'.[153] Authority, the dignity of age, tradition were threatened with disruption by the unruly pronunciation of Greek dipthongs. (More had used the same rhetoric against Luther's revolution: 'Yonge scolers be somtyme prone to newe fantasyes' especially those who are 'properly wytted, fetely lerned, and newfangly minded.'[154]) Cheke, Smith and others began a pamphlet war which escalated from a polite exchange of letters to the publication of lengthy technical treatises

---

[151] Hudson (1980) 35.
[152] *De recta pronunt. CWE* 26: 474. For a parallel Greek speaking club see Saladin (2000) 97–9.
[153] Documents translated briefly in Brewer, Gardiner, and Brodie (1862–1910) vol. 17. See Muller (1926) for discussion.
[154] *Dialogue Concerning Heresies* 1.1 (*CWM* VI. i. 34) and 3.4 (*CWM* VI. i. 269).

and polemics.'¹⁵⁵ 'Those Cambridge men'¹⁵⁶ who were active in the Religious Settlement were together opposed to Gardiner's high-handed intervention. 'Piquancy and excitement were added to the enthusiasm [for classical study] when the "radicalism" of the most admired circle of friends brought them into conflict with Stephen Gardiner, the Chancellor of the University, who considered their ideas "subversive of all good order".'¹⁵⁷

It is worth recalling who the players in this bizarre row were. Gardiner was not merely Chancellor of the University. He was also Master of Trinity Hall, the Bishop of Winchester (an important see), and, above all, chief Minister to the King. Cheke, Provost of King's College, was tutor to Edward VI, and a courtier who prominently played the role of advisor to the throne (and was Secretary of State for the nine days of the reign of Lady Jane Grey). Smith was the first Regius Professor of Civil Law, Principal Secretary to Edward VI and Elizabeth I, a Member of Parliament, Privy Councillor, Chancellor of the Order of the Garter, Ambassador to France (and went on to be Chancellor of the University after Gardiner). These are not academics remote from the Real Life of power and politics. John Strype is certainly quick to see 'secret malice and hatred against them in the minds of the rest of the University' because of the 'distinguishing favour of the King' as the source of this trouble over pronunciation.¹⁵⁸ The personal politics, however, are a stake in the wider power plays. 'The controversy over Greek was no "tempest in a teapot".¹⁵⁹ It was more than even simple control of a university. It was part of a larger battle for control of England.'¹⁶⁰ I hope that doesn't sound too grandiose a way of putting it. For as Erasmus' arguments with Luther about Lucian bring the most powerful theological teachers into battle over a Greek text, a battle which is also for the minds and souls of the Christian West, so this argument over pronunciation engages some of the most powerful figures in England, who are fighting precisely over who rules England and how. Or, at one level, with what advice, with what education should a Christian Prince rule? 'The issue of Greek pronunciation was of great symbolic importance as a tag by which one's loyalty and stance on other issues could with some assurance be ascertained.'¹⁶¹

---

¹⁵⁵ Collected usefully in Havercamp (1740). Cheke's *de pronuntiatione* has been reprinted in facsimile (Meriston, 1968).
¹⁵⁶ Phrase – *istis Cantabrigiensibus* – lifted from Colet, *EE* 1: 470 [*ep.* 230] September 1511, from John Colet.
¹⁵⁷ Hudson (1980) 35.   ¹⁵⁸ Strype (1821) 7.   ¹⁵⁹ Hudson (1980) 43.
¹⁶⁰ Hudson (1980) 46.   ¹⁶¹ Hudson (1980) 45.

When you opened your mouth to speak Greek, or when you defended a way of speaking Greek, you were taking sides. Greek, your knowledge of Greek, was an emblem in the personal politics of the Elizabethan regime. And once again, it was a text of Erasmus that started the disquiet.

VII

For Erasmus' Europe, then, learning Greek became a fundamental element of a cultural identity. Perhaps even more. When Standish attacked Erasmus' translation of the Gospel, he called it the work of 'some little Greek'.[162] Erasmus himself wrote to Latimer in 1517: 'Anyone is a Greek who has worked hard and successfully at Greek literature, though he may not wear a beard.'[163] He loved to refer to his own work as the labours of Heracles – and his assistants thus as 'Theseus'. His friends promised to be an Alcibiades to his Socrates.

The revolutions of the sixteenth century were enacted in Greek dress.

That's what I mean when I said Erasmus made learning Greek sexy. Under his influence, your relation to Greece, to knowing Greek, inevitably now played an integral part in your personal politics, in your engagement with religion, in your sense of self. It was also risky. The conflicts of the Reformation and the power struggles around the monarch at court made your dealings in Greek a marker of your performance in the pursuit of authority and position. Always alongside Erasmus' mission for Greek there ran consistent vocal and physical opposition to the study of Greek, to the study of particular Greek authors, even to the Erasmian sound of Greek. In this period of self-conscious rapid cultural change, Greek knowledge constitutes a fundamental site of cultural conflict. Between the injunctions to 'Embrace the Greeks!' and 'Keep your children away from Greek learning!', a revolution was being acted out.

---

[162] *EE* 4: 309–18 [*ep.* 1126] to Hermann Busch, 31 July 1520.
[163] *EE* 2: 486 [*ep.* 540], February 1517, to William Latimer.

CHAPTER TWO

Becoming Greek, with Lucian

I

Lucian, however, is extremely chary with *his* name.

'Erasmus' – 'that *great, injur'd* name'[1] – is blazoned across every production of Erasmus, printed, circulated, obsessively attacked and defended by his contemporaries as the Sign that encapsulates a movement, a scandal, a contest, a hero. This triumph of *publicité* fulfils one of the constant aims of performance in the traditions of Greek and Roman cultural life from the beginnings: the preservation of your name. The desire 'to be sung', 'to be on the lips of all', is the motivational drive of hero and writer and family man alike. From epic to history, from gravestone to the huge letters M. AGRIPPA L.P. COS. TERTIUM FECIT on the Pantheon in Rome, making a name solid, permanent, an inheritance to pass on, is the express aim of social ambition.

Alongside this, a constant parasite on the monuments of naming, there runs also another, more sly tradition. I don't mean the joke that Ovid plays when he promises a girl eternal fame if she will sleep with him – in a poem which deliberately 'forgets' to record the girl's name.[2] Nor Theognis' grand promise to his lover, Cyrnus, that 'I will give you wings to soar over the uncharted sea, raised over the earth with ease. You will be at every feast and party, lying like a treasure in the mouths of many . . . ' – in a poem which immortalizes Cyrnus as an unfaithful cheat.[3] Nor even do I mean the *Odyssey*'s celebration of the trickster hero, Odysseus, who so often conceals his name and identity in his pursuit of lasting name.[4]

---

[1] Alexander Pope *Essay in Criticism*: '*Erasmus*, that *great, injur'd* name/ (The *Glory* of the Priesthood, and the Shame!)'

[2] *Amores* 1.3.

[3] Theognis 237–54, on which see Goldhill (1991) 109–16.

[4] See Goldhill (1991) 24–36 for discussion and bibliography.

Rather, I mean the silence of Homer on Homer. The most celebrated of all Greek poets does not name himself nor describe himself in either the *Iliad* or *Odyssey* (bar the less than informative, 'speak to me too, Muse . . .) – a silence which allowed the extraordinary proliferation of fictions about the now blind, now hairy, now Egyptian, now female Bard.[5] The founder of pastoral poetry from Alexandria, Theocritus, also knowingly refuses to name himself in his poetry, even – especially – when writing in the first-person about becoming a poet, or being a lousy lover: a paradigm of the ironic indirection of Hellenistic poetics.[6] And not only of Hellenistic poetics. Plato names himself as *absent* from the scene of Socrates' last conversation, and in his dialogues he offers a play of different masks, from the intimate impersonation of Socrates in the first-person to the studied anonymity of the 'Athenian Stranger'. (How *is* philosophy (to be) internalized?) Plato is veiled – absent and all-seeing – in 'Plato'.

All of which throws a sharp light on Lucian's individual hesitation. Over eighty prose works have come down to us under the name of Lucian, a handful of which may be spurious. Yet in this very extensive body of writing the name 'Lucian' occurs barely *six* times, and four of these are in titles or headings of one sort or another. This, despite the fact that many pieces are written either in the first-person or as dialogues, and feature a Syrian, trained in rhetoric, writing in Attic Greek, writing for Roman patrons, in both the Eastern and Western Empire, in the second half of the second century CE – that is, a figure rather like (a/our) Lucian.

Something particular and fascinating is going on with Lucian and the act of naming himself. It isn't a casual gesture[7] and exploring it properly will lead to the very heart of the issue of cultural identity, and to the continuing importance of 'being Greek', not just for Lucian but also, more surprisingly, for some of the most unpleasant racist and nationalist ideologues of the nineteenth and twentieth centuries. For Lucian's veiling of his name turns out to be a factor in a much more broad question of self-representation as an embodiment of cultural value. And who doesn't have a stake in cultural value?

For Erasmus and his contemporaries, it will be recalled, Lucian was a name to conjure with because his unsettling satire had a precarious

---

[5] See Graziosi (forthcoming).   [6] See Goldhill (1991) 223–83.

[7] Ancient prose and verse authors often 'seal' their texts with their name e.g. Thuc. 1.1; Her. 1.1; Theognis 19–30; Josephus *Jewish War* 1.1; Heliodorus x.3.4.; or use their name in the third person (e.g. Xenophon). Some genres, of course, do not tend towards the proclamation of the name of the author.

moral purchase and because his ancient, and thus authoritative, comments on Christianity were dismissive. Both of which qualities sat awkwardly with the didactic value of his pure, clear Attic Greek. The very fact that Lucian even mentions Christians in his well-populated rogues' gallery of charlatans, philosophers, intellectuals and power-brokers, does emphasize the extraordinary excitement and volatility of the social and intellectual context in which Lucian was writing and performing. Although the second-century Roman Empire enjoyed the apparent institutional stability and material benefits of the Pax Romana, it was also a period of intense cultural conflict. Christianity was only one, particularly radical, growing minority movement which demanded a new sense of how you engaged in society, in your life – a new sense of the person, the self. Michel Foucault and Peter Brown (among others) have investigated in a most stimulating way how philosophers' obsession with care of the self and religious leaders' promotion of different, often anti-social spiritualities provide one crucial strand of this battle over the individual in society.[8] At the same time, the education system, that dominant institution of acculturation, provides a model of social continuity and stability, and a means of social mobility from the edges of Empire towards the centres of power.[9] This period is also often known as the 'Second Sophistic' because so much cultural effort was dedicated to promoting and projecting an image of classical Greece (when the first sophists had flourished): re-reading the classics of the fifth and fourth centuries BCE, and learning to write and speak the Attic of that period of five or six hundred years earlier, and investing huge energy and capital in rhetorical and philosophical performance, dominated elite education.[10] The tension between this Greek education – an education in Greekness – and Roman authority provides another crucial strand of second-century Empire society.

The cultural clashes of the second century – to hazard the short and sweeping version of why this period really matters – are formative in the development of Christianity, the idea of the Classics, the very idea of the (modern, Western) individual in society. Lucian is a revelatory figure for this formative era, not least because he straddles so many boundaries. He is a Syrian (from Samosata) who is educated in Greek (and Greekness),

[8] Foucault (1986); Brown (1988); see also Lane Fox (1986); Clark (1992); Gleason (1994); Francis (1995); Cooper (1996); Frankfurter (1998); Woolf (1999); Goldhill ed. (2001).
[9] See Morgan (1998); Anderson (1989); (1993); Reardon (1971); Too ed. (forthcoming).
[10] Bowersock (1969); Bowie (1970); Jones (1986); Gleason (1994); Flintermann (1995); Swain (1996); Whitmarsh (forthcoming).

and travels the Empire as far West as Gaul in pursuit of a career as an orator and intellectual superstar. He writes from the fringes of the Emperor's court and from the prostitute's bedroom. At the same time, he offers a constant, satiric running commentary on those who are trying to make it as intellectuals in the Empire, those who are engaged in the life-changing claims of philosophy and religion. Lucian's ironic, distorting, funny gaze is repeatedly directed at how the individual behaves in society, talks about his behaviour, hides his behaviour; he mocks your aspirations, desires, ambitions. It is because Lucian thus satirizes the self-serving, self-promoting individual in this age of care for the self that his disinclination to use his own name may seem a rather charged gesture.

Indeed, each time the name 'Lucian' appears in Lucian it is discon-certingly hard to see it as a straightforward act of self-identification, a seal of identity on a text. For Lucian's general unwillingness to name himself is coupled with a playfulness that requires from you a certain sophistication when you do come across any of the handful of times he lets slip the L word. Lucian seems to have learnt a lot from his great predecessor in dialogue writing, Plato, when it comes to ironic hedging and careful withdrawal behind a mask (or two).

I had better provide first a brief look at the Facts on The Name (we will come back to the stories later, inevitably) to get a sense of how his point-edly low-key wittiness plays off the tradition of striving to immortalize oneself in stone or word.

First, there are the four headings (which, it should not be a surprise to find, are the least marked examples). Two of these cases are also textu-ally uncertain too. 'Lucian' appears in one subtitle, *The Dream; or, Lucian's Life*. Now subtitles (like titles) are often later editorial additions (especially when, as here, there are two works in the corpus with similar primary titles).[11] Here, however, there is another twist. For this apparently auto-biographical work about how the author became an orator, does not get round to naming the subject of the autobiography, or any member of his family, even when a figure in the dream is said specifically to utter his grandfather's name. What's more, even if the subtitle was penned by Lucian, the suggested equivalence between the insubstantial vision of a dream and a life-story should make one hesitate before unreservedly

---

[11] 22: Ὄνειρος ἢ Ἀλεκτρυών, *The Dream, or The Cock*; 32: Περὶ τοῦ Ἐνυπνίου ἤτοι Βίος Λουκιανοῦ, *On the Dream, or The Life of Lucian*. We are told explicitly that one of the most famous titles of ancient drama – *Oedipus Tyrannos* (*Oedipus Rex*/*Oedipus the King*) – was added to distinguish it from the other *Oedipus*, and was sometimes called *The Earlier Oedipus* (*Hyp* II).

taking the autobiography at face value. ('What is a someone? A no one? Man is the shadow of a dream.')[12] Indeed, the Dream here is introduced with a quotation of a pair of lines from Homer, which in the *Iliad* introduce Agamemnon's *false* and *misleading* dream![13] In another text, a dramatic dialogue, one character is labelled 'Lucian' (though never addressed as such in it). Editors, however, some of whom do not believe this piece is written by Lucian, often change the name to 'Lycinus'.[14] Amusingly enough, this dialogue, the *Pseudosophistes*, is about catching linguistic errors, and mocks a character who pretends to be especially good at policing linguistic impropriety. Which puts a nice gloss on getting the (silent) name just right.

On two other occasions 'Lucian' appears as the first word in the heading of epistles: 'Lucian to Cronios: greetings', 'Lucian to Nigrinus: greetings'.[15] There is a long tradition in Greek and Roman cultures of philosophical Letters which use the fiction of intimate exchange to discuss the care of the self and the dynamics of interpersonal relationships. Lucian draws on such a tradition here – in his sarcastic and biting style; but strikingly and typically, he also turns each letter into a dramatized dialogue where the question of who speaks for Lucian becomes much harder to determine.[16] The use of Lucian's name in the letter heading becomes in this way part of the work's interest in what being true to oneself – and speaking out – might involve.

Apart from these four headings, Lucian identifies himself by name only twice. The *Alexander* is an exposée of a sham holy man, called 'Alexander', who set up an oracle at Abonuteichos. The narrator has sent various trick questions to unmask the oracle's pretensions, and then arrives at the city himself. 'When Alexander discovered that I had come to the city, and when he had learnt that I was that man, Lucian, he invited me with all due politeness and kindness.'[17] Lucian, offered Alexander's hand in greeting, promptly (and without explanation) 'gave it a good bite

---

[12] Pindar *Pyth* 8. 95–6.   [13] 32.5 cites *Il.* 2. 56–7; see Saïd (1993) 268–9.

[14] See Hall (1981) 298–307; Swain (1996) 49–50. A few editors also put the name 'Lucian' in 28 (*The Fisherman*) (following ms. tradition Γ) but not most, including Macleod in the *OCT* who follows Ω.

[15] (55.1) *De Morte Peregrini*; (8.1) *Nigrinus*.

[16] In the *Peregrinus*, as is often noted, the anonymous 'stranger' who speaks out with laughter at the funeral, seems to 'speak for Lucian': see e.g. Jones (1986) 117–32. The dialogue of the *Nigrinus*, as well as the image of 'an eye cure', is regularly seen as ironizing the 'conversion' narrative: see Robinson (1979) 52–4; Hall (1981) 157–64, Saïd (1993) 264–6; and on the form of the letter Anderson (1978).

[17] 42.55.

and nearly crippled it'.[18] Lucian is identified to Alexander (and to us, the readers, after fifty-five chapters) as he is attempting to unmask Alexander by a deceptive ruse (which also bizarrely literalizes the 'bite' of the Cynic philosopher). Revelation of identity through the name is here part of a deceptive attempt by the narrator to uncover a false appearence.

The final example of Lucian's self-naming is by far the most emphatic, and it is my favourite. In the *True Histories*, the previously unnamed narrator has visited the Isles of the Blessed where the dead heroes live. In order to memorialize his trip, he asks Homer (who else?) to write an epigram to be set up on a pillar. Homer comes up with:

> Lucian, dear to the blessed gods, saw all this,
> And back again he went to his dear homeland.[19]

This trashy pastiche of the *Odyssey*'s opening is inscribed on a column of beryl and set up by the harbour. The *True Histories* is introduced by Lucian with the declaration that he will claim the mythographer's privilege of lying and that 'the only bit of truth I will tell is that I am lying'.[20] And he singles out Homer's Odysseus for starting the disreputable trend of travellers' fibs. That Lucian immortalizes his name thus in a third-rate epigram by a fictionalized and untrustworthy poet on a monument in an unseeable afterlife, recorded in a work which boasts of its own falsehood, neatly summarizes Lucian's oblique and funny stance towards proclaiming and preserving the glory of his name. M. AGRIPPA L.P. COS. TERTIUM FECIT this isn't.

Lucian, then, has some pointed fun being chary with his name.

And in what has come down to us from the second century, which is, of course, a very fragmentary archive, everyone else is extremely chary with it too. There's no reference to Lucian in the work of any contemporary intellectual or in any material source. Unless the Lucian mentioned in a ninth-century Arabic translation of a now lost Greek commentary, written by his contemporary, the doctor, Galen, is our Lucian.[21] It may well be, not least because Galen's Lucian produces a hoax (lost) book of Heraclitus and tricks a bunch of posey academics into humiliating

---

[18] On the *Alexander* see especially Jones (1986) 133–48; Branham (1989) 181–210.
[19] 14.28.   [20] 13.1–4.
[21] Strohmaier (1976) 117–22; see also Nutton (1972) 58–9; Hall (1981) 4–6.

themselves by commenting on its nonsense. Making intellectual superstars look silly is one of Lucian's favourite activities. Otherwise, it is only
through later Christian and Byzantine authors that Lucian emerges as a
presence in other ancient writing.[22] In short, I can't give a snapshot of
Lucian's biography and cultural importance within his society, save to
say that he was a snidey intellectual from Syria, writing in the later half
of the second century CE, in Greek, for a Roman audience, at least in
part. Each element of that sentence, however, will become a significant
topic in the issue of why Lucian's writing matters, and why his hesitation
around the act of self-identification is telling. Lucian's name games are
part of his staking out a position on what it might mean to be a somebody
in Empire culture.

There will be no learned and serious biographies of Lucian, then,
to match those of Erasmus and More, no kaleidoscope of contemporary
reactions, no life of words through the exchange of letters and polemic.[23]
Yet Lucian often writes in the first-person, often dramatizes a life, and,
most often, offers a series of characters who act as protagonists in dialogues and narratives, who, as educated, rhetorical Syrians writing in
Greek might seem close to the author. The unwillingness to use the
name 'Lucian' is matched by a multiplicity of other names. In particular, 'Lycinus' [LUKINOS] puts in several heroic appearances – a name
which is only two vowels short of 'Lucian' [LOUKIANOS].[24] So too does
an unnamed 'Syrian'; a figure called 'Tychiades' ('Son of Fortune'), and
'Parrhesiades' ('son of Free Speech'). In the first person, Lucian tells of his
dislike of intellectual snobs and poseurs, of his hatred of the mercenary
life of learning, of his distaste for superstition, of the folly of human desire. So too do Lycinus, Tychiades, Parrhesiades and the Syrian. Lucian,
in the first-person, displays an educated, witty, rhetorical persona. So
too do Lycinus, Tychiades, Parrhesiades and the Syrian. Whose, then, is
the story of the Syrian's turn from rhetoric to philosophy at age forty?
Whose is the praise of the Emperor's mistress which Lycinus so cunningly
articulates and defends?

Scholars have often wanted to cut through all of Lucian's playing with
the dressing-up box, and declare dismissively that Lucian sometimes
calls himself 'Lycinus', ('Tychiades' etc.). Lucian a.k.a. 'Lycinus'. And
not ask why. Or, better, it is possible to hazard a more sophisticated

---

[22] Testimonia easily available in Hall (1981); Schwartz (1965); Baldwin (1973) 7–11, 98–103.
[23] Croiset (1882); Schwartz (1965) and others who have none the less tried such a project are well
criticized by Hall (1981).
[24] Bowie (1970) calls 'Lycinus' a Hellenization of 'Lucian'.

version of role-playing, that sees self-dramatization and imagined voices
as an integral element of the art of rhetoric (*prosopopeia*). But I don't
think we should rush simply to do either. There is more at stake in
the question of why this scourge of hypocrites and imposters adopts
so many voices, why this learner of Greek mocks learning, why this
intellectual who writes in the language of five hundred years earlier,
teases antiquarians who are so obsessive about the past. No less than
Erasmus, Lucian constructs a fascinating repertoire of strategies of self-
presentation – a self-presentation which sets at stake what you might
imagine it means *to be Greek*.

What Lucian's writing engages with, thus, is the projection of a cultural
identity.

II

So how does Lucian construct a picture of himself?

Let me select four of his most direct portrayals, which should provide a
good sense of the sophistication, amusement, and twistiness of Lucian's
self-portrait. This will be the longest section of this chapter, not least
because this aspect of Lucian's writing has been so poorly – naively –
served by critics over the years. But it will become clear why Erasmus was
so attracted to play with fire by Lucian. We can begin with the speech that
is often described as Lucian's autobiography. Lucian starts *The Dream; or,
Lucian's Life* not with the details of date, birth, provenance, parentage that
you might expect for a life story, but, suitably enough for a tale about
coming into culture, with a crucial juncture in his education: 'It was just
after I had finished going to school and was now a young man that my
father began considering among his friends what he might apprentice me
to.'[25] The somewhat straightened family circumstances preclude higher
education, and so a career in sculpture with his uncle is chosen. The
narrative continues – in a gripping Dickensian style – with the youngster
breaking the first piece of marble he is set to work on and being beaten
harshly by his stern employer, so that he runs away. In hiding, he falls
into a tearful sleep, and has a life-changing dream. Two women appear
to him, one The Art of Sculpture (rather shabbily dressed), the other
Paideia (education/culture[26]) – in a rather more fetching outfit. Each

---

[25] 32.1.
[26] For the importance of *paideia* in this period – of becoming a *pepaideumenos* – 'educated', 'cultured'
see in particular the fine work of Bowie (1970); Reardon (1971); Anderson (1989); Gleason (1994);
Flintermann (1995) and Bompaire (1958) from which I have learnt much.

advises the dreamer of their benefits and aspirations. The young man chooses *Paideia*, and the rest is . . .

You can read in almost any book on Lucian that he started life as a sculptor before turning to Rhetoric. A good story should, after all, be believable. The speech – addressed to 'gentlemen' – does indeed finish with an encouragement to remember 'what sort of a fellow I was when I pursued the noblest of callings and desired Culture, despite my then poverty; and how I have come back to you, if nothing else at least no less worthy of honour than any carver of stone'.[27] You can probably flesh out the story for yourself easily enough. The flight away from home, westward towards opportunity; somehow winning an education for himself; becoming a successful orator; coming home triumphantly to show the hometown boys how he has made good.

Lucian, however, interestingly also writes a sneering audience response into his own tale: 'As I was speaking, "Hercules!", someone said, "The dream is so long and so annoying!" Another butted in: "It's a midwinter night's dream, when nights *are* long . . . But why on earth did it occur to him to babble on about this to us and recall his nights as a child and old dreams that are over and done with. How stale! How stilted his speech is! He can't really think we're dream-analysts!".'[28] People who tell you their dreams are never as interesting as they think they are. But Lucian (of course) has set himself up to come back with the moves of any well-educated chap in the Empire. First he appeals to a classical text: don't they remember Xenophon – favourite soldier, huntsman and writer of the classical era – and how he experienced and expounded Useful Dreams even in desperate times of war? Second, don't they see that his Dream has a didactic moral message, encouraging the young not to be put off from doing the right thing and getting Culture? This Dream, now properly buttressed by Classics and Morality, is meant as a didactic talk about learning. It's a myth (*muthos*), a paradigm (*paradeigma*), for any faint-hearted budding scholar. Not for nothing was this piece a set text in the compulsory Greek entrance exam to Cambridge in the nineteenth century![29]

The Dream is indeed made up of standard allegorical elements from a range of possible sources in philosophy, drama and rhetoric.[30] Not

---

[27] 32.18. [28] 32.17.

[29] W. Heitland's 1877 edition of the *Somnium* (Cambridge, Cambridge University Press) which was specifically designed for those taking that exam, went through thirteen editions by 1905.

[30] See Bompaire (1958) 258–64. For Lucian's account of the world of Dreams in his *True Histories* and general background see Miller (1994) esp. 26–8.

only do tall women in special dress, often in pairs, repeatedly pop up in dreams and visions (I mean *classical* dreams), but also the opposition of working in stone and working in words, or painting and literature, has a very long tradition back to Simonides' *bon mot* that painting is silent poetry, poetry speaking painting, or Pindar's boast that he has made a song more lasting than a marble monument.[31] As Hercules is directed to the path of virtue, or Parmenides away from the Path of Seeming by suitably attired ladies, so Lucian's Dream is self-consciously a Calling to a way of life.

The dress of allegory should make it harder to read *The Dream* simply as autobiography (even when starting from the knowledge that autobiography is rarely as transparent a genre as some would want it to be). Is the flight of the tearful apprentice part of the didactic tale – the painful struggle which education demands? If it is part of an allegory, does that necessarily mean that it has no historical basis? (The lack of a name helps allow these questions.) Lucian, it seems, rather enjoys juxtaposing the reality effects of a life story with the traditionally fictional elements of a literary dream – and dramatizing different responses. 'The dream may be odd', he teases, 'but don't disbelieve it. . . .'[32] *The Dream*, then, does not simply tell a life story, but flirts with making an allegorical paradigm out of fragments of a life.

If *The Dream* adapts the language of allegorical moral instruction to suggest a grander generality than a story of a Syrian made good, our second autobiographical text, *The Apology*, takes up the polemical language of the philosopher accused – though it will quickly be appreciated that we are a fair way away from Socrates in court. In his earlier, very funny satire *The Hired Academic*, Lucian had sneered and railed against the life of the impovershed intellectual whose pursuit of material security leads him into the humiliation of 'willed slavery' – employment in the house of a Roman patron. Late in life, *The Apology* declares, Lucian has taken a post in the Emperor's civil service in Egypt. Shouldn't he be hoist on his own petard? *The Apology* is addressed to one Sabinus, and it imagines him giggling at *The Hired Academic* but then snorting at Lucian's present behaviour – which can only be seen as a sign of *diaphônia* – 'dissonance', 'different-voicedness'.[33] This is no literary game, but a real disjunction

---

[31] Lee (1967); Praz (1970) for the big picture; for more detailed classical material, Svenbro (1976); Goldhill (1994); Steiner (forthcoming); and on Lucian, Romm (1990); Goldhill (2001).
[32] 32.14.   [33] 65.1.

between words and behaviour, exactly the sort of hypocrisy which Lucian so often rants against.

How are the charge and defence expressed, however? By a drama in which Lucian plays all the parts... The charge he thinks Sabinus reasonably would make, he declares, is fitting for a friend and a proper philosopher, so 'if I put on your mask properly and act out the role in response, then everything would be fine and we will sacrifice to the God of Logos. If not, well, you will add what's needed. Time for a scene change...'[34] Lucian will adopt the *mask* of a good friend in order to *act out* his role in a new *scene*. The verb here, *hupokrinomai*, can mean both 'to act' and 'to reply' (as in court) – and it is, of course, the etymological root of the word 'hypocrisy'. There is going to be a change of set, a new scene, and if all goes well, they will offer their sacrifice of thanks to the god of Logos (*ho logios*). Elsewhere in Lucian this expression is used to refer to Hermes, the god not just of communication, but of false messages, lies, deception and corrupt exchange.[35]

With such a self-conscious performance of preparation, Lucian ventriloquizes a rather sharp attack which has Sabinus mock Lucian for living a life that contradicts his own precepts – like a tragic actor who looks like the hero Hercules, till his mask comes off and he is just some Joe playing a part for money; or like Cleopatra's monkey, which could dress and act like a trained human dancer, till it saw a fig on the ground, whereupon it threw off its mask to grab it.[36] So Lucian, who always professed precisely to be no actor but a poet of the noblest sentiments and a moralist of high seriousness, is proven a monkey by the fig of a job in Egypt.

Lucian is enjoying a self-reflexive joke here: the accusation of hypocritically playing a part like an actor is acted out as a scene by Lucian in a mask...

The defence? Lucian first suggests but rejects several possible standard moves. He could, for instance appeal to Fortune, or Fate, or Destiny (too vulgar); to the patron's exceptional qualities (too much like flattery); or to old age or poverty (not a pretty reason).[37] But then he tries to distinguish *his* noble labour in public service from the sort of hiring he had previously mocked, and adds that everyone works for *some* reward: the question is only whether the activity and the reward are noble. He ends with the

---

[34] 65.2.

[35] Kilburn in the Loeb translates it as 'The God of Reason' which misses the point. Fowler, correctly, 'the God of Words'. On Hermes' untrustworthiness see especially Kahn (1978).

[36] 65.3–7.

[37] None of the reasons offered, comments the speaker (65.11), is εὐπρόσωπον: 'with a nice face', 'good mask' – a term which picks up the 'mask' he puts on 65.2.

hope of securing acquittal from Sabinus. But 'as for all the rest, even if they all condemn me to a person, it would be quite enough for me to say "No matter to Hippocleides" '.[38] So if you are unconvinced by Lucian – and thus outside the little group of Lucian and Sabinus – Lucian is giving you the finger. 'No matter to Hippocleides' is the celebrated retort – now a proverb – of an Athenian aristocrat, Hippocleides. He had won a noble bride in competition, but his lewd dances in celebration at his stag-night so appalled his prospective father-in-law that he declared 'You have danced away your marriage.' To which Hippocleides replied, 'No matter to Hippocleides'.[39] Lucian ends his defence with a classical tag, but also with a testy rejection of the aims of persuasive oratory. You can think him a hypocrite, for all he cares.

Lucian's *Apology*, then, may tell us he once worked as a successful orator in Gaul and took a job in Egypt later in life – and you may take that as fact if you wish; but what is central to this text – and fun for you to watch – is the wittily self-conscious play with the strategies of self-justification. Self-revelling rather than self-revealing. In a defence against being a hypocrite, Lucian stages and acts out an attack on himself for himself, tries some defences on for size, before hazarding his justification, which he doesn't care if anyone but Sabinus accepts. Or so he says. Trying on masks is an integral part of Lucian's self-presentation here. Taking a job in Egypt prompts a reflection on self-consistency, social performance, and self-dramatization. Lucian finds it rather difficult to talk about himself without this sort of clever(-clever) game.

The Apology's language of accusation and defence becomes a fully fledged scene of philosophy in court in our third text of self-presentation, the *Twice Accused* – which also explicitly brings to the fore the issue of Greekness itself. This text is a long dramatic dialogue, set first on Mount Olympus, the home of the gods. It begins with the King of the Gods, Zeus, moaning that philosophers are quite wrong to think that divinities live in bliss and quietude. Like all the gods, he has nothing but hassle. As Apollo has to keep rushing from oracle to oracle to keep the prophecy business running, so he is kept constantly at work in the administration of Divine Sovereignty. Just too many committees and meetings. This opening speech constructs a sweetly sophistic version of the first speech of Homer's *Odyssey*.[40] There Zeus sets the agenda for the epic of retribution by reflecting on how foolish humans are constantly to blame the

---

[38] 65.15.   [39] Herodotus 6.127–9.   [40] *Odyssey* 1.32–43.

gods, when their avoidable sins are punished. Now, it is academic philosophical misconceptions of the divine that are corrected, and it is the bureaucratic backlog at the divine court of justice that is causing the difficulty with the justice system. (With its administrative delays and legal gerrymandering, this is a heaven based firmly on Empire culture.) With a swift scene change to Athens, the court is soon in session, however, and a series of trials begins. The backlog means the whole history of philosophy is fair game. With Hermes as herald, and Justice herself in attendance, a stereotypically raucous and self-interested Athenian jury is convened on the Areopagus to hear a string of cases.

The first is Drunkenness against the Academy *in re* Polemo, on a case of kidnapping. Polemo was a reprobate who went to a lecture of Xenocrates to cause a disturbance (like an Oxford Trojan), but who was converted by what he heard (like a Cambridge Reformer). The Academy gets to argue both sides of the case (in best sophistic fashion) because Drunkenness is too drunk to speak. The Academy easily justifies the change of Polemo's character from drunk to temperate citizen – but has much more fun lampooning Polemo's exchange of garlands, wine, women and song for a philosopher's syllogisms and shrivelled body.[41] The second case is the Stoics *v* Pleasure *in re* Dionysius. Dionysius had been a Stoic, but his sore eyes hurt him so much that he could no longer maintain the Stoic principle that pain doesn't matter. Epicurus appears to argue the case for pleasure, the Stoics argue for the hard-man school of philosophy and social restraint. Since this *is* Lucian, Pleasure wins the case unanimously.[42] The third case (Virtue *v* Degeneracy *in re* Aristippus) and the fourth case (Painting *v* Pyrrho) swiftly end on technicalities.[43] This fizzing mixture of easy parody of doctrine, caricatures from anecdote, and knock-about legal humour prepares for the final case – the double accusation of a Syrian orator by Rhetoric and Dialogue, for neglect and abuse.

Justice herself is the first to complain that the Syrian isn't named: 'Who is this man? There is no name on the indictment.' Hermes – ever unreliable – 'Assign the court as it is in the writ: "Against The Syrian Orator". Nothing will stop the trial going ahead without a name.'[44] Justice notes somewhat sniffily that a Syrian case should probably be heard on the other side of the Euphrates, not in Athens, but demurs. This short introductory exchange by the divine court officials draws careful attention to Lucian's namelessness game – even, ludicrously, in court – but it also underlines the invasion of the Athenian history of philosophy

[41] 29.15–19.   [42] 29.20–22.   [43] 29.23–25.   [44] 29.14.

by a foreign outsider. Lucian's name may be silenced, but this Syrian orator is also written into the grandest line of Greek philosophy and speaks as the subject of a divinely administered trial, where abstract figures of genre debate his work and worth. Ostentatious modesty suitably marks this self-defence as self-promotion.

Rhetoric's accusation of neglect certainly plays the Greek and Barbarian card fully. After an introduction, cobbled together from Demosthenic prologues, she begins her story of marital abuse:

I found this man, gentlemen of the jury, when he was but a youth, a barbarian still in his voice, and all but wearing a caftan in the Assyrian style. He was still wandering about Ionia; he didn't know what to do with himself. So I took him up, and educated/cultured [*epaideusa*] him.[45]

Rhetoric portrays the Syrian as a foreigner at a loose end on Greek soil, marked out by his dodgy language and dress sense. He lacks *paideia*, culture/education, and that is what she offers him. Indeed, she marries him (despite her other richer lovers) and 'after I had married him, I improperly registered him among the members of my tribe and made him a citizen'. Like a Henry James couple, they travel Europe together, finely attired and winning fame and wealth – until he meets an Older Man, Dialogue, who seduces him away from the successful marriage.

From uncertain foreigner to irregular citizen, then, this story of a union is indeed confirmed by the Syrian in his defence speech:

Yes, she did educate me and we travelled abroad together, and she inscribed me in the class of Greeks. For this at least, I owe her thanks for my marriage.[46]

It is, he continues, his wife's descent into cheap whoring and public lack of decency – the constant complaint against the Rhetoric of Today, whenever today is – that makes him flee to the more austere home of Dialogue. And that is his (winning) defence against the charge of neglect.

Although the parody of juicy sex and citizenship trials is evident enough in this account of intellectual development (within the comedic frame of a woman's speech), none the less there remains a nagging question of exactly how the Syrian's cultural identity is being projected. As the elegant classical Greek narrative produces a list of Greek philosophers and schools into which the Syrian's work is inscribed, and as his trial in racy and satiric style describes his 'enfranchisement' as Greek, how closely is the idea of 'becoming Greek' to be pressed?

---

[45] 29.27. 'Caftan' translates κάνδυς, a specifically 'barbarian' outfit.
[46] 29.30.

The higher education of the elite in the Roman Empire of the second century, as I have already mentioned briefly, was based largely on a Greek-dominated syllabus.[47] The so-called *enkuklios paideia* – the cycle of culture – linked the most educated members of the powerful classes from East to West. The syllabus expected performance in the arts of rhetoric and philosophy and knowledge of what were already the Classics: (highlights of) Homer, classical tragedy, old and new comedy, and the rhetoricians and philosophers of the Athenian heyday were required cultural markers, a shared and self-defining possession of the educated elite. The institutions of symposium, gymnasium and theatre – the very signs of Greekness – spread quickly through the Eastern Mediterranean in the wake of Alexander's conquests in the third century BCE, and more gradually and in changing form throughout the Empire. Greek learning retained a huge cultural capital in these elite circles, whatever the inevitably different levels of attainment in and commitment to such an agenda. This, despite and in tension with repeated Roman suspicions of such Greekness, which erupted in regular, highly conservative tones. Indeed, the social and intellectual networks of the Empire in the second century constantly articulate this complex dynamic between the institutional and social centres of Roman power, on the one hand, and, on the other, the different engagements with both influential and marginalized intellectual activities focused on Greek cultural value.

This dynamic has its paradigmatic (problem) cases. It is in the second century that the Roman emperor, Marcus Aurelius, can write his Meditations in Greek, deeply imbued with a philosophical training[48]; or another emperor, Hadrian, a military hero from Spain, can grow a beard like a Greek and take a young male lover, at whose death he demanded and received rituals designed to throw his extreme grief in everyone's face, as if he were Alexander mourning for Hephaestion.[49] The Gospels, written in Greek, as were the Pauline letters, were circulating in the East (and elsewhere) as early testimony of the the religious upheavals which would shortly convulse the Empire – taking a revolution from Aramaic-speaking society into Greek culture and thence into Rome. Juvenal, meanwhile, the satirist at the very centre of the Empire at Rome, has the conservative posture of his verse violently dismiss the 'hungry little Greek' who promises any trendy skill to make a buck, and laments that the river Orontes – Syrian like Lucian – has been pouring its

---

[47] See above n. 8 for discussion and further bibliography on the following picture.
[48] See Rutherford (1989); Brirley (1987).   [49] See Vout (2000).

sewerage of Eastern language, art, and music into Rome.[50] In short, the cultural conflicts of the second-century Empire are focused on negotiating positions within the matrix of what Greg Woolf nicely calls 'Becoming Greek and Staying Roman'.[51] The cultural capital of 'becoming Greek' is constantly framed by the authority of being and staying Roman – and the consequent worries of being 'too Greek', or 'not Greek enough'. It is within this light that Lucian's education into culture (from Caftan to Rhetoric) must be viewed. 'Being inscribed in the class of Greeks' is a charged cultural claim.

By way of a more detailed contrast, let's take another rhetorician, contemporary with Lucian, who loves to play with a sense of belonging and with the paradoxes of boundary crossing, namely, Favorinus of Gaul. He was celebrated – or celebrated himself – for a triple paradox: 'A Gaul who was Greek; a eunuch who was prosecuted for adultery; a man who disagreed with the emperor and lived.'[52] The emperor in question was Hadrian, and Philostratus whose *Lives of the Philosophers* includes Favorinus, points out with testy imperial flattery that the tale of survival should really be put down to the emperor's proper, philosophical leniency.[53] Favorinus was born a hermaphrodite, Philostratus also declares, hence his beardless face and high-pitched, oddly modulated, voice, but he was 'so hot a fellow in erotic matters that he was charged actually with adultery by a senator'.[54] Favorinus came from Arles in the Rhone Valley, a Roman citizen of Gaul, but when he delivered his Greek orations in Rome, there was such enthusiasm for his performances that 'even those who did not understand the Greek language listened with pleasure to them'.[55] The verb *hellenizein*, which I translated 'was Greek', most often implies 'to speak Greek'. But in Favorinus' self-presentation it indicates more than learning a foreign language, which is not a frightfully impressive paradox (even for a Frenchman). Rather, *hellenizein* means to be fully educated into the cultural status of Greekness – to become Greek.

Maud Gleason has written a wonderful account of the self-presentation of this polemical and florid character, through his own and others' outraged and entranced portrayals.[56] 'Embalmed in a mythology that was partly his own creation',[57] Favorinus embodies a performance of physical, rhetorical and sexual attributes that together make

<hr />

[50] Juvenal 3. 62–78.   [51] Woolf (1994).
[52] Philostratus *Lives of the Sophists* 489.   [53] *Ibid.*   [54] *Ibid.*
[55] Philostratus *Lives of the Sophists* 491–2.   [56] Gleason (1994).   [57] Gleason (1994) 6.

up his particular version of Greekness (much as Lucian's picture of the Syrian's enrolment in Hellenism also is represented through a heady brew of erotic, intellectual and cultural elements). I want to pick out two particular moments in the representation of Favorinus that are especially relevant to my current argument.

The first moment is taken from Philostratus (again) and concerns an Indian servant called Autolekythos, whom Favorinus left in his will to the famous sophist, Herodes Atticus. Autolekythos 'was an Indian, pretty well black, and a plaything of Herodes and Favorinus. When they were drinking together, he would amuse them by mixing Attic words with his Indian, and by speaking his barbarian language with a tongue that was all over the place.'[58] Herodes Atticus was a major patron and educator, who, as well as being an associate of Hadrian, is said to have taught Marcus Aurelius and Lucius Verus (the emperor whose mistress Lycinus praises). As Gleason says, 'A friendship with Herodes Atticus was not just a friendship; it was, to use the language of Madison Avenue, a statement.'[59] This epitome of Hellenic culture, then, the teacher of Romans, and his drinking partner the Gaul, who has become Greek, take amusement in the Eastern slave's mixture of Attic and Indian, and his barbarisms of the tongue, 'all over the place'. There is a scale of 'being Greek': some are more Greek than others.

Herodes Atticus himself delighted in a farm-worker, 'as big as a Celt', known as 'Heracles', who spoke remarkably pure Greek.[60] He came from the interior of Attica, and, unlike his lord, Atticus, or Favorinus, he would not go to the City, because all sorts of Thracians and other foreigners had flooded it, and thus the Athenians have been corrupted in their speech more readily than they can help the barbarians towards proper diction. In contrast, 'the interior is untainted by barbarians and its language is healthy, its tongue rings pure Attic'. This man from deepest Attica has a pure, healthy Attic tongue for the landowner, Atticus – suggesting an inherent and integral tie between place and purity, just as the dark Indian's mixed up tongue wanders 'all over the place'. Yet how does Favorinus – or Lucian – fit with such a topography? The paradox is not just that the Gaul (or Syrian) can 'become Greek', but also that he sits and laughs with the most completely Greek protector of true Greek culture about getting Greekness just right.

---

[58] Philostratus *Lives of the Sophists* 490.   [59] Gleason (1994) 145.
[60] This story is taken from Philostratus *Lives of the Sophists* 552–3. For the rest of the story of 'Heracles' and his connection with Lucian, see Swain (1996) 80–4.

My second moment comes from a speech of Favorinus himself on the subject of his own statue, which the Corinthians, who erected it, have decided to tear down.[61] In the culture of public honour and self-promotion, to see one's own memorial thus destroyed with public pomp is indeed a crisis of self-presentation — on which Favorinus discourses with some horrified commitment. He once again boasts of how, despite being Roman, he has been 'zealous in pursuing not merely the language but the attitude, way of life and bearing of the Greeks'.[62] This, he declares, is all the more remarkable since even the best Greeks, in contact with Roman power, incline towards The Roman Way, while he has sacrificed everything 'to seem and to be Greek'.[63] One might have thought that 'appearance' ('to seem') and 'reality' ('to be') should be opposed, but their accumulation in Favorinus' self-conscious performance apparently makes him just more Greek than even the best Greeks. He should, he declares roundly, be honoured for his Attic speech in Athens, for his support of athletics in Sparta, for his philosophical prowess in all Greek cities – rhetoric, sport and philosophy, the very signs of Greekness each in its home territory. His divinely granted mission is to be the sort of example that an honorary statue proclaims. I come, he announces climactically,

for the Greeks, so that natives of Greece might have an example that in glory there is no distinction between being born a Greek and being made Greek by education. For the Romans, so that even those who are obsessed with their own worth may not ignore such education when it comes to esteem; and for the Celts, so that no barbarian might despair of attaining an education in Greekness, when he looks at this man, me.[64]

Favorinus' wonderfully bombastic self-promotion demands that the whole world stare at him as the paradigm of how a man can become by cultural education fully Greek. Every race – even the Greeks – can aspire to the Greekness he personifies.

Favorinus' brash demonstration of how he has become so Greek highlights the particularity of Lucian's self-representation. Where Favorinus stands up in a public arena to debate his own threatened memorial by demanding international recognition of his specific achievement and worth, Lucian writes a mythological drama in which an anonymous Syrian stage-manages a winning story of his married life with Rhetoric and his comic undermining of Dialogue's seriousness. In a culture of spectacle – and Roman power loves to make a spectacle of itself, as do the elites of

---

[61] This whole incident is well discussed in Gleason (1994) ch. 1.
[62] [Dio] 37. 25.   [63] *Ibid.*   [64] [Dio] 37. 27.

the Greek East – Lucian's indirectness stands out. The *Twice Accused* is a comic dialogue with a witty (anti)rhetorical flair and thus *performs* what it sets out to defend. It is written in sophisticated literary Greek, and alludes knowingly to the status of the educated Syrian's enrolment in the history of Greek scholarship. It is a text which flaunts and flourishes its author's literary achievement. Yet it does so without blazoning a name, inscribing a monument. Where Favorinus struts, Lucian sidles – with a certain panache – towards his glory.

This seductive combination of indirection, literary sophistication, and a fascination with what it means to be Greek runs throughout Lucian's corpus, but perhaps nowhere more tellingly than in my fourth text of self-presentation, *On the Syrian Goddess*. This is a quite extraordinary piece, which uses its sense of topography and literary heritage to create a re-markably poised and challenging presentation of cultural identity.

On the Syrian Goddess is an account of pilgrimage to a temple in the city of Hirê (also known as Hierapolis) in Syria, which includes details of the ritual in the temple and in the surrounding territory, as well as the mythic tales which act as explanations for the temple's construction. As Jas Elsner writes (in what is by far the most sophisticated and extended dissection of this text), the very act of writing this pilgrim's narrative in Greek is an act of 'cultural translation' – from the Syrian East into the cultural values of Greece, a Greece which enjoys the Pax Romana (which remains an unmentioned frame here).[65] Yet the Greek in which this text is written is the Ionic dialect, which, although it was once the Greek of the seaboard of Asia Minor, by Lucian's time was associated very strongly with the archaic historian, Herodotus. Since Herodotus was especially celebrated for his anthropological excursuses of the Mediterranean world, and his history of the clash of East and West was so interested in Asian matters that he was readily known as a 'lover of barbarians' (as well as the father of lies and malignity),[66] it is a pointed and unusual choice of language for *On the Syrian Goddess*. It is written as if it were an early Greek historical document relating contact with the unfamiliar Eastern Other. But the narrator of the text declares firmly that he is Assyrian, and has participated fully in the rites of pilgrimage himself. This is (also) an Insider account of Syrian religion. How is the Greco-Roman audience (or audiences) to respond to this tension between the commitment of Syrian pilgrimage and the

---

[65] Elsner (2001). The edition of Jane Lightfoot is forthcoming.
[66] These phrases are taken from Plutarch.

distancing of Greek literary portrayal? How does this text address its reader(s)? Can you place yourself in its cultural topography?

The opening paragraph of the work introduces the city and its temple, and ends with a strong statement of authorial positioning which sums up from the start the doubleness of this first-person narrative. I will cite it in a translation which makes no attempt at reconstructing the distancing of the archaic Herodotean discourse. Perhaps it could be imagined as a cross between Mandeville and Burton.

I write as an Assyrian. Some of what I recount I have learnt from witnessing it myself; but the history of what happened before me, I learnt from the priests.[67]

The historian marks himself as a Syrian writing in Greek for Greeks (at least at one level). But both his claim of 'autopsy' and of priestly sources immediately recalls the archetypal self-representation of Herodotus (who loves to tell you what he saw with his own eyes and whom he learnt his religious information from). Indeed, the second chapter of *On the Syrian Goddess* begins 'The first men we know to have developed a conception of the gods were the Egyptians' – thus taking us back to Herodotus' most famous disquisition on religious history, his account of Egypt. Bringing Herodotus on stage in so marked a manner, however, is, as Elsner notes, scarcely 'a neutral act. To affirm a literary ancestry in Herodotus was in this period to profess at the very least an ambiguous, if not downright controversial genre for a book.'[68] This combination of self-presentation as authority and self-undermining as Herodotean pastiche is unsettling. One constant strand of humour (and virtuoso brilliance) in this text is the 'comic homage'[69] to Herodotus in the language used, stories told, stance adopted. It is disquieting comedy, however, because of the shift of positions between insider and outsider. This is not a Greek intellectual coming into contact with the East, but an Eastern intellectual writing in the style of an archaic Greek historian coming into contact with the Other – which is himself. 'We can never be quite sure when it puts "Syria" or "Greece" under the humorous (and deliberately distorting) light of irony; we can never be certain whether the authorial voice is reliably direct or whether it is poking fun.'[70] This uncertainty stems from the uncertain self-presentation of the narrative

[67] 44.1. 'Assyrian' and 'Syrian' are used interchangeably.
[68] Elsner (2001) 128.
[69] A phrase taken from Branham (1989) 159 – a very fine discussion of Lucian's humour from which I have learnt a great deal. See also Jones (1986) 41–2.
[70] Elsner (2001) 128.

voice – but it spreads to you as a reader and threatens to disrupt your cultural map.

The final sentence of the work attests to the Syrian author's full participation in the rites of the temple. He describes how the young men of Syria make offerings of their beards and locks of hair in golden and silver containers, and inscribe their names in the temple. This is a rite practised in Greece only at Troezen, he notes. (Which is the dominant model? Which the analogy? Greek or barbarian?)[71] He concludes: 'I too completed this ritual when I was a young man, and in the temple still there rest my hair and my name.'[72]

The author's name is inscribed in the temple as a memorial to his ritual fulfilment. The last word of the book is 'name', but as you should by now expect for Lucian, the name itself is withheld. The key marker of the author's identity is preserved in the temple, but since we have only this text, we can't read it. Not even the language of its letters.

This final moment of an unknown name has been sophisticatedly prepared for in the text. We are offered, in good anthropological style, a discussion of the temple's cult statues and their names. There are two statues in the inner sanctum:

> One is Hera and the other is Zeus, whom, however, they call by another name. The statue of Zeus looks like Zeus in every respect; his head, clothes, throne. Nor will you, even if you want to, liken him to any other figure. As you look at Hera, she reveals a multiform shape. On the whole she is Hera by accurate reckoning; but she has something of an Athena, and Aphrodite and Selene and Rhea and Artemis and Nemesis and the Fates.[73]

The stance of the Syrian, writing as if he were a Greek explaining an alien culture to a Greek, dances along the fault lines of the reader's cultural surety. The Zeus looks exactly like a Zeus, and you couldn't, even if you wanted to, compare it to another divinity – except that it has another name (and identity?), which we are not told. The Hera, certainly Hera, shades away into a mess of other images – she has 'something of' a ludicrously long list of other goddesses. (Can you picture her?) Nor does he tell you whether this figure was called 'Hera'. As Elsner happily comments, the problem of cultural translation here reaches something of a climax.[74] How can you envisage these statues? With whose eyes are you looking?

A similar problem of identity and and naming is evident at the beginning of the work where we are told that the Sidonians call the

[71] 44.60.   [72] 44.60.   [73] 44.32.   [74] Elsner (2001) 137.

goddess of their great temple 'Astarte', while the author thought it was 'Selene', but one of the priests told him it was 'Europa'. Any authoritative choice between Syrian goddess, Greek goddess, or human founder of – precisely – Europe is left quite unclear.[75] Most strikingly, however, between the two statues of 'Zeus' and 'Hera' there stands a third image:

> It does not have its own form but bears the qualities of the other gods. It is called 'Sign' [*semeion*] even by the Syrians themselves, and they do not give it any specific name. Nor do they have a story of its origin or form.[76]

Religious historians have had a field-day with this.[77] Representations of the cult at Hierapolis show an aniconic image that looks rather like a Roman legionary standard (called *semeion* in Greek). The semitic word for this object [CSMY'] sounds similar to *semeion*. So, it is argued, Lucian has not mistaken an unfamiliar Syrian goddess' name for a familiar Greek word (like a Greek meeting the Other), but rather the 'homophony [has] allowed him to include the Aramaic word in his Greek'.[78] Yet even such sensitive archaeology does not remove the difficulty here, as the Greek struggles to express what the Syrians – 'them', not 'us' – do not have a story or a name for, except the word 'sign' (in Greek). 'Cultural translation' has become a highly convoluted and blocked process.

On the Syrian Goddess dislocates a topography of the self. The Syrian first-person narrator declares himself to be an insider of the cult of this temple, but describes its artefacts and myths as if he were a Greek anthropologist striving to understand an unfamiliar Other. Yet the Greekness of the narrative voice not only sits awkwardly with his Syrian identity, but also undermines its own authority by its virtuoso pastiche of the unreliable Herodotus. 'Becoming Greek' and 'staying Syrian' are mutually implicative – and ironized – problems. The self-implicating difficulties of finding your place, expressing your cultural identity – this is what Lucian is holding up to wonderfully engaging scrutiny – as if in his own cracked looking-glass. Lucian's first-person story of his religious life oscillates and agitates between different cultural positions, different intellectual masks. If you try to fit this story into a model of straight, confessional, religious autobiography, it can only make you appear a more than usually unsophisticated Procrustes. For Lucian, telling the story of the self

[75] 44.4. [76] 44.33.
[77] Good summary with bibliography in Swain (1996) 304–8.
[78] Swain (1996) 306.

is a tricky, alluring, implicating rhetorical activity. So: 'Be sober, and remember not to believe.'[79]

These four (self-)portraits, then, reveal a dazzling repertoire of strategies for manipulating and ironizing the performance of self-presentation. One could read Lucian's first-person writing to extract what look like nuggets of secure biographical data. Many have. Yet it is hard not to feel that such an agenda is a rather crude approach towards this writing and its cultural import. The inclusive policy of the Roman Empire meant that its subjects could and did become Roman citizens. Yet this did not assuage the competitive tensions of localism, or the pull of the centre of power. Greek culture could be promoted as the educational glue binding the elite of Empire. Yet not only did different commitments and resistances to such education allow for a multiplicity of styles of engagement in elite society but also to speak from within Greek culture required an intricate process and policing of self-fashioning. And it should not be forgotten how momentous the possibilities of this self-fashioning are for the history of Western culture. It is this process of self-formation – its narratives, lures, and deceptions – that Lucian portrays in his first-person writing. His sophisticated feints, deferrals and multiple voicings make this writing of the self a wonderfully intricate game of masks. It should not be thought that being a somebody is an easy or self-evident matter. Lucian may be playful (in all senses), but there is a very serious motivating question that gives his work its force: how is your cultural identity *made up*?

III

How, then, do you become a somebody, a Greek somebody, in Empire culture?

You have to know, properly, how to walk, talk, think, and act Greek, and how to take up your role in Greek social institutions and rituals. That will do for starters.

Let's imagine you are in an art gallery, or museum, or patron's wealthy home. How should you behave? If you wish to appear boorish, unsophisticated and uncultured, you will stand quietly, you will just look, and stare around, you will raise your eyes towards the roof, and wave your hand ineffectually; you will enjoy the art in silence, out of fear of having nothing

---

[79] 70. 47. Lycinus quotes Epicharmus (fr. 250 Kaibel) as his advice to Hermotimus when faced by the teachers of philosophy.

to say worthy of what you are looking at. There is an alternative: to desire to deliver a speech of praise, to honour, to glorify, to fill the space with upraised voice. To fulfil the orator's duty of requiting beauty with words. It should be clear that 'when it comes to looking, there is not the same law for for the ordinary fellow and for men who have been educated/cultured'.[80] Where there is law, there is policing. How you stare, how you hold your hands, and, above all, how you respond before the spectacular possessions of Roman patrons or local big-wigs *matters* and is open to scrutiny. If you read Lucian's *On the House*, or *On Images*, or *In Defence of Images*, you will see this regulating at work.[81]

How you walk is a repeated topic of commentary by Lucian. You should hope to 'walk like a man' (which is linked to a body bronzed by the sun, a masculine glint in the eye, an alert appearance).[82] You don't want to walk 'with an unsteady shimmy' (which is linked to a floppy neck, a woman's glance, a soft voice, the smell of perfume, scratching your head with one finger, and carefully coiffed curls).[83] The figure of Blame in one of Lucian's divine comedies attacks even the god Dionysus for his 'walk': 'you all know how female and girly he is in his nature . . . '[84] In particular, however, it is philosophers who seem to have a specially noticeable style of walking (which you may think harder to spot these days around the university or on the street). Thrasycles' walk is 'orderly' (eye-brows high, fierce gaze, elegant turn out);[85] Diogenes' walk matches his intense expression.[86] The uncultured book-buyer is mocked for imitating the walk of a philosopher;[87] and a string of philosophers are immediately distinctive because of their gait. The longest description of what 'the walk' should be like is this:

I saw them walking in an orderly fashion, decently dressed, always in thought, masculine, mostly with close-cropped hair: nothing degenerate, none of that hyper-indifference which marks the simply mad Cynic, but of middling constitution, which everyone says is best.[88]

This description of Stoics on the street is offered as a reason for taking up Stoic philosophy by Hermotimus. But he is immediately ridiculed by Lycinus who finds it hard to believe that anyone would make even an initial judgement about philosophical value by a man's *walk*.[89] Typically,

---

[80] 10.2: the remarks of this paragraph paraphrase these opening paragraphs of the *de domo*.
[81] Discussed in Goldhill ed. (2001).   [82] 41.9.   [83] 41.11.   [84] 52.4.
[85] 25.54.   [86] 27.10   [87] 31.21.   [88] 70.18.   [89] 70. 18–19.

Lucian can obsessively observe a walk and scoff at its effeminate or floppy appearance, but that doesn't stop the mockery of anyone who judges by appearance!

Lucian also describes what it feels like to make a social gaffe in this atmosphere of scrutiny – to be on the receiving end of society's collective commentary. He has inadvertently used the wrong word of greeting in that public display of power, the early morning visit of clients to their patron – an inexplicable and embarrassing slip which he tries at length to apologize for. He recalls:

I began to sweat and went pink with embarrassment, and was all over the shop in my confusion. Some of those present thought I had made an error, naturally enough; others that I was babbling from age; others thought it a hangover from yesterday's wine-drinking.[90]

The intense physiology of social discomfort is framed by a vivid aware-ness of the audience's shocked observation and prurient interest. More often, however, Lucian – or his Lycinus, or Parrhesiades etc. – plays the role not of victim but of satirical cultural policeman. Indeed, the prestige of *Paideia* (culture/education) makes it a charged site of contest, mockery and display, with all the attendant worries and boundary disputes.

So, Lucian attacks one fellow – we have already met him – who wants to gain a reputation for *paideia* by collecting books, but who gets little but Lucian's scorn. Lucian excoriates not just his insufficiently intellectual appreciation of these luxury objects, but even the very way he reads:

You look at your books with your eyes open, and, by god, you look at them more than enough. Some you read with loads of fluency, with your eye ahead of your mouth. But this is certainly not enough yet, I think, if you don't know the value and defects of each thing written in them, what is the intention of every utterance, what the order of words, what has been accurately turned by the author in accordance with the canons of propriety, and what is false, base, counterfeit.[91]

Even if this would-be intellectual can manage to pass muster as a reader physically, Lucian's scrutiny can reveal his internal insufficiences, his lack of knowledge of the rules of the canon, that is, the technique of really critical reading. Lucian's patrolling of the boundary of insider and outsider is strict: 'Well then? Do you declare that you *know* if you haven't learnt the same things as us?'[92] The satirist expects you to (try to) join the 'we' of those who are in the know – or to suffer the same scorn. Fitting

[90] 64.1.   [91] 31.2.   [92] 31.2.

into the clique of superstar intellectuals is a hard-fought and precarious enterprise.

The satire *On the Hired Academic* is full of the excruciating tensions of social awkwardness. Lucian imagines the academic's first dinner party in the house of the grand patron:

> You are agog. Everything is strange and unfamiliar to you. The servants stare at you, everyone at the party scrutinizes your actions. Even the rich man is concerned. He has told some of his servants to watch to see if you stare from afar at his boys or wife. The attendants of your fellow diners see that you are out of your depth and mock your inexperience about what's being done.[93]

A room full of staring eyes . . . Caught in the glare of a critical gaze from all sides – mocking servants, suspicious host, judgemental guests – the socially inexperienced academic breaks into a humiliated sweat, but is too nervous to take a soothing drink. He watches those around him (everyone is observing everyone else . . .) to get the correct order of food, but when it comes to the toasts and the master drinks his health, he is once again firmly in the spotlight. 'You take the cup but you don't know how to reply because of your inexperience and you earn yourself a bad name because of your lack of culture.'[94] You just can't win by the rules of the (power) game. Lucian seems to address the reader directly as the potential victim of this wretched social circumstance of being a Greek intellectual under Roman power: 'The whole story', he announces, 'is perhaps told for *you*' – not only 'you, the philosopher', but also 'you who have chosen a more serious path in life, including grammarians, rhetoricians, and all who think fit to take a position and accept a wage on behalf of culture/education'.[95] Which reader isn't included in that list? Remember, though, that even success will not bring the comfort of being an insider. Immediately the gossip of a Juvenal begins: 'It's only those Greeks for whom the door is open in Rome. Why are they preferred? . . . He's an unsophisticated fellow, constantly hungry!'[96] Indeed, being an insider brings its own worries. 'People on the outside envy you when they see you living within the Pale and entering fancy free, and being really quite the insider.'[97] But you, of course, miserably worried about holding your position, are unaware that you appear lucky to those outside the charmed circle. Being within the Pale, it seems, cannot make you feel like an insider – just the miserable victim of the outsider's jealousy. All this, to make the patron seem 'a cultivated man of education'

[93] 36.15.   [94] 36.16.   [95] 36.4.   [96] 36.17.
[97] 36.21: 'within the Pale'= ἐντὸς τῆς κιγκλίδος, 'inside the gate of the jurors' enclosure in court'.

by running a salon of intellectuals. It is, finally, the patron who has the kudos of 'possessing education'.[98]

Lucian's satire cruelly exposes the threats and miseries of preferment in the casually humiliating context of Roman authority. Being a somebody, an intellectual, Greek somebody, for Lucian here means the freedom of distance from Roman power. The painful portrait of the academic in the house of the great Roman patron sharply focuses how difficult it is to become Greek without being degraded by The Roman Way. It is this biting satire that requires the *Apology* when Lucian accepts a job with the Roman civil service, Egypt branch.

Of course, Lucian also writes to win patrons for himself, and writes to Roman addressees, and writes in praise of grand houses, and of the beautiful mistress of the visiting Emperor. (But how much is consistency a requirement of satire?) And Greek dinner parties too can produce a sardonic leer from Lucian. His *Symposium*, whose title inevitably recalls Plato's and Xenophon's philosophical versions of that central institution of Greekness, is subtitled *The Lapiths*, and it depicts philosophers arguing and misbehaving in a Rabelaisian parody of the Good Form and Decency expected in such social ritual. (It includes the edifying image of one Cynic waving his willy at the ladies, and later urinating in the middle of the room.)[99] *The Parasite*, in a gentler inversion of the *On the Hired Academic*, takes a different view again – arguing that the art of a parasite is a discipline (*technê*) in a fully philosophical sense, and indeed the parasite is a nobler soldier in war and a better citizen in peace than the self-interested rhetorician or greedy philosophers. The rich actually *need* the parasite, since there is no pleasure in dining alone.[100] *The Parasite* revalorizes a stereotypical Greek character – within the same frame of power relations which made the *On the Hired Academic* so bitterly funny. Knowing how to behave like a Greek, in Greek institutions, often goes awry also for the (over)educated Greek characters of Lucian's little social dramas.

If 'being Greek' means knowing how to lie down to drink of an evening, it also means going to the gym of a day. The dialogue called the *Anacharsis* shows wonderfully well how Lucian combines his provocative questioning of what being Greek implies, with his love of the (classical) past, and his dramatic ability to make figures of myth and history speak – now all turned towards gymnastic exercise as a mark of cultural performance.

[98] 36.25.   [99] 17. 16; 17.35.
[100] 33. 55–7; 33. 58–9. For everything you want to know about *The Parasite*, see Nesselrath (1985).

How did the archetypally Greek institution of the gymnasium show its Greekness?

The *Anacharsis* has a dramatic setting in Athens of the sixth century BCE, and is a dialogue between Solon, one of the founding fathers of classical democracy, and Anacharsis, a visiting Scythian sage, about athletic exercise.[101] Anacharsis, seeing citizens roll around in the dust naked, fighting, hitting each other, 'like pigs', wonders why on earth the Athenians allow such bizarre behaviour. Solon tries to explain the rationale of the gym to the incredulous Scythian, who points out sharply that in Scythia anyone who physically abused a citizen like that would be severely punished. Lucian is only one of a string of Greek and Roman writers who debate the gymnasium's value,[102] especially in Roman society, but he avoids any obvious contemporary polemics by creating what will by now be recognized as a typical highly ironic satiric pose through the layerings of his prose: the foreigner, Lucian, from the East, writing in Greek for a cultured audience in the Roman Empire, imagines an ancient Eastern foreigner's bemused reaction to a central – but now contested – Greek institution. How, then, does the gym make a Greek man of you? The play of insider and outsider, ancient and modern, knowingness and naivety, constructs an intricate and ironic position for author *and* reader alike.

The set-up of the dialogue – its dramatic staging – knowingly disports with these frameworks of identity and cultural value. Anacharsis suggests finding a shady spot for them to discuss Greek training. After Plato's *Phaedrus*, it becomes a commonplace that philosophical discussion needs 'a tree-shaded spot'. But this literary expectation is immediately replaced by the more mundane reason that Anacharsis finds the heat difficult with a bare head. For he has not brought his Scythian hat from home because he did not want 'to be the only person among you to be a foreigner in appearance'.[103] Anacharsis wants to fit in, not to be (pre)judged a foreigner by his appearance, dress, attitude. What is it to look like an Athenian, a Greek? Anacharsis may have left his give-away Scythian hat at home, but he is sweating and uncomfortable in the heat. His body indeed thus marks him as not an Athenian, as Solon promptly points out: gymnastic exercise, he declares, is precisely what has trained

---

[101] This dialogue is well discussed by Branham (1986); my discussion here is drawn from Goldhill (2001b).

[102] I have learnt from Jason König's fine thesis (2000) on this.

[103] 37.16.

Athenians to survive the sun's rays without a hat! The standard apology
of athletics – that it prepares a man to withstand extremes of condition
in war – even in this less exalted form of whether to wear a hat to the
gym, functions to establish an 'us' and a 'them'.

As they walk to the shady spot, Solon's talk is designed to show him
off as a Greek culture hero. Good Athenian to the core, he promises
Anacharsis a (democratically) fair debate, and even offers to honour
Anacharsis publicly in the Assembly if he can point out what's wrong
with Athenian education and training in the gym: 'You may be sure
that the city of Athens will not be ashamed to learn fully what is advantageous from a barbarian and foreign guest.'[104] This is real Greek
talk indeed: adding 'barbarian' to 'foreign' makes sure the reader picks
up the full ideological weight of self and other so familiar from classical
rhetoric. (Anacharsis will turn this back on him, though: 'Since I am
a barbarian, don't make your explanation too complicated or long', he
asks disingenuously, before trashing athletics as 'foolishness for young
men with nothing better to do' – a Roman moralist's point of view.[105]).
Solon's grand promise 'to learn fully what is advantageous' from whatever source rings with the openness Athens so often boasts of displaying.
Where wisdom comes from – whether it comes from the East, indeed –
is also a question of long pedigree. (Herodotus on Egypt is a *locus classicus*
we have already met.) Solon, then, speaks for Greek culture and in the
privileged terms of Greek cultural tradition.

Anacharsis responds, however, with a rather different take: 'Now I
see! That's exactly what I used to hear about you Athenians, that you
are ironical in discussion!'[106] How could he, a wagon-dwelling nomad,
teach those educated in the city-life of Attica? The foreign guest (writes
the foreigner in his best Greek) notes that it is a sign of being Athenian not
to say what you mean. Especially when claiming to be open to learning
from foreigners. (In a neat symmetry, the Greek proverb 'to speak like
a Scythian' means to speak the blunt truth – and had Anacharsis as its
model. And Lucian himself elsewhere takes Anacharsis as a model for his
own story of a foreigner's reaction to the Big City).[107] So what is the reader
to take from this foreigner's lesson? The (foreign) ironist's discussion of
Athenian irony seems designed to make the scene of learning the site of
a playful confusion of voices.

---

[104] 37.17: he imagines the speech in which he claims to have been re-educated about training.
[105] 37.18.   [106] 37.18.
[107] Diogenes Laertius 1. 101 for the proverb; 68. 9 for Lucian's use of it.

Lucian makes a *question* of Greek culture – its signs, value, enactment. His Anacharsis remains unconvinced by Solon's case. His prose mobilizes a cultured, educated layering of literary reference; but this knowingness frames the naivety of the outsider's questioning of what is a normative commonplace for the insider. The silly outsider's non-comprehending question cracks the cultural composure of the insider. Lucian utilizes the voice of the outsider and the setting in the distant past not only to dramatize in an ironic way the old arguments about physical training, but also to comment on the contemporary tension within the valuing of Greek exercise in the Roman Empire. He slyly allows his authorial stance – his foreignness, his commitment to Greek culture – further to vein his cultural politics with a destabilizing irony. For Lucian, in the Roman Empire, speaking to Greekness is a complex business.

It is not easy to become a Greek somebody in the Empire, then. Being a Greek is quite a performance.[108] And Lucian should make you very self-conscious, as well as rather leery, about the whole process and its agenda. From how you walk to how you read to how you exercise to what you do to get a salary. The passionate commitment to being born anew in Christianity – 'Walk Humbly!'; the seriousness of the philosophers' claims on the individual's soul – 'Look at Yourself!'; the manicuring of the politician's self-image – 'Authority! Dignity! Discipline!'; all find in Lucian a running – dancing, laughing – commentary. Lucian's writing is constantly teasing you and provoking you about your acts – in all senses – of self-formation.

IV

But above all, being Greek is speaking Greek.

It will be recalled how madame Rhetoric found the narrator of *The Dream* wandering around Ionia still speaking 'in a barbarian's voice', and how a slip of vocabulary before a patron left Lucian in a sweaty embarrassment. This anxiety about a proper Greek voice needs to be contextualized both by the extensive interest in Attic Greek in intellectual circles in the Empire, and by Lucian's own specific and highly articulate concern.

The parameters of the issue of Greek language usage are easy enough to draw, but the detailed negotiations turn out to be highly complicated and one of the most hotly debated of scholarly questions – both

---

[108] 'La seconde sophistique performe l'hellénisme'. Cassin (1995) 451.

then and now.[109] The Greek that was generally spoken in the Eastern
Mediterranean in the second century CE was *koinê*, 'common' Greek, a
descendant of the Attic of the fifth century BCE. Most elite writing, certainly most intellectual activity, including rhetorical performance, was
conducted in versions of Attic Greek of the classical period. Two obvious
and important exceptions may be due to genre: a doctor such as Galen,
and the philosopher/emperor, Marcus Aurelius, each write in a sophisticated literary Greek which does not closely immitate classical Attic,
though it is still removed from *koinê*. Many Greeks display no knowledge
of Latin, even when it is very likely that Latin was a spoken language necessary for interaction with the authorities of the Empire. Some of those
who have left sophisticated works in Greek spoke other native languages
(such as Aramaic) as a first language or alongside Greek. Many Romans
in the elite spoke and wrote in Greek as well as in Latin. The Latin
of the Empire, too, varied considerably in sophistication and practice
according to class and provenance.

Those general parameters would probably meet with shrugs of approval from our contemporary scholarly community, and – to take the
general model a step further – the best recent discussion of the issue
is rightly keen to see such varied usage of Greek as a sliding scale of
stratification and differentiation (with correspondingly overemphasized
high points of conflictual disagreement) rather than as firmly defined
sectarian groups with highly specific agendas.[110] It remains hard, however, for us to pin down with any precision the social and intellectual
significance and effect of particular practices (in the way, for example,
a dropped 'h' can be so precisely telling in the fiction of the nineteenth
century).[111] The slave of Herodes Atticus who spoke such pure Greek is
a case in point. Purity of Attic is certainly an issue. As we will see shortly,
Lucian attacks one writer for his excessive Atticism, and is attacked himself for making mistakes in his Attic vocabulary. The doctor Galen, who
does not write his medical text books in 'high' Attic, none the less wrote
extensively on the need for 'exact language', and 'pure Greek'. 'Unlike
some people of today', he writes, 'who give out orders, we do not require
everyone to atticize in speech just because they are doctors, or philosophers, or geometers, or musicians, or lawyers or even if they are none
of these professions but just happen to be rich or well-off.'[112] How pure

---

[109] The best recent discussion – with full bibliography – is Swain (1996) 1–131.
[110] Swain (1996).   [111] See especially Mugglestone (1995).
[112] Galen *On the Order of His Own Books* 19. 60. This is well contextualized by Swain (1996).

your Attic Greek is expected or recognized to be is a source of conflict and contention between elite practitioners. So is Heracles' remarkable purity of language – especially when associated with his master's reputation as a cultural arbiter and his master's name, Herodes *Atticus* – an ironic anecdote by Philostratus? If what is wanted is pure language, then it must be rustic, not educated; a poor man's not a master's; a man who has no contact with city life. Or is it a comment on Herodes Atticus' exquisite taste and perception? He is the sort of man to have a slave who is not a barbarian in speech, but of the finest possible linguistic skill, a paradoxical wonder that only a Herodes Atticus could possess. And one can imagine other possible reactions – and combinations of reactions – to the tale, too.

Similar difficulties can arise with even the broadest categories. Latin writers in particular (and some Greeks too) opposed 'Attic rhetoric' as a style to 'Asiatic rhetoric'.[113] The vocabulary of the opposition depends on a familiar Orientalism: the Atticist is simple, clear, direct, controlled, manly, unaffected; the Asiatic is florid, effeminate, excessive, uncontrolled. Claims and accusations fly in the competitive world of oratorical performance, and consequently many modern, and some ancient scholars have been keen to divide orators into 'schools' of Asiatic and Attic styles. Yet it is hard to find any writer claiming himself straightforwardly to be Asiatic in style. Indeed, to take one pointed example, Hegesias who was singled out by later histories as the epitome of 'the affected and corrupt style' of oratory, 'apparently thought of himself as an imitator of Lysias',[114] the archetypally simple and pure *Attic* orator. It might be better to think of 'Asiatic' as an insult to throw at your enemy, a term persuasively to define yourself and your friends, a glib way to distinguish your tongue from another's verbal habits, rather than as a school or policy to which you could affiliate yourself. What opponent could not become a florid and uncontrolled Asiatic in your vitriolic – critical – view?

How you speak or write Greek is a fundamental cultural issue of the second-century elite, on which almost every author has something to say, whether it is Josephus' bare declaration that he first wrote *The Jewish War* in Aramaic for the 'upland barbarians' and then translated it into Greek (for you, the reader, he says),[115] or whether it is Galen's (lost)

---

[113] Evidence and bibliography in Swain (1996) 17–27: my conclusions are quite different from his, however, on this issue.
[114] Swain (1996) 22.   [115] Josephus *Jewish War* 1.1.

forty-eight volume book on Attic usage (coupled with tomes on *Fake Attic Usage* and *On Clarity and Obscurity*). The differentiation and stratification of such debate runs throughout the personal politics of Empire society. The time and leisure to learn Attic required already a certain social and financial position, and, as with 'courtly' language, its correct usage – carefully scrutinized – acted as a badge of elite identity and exclusion. What is more, the use specifically of this antique language linked its speakers to a particular image of Greece – an idealized, Classic image. Writing Attic Greek declared the writer to be the heir of a glorious tradition, the representative of the celebrated history of Greece. The turn back to the past, as ever, is a statement in the politics of the present.

Even within this milieu, Lucian's concern with speaking Greek properly stands out. He more than once worries that a Syrian will be accused of speaking in a slightly weird way, however educated he is: 'I am a Syrian..But what of it? . . . For you at least, it shouldn't matter if a person's speech is barbarian if his judgement is sound and patently just.'[116] That's Parrhesiades, 'Son of Free Speech', defending himself to the figure of Philosophy. The speech, *The False Critic*, is a sixteen-page rant against some scholar who had apparently mocked Lucian for using the word *apophras*, 'nefandous', to describe him. Lucian calls the fellow 'ill-educated', 'ignorant', and the whole gamut of insults that point to the spiky infighting of intellectuals – and he seems particularly upset at the implication that any error stems from his country of origin: 'Your laughter was because of my barbarism, and my alienness, and my transgression of Attic boundaries!'[117] Speech and identity, as ever, are linked in the topographical discourse, and Lucian is acutely conscious of the slur of being out of place.

Lucian also writes a mock law-court speech on behalf of the letter 'sigma' against the letter 'tau' on the grounds that the spread of Attic dialect has led to an encroachment by the 'tau' on 'sigma's territory. (Attic often uses 'tt', where earlier Greek had 'ss'.)[118] There is a dialogue between 'Lucian' and a sophist (*The False Sophist*) which makes fun of the sophist's constantly failing attempts to spot the errors of Greek which he so boastfully claimed to be able to do. Since Lucian does not always point

[116] 28.19.
[117] 51.19. It has been suggested that the sophist in question was Hadrian of Tyre: Jones (1986) 113–4; Swain (1996) 48.
[118] 16: this dialogue was taken up by Richard Pace in *de fructu* as part of his fun with the new Greek: Manley and Sylvester eds. (1967) 101–2.

out exactly what the errors are, the reader is put in the same position as the sophist, with his education under observation, at risk (though with at least the chance of joining in the joke). Since some of the apparent errors are also found elsewhere in Lucian, some editors have been happy to declare that this work is not by Lucian. How could he make fun of his own obsessiveness? How could he be inconsistent?[119] The *Lexiphanes*, however, is a dialogue in which Lycinus meets a 'hyper-atticist', Lexiphanes, who reads him a section of his new work, a 'Symposium'. This is a piece of excruciatingly arcane vocabulary and ridiculous expression, which prompts Lucian to bring in a doctor to cure the poor pretentious writer. He has to stick his fingers down his throat and vomit out his word lists; take the pills of Good Authors; and he will rejoin the ranks of the properly cultured. You can easily go too far with your Atticism.

The different worries about language use, the petty or passionate scenes of argument about linguistic error, the challenges to character and education that such scenes enact, the social discomfort and power that such investment produces, all show how deeply engaged with speaking (like a) proper Greek Lucian is. Yet you shouldn't try to forget that this satire is also aimed at you, the reader. It is not just that whenever you open your mouth, your education and cultural status too are revealed (Lucian should make you fully self-conscious about this). It is rather that his elaborate speeches and dramas suggest that you are missing the joke if you don't pick out every slip of too much or too little Attic flavour, every pretentious pose, every mockery of pretention. You need to be very sure indeed of your cultural acumen, your education. And he does make especial fun of those who think they are arbiters of linguistic nicety. (The uncertainty about who the butt of the joke is, was one thing which so upset the first readers of Erasmus' Lucianic *Praise of Folly*.) Your role as an educated, cultured reader is what's on the line here. Lucian is putting you in the picture. He depends on your complicity, on you being in the know; but you are also a figure in this drama of the fragility of culture. Are you sure you are reading properly, right now?

V

It is not without irony, then, that it is Lucian who should so often have been chosen in modern Europe as the text with which to teach Greek, and who should have been so important as the epitome of Greekness

---

[119] For such debate see Hall (1981) 298–307.

for Erasmus, locked as he was into such battles over translation and 'proper' language. Lucian continues, however, to act as a lightning rod for concerns over purity of culture and the language of Empire. If the Renaissance shows one critical juncture of the engagement with Lucian, the turn of the nineteenth century shows another equally turbulent and disturbing conflict of re-evaluation – which critics are still working through today. In 1899, Houston Stewart Chamberlain published *Die Grundlagen des 19 Hunderts* (*The Foundations of the Nineteenth Century*). This massive two-volume blockbuster, scarcely read these days, was a major bestseller (over 100,000 copies in Germany by 1915). The first 'popular edition' sold 10,000 copies in ten days in 1906, and it was reprinted twenty-four times. It 'caused more of a ferment than any appearance on the book market in recent years', according to the *Frankfurter Zeitung*. The book was a favourite of Kaiser Wilhelm, who entertained the author publicly and with deference. It became not merely a *cause célèbre*, but a book of fundamental influence on the development of the twentieth century.[120]

Chamberlain was an Englishman brought up in France, who was a passionate German nationalist, and who lived in Germany and wrote in German. He had been closely associated with the cult of Richard Wagner and the Bayreuth Festival (he eventually married Wagner's daughter and his first published works were on Wagner). *The Foundations of the Nineteenth Century* is an account of the history of Europe – originally planned so that 'thirty centuries of human development would culminate gloriously with Richard Wagner'[121] – which sees the development of civilization as a clash of race: 'European history had arisen out of conflict of the major racial forces: a chaos of mixed races, and two "pure" races: the Teutons and the Jews.'[122] The argument of the book served to laud the Teutonic race – 'the leitmotiv that runs through the whole book is the assertion of the superiority of the Teuton family to all other races in the world'[123] – and to see the Teuton race threatened on the one side by the Jewish race, whose physical, mental and moral characteristics he outlined at length, and, on the other, by the danger of *Völkerchaos* – which became a buzz word in the extraordinarily extensive debate he prompted – 'A chaotic mix of people'.

---

[120] The facts in this paragraph are culled from Field (1981) 224–77.
[121] Field (1981) 171.　　[122] Field (1981) 184.
[123] Redesdale (1921) xxxiv. I cite Redesdale's pamphlet from this reprinted introduction rather than from its original private publication (1909) because it is probably easier to consult.

It is certainly true that 'racial theory was well established before Chamberlain wrote the *Foundations*'[124] – Gobineau and Lagarde are particularly influential in this context – and race had already been the subject of much detailed scientific, academic, and technical discussion (as well as murderous social display).[125] Yet Chamberlain proved to be a great synthesizer and popularizer: 'the publication of the *Foundations* turned Chamberlain almost overnight into the prophet of race for educated laymen in Central Europe'.[126] He avoided the violence and extremism of the most vulgar anti-semitism – he made few if any positive recommendations for action or policy – and he also by-passed advanced contemporary science, to the dismay of professional scholars, while giving his book a constant and persuasive patina of academic expertise. It was a book which was extraordinarily popular with academic youth, and widely debated among the professional middle classes. It was often disagreed with, and its sweeping mixture of generalizations and mass of detail across a wide range of subjects – from Homer to Wagner – provoked a varied response. But it set an agenda. In 1927, Alfred Rosenberg, one of the leading ideologues of the Nazi movement, saw it as 'an indispensable accompaniment in the coming struggle for German freedom'.[127] With customary sense of theatre, Hitler visited the dying and paralyzed Chamberlain, and kissed the hands of this 'apostle of Germanism'.[128] Its images of the Teutonic race and its enemies fuelled and focused the German imagination.

In England, *Foundations* was published in translation in 1910, and seen through the press with an introduction, and privately printed pamphlet of praise, by Lord Redesdale, A. B. F. Mitford (one of whose daughters married Oswald Mosley, the leading English fascist of the 1920s and 1930s). It was avidly read – usually with something of the distance of the English gaze at the obsessions of the Continent. Redesdale is proud to report to Chamberlain that Winston Churchill had it open on his desk and had praised it to him lavishly.[129] Perhaps its most remarkable imprimatur – which reads chillingly now – came from George Bernard Shaw. Writing for *The Fabian News* of 1911 he declared, 'It really is a magnificent manifesto' which 'all Fabians should read'. 'It is a masterpiece of really

---

[124] Field (1981) 178.
[125] See Mosse (1964); Stern (1961), who (90) calls Lagarde 'the patron saint of the emergent anti-semitic or *Völkische* movement'; Volkov (1978); Rose (1990); Le Rider (1993).
[126] Field (1981) 214.   [127] Rosenberg (1927) 29.   [128] Mosse (1964) 93.
[129] Quoted, from a letter from Redesdale to Chamberlain of 25 Jan. 1912, by Field (1981) 463.

scientific history'. 'Anyone who has not read it will be rather out of it in
political and sociological discussions for some time to come.'[130] It is also
interesting that both Redesdale and Shaw distanced themselves from the
image of the Jew that Chamberlain offered. Redesdale, although he calls
the Jew 'the born rebel against State law', essays the customary sop of
'some of my best friends are Jews' by declaring that not all individual
Jews need instantiate the type of the Jew ('race and purity of blood are
what constitute a type'); and Shaw sees the enemies of civilization – by
which he means the enemies of Fabianism – not as 'the Basque or the
Jew' but – never one to miss an opportunity for his snobbery – 'the
English greengrocer', who won't vote for Shaw's party.[131]

When it came to the central category of 'race' itself, Chamberlain's
book demonstrates a 'mixture of evasiveness, bold assertion, and
contradictions'.[132] It is something of a surprise to learn that Thomas
More is an archetypal Teuton; and that Christ was certainly not a Jew.
Nor is race consistently a matter of biological determinism: one's racial
characteristics may slip or become concealed. 'It is comparatively easy
to become a Jew; difficult almost to the point of impossibility to become
Teutonic.'[133] The paranoid exclusivity, with its accompanying need for
scrutiny and protection, is clear enough. And indeed the threat of the
disguised Jew, and the insistence on constant suspicion, along with the
asserted inevitability of racial characteristics coming out, became a dominant rhetoric of later German nationalism, epitomized in the film *Jew
Suss* – which itself was buttressed by a ream of moral and physiognomic
guides to recognizing deceptive Jewishness.

It is, then, particularly striking that Chamberlain's test-case example of the horrors of *Völkerchaos* is Lucian. Introduced as the 'witty
Heinrich Heine of the second century',[134] Lucian is treated to a brief,
new biography. 'In addition to the Syrian *patois*, the boy began to murder Greek'; money led him to reject sculpture as a career. 'During his
whole life . . . this desire for money remained the guiding star – no, that is
too fine an expression – the driving impulse of this gifted Syrian.'[135] He
failed in Athens and left for Marseilles, 'a place where taste was not so
indispensable. This sea-port of the Phoenician diaspora had just received
by the arrival of thousands of Jews from Palestine such a clearly marked

---

[130] Shaw (1911) 52; 53.   [131] Redesdale (1921) xxiii; xxxiv; Shaw (1911) 53.
[132] Field (1981) 215.   [133] Chamberlain (1921) 491.
[134] Chamberlain (1921) 78.   [135] Chamberlain (1921) 302.

character that it was simply called "The City of the Jews".[136] His career and writings reveal his character. Break the shell, look for the kernel and what will you find? 'Nothing. Of course nothing.' Because of his racial mix, he has 'no noble aim, no profound conviction, no thorough understanding'; all he can reveal is himself: 'a clever Syrian mestizo, a bastard born of fifty unrecorded crossings'.[137] At best a journalist who 'scoffs like Heine' (except that 'Heine did belong to a definite people and in consequence possessed a more definite physiognomy'),[138] the only positive thing to be said for Lucian was that 'he understood the spirit he resembled, namely, the totally bastardized, depraved and degenerate world around him'. In short, Lucian, like St Augustine with whom Chamberlain bizarrely couples him, is 'cut off from all racial belongings, mongrels among mongrels'.[139]

Chamberlain sees in Lucian, then, not merely the slide away from the glory of classical Greece, which is a charge so often thrown at the Second Sophistic, but also and most importantly, the embodiment of a racial chaos which dooms the author to a journalistic display of his own degenerate foulness. Lucian's 'becoming Greek' has become the very sign of his corruption of his racial and (thus) cultural identity.

I still find it unpleasantly alienating to see what looks like the direct influence of Chamberlain's book on classical scholarship, particularly in the early twentieth century in Germany. These scholars, moreover, are still blithely quoted today in Lucianic studies. (It's one of the places where claims about objective and apolitical scholarship look least convincing.) Niklas Holzberg has pointed out tellingly how Wilamowitz's description of Lucian in a big, multi-authored volume on the history of Greek and Latin literature and language (published in 1905) had a profound and negative effect on German scholarship's view of the author.[140] It is perhaps not surprising that this immensely powerful doyen of the discipline of classical scholarship should have had a deep influence on his colleagues on this topic too. Yet as Holzberg tells the story, Germany's Lucianic scholars were immediately converted to a 'new, unanimously accepted assessment of Lucian's literary and intellectual significance'.[141] The story may well be more complicated and nuanced – as stories of intellectual influence tend to be – but the echoes Holzberg traces in

---

[136] Chamberlain (1921) 304; 308.   [137] Chamberlain (1921) 307.
[138] Chamberlain (1921) 308. The word 'journalist' will become a leitmotiv in Lucianic studies: see below p. 98. On Heine's scoffing and its background see Chase (2000).
[139] Chamberlain (1921) 320.   [140] Holzberg (1988) 205.   [141] *Ibid.*

these scholars do look damning. Wilamowitz, like Chamberlain, called
Lucian a 'journalist' with 'no thoughts of his own';[142] Schmid, upping
the ante, called him a 'light -fingered, sensation-mongering, irresponsi-
ble columnist'.[143] Helm, who wrote a big and still much cited book on
Lucian, as well as the entry in the authoritative encylopaedia of Pauly-
Wissowa, declared him not to be man of character; he used the full
battery of his (Germanic) scholarship to prove Lucian's 'lack of originality', and he also likened him to Heinrich Heine. Holzberg's story
should be nuanced by the observation that using Heine as the example
of the dangerously Semitic/Eastern in culture was a commonplace,[144]
as was a post-Romantic aggression towards perceived lack of originality;
but tellingly, in the Pauly-Wissowa article, Helm cites Chamberlain as a
supporting authority for his views. Geffcken – a distinguished historian
of the later Empire – calls Lucian 'a disgusting Semite'; and Capelle in
1914 states that this 'Syrian scribe' could have 'little lasting appeal for
the truly Germanic soul'.[145]

   To complete this trajectory, in 1936 Eduard Wechssler not only dismisses Lucian for (again) his 'humorous journalism', but also calls him
bluntly 'The Jew Lucian' – 'der Jude Lukianos'.[146] All readings are, of
course, political (we have become accustomed to saying) – and no doubt
how seriously *you* engage with Lucian's games of masks and identity depends to a degree on your own (political) ideas of how cultural identity
is conceptualized and formulated – but I do hope that I do not have to
emphasize that Wechssler's identification of Lucian as 'The Jew' encapsulates a horrific politics of race and nationalism – and religious hatred.
Wechssler writes as a committed, evangelical Christian and Professor
of Theology (though it's worth knowing that his earlier work includes a
study of Wagner and the Holy Grail); his book, *Hellas im Evangelium*, like
Chamberlain's *Foundations*, sets out with the grotesque agenda of removing 'Jewishness' from the thought of Jesus in favour of the acceptably
Aryan roots of Zoroastrianism and Greek philosophy. (The religious
roots of arguments about Greek in Luther and Erasmus find particularly sick fruit here.) It is sobering to reflect on the fact that this book was
re-published in a second edition (with corrections!) in 1947, after the war.

---

[142] Wilamowitz (1924) 249.
[143] Von Christ (1924) 740; cited by Holzberg (1988) 206. Schmid will re-appear in chapter 3 below,
    pp. 159–60.
[144] Heine is 'the touchstone in the late nineteenth century for Jewish originality': Gilman (1996) 46.
    See also Chase (2000) with good further bibliography.
[145] Cited from Holzberg (1988) 206–7.   [146] Wechssler (1947) 105.

German attacks on Jewishness also privileged language in a particular way. Partly it was a general concern about Jews fitting in to cultural norms. Wagner himself sums this up in a paradigmatic manner: 'But the Jew has stood outside the pale of any such [German] cultural community . . . just as even the peculiar (Hebraic) language of that stock has been preserved for him as a thing defunct . . . Our whole European art and civilization, however, have remained to the Jew a foreign tongue . . . In this Speech, in this Art, the Jew can only mimic and mock.'[147] The slides between language as linguistic form and language as cultural expression are telling. The Jew, debarred by his stock from authentic speech, is forced into mimicry and mockery – remember the descriptions of Heine and Lucian, inveterate mimics and scoffers both. But there is a more invidious recognition of the Jewish *phônê*. 'Mauscheln', or 'jüdeln', 'to moish', or 'to jew', means to speak improperly like a Jew. ('Mauscheln' is derived from 'Moses', or 'Moishe' in Hebrew.)[148] To hear the corrupting sound of Jewishness within German disgusted, dismayed, or amused Germans and became a source of constant agitation for Jew and non-Jew in social exchange. (It is a repeated scene of anxiety captured vividly in Gregor von Rezzori's fine novel, *Memoirs of an AntiSemite*, where it is translated 'to yiddle'.) This pervasive and corrosive image of a mimicry of proper language which can never quite conceal its barbarous corruption, made the association of Lucian and German anti-Semitism all too easy.

The less organized anti-Semitism of Victorian and Edwardian English society often also focused – particularly after the wave of Jewish immigration in the 1890s – not only on physiognomy and morality but also specifically on accent. Dickens' portrayal of Fagin influentially projected such stereotypes, as did cartoons and other writing.[149] The Anglo-Jewish community itself, in its drive towards acculturation, also resisted any influx of Yiddish – 'that miserable jargon that is not a language at all', merely 'an uncivilized, uneducated jargon'[150] – and despite the long-running and often intense rows over the Aliens Act (finally passed in 1905), there was surprisingly little struggle over the act's literacy

---

[147] Wagner (1912–29) III, 84–5.

[148] Gilman (1986) 139–48; and more generally, 68–107. See also Gilman (1991) ch. 1: 'The Jewish Voice: chicken soup and the penalties of sounding Jewish'.

[149] See Cowen and Cowen (1998); Baumgarten (1996); Steyn (1995); and, most generally, Cheyette (1993).

[150] First quotation from the end of year speech of Louis Abrahams, Headmaster of the Jewish Free School, in 1905: see Black (1988) 110; second quotation from *Jewish Chronicle* 23 May 1917 (cf. 8 June 1923): see Livshin (1990) 82.

requirement for Naturalization, which stipulated that one test for Naturalization should be the ability to read an English newspaper – a test administered in a police-station by the police force. In England indeed the interest in accent was far more than part of the Jewish question.[151] *Punch* is full of cartoons making fun of Irish and Scottish accents, and, above all, of laughable working-class mistakes. As George Bernard Shaw's *Pygmalion* dramatized, social persona in English society was integrally linked to the English you spoke. While this fascination with accent often appears in gestures of snobbery or humour, it is also a fundamental element of a much wider debate about education and language, the influence and importance of which is still being felt. This debate frames a rather English Lucian, towards which the following paragraphs are leading.

Whether English should be taught in schools in England, and what form such teaching should take, was one of the most earnestly and widely discussed issues surrounding the Education Act of 1918. It led directly to the Government Report of 1921, 'The Teaching of English in England'. The Education Act of 1918, part of a long history of reform starting with Forster's Act of 1870 which introduced State elementary schools, expressly put class and nationhood at the centre of the Education System.[152] It was to be a National system (Col. Wedgwood: 'This is not a national system because it does not include the children of the rich.')[153] From one side, parliamentary debate invoked the support offered 'in the strongest possible terms and unanimously by the Workers' Educational Association'[154] (Col. Wedgwood: 'And they call that education! To my mind it is a travesty of education. It is the vocational education . . . which Germany invented.')[155] It aimed to raise the standards of education for all throughout the country (Col. Wedgwood: 'It is rather a scheme for training children to become useful producers of wealth than a scheme for producing a national improvement in the real education of the people of the country.')[156] The politics of education here inevitably debate the role of training in class formation, wealth production, and

---

[151] See Black (1988) 243–332, esp. 317–21; Feldman (1994). Chamberlain's war-time essays, published in translation under the title, *The Ravings of a Renegade*, emphasizes the obsession with accent as particularly English (Chamberlain (1916?) 119).

[152] See in particular Baldick (1987).

[153] *Parliamentary Debates* 1918 vol. 105, 7 May 1918: 1999.

[154] *Parliamentary Debates* 1918 vol. 105, 7 May 1918: 2006.

[155] *Parliamentary Debates* 1918 vol. 105, 7 May 1918: 2037.

[156] *Parliamentary Debates* 1918 vol. 105, 7 May 1918: 1999.

the control of social mobility. It is about what England and the English should become.

Hence the passion surrounding the publication of the report 'The Teaching of English in England' (it was even, in a rather ridiculous gesture, burnt, in the forecourt of the usually rather more staid University of London).[157] This finely written report was produced by the typical government committee (friends, lackeys, professionals, amateurs, vested interests: Quiller-Couch, professor of English at Cambridge, refused to attend any meetings after the first because no alchohol was served).[158] When it appeared it 'sold like a novel', 'like a "bestseller"' indeed. 'It was widely read in business as well as eductaional circles.'[159] It had a lasting effect, not merely in the determination that English and English culture should be a school subject and discussed as such, but also in its questioning of the role of teaching Greek and Latin in schools. It makes a careful and firm case for Classics to be displaced. 'We do not believe that those who have not studied the Classics or any foreign literature must necessarily fail to win from their native English a full measure of culture and humane training. To hold such an opinion seems to us to involve an obstinate belittling of our national inheritance.'[160] Indeed, English is 'the most analytical language in modern Europe'[161] – and it is important to get such nationalist linguistics just right: 'the comparison between the sturdy integrity of the German tongue and the decadent Teutonic speech of modern England was an important element in "the German legend" which led directly to the Great War'.[162] (Philology has a lot to answer for.) English, in short, is 'decidedly more suited [than Greek or Latin] to the necessities of a general or national education'.[163] The report's easy nationalism, its overlap of linguistic and cultural expression, its polemical force within educational debate, spoke strongly to interwar English society. Any attempt of the committee to keep its polemics nuanced was compromised when one of its members, George Sampson, published in the same year an even more aggressively expressed manifesto, called bluntly and pointedly, *English for the English*.

On the fringes of such government policy making, societies like the *Society for Pure English* published and encouraged debate into English and how to prevent the 'active force towards degeneration' in its use in

---

[157] Wilson (1969)   [158] Wilson (1969) 86–102 tells the inside story.   [159] Wilson (1969) 98; 99.
[160] *The Teaching of English in England* HMSO (1921) 18.
[161] *The Teaching of English in England* HMSO (1921) 288.
[162] *The Teaching of English in England* HMSO (1921) 286.
[163] *The Teaching of English in England* HMSO (1921) 15.

society.[164] J. Reith, the founder of the BBC, wrote that 'one can place a man socially and educationally from the first few dozen words he utters', and since 'I do not suppose that any man wishes to go through life handicapped by mistakes or carelessnesses of his own pronunciation . . . We have made a special effort to secure . . . men . . . who . . . can be relied on to employ the correct pronunciation of the English tongue.'[165] Reith was proud of how the BBC had become a model and arbiter for English usage. Between elocution lessons, the spread of BBC English through radio into so many houses, and the changing education system in the strife-ridden years between the wars, how English is (to be) spoken became a charged issue of national cultural importance.

It is in such a context that there emerges one particular book and author, towards which these last few paragraphs of contextualization have been travelling, namely, H. W. Fowler and his *Dictionary of Modern English Usage*. The *Dictionary of Modern English Usage*, a series of articles on how English should be used, was a runaway success. Over half a million copies were quickly sold, in thirteen impressions, and it is still widely consulted, or at least owned (as if 'Modern English' still meant the 1920s).[166] In the debates about how English is to be used, Fowler became an instant and awesome authority. Fowler himself wrote that 'we have our eyes not on the foreigner, but on the half-educated Englishman who wants to know Can I say so & so?..Is this use English?..Not but what we may be of use to the foreigner who knows English pretty well.'[167] And indeed, especially in the colonies and the former countries of the (collapsing) British Empire, Fowler provided the privileged means of checking whether your English had the imprimatur of propriety. In the fragmented and conflictual world of English usage – in becoming English – Fowler offered a touchstone. What I find fascinating, however, is Fowler's lifelong engagement with Lucian, and how the great satirist of language and cultural identity found a champion in Fowler, whose own work was successful to a large degree precisely because he 'detest[ed] affectation, preciosity, and humbug', and because he wrote 'as if [he] were seized from time to time with an irresistible impulse to laugh at his own too solemn self'.[168]

---

[164] For insider history of the society see Smith (1931) who notes (484) that the title was chosen 'to protest against current notions of purity in language, and to suggest, ironically and perhaps too subtly, the great linguistic truth to purists that in their discriminations and denunciations they are almost always wrong'. 'Active force for degeneration' is cited from *SPE* tract 1 (1919) 7 – against the use of italicized French words in English prose.

[165] Reith (1924) 161.

[166] Updated, of course, with some awkwardness in a third edition by R. W. Birchfield.

[167] Cited by Birchfield.   [168] Gowers (1957) 8.

Fowler was an eccentric character, even for Victorian England. 'Victorian in essence ... down to the very end' and 'how English ... to the core',[169] he first worked as a classical schoolmaster ('smelly Joe') in Yorkshire. He resigned when his unwillingness to train boys for confirmation led to him being passed over for the position of housemaster. He lived briefly in London on a small private income, writing occasional journalistic pieces, before taking up a hermit-like existence on the island of Guernsey, where he lived alone in a small cottage near his younger brother's own small cottage (where he, who had also been a classics schoolmaster at Manchester Grammar School, also lived on his own). There, he exercised religiously every day, and read and wrote, usually sitting in the door of his cottage. He decided to marry a local nurse (whom he had met because she tended a friend of his) on his fiftieth birthday. At fifty-four, he – like his brother – volunteered to fight in the first world war, pretending he was forty-one (the regular exercise enabled the pretence). He wrote home to his wife – usually in pencil – almost every day, and sometimes more than once a day, signing every letter 'Your loving Dux', and then, with sweetly bizarre etiquette, adding in brackets: '(H. W. Fowler)'.[170] When he was not allowed to the trenches because of his age he disappointedly wrote to his command asking to be returned to England since he was doing work there of national importance on a dictionary (he also produced the *Concise Oxford English Dictionary*).[171] (When he died, *Punch* published a poem in his honour which ends by praising how all his linguistic labour had been 'To serve his country in her hour of need', recognizing the connection of the Dictionary and nationalism with that journal's usual *in joco veritas*.)[172] His brother died shortly after the war. The *Dictionary*, a work which they had planned together, was thus completed alone. He enjoyed fame on the page alone, nor did he receive many guests in his new home in Somerset. He remained 'a figure so shadowy that even at the Clarendon Press there were only two people who had just once seen his face and heard his voice.'[173] His marriage was reputed to be happy, his very few friendships intense, his love of swimming and jogging unquenchable, and his sense of etiquette punctilious.

The *Dictionary of Modern English Usage* (1926) was the culmination of his earlier writing. *The King's English* (1906), which according to a rather

---

[169] Coulton (1934) 99; 123.

[170] These letters, along with the letters from his school-teaching career, are in the library of St John's College, Cambridge.

[171] On dictionary writing in this period, and the *OED* in particular see Murray (1977) and Willinsky (1994).

[172] *Punch* 186, 10 Jan. 1934: 36.   [173] Coulton (1934) 99.

overheated obituary in *The Times*, 'took the world by storm',[174] was a first large-scale attempt to engage in the cultural battles over English with a mixture of satire and normative advice. He continued this critical polemic with regular articles on language use for *The Society of Pure English*. Fowler also published a brief book of essays in 1907 called *Si mihi – !* (which completely failed), which he republished in 1929 under the title *If Wishes Were Horses*. These little essays of human desire and frailty are Lucianic in tone – down to the self-mocking publication of insulting Press notices ('We feel that we are not supposed to know what he means and that he does not mean it' *Irish Times*); but also he quotes Lucian in the introduction and elsewhere in the text – always on how you shouldn't read what he writes at face value. (Lucian too wrote a piece subtitled 'The Wishes'.) His first large-scale project, however, shared with his brother, and completed in 1905, was the four-volume Oxford translation of the works of Lucian.

The Fowlers see Lucian as very much speaking to their own time: 'a twentieth-century Englishman and a second-century Greek in Rome would be much more at home in each other's century, if they had the gift of tongues, than in most of those that have intervened';[175] and they run through a list of the similarities (the *Anacharsis* recalls modern obsessions with sport, and so on). And indeed the mocking of the 'purist' who thinks himself 'blunder proof' in 'The Purist Purized' (*The False Sophist*) brilliantly captures the tone Fowler himself will adopt in the *Dictionary*. Indeed, Fowler's writing again and again shows the satiric strategies and critical élan of his Lucian.

As with Lucian's writing, Fowler's reflections on usage are shot through both with a strong sense of how language functions as a social marker, and with a sharply comic sense of the ridiculousness of excessive regulation – in a not wholly consistent manner. His famous article on the 'split infinitive' divides the English-speaking world into five categories: '(1) those who neither know nor care what a split infinitive is; (2) those who do not know, but care very much; (3) those who know & condemn; (4) those who know & approve; (5) those who know & distinguish'.[176] How you are in the know is what counts, and having the judgement to distinguish is what the article demands (and offers). He gently taunts the reader with slipping into the wrong group. He mocks 'the bogy-haunted creatures' who are so 'deaf to the normal rhythms of English sentences' that they allow 'the tame acceptance of the misinterpreted opinion of

---

[174] *Times* 28 Dec. 1933: 12.   [175] Fowler and Fowler (1905) xviii.   [176] Fowler (1926) 558.

others' to militate against 'instinctive good taste' in favour of 'the queerest distortions'. And he ends his six column entry by pushing you, the reader, firmly into the spotlight: 'After this inconclusive discussion, in which, however, the author's opinion has perhaps been allowed to appear with indecent plainness, readers may like to settle for themselves [which expression] in the following sentence . . . should have been preferred.'[177] If the author's 'indecent plainness' has poked out of his 'inconclusive discussion' adequately, you should have no difficulty in demonstrating your 'instinctive good taste' in his little test. (Or are you still in the limbo of the 'half-educated'?) His *Dictionary* does not just tell you what is right, but playfully engages you in the difficulty of demonstrating the lesson taught.[178]

His entry on 'Genteelism' shows his socio-linguistics at its most scornful.[179] (Immediately above on the same page, his entrance on 'genteel' reads: '**Genteel**: is now used, except by the ignorant, only in mockery.') With a wonderfully self-aware performance, he attacks anyone who avoids a 'natural word' with a 'synonym that is thought to be less soiled by the lips of the common herd, less familiar, less plebeian, less vulgar, less improper, less apt to come betwixt the wind and our nobility'. (Enough synonyms . . .) So 'the truly genteel do not offer *beer*, but *ale*' – and so forth. He adds a list of in and out words, which the reader 'will easily increase for himself' – a list which denigrates not only the use of 'perspire' for 'sweat', 'preserve' for 'jam', 'odour' for 'smell', but also the (shocking) habit of saying 'mirror' for 'looking-glass', or 'stomach' for 'belly'. Fine lines . . . The reader is invited to smile with the author at the pompous snobbery of the genteel – but also to police his own vocabulary with some care. Fowler's sharply humorous satire and his engagingly rigorous regulations speak to the anxiety of what proper English is – as Lucian's satiric humour and badgering mark the social pressures surrounding Greek and Greekness. Fowler offers to educate the reader in the instinctive and natural use of English – to speak like a real Englishman.

Fowler's philology in the *Dictionary of Modern English Usage*, with its mocking of genteelism, of pomposity, of excessively 'pure' English, draws fully on his Lucianic reading – and, like Lucian, he speaks directly to the

---

[177] Fowler (1926) 560.
[178] Cf. *SPE* x (1922) [*On Grammatical Inversion*] 10: 'The reader is invited to decide for himself whether it would not have been in all these instances clearly better . . . '.
[179] Fowler (1926) 212–13.

cultural crisis of language and power in Empire society. Chamberlain and Fowler, roughly contemporary Englishmen, each made his Lucian, and each used his Lucian to produce a significant and lasting contribution to the politics of language, nationhood, and cultural identity. Lucian's concerns with 'becoming Greek' were good to think with. At this crucial juncture in the history of Europe, Lucian does not merely function as a counter in academic or intellectual discussion. Nor is this a story of 'reception'. Rather, the work – the figure – of Lucian both informs and is informed by nationalist debate about language and the privilege of Greekness. For Fowler and for Chamberlain, finding the cultural identity of 'being English' or 'being German' travels through Lucian's project of 'becoming Greek'.

VI

Lucian's writing could, of course, bear more framing. My strategy has been to contrast Lucian with Favorinus in order to emphasize as strikingly as possible the particularity of Lucian's indirectness and irony. This particularity would be further underlined if we compared his first-person narratives with other second-sophistic writers – notably the hypochondriac and obsessively self-observing Aelius Aristides, or the rhetorician who positions himself close to the throne, Dio Chrysostom, or even Josephus and his account of his own political career as a Jew in the Roman Empire.[180] The ancient Christians who do talk, with some distaste, about Lucian also have a tradition of first-person confessional prose which reaches its acme in Augustine's epochal *Confessions*. Similarly, I have juxtaposed the different conceptualization of Lucian first among Erasmus, Luther and their contemporaries and second among Chamberlain, Fowler and their contemporaries to stress most vividly the radical shift in the image and status of Lucian before and after the Enlightenment. (A history of reading Lucian would have to include also Fielding, say, or Swift or Rabelais.) But one framing that I have been perhaps too coy about is my own. I am certainly acutely aware – and happy enough – that my delight in Lucian's satirical prodding of identity politics will be seen as having its own contemporary agenda. (So, too, no doubt, will its background in empire/colonial writing, and its interest in the strategies of self-representation and the seriousness of jokey dialogues

---

[180] See Whitmarsh (forthcoming); Gleason (2001); Miller (1994) esp. 184–204; Brown (1978); Bowersock (1969), Baslez, Hoffmann and Pernot eds. (1993) and in general Edwards and Swain eds. (1998).

about what makes a somebody a somebody.) I have cared to trace how Lucian's humour makes a serious point about the stories that are told of the self because the consequences of not thinking hard enough about such stories seem to me to be intellectually and politically impoverishing. How the stories that fashion the self are modelled, needs scrutiny, if there is to be adequate comprehension of one's own social and cultural engagement. And I find Lucian's ironic provocation stimulating to that end. As my examples of Erasmus and Chamberlain show most vividly, it is how Lucian engages you in the politics of the person that has made him a figure to fight over. And who stands outside that fight?

CHAPTER THREE

Blood from the shadows: Strauss' disgusting, degenerate 'Elektra'

I

In 1910, the same year in which the translation of Chamberlain's powerful and horrid *Foundations of the Nineteenth Century* was published in England, a different cultural production in Edwardian London provoked the widest and most passionate debate about nationalism, modernism, degeneracy and Germany. It is an event which dramatically exposes the fissure between nineteenth-century classicism and a modernist view of ancient Greece – and thus makes it a particularly important case for my book. In a quite different manner from contemporary German re-evaluations of Lucian, arguments about the true Greece, the true England and the true Germany were polemically thrust into the public domain. This story will provide not only a continuation of the narrative of the previous chapter from Chamberlain into the heart of German-speaking nationalism and modernism, but also a paradigmatic demonstration of how the Greek Question is expressed at all levels of culture, from dress, to psychoanalysis, to music to politics – and how a truly interdisciplinary study is needed to comprehend such a cultural transition. This chapter will explore the modernist assault on the bastion of Victorian Hellenism: the following chapter in turn will show how the construction of Victorian Hellenism was far more contested and difficult than suggested by modernist dismissiveness. Together, they offer an extended historical context which is fundamental to any explanation of Lucian's change in status, and, indeed, any explanation of the shifting values of modern Hellenism.

The production I will be discussing is the first performance of Richard Strauss' latest opera, *Elektra*. It was *the* event of the season. 'Excepting the death of King Edward, which occured the following spring, it was the most discussed event of the year', recalled Sir Thomas Beecham, who conducted the performance.[1] Beecham was trying to establish for the

---

[1] Beecham (1944) 89.

first time a national opera company in London with a season to rival
the great houses of Paris and Berlin and other European capitals – after
much public debate about the need for such a national project; and he
was both central to the opera's impact and an adept self-publicist. But
his claim that the *Elektra* was a major turning point in English cultural
life was shared. George Bernard Shaw – another great manipulator of
the media and his self-image – called it 'a historic moment in the history
of art in England, such as may not occur again in our lifetime'.[2] Even
The Tatler from its less exalted, indeed frankly ephemeral perspective
noted that 'the opening of the Beecham opera season is the social event
of the week. The theatre was simply crammed with well-known people
on opening night.'[3] Indeed, in the presence of the King and Queen,
with tickets in such unprecedented demand that journalists could not
get seats, 'an overwhelming audience' of 'all London' was participating
in a 'sensation'. 'They cheered and cheered and cheered again till from
sheer bowing Mr Thomas Beecham... the singers and the rest must
have increased the enormous physical weariness that could not have
failed to have attended their efforts to present *Elektra*'[4] – and Beecham
was presented, symbolically enough, with a large laurel wreath. What
was it about this modernist musical performance of a German version
of an ancient Greek tragedy that made it such a moment in Edwardian
London? What made so many writers, so many politicians, so many
concerned citizens care about this opera?

'Expectation had been raised to the highest pitch by unprecedented
preliminary newspaper articles', commented *The Musical Times*, 'many
of which gave absurdly exaggerated and inaccurate accounts of Strauss'
work'.[5] Beecham too noted with some satisfaction that 'weeks before the first performance newspapers vied one with another in drawing the most lurid picture of what was happening on stage'.[6] (I have
traced over seventy-five articles 'announcing' (or denouncing) the coming performance. Before film and television, the importance of the
stage in the cultural imagination was huge: 'Who shall deny the immense authority of the theatre', wrote Henry James, 'or that the stage is
the mightiest of modern engines?')[7] In a process familiar from the press
today (and familiarly lamented as a modern decline), rampant rumour,
laced with nationalist cant, produced increasingly baroque speculation,

[2] Shaw writing in *The Nation* for 1910, 969; reprinted in Shaw (1960) 263.
[3] *Tatler* 452, 23 February 1910.   [4] *Daily Telegraph*, 21 February 1910.
[5] *Musical Times* 51 (1910) 158.   [6] Beecham (1944) 90.
[7] Quoted by Tóibín (2001) 11.

which became the source of *de haut en bas* commentary by the 'better' papers (which also thus increased the sense that the peformance needed to be discussed). That 'everyone was talking about' the *Elektra* rapidly became a self-fulfilling *topos* of press reporting. Most bizarrely – though the story shows well how far the gossip penetrated beyond intellectual circles in London – anticipatory accounts of the sacrificial procession which Clytemnestra inaugurates became sufficiently grandiose and confused that a farmer sent a bull to the opera house to indicate his willing support for the project. (Beecham drily remarks that 'as we could not employ him in the service of art, [we] put him to the next best purpose'.)[8] *Salome*, Strauss' previous opera, was still banned in England by the Chancellor's censorship, a scandal which added to the salacious anticipation.[9] The rapid and extensive circulation of press reports was a condition for the excitement around *Elektra*, but it was not this, I think, which made its performance an event of cultural significance. There was much more at stake in the issues it helped focus. The process of understanding what made this such an event will indeed require me to trace a series of overlapping contexts, intellectual and social frames, built up through 'low' and 'high' cultural materials, from several countries.

Elektra opened on Saturday night, 19 February. On Friday, 18 February, in His Majesty's Theatre the distinguished composer, teacher and conductor, Sir Charles Villiers Stanford – who had written music for the Cambridge Greek Play in both 1885 and 1887 – conducted a performance of Gluck's *Iphigenia in Tauris*, performed by the semi-professional students of the Royal College of Music. It starred Viola Tree, the daughter of Sir Herbert Beerbohm Tree, perhaps the grandest grandee of the turn-of-the-century theatre, a larger-than-life figure who had at least two families (at the same time), at least ten children, and who used his powerful connections from the Royal family down to help advance his beloved daughter's career.[10] Gluck's eighteenth-century classicism by now conformed perfectly to the expectations of the conservative musical establishment. It was, however, not always so, and Stanford himself had been instrumental in this new-found status of Gluck. In 1890, as Professor of Music, he had conducted in Cambridge an amateur performance of Gluck's *Orphée* (always the composer's most celebrated work) with one

[8] Beecham (1944) 90–1.
[9] Beecham (1944) 99 reports how he visited the Prime Minister to get the ban lifted.
[10] On Beerbohm Tree's life, see Bingham (1978).

Mrs Bovill in the starring role.[11] As several national newspapers noted with surprise, this was the first fully staged performance of this master-piece since 1830 (when it had briefly and unsuccessfully been staged in London). The performance was produced by a committee headed by Sir Richard Jebb and including A. W. Verrall (two immensely distin-guished classsicists who both played a large role in Victorian public life, and who will reappear later in this book). It also included John Willis Clark (who with them had been instrumental also in starting and main-taining the Cambridge Greek play). There was also an extensive Ladies' Committee including Lady Jebb, Mrs. Verrall, Mrs Stanford, who also sang in the chorus, and other Cambridge worthies. These distinguished committee lists inevitably played a role in the play's publicity.

Not only did this amateur performance receive national coverage – international, if you count *The Scots Observer* as such – but also the inter-est was so great that special trains were put on for the audience from London. 'That the dresses were as far as possible archaeologically cor-rect', observed *The Daily News*, 'may be judged from the fact that they were passed by a committee at the head of which was Professor Jebb',[12] and *The Guardian* commented that 'the frequent performances of Greek plays which have taken place in Cambridge of late years have famil-iarised the Cambridge public with classical drama, and on this occa-sion great care was taken to ensure accuracy in the matter of dress and movement'.[13] ('Accuracy' here means, of course, to classical Greece, without reference to eighteenth-century France). The excitement of this production was not just the revival of a musical masterpiece of the previous century, but also the thrill of an 'archaeologically correct' classicism which the Cambridge Greek play (which also needed spe-cial trains from London) inaugurated.[14] The extensive overlap between the Greek Play Committee and the Orpheus Committee helps empha-size this Hellenism. Furthermore, in 1895, Ernest Newman, the leading music critic whose response to the *Elektra* will prove so important, wrote

[11] There is a delightful small archive on this performance, including pictures of Mrs Bovill, in the Cambridge University Library, in the local collection (Cam.b.890.5). Oddly catalogued, it has not previously entered the discussion of Gluck or the Cambridge Greek Play.

[12] *Daily News* 14 May 1890.   [13] *Guardian* 21 May 1890.

[14] See Easterling (1999) for a fine account of the beginnings of the Greek Play, including a wonderful picture of Sir Charles Stanford with the Furies. One of the earliest performances in Cambridge was in 1883 by the women of Girton – of Sophocles' *Electra*: see the fine discussion, with pictures, Hall (1999a). The Oxford production of *Agamemnon* in 1880 which launched the career of the actor-manager F. R. Benson (who helped Tree) was a similar success – and had costumes designed with advice from Burne-Jones, Alma-Tadema and Frederick Leighton (Trewin (1960) 9) to guarantee their (Victorian) authenticity.

the first important English book on Gluck, which not only called *Iphigènie* 'the last of Gluck's great operas and the finest', but also quoted with approval Grimm: 'when I hear *Iphigenie*, I forget I am at the opera; I seem to be listening to a Greek tragedy'.[15] Gluck's classicism encapsulated an image of true Greece for the late Victorian music world. In 1910, a major production of *Orphée* was also staged at the Savoy (with Viola Tree as Eurydice: its run was extended due to popular demand), and Stanford's *Iphigeneia* with the Royal College of Music received a good number of laudatory reviews (many attached to the performance of the beautiful and publicity-hungry Viola Tree).

Gluck's classicism had become paradigmatic: but the association of Greek drama with Victorian music was surprisingly pervasive.[16] In particular, the most popular translation of a Sophoclean tragedy – Trieck's *Antigone* – was so associated with Mendelsohn's music for it that this play – perfomed widely thoughout Europe – could be known simply as Mendelsohn's *Antigone*.[17] Jebb observed in 1900 that two generations of audience by now were so at home with the musical *Antigone*, that it was 'too familiar to permit any word of comment'.[18] Although Trieck's connection with Wilhelm IV of Prussia and with Hegel's reading of *Antigone* make this a fascinating text for considering the politics of drama in the mid-century, its wide circulation as a production with formal, classical dress, formal classical sets, and formal classical music made this also an icon of Victorian staged Hellenism – against which Strauss and Hofmannsthal will violently rebel.[19] Mendelsohn's *Antigone*, like Gluck's classical operas, forms an important horizon of (comfortable) expectation for the Victorian audience.

It was not, however, just that the combination of Sir Charles Villiers Stanford, the Royal College of Music, together with the daughter of the famous Sir Herbert Beerbohm Tree and Gluck's classicism, inevitably attracted solidly respectable reviews for its solidly respectable project. Every reviewer also had an eye on the opera to come the following night. 'It is good to consider how perfect is the adaptation of the simple means available to the composer's purposes and how he attains a truly Greek horror while hardly ever transgressing the operatic conventions of his day', declared the music critic of *The Times*, who would go on to

---

[15] Newman (1895) 187, 189.

[16] On burlesques, see Hall (1999b); Mackintosh (2000); and general background in Mackintosh (1997); see also Beecham in Walton ed. (1987). For an account of the earlier period of the eighteenth century, see Hall (2000).

[17] See Mackintosh (1995).   [18] Jebb (1900) xlii.

[19] For an account, with pictures, of Trieck in London, see Mackintosh (1997).

excoriate the *Elektra* (and knew he would when he reviewed the performance of Gluck).[20] 'The simple means' of Gluck is a pointed rejoinder to Strauss' scandalously huge orchestra (111 pieces), his aggressively new and loud orchestration, and the shocking staging of violence. 'Truly Greek horror' makes a stark claim of what is the true Greece (for Edwardian England), in contradistinction to Strauss' modernist vision. 'While hardly ever transgressing the operatic conventions of his day' not only promotes the *Times'* sense of the value of convention, but also again is aimed against Strauss, who is nothing if not 'transgressing the conventions of his day'. *The Times* is staking out the territory on which the comprehension of Strauss will be fought out: the horror and conventions of (representing) Greece in music and on stage.

Viola Tree herself projected an image which encapsulated a particular version of Edwardian classicism, a particular, idealised, Grecian style. The rather wonderful pictures in plate 3 are taken from *The Tatler* of 23 February 1910, the week after *Elektra* opened and *Iphigenie* played.

Headed by a suitably English version of a classical-sounding tag – it quotes, rather nicely, the poet laureate of the previous generation, Tennyson and his description of, precisely, Iphigeneia – Viola (a suitably Shakespearian name for the daughter of a theatrical giant) is depicted in three 'beautiful portrait studies' as a Greek goddess or princess – reaching for a garland (intent and observed by the viewer); posed like a frozen stately dancer from a classical relief (staring out of the frame); decorously resting, and staring dreamily (but self-conscious of your gaze?) into the distance. Her classical robes, poses, and hair style construct a familiar and fashionable Edwardian image (which need not be in tension with her advertised previous roles in *Trilby* and *Pinkie and the Fairies*, a popular show for younger audiences).[21] Viola Tree much later in life described herself – quoting in part the heading of this picture – as a girl 'with a "take the wind out of your sails" manner, a prey to the nearest emotion, neither sensitive nor reticent, divinely tall and fairly fair, a loud voice, overwhelming health, a superb sleeper. Her only delicate things were her ankles and her vocal chords'.[22] She went on to train unsuccessfully in Italy to become an opera singer (writing home daily to her fiancé about which boy was going to fall in love with her and

[20] *Times*, 19 February 1910.
[21] On the same day a similar three-picture-spread appeared in *The Sketch* (23 Feb. 1910, suppl. 4), under the heading 'Viola, vocalist, the "O'Flynn's" fair daughter'. Her father and mother were appearing in a play as 'the O'Flynn's'.
[22] Tree (1926) 13–14.

3. Viola Tree, from *The Tatler*, 1910

whom she found attractive today). She auditioned for Richard Strauss for the London premiere of *Rosenkavalier*, only to be told (partly on the strength of Strauss' wife's judgement) that 'you sing like a good actress – not like a singer'. She finally landed the role of Salome in Genoa, but her voice collapsed before any performances and she returned home to a family life with the waiting fiancé (*The Times* listed the wedding gifts three days before her marriage, including presents from more than one Prime Minister).[23] This potted biography of an exciting life in music theatre may help emphasize how carefully fashioned the Grecian imagery of her fashionable *Tatler* portraits is.

A further figure who must lurk behind this construction of image is the dancer Isadora Duncan. She was described as 'like a Greek goddess come to life',[24] and her diaphanous Greek costumes, and 'flowing, unhurried, gentility'[25] self-consciously aimed at the re-invention of Greek dance. Isadora Duncan herself offered many theoretical bases for what she called in rather grand homage to Nietzsche and Wagner the 'dance of the future' (Der Tanz des Zukunfts): she claimed Rousseau, Whitman and Nietzsche were her only dance-masters, and, in her autobiography, describes her real inspiration for her movement coming from reading (with a glass of milk in bed) Kant's *Critique of Pure Reason*, something lost on most audiences, I expect, and hard to imagine, I confess, for me at least.[26] (She also on occasion claimed to be really an American dancer, taught on the pioneers' journey across the plains to California – though she insisted it was American puritanism that led her to live most of her life in Europe.)[27] But to audiences and critics it was the revivification of Greek dance that she epitomized (and her gushing love of Greece and Greek culture does nothing to dispel such an image).[28] In particular, she premiered a show in 1905 in Amsterdam, which she took to New York in 1908/9, on Iphigeneia, based on Gluck's music (from *Iphigenie en Tauride* and *Iphigenie en Aulide* and even *Orphée*), in which she danced various roles and scenes. It was described as 'bringing a classic frieze to life',

---

[23] Anecdotes all taken from Tree (1926) (on Strauss 126), crosschecked with Bingham (1978).

[24] Irma Duncan (1965) 6, 10. Irma Duncan took Isadora's last name as a gesture of love and 'elective affinity'.

[25] Daly (1995) 115. 'Extremely simple, natural and unaffected', as the *Philadelphia Telegraph* put it (quoted Daly (1995) 90).

[26] Duncan (1968) [1928] 89, 151.

[27] Sensible remarks on Duncan's self-formation in Daly (1995).

[28] See especially Duncan (1968) [1928] esp. 60, 97–9, 126–46 – crying at the story of Winckelmann's death; sobbing at Oedipus; sailing to Greece, quoting Byron and Homer – and so forth. She does finally note (146) 'I look back at our youthful aspirations [to build a Greek temple and revivify the Greek chorus] as really curious phenomena.'

and was a huge success with audiences (if not the sniffier critics).[29] She
and her family will re-appear again in this chapter, not least for her
connections with dance and German culture: but for the moment it
is enough to note that she had danced for Viola Tree's father (who
apparently took little notice, though they became fast friends later[30]), and
had produced a particular and celebrated classicizing image of dancing
Greek womanhood through Gluck's *Iphigeneia*, against which Viola Tree
is forming her own Grecian image.

Plate 4 – from the week before the *Elektra* – shows this Grecian fashion
in a further guise.

The young American gentleman is wearing an art-deco version
of Greek dress; he is bare-footed and garlanded, and carrying a frond –
in which costume he took part in a 'remarkable Greek pageant' in
New York. (Master Christian Herter, one might not have guessed, grew
up to become the Secretary of State in the 1950s, and a major figure in
International Relations, particularly between Germany and the USA.[31]
This snap does not seem to appear in his later press packs.) This picture
is surrounded by short, witty paragraphs mocking a new book on etiquette, *Manners and Rules of Good Society*, teasing its earnest advice on how
to cut cheese, eat asparagus, or enter a drawing room. The humorous
treatment of these proposed rules – itself one of the rules of responding to
such books – invites the reader's complicity in a self-conscious assurance
about social performance, which assuages and marks the anxiety which
a book of etiquette embodies. The complicity demanded by such social
humour combined with the lure of the photograph's 'true representation' of reality makes such magazine pages culturally normative – and
sets an image of Greekness within the promotions of propriety. A certain
Greekness is part of Edwardian knowingness.

It is a knowingness that requires the right staging. Raymond Duncan,
the brother of Isadora Duncan, went on a lecture tour to America in
January 1910. When he arrived with his son, Menalcas (*sic*),[32] both
dressed, as was their wont, in ancient Greek clothes, he was arrested
in New York, for cruelty to children, and the four year old Menalcas
was arraigned for not having proper guardianship. Behind the arrest
was the Gerry Society (the Society for the Prevention of Cruelty to
Children), which feared that the boy would get cold. 'Do you feel cold?',

---

[29] Daly (1995) 146–54, quotation (from Irma Duncan) (146). For the critics see van Vechlen (1977).
[30] Stories in Duncan (1968) [1928] *s.v.* Tree.   [31] See Noble (1970) for the diplomacy.
[32] Gertrude Stein (1933) 53 recalls, perhaps cynically, that he had been legally registered as
    'Raymond' and hated being called 'Menalcas' as his family insisted!

THE TATLER [No. 450, February 9, 1910]

Some Timely Reminders : By S. L. Hughes.

PROBABLY even the most patient and gentle reader has by this time had enough of the General Election and is weary of those ladders, races, or diagrams in the papers which were supposed to indicate the state of parties, but which may well puzzle and bewilder plain men. It is fortunate therefore that at a time like this the thoughtful people who decide what is the correct thing in the way of etiquette should produce a new edition of "Manners and Rules of Good Society." Many of us need some such reminders just at present, for whatever else may be true about a general election it has most certainly a disastrous effect on what may be called the amenities.

A Sound Old Rule.

MOST of us have been very rude during the last month, and it may be well therefore if we study this little book in order to recover some of the repose which is supposed to be the strong point with the Vere de Veres. I am immensely relieved to find that no change has been made in regard to one sound old rule, for I find it laid down here that "peas should be eaten with a fork." The people who decide such matters for us have a way of altering their rules every now and then, and that which is "doo rigger," so, use a phrase I have heard employed by a friend in the House of Commons, one year may be horribly incorrect the next. But there has been no tampering with this peas problem.

A Word for the Peers.

AND here let me put in a word for the peers, against whom so much has been said of late. They are quite sound in this respect; even the humblest baron would scorn to shovel peas down his throat with a knife. There are commoners who are not so delicate in their methods; I have seen them pursuing the elusive pea round and round the plate, and finally scooping it up on the glittering blade, and then darting that blade into their open jaws with a skill rivalling that of a professional sword-swallower. But the peers to a man rely on the fork; and let us therefore give honour where honour is due.

I Object.

LET it not be thought that while I rejoice in the firm stand made by this teacher of etiquette in regard to eating peas that I therefore bow down to him and accept all his dicta, for this is not the case. Thus I notice that he has the assurance to say that "in eating asparagus a knife and fork should be used, and the point should be cut off and eaten with the fork." Well, all this I flatly deny, regarding it as a pestilent heresy. Whenever I eat asparagus I pick it up and suck away at it, and I shall continue to do so. Therein lies half the pleasure. I will undertake to say that when Charles Lamb found that asparagus "inspired gentle thoughts" he did not hack it to bits with a knife.

Concerning Cheese.

IN another respect I am quite an impenitent offender against the laws laid down in this book, for here I find it taught that in eating cheese you should place a small piece on a little bit of bread

and convey the two into your mouth by using finger and thumb. Well, I decline to do anything of the sort. I prefer the old style of dabbing my knife into the piece of cheese, and in this way getting it to the mouth. Some of the best and bravest men in our empire have eaten their cheese in this way, and I decline to alter my methods because some etiquette crank chooses to alter the rules of the game.

Haut Ton.

WHENEVER you happen to be entertaining a royal personage it seems that you should be sure to conduct that personage

MASTER CHRISTIAN HERTER
Who took part in the remarkable Greek pageant arranged by his father in New York recently

to his or her carriage when the visit is over. It is a mistake to suppose this is done in order to see that the exalted one gets past your umbrella stand without annexing anything. That is an unworthy suggestion which must be dismissed at once. Some difficulty may be experienced in regard to royal personages who do not happen to have a carriage, but tact will enable that difficulty to be surmounted. By putting two fingers in the mouth a shrill whistle may be produced, and a taxi will turn up to convey away your illustrious though possibly impecunious guest.

Drawing the Line.

THE author of this book is careful to explain that all this attention need not be paid to foreign princes. It is quite enough if the host accompanies them to the door, and the reader will see that this is quite reasonable, for the phrase, "foreign prince," may cover a multitude of quaint people. It may, for instance, be applied to a man and brudder, a gentleman of colour, a doo-dah-doo-dah-day sort of potentate whose cheek is as black as night or as black as Day—and Martin. It would be absurd to pay real deference to such princes. Let them have a good time in the servants' hall, of course, but beyond that I think the host need not feel himself called upon to do anything.

A Fine Point.

I fear I may be revealing some plebeian strain in my blood when I confess that I have never been able to recognise the true significance of the elaborate instructions given in etiquette books in regard to "how to enter a drawing-room." Of course, I admit that it is not desirable for anyone to pop down the chimney or to swarm in at the window, but I have always been content to walk in through the door, and I am given to understand that this is not quite "classy" enough. The man of blue blood is supposed to glide in, or prance in, or possibly to roll in; that is to say, he must avoid simple walking as a method belonging to those terrible people known as the middle classes.

On Hand-shaking.

THERE are some elaborate instructions here on the correct manner of shaking hands. You have to project your right hand on a level with your chin and take the tips of the fingers of the other person in a style that may be described as frigid and calculated. This may be all very well in the drawing-rooms of Suburbia, but a man who has just been through a contested election knows well enough that such methods would never satisfy his stalwarts and his warm-hearted and loyal supporters. At times of political excitement you must be prepared for a bone-crushing grip, followed by a hearty jerk which almost dislocates the shoulder. There is no simpering nonsense about such proceedings, and unless a man is prepared to show that he enjoys such attentions he will do well to keep outside electoral contests.

Note this Carefully.

HAVING declined to accept the instructions here given in regard to eating asparagus with a knife and fork I have pleasure in entirely concurring with the directions in regard to cucumber. This should be eaten "from a plate" according to the book before me. I believe there is a school of thought in which it is held that cucumber can be eaten on the mat or on the floor, worried and wolfed to an accompaniment of quasi-canine growls. Such proceedings are, however, frowned upon in decent society. And I hope I need not add that though flinging pats of butter about was once regarded as quite the correct thing in smart-set circles it has long been abandoned, and even the other trick of squirting soda water across the table from a syphon is gradually falling into desuetude.

150

4. Christian Herter, from *The Tatler*, 1910

the magistrate asked the boy in court. '"No", responded the young-ster, who speaks French and Greek with the same fluency that he does English'.[33] Duncan defended his dress on the grounds that 'we live ac-cording to nature as did the ancient Greek'. Not only is there 'nothing immodest' about the garb, he claimed, but to dress conventionally is to be 'not rationally clothed', because it is unhygienic not to be able to wash one's clothes with great frequency.[34] The claim that Greek dress was 'rational' had been made by Oscar Wilde back in 1884, in a lecture which he toured round Britain and which prompted a brief exchange of letters in the *Pall Mall Gazette*.[35] (Having Wilde as a figure-head in a matter of dress may not have helped the acceptance of the propriety of Greek clothing.) The case was dismissed, however, after medical reports confirmed the child's healthy prospects, with a brief flurry of coverage, including plate 5 from an English journal, *The Sketch*.

The contrast with the little girl on the left of the picture with her muff, layered coat, boots and hat is an editor's dream – though the caption writer is more interested in snide commentary than accuracy of report-ing. It is both in England and America where such dress 'caused a stir', though the over-reaction of the American policeman is clearly thought pretty funny. (We, on the other hand – the implied audience of sophisti-cation – can share the joke about Theocritus, the pastoral poet, where the shepherd boy, Menalcas appears . . .) The caption refers back to 1909 when *The Sketch* had run a full-page spread with three (posed) pictures of the Duncan family, headed 'ANÊR, GUNÊ KAI PAIDION' (which is, of course, transliterated Greek for 'husband, wife and child' – note the hyper-correct indication of length of syllables), with the subtitle: 'Greek to Londoners; yet popular in the park'.[36] Their appearance in Hyde Park was said to be a sensation (but one whose joke in the reporting depends on your knowledge, not your ignorance of Greek). The group was not named but left (mysteriously) vague as 'members of a wealthy Greek family'. This spread was juxtaposed nicely to four pictures of risqué and exotic Parisian dancers from Massenet's Paris production of *Bacchus* (headed 'Defeated by Monkeys: Bacchantes in India'), and preceded by

[33] Reports in *New York Times* for Saturday, 8 January 1910; Monday, 10 January; Tuesday, 11 January; Wednesday, 12 January. The quotation on the boy's monosyllabic linguistic prowess is taken from the article on Monday.

[34] *New York Times* 10 January 1910.

[35] Wilde (1966) vol. 15, 47–51 is his reply to a letter on 7 Oct. from 'A Girl Graduate' in response to original reports on 2 Oct.: Wilde returned to the theme of 'Rational Dress' on 11 Nov. (Wilde (1966) vol. 15 52–67. See Ellmann (1987) 245–7.

[36] *Sketch* 854, 9 June; Supplement: 9.

[Photograph by the Fleet Agency.

WHEN GREEK JOINS GREEK, THEN COMES — THE POLICEMAN :
MENALCAS MISUNDERSTOOD IN NEW YORK.

Our readers will remember that last summer little Menalcas Duncan and his parents, in their Greek attire, drew much astonished attention in London. On a bleak day in New York of late a policeman, unversed in the Idylls of Theocritus, met Menalcas, clad as above, in company with two artists, and, thinking him insufficiently clothed, bore him away to the offices of the Gerry Society, which exists to prevent cruelty to children. His father, Raymond Duncan, having explained that the costume was designed for health, and not for discomfort, was allowed to bring Menalcas away, as shown in the photograph.

5. Raymond Duncan, from *The Sketch*, 1910

a fetching double spread of Miss May Kinder as 'Chrysea' in 'The Arcadians' – a play which knowingly transformed coy shepherdesses and shepherds into 'modern men and maidens of this world'. In the USA, however, such shocking dress was too much: the 'young women students of Bryn Mawr' cancelled Duncan's lecture because of his 'Grecian garb', and even the faculty of Harvard held a special meeting to debate whether the invitation to lecture on Greek music should be rescinded.[37] Greek dress in pageant and theatre, it would seem, did not lead easily to Greek dress on the street. The divide between the 'imaginary' world of dressing up and the 'real' world (of . . . ?) should not seem too permeable. Oscar Wilde may have theorized that 'some modification of Greek costume is perfectly applicable to our climate, our country and our century', but living out the theory was something else.[38] The juxtaposition of the acceptable Greek pageant of the 'young gentleman' and the unacceptable Duncan, father and son, reveals a watchfully monitored boundary in the act of 'being Grecian'.

Duncan continued on his way back to California (where he had been brought up, and had gone to school with Gertrude Stein). There, with Penelope Sikelianos, his wife, and various other members of the family and friends of the famous poet, Angelos Sikelianos, 'his small troupe of Greek performers presented the play "Electra" dancing in a sort of "statue" style copying poses on Greek vases in a mode two-dimensional and almost Egyptian'.[39] This, like his production of – again – Sophocles' *Electra* in Paris in 1912 with choral dances and music, did little to 'revive interest in the arts of ancient Greece',[40] or, indeed, to attract any audience. He ended up a rather sad and deeply eccentric figure in Paris. Gertrude Stein, when he arrived at her house to eat pastries, cackled at him: 'Why . . . before you became a Greek..you used to wear carnations in your button-hole and smoke long cigars';[41] and in 1922 he set up a claque to boo Cocteau's *Antigone* for its (unacceptably modern) Greekness. He had a small commune and dodgy shop which sold Greek clothes and

---

[37] *New York Times* 12 January 1910.

[38] Wilde is cited from Jenkyns (1991) 295 who suggests Wilde is following the theories of the architect E. W. Godwin, who thought 'Greek dress should be the model for modern costume'. Godwin, who had a long affair with the actress Ellen Terry (who dressed in private in a loose Greek robe), was the father of Craig, the lover of Isadora Duncan. A nicely Freudian son and father thing, falling for women in Greek clothes.

[39] Roatcap (1991) 16 quoting Lois Rather, *Lovely Isadora* (1976) 67–9.

[40] As the newspapers promised. See Roatcap (1991) 16. Eva Palmer-Sikelianos also recalls the Paris performance: Palmer-Sikelianos (1993) 55.

[41] McAlmon (1997) 262–3: the recollection is Kay Boyle's.

sandals,[42] but his becoming Greek, once a sensation, finally became seen as harmless 'existential delusions'.[43]

It was not only men in Greek costume that could cause disruption. One of Penelope Duncan's close friends, who married her brother, the poet, Sikelianos, was the classy New York lady, Eva Palmer (who would go on to found and direct the Delphi Festival of ancient Greek drama in 1927). She returned home to New York from Greece, where she had been staying with the Duncans, also dressed in Grecian style. ('For many years, I had made ever renewed efforts to imitate the Greek clothes we see on statues, bas-relief, and vases.')[44] The Press arrived at the gangplank, but could not get a picture of the suddenly shy Miss Palmer. This did not deter them: they dressed models in Greek clothes and published pictures as if they were the shocking 'Eva Palmer in Greek toga' anyway.[45] Her family were distinctly upset: 'I had delegations of my relatives and friends who tried to impress on me the evil and selfishness of my ways', she recalls, but she declared with proud early eco-warrior spirit that 'I would never again be touched by stuffs turned out by machines, machines of metal, and machines of flesh and blood.' Her long-suffering mother tried to find a compromise – and set a limit: 'she felt there was nothing wrong in what I was doing if only I would stop wearing sandals in New York'.[46] The power of sandals to shock New York has probably been lost for ever, but the nervousness with which such a sign of Greek dress is received among New York ladies is revealing.

If Raymond Duncan and Eva Palmer seem (comically or threateningly) to have transgressed Edwardian mores, Lady Constance Stewart-Richardson is more risqué – that is, more daring within the recognized rules (see plate 6).

Carefully posed between columns (and on the cover), she will, it is promised, 'electrify London' with 'a series of Classical Dances'. The puns on 'Electra' and 'electrify' are a commonplace in reporting the effect of Strauss' and von Hofmannsthal's work – whose most famous scene is Electra's final dance of death while her mother is being slaughtered. But Lady Constance is drawing on a different repertoire of images

---

[42] See McAlmon (1997) 311–25.

[43] Roatcap (1991) i. His work for Albanian refugees had been distinguished; but his attempt to build a Greek temple and community on a waterless mountain near Athens less successful.

[44] Palmer-Sikelianos (1993) 47.

[45] Palmer-Sikelianos (1993) 81–5. She was rather annoyed, though not baffled as she had been when laughed at in Athens for the same garb (54–5).

[46] Palmer-Sikelianos (1993) 82–5.

6. Lady Constance Stewart-Richardson, from *The Tatler*, 1910

and is framed by a different discourse. As with the famous pictures by Lord Leighton, the classical scene enables sexually titillating material to be displayed through the culturally validated veils of classicism. Lady Constance's loose hair, short skirt, revealing her calves (compare the demure Miss Tree's floor-length robe), and knowing over-the-shoulder look at the camera, are designed to encourage the reader to pursue the further 'beautiful pictures of this versatile and accomplished lady'. You should also note, however, that she is offered as 'a delightful answer to Lloyd-George and Co.'s allegations as to our idle aristocracy'. The year 1910 was a general election year (the new parliament was opened the same week that the *Elektra* was performed) and one of the hot issues of the political campaigning was the political challenge to the authority of the aristocracy in the House of Lords, led by Lloyd-George. (We will see how such consitutional debates become intertwined with the *Elektra* later.) *The Tatler*, with customary trivialization, offers Lady Constance's proposed music-hall career – inevitably touched with scandalous overtones – as a 'delightful' demonstration of the usefulness of aristocrats.

This delight in Lady Constance's 'unorthodox' self-image is developed in the photo-spread inside the magazine (which is plate 7 – I wouldn't want anyone to be disappointed of the voyeuristic promise of the magazine's cover).

This triptych contrasts neatly with the 'beautiful portrait studies' of Viola Tree. In the first, Lady Constance is depicted in rapid dance, with an exaggerated and stretched pose (as opposed to the statuesque Tree). In the second, which rather shockingly reveals even more of her legs, she is seated imperiously on a throne, from which she stares directly at the viewer (as opposed to the ever unthreatening and passively observed Viola). In the third and largest picture, she is on the floor (as was Viola Tree), but unlike the demure and dreamy Iphigeneia, Lady Constance leans towards the viewer intently, full-face. There is a carefully controlled brashness to these poses which is matched by the daring prose. 'She is delightfully regardless of "what other people will think"'; she is a madcap dancer who has kept snakes, shot big game and has a total absence of 'feminine pettiness'. The worry about her appearing as a professional dancer is tempered, however, by its basis in a wish to found a school for boys in Scotland 'where an active form of physical development shall be one of the principal items in the curriculum'.

The papers loved Lady Constance and her carefully controlled oddity (and her dances were even reported in New York). Plate 8 captures this paradox wonderfully well. Here Lady Constance is posed in a thoroughly

No. 446, JANUARY 12, 1910]   THE TATLER

THE PALACE SCORES AGAIN

Lady Constance Stewart-Richardson to Dance there Shortly.

The Lady Constance Stewart-Richardson, who will shortly make her first professional engagement at the Palace Theatre, is considered by many people to be a serious rival to Miss Maud Allan in this country. Lady Constance has already appeared in the rôle of classical dancer at several charity functions in America, but this will be her début in the regular programme of a variety theatre. Two seasons ago Lady Constance gave a private performance as Salome before a great personage, and, rumour says, kept up the name-part by demanding the head of one of his intimate friends as her reward. In private life Lady Constance is the wife of Sir Edward Austin Stewart-Richardson, 15th baronet, and before her marriage, in 1904, was the beautiful

daughter of the Earl of Cromartie and sister of the present countess. She is possessed of great originality, has kept snakes as pets, shot big game, tried to get in the fighting line during the recent "Mad Mullah" campaign, is delightfully regardless of "what other people will think," and her large heart and total absence of feminine pettiness have given her a host of friends who will wish her well in this or any other venture she attempts. Her professional appearance in the capacity of danseuse is founded on the desire to found a school for boys somewhere in Scotland where an active form of physical development shall be one of the principal items in the curriculum

39

7. Lady Constance Stewart-Richardson, from *The Tatler*, 1910

No. 449, FEBRUARY 2, 1910]

THE TATLER

HAIL! UNCONVENTIONALITY, HAIL!

A NEW PORTRAIT OF THE LADY CONSTANCE STEWART-RICHARDSON

Lallie Charles

Whose dancing at the present moment is drawing society, slightly shocked but wholly amused and bewitched, to the Palace Theatre. Lady Constance may not have the art of Maud Allan, but she has great vivacity and charm and a beautifully graceful figure. Her present engagement is only of four weeks' duration, but so great has been her success that it will in all probability be considerably prolonged

113   b

8. Lady Constance Stewart-Richardson, from *The Tatler*, 1910

elegant and fashionable gown, carrying a posy of flowers, against a decorated wall which frames her as if a painting. This could be one of any number of society portraits. The banner headline, however, proclaims: 'Hail! Unconventionality, Hail!' The combination of absolutely traditional picture with self-congratulatory boast of 'unconventionality' shows how easily contained such transgression is. We can, however, move slightly further down the scale of social class. Miss Maude Odell is pictured (plate 9) in four classical poses. She is a professional 'beauty queen', who had been to America 'to pose in vaudeville',[47] here appearing under the headline, 'A Perfect Woman Nobly Planned' (in case you ever wondered what a perfect woman might look like). Indeed, the caption tells you that Mr Sandow has declared her to be 'the most perfectly proportioned woman in the world'. You are being encouraged to look closely at this woman, to judge her proportions, to gaze at her leg carefully exposed in the final image, to play Paris in judging perfect beauty. The professional 'beautiful woman' is exposed in a way which even Lady Constance is not – as the scale of the risqué is precisely calibrated.

These images of Viola Tree, Lady Constance Stewart-Richardson and Maude Odell indicate something of the pervasive but carefully controlled classicism in public Edwardian culture, especially in the representation of women associated with performance.[48] The demure elegance of Tree and the gay bravura of Stewart-Richardson mark the patrolled limits of how an ideal of Greekness informs such representations. It is, of course, possible to have far more exotic images, even within *The Tatler*, but these pictures are distinguished by the easy Orientalism of Empire. Consider plate 10: the Eastern princess and priestess, in strange costume and set amid smoking urns, dances smilingly with snakes. The text focuses explicitly on her body and its proximity to the monstrous snakes and uncanny smoke effects. (The body of either Viola Tree or Lady Constance is not explicitly mentioned in the captions to their portraits. The physicality of the other is different.) Princess Mahara is 'a sensation in Vienna', where 'distinguished audiences' have witnessed her otherness. She, too, electrifies. The imagery of snakes, dancing and the East (not to mention Vienna) all play a part in the uneasy response to *Elektra*. What is clear and important, however, is that in the ideological world of *The Tatler*

[47] *New York Times* 9 November 1908, 4.
[48] On classicism in Victorian through to Edwardian culture, see especially Turner (1981); Jenkyns (1981) and (1991); Clarke ed. (1989); Dowling (1994); Gregory (1997); Stray ed. (1998); Leoussi (1998); Prins (1999). For the earlier Victorian period, see the following chapter and its bibliography.

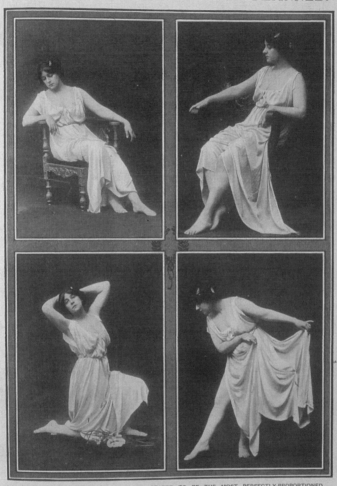

No. 453. MARCH 2, 1910] THE TATLER

A PERFECT WOMAN NOBLY PLANNED.

MISS MAUDE ODELL, WHO MR. SANDOW STATED TO BE THE MOST PERFECTLY-PROPORTIONED
WOMAN IN THE WORLD

Miss Odell is appearing with enormous success in vaudeville in the United States

217 b

9. Maude Odell, from *The Tatler*, 1910

NO. 447, JANUARY 19, 1910]

THE TATLER

FROM THE TEMPLE TO THE THEATRE.

THE PRINCESS MAHARA, AN EX-PRIESTESS, ELECTRIFIES VIENNA

An Indian princess, Mahara, whose portrait is seen above, is at present making an enormous sensation in Vienna by her wonderful snake dances. Princess Mahara, who is of the highest caste and has been a priestess in India, has complete control over very large snakes, which follow every one of her movements without harming her. The princess handles these powerful snakes with ease, laying them around her neck like a boa and round her body like a chain, until the reptiles literally cover her from head to foot. Dancing between lighted braziers the movements of her dance cause the smoke to appear as following her, producing a very novel effect. Princess Mahara is a most interesting artist, and her appearances have brought together some distinguished audiences. At the Court Theatre, Coburg, all the members of the royal court were present to witness her dances

75

10. Princess Mahara, from *The Tatler*, 1910

(which despite – or because of – its triviality seems to offer an exemplary guidebook to Edwardian ideological positioning), there is a clear divide between the ideals of Hellenism which British women can embody, and the dangerous exoticism of an Oriental otherness. For all the possibilities of dressing up, you could not, and should not confuse the Princess Mahara even with Lady Constance Stewart-Richardson.[49]

In this regime of visual display, the ideological interface of gender and Hellenism is glaring to modern eyes. While men continue to struggle over learning Greek, the high peaks of sublime knowledge still largely fenced off from women (as we will see in the next chapter), the cultural privilege of Hellenism also allows a regulated ogling of different classes of female bodies. The orientalism of Princess Mahara and the dubious and laughable status of Raymond Duncan provide limit cases to frame the images of British women in their Greek dress. That 'Greek[ness]' can be used to encode more secretive counter-cultural male homosexual behaviour must also be seen to help enforce the normative value of these female embodiments of Greek beauty. At each point in my story of caring about Greek, gender – always an implicit issue – can flare into crisis. Yet here, the fashionable world seems all too comfortable with its display of women through the veils of Hellenism for a fully complicit audience. Happily setting the standard.

It is through this iconographic and ideological repertoire that the shock of the *Elektra* is represented in the newspapers. My brief detour through *The Tatler* and Stanford's *Iphigenie* has been leading up to a remarkable and paradigmatic pair of images from *The Illustrated London News*. On 26 February, it carried its review of the *Elektra*. The whole page is plate 11. I will discuss the text more fully in a while, but first I want to look at how the imagery is constructed.

The text is framed by a series of portraits of noteworthy figures from the contemporary theatrical and musical world of London. Most are still familiar in literary history, headed as they are by Henry James and Sir Arthur Pinero; Shaw, Murray (whose Euripidean *Iphigeneia* was about to be produced) and Galsworthy will each reappear in this chapter. The review is surrounded by busts of grandees of the literary world, like a courtyard surrounded by classical heads. In the middle, like a statue, in her most demurely dramatic pose, stands Viola Tree in the role of Iphigenia – again the very embodiment of a virginal, white classicism.

---

49 It is, I take it, important that a dancer like St Denis who did an 'oriental dance' had a dark body suit but white face to emphasize the dressing up involved in such self-conscious exoticism: see Daly (1995) for a picture.

11. Viola Tree, from *The Illustrated London News*, 1910

The text around this image describes the *Elektra* as 'crude and brutal'; Elektra as 'wholly possessed by the lust of vengeance' which is 'frankly horrible'. The pictures frame the text, in all senses.

Look now, however, at plate 12 – the next page from *The Illustrated London News*. This is a remarkable image indeed, which, more surprisingly than the other images in this chapter, also has not been reproduced in any of the books or articles on this opera.[50] Elektra – Edyth Walker as Elektra – is represented not in demure white, but in black rags. Her hair, completely unrestrained – even wilder than Lady Constance's – runs in the image in an unbroken sweep into her robes. But it is her hands and face which are so striking. Wild, staring eyes, grabbing, talon-like hands, half open mouth – an image of despair and horror and violence, which draws fully on the imagery of the mad woman both in popular culture and – perhaps even more fascinatingly – from Charcot and other medical text books.[51] She is not set amid stately columns but against a (Cyclopean) wall, as much like a prison or a tomb as a standard image of ancient Greece. As we will see from the more informed contemporary discussions of Hofmannsthal and Strauss, the connection between Electra and mental disease, especially Freudian psychoanalytic uncovering of the psychopathology of sexual desire, was instantly and powerfully appreciated – and the artist here has striven to portray the dangerous threat of this conceptualization. With her white, white arms and face against the black robes, this is like a photographic negative of the classicism of the previous pages. Classical, Edwardian femininity has been twisted into a disturbing portrayal of disease (to the viewer's lack of ease). The shock of *Elektra* is wonderfully well captured.

The image is further framed by its inscriptions, base and head, pedestal and capital. Above, in stark Greek lettering is (misspelled) 'Electra'. The misspelling (the first letter should be 'eta' not 'epsilon', H not E) may

[50] Puffett ed. (1989)] (pl. 4) reproduces the one familiar picture of Clytemnestra, from the Covent Garden archive [in fact, from *The Sketch*]. Gilliam (1991) and Mann (1964), though basic for criticism of the music, are not very interested in the production or its impact. Wilhelm (1984), despite its wealth of pictures, is, of course, concerned with a delimited version of Strauss' biography. The works cited below are concerned with the libretto or music or both, but not with the performance. It is noticeable that none of these works has considered the other productions contemporary with the *Elektra*, the material surrounding the reviews, or the range of reviews themselves.

[51] On Charcot, see especially the now standard work of Didi-Huberman (1982); and the useful survey of Micale (1995); see also Bernheimer (1989) 234–64; Harris (1989) 160–84; Goldstein (1987) 322–77; and, most relevantly here, Gilman (1993); the pictures from the Salpêtrière were published as early as 1878 [Bourneville and Régnard (1878)]; on mad and fallen women, see especially Nead (1988); Showalter (1985); Dijkstra (1986); Oppenheim (1991) 143–80. A significant overview of 'murders and madness' in this period is provided by Harris (1989).

12. 'Elektra' [Edyth Walker], from *The Illustrated London News*, 1910

testify to the lack of education of the artist or his editors, but it also makes the Greek letters more easily assimilable to an audience without Greek (which may be the intended readership of *The Illustrated London News*, which is at the opposite end of the spectrum from *The Times*, with its celebrated refusal to carry pictures on its front pages).[52] This misspelling is also added above the much-reproduced photograph of Clytemnestra, and, tellingly, a portrait of Anna Pavlova in the same series has Cyrillic letters which badly misspell her name in such a way as to make the foreign letters more 'readable': 'АИИА' would spell 'АПА' not 'ANNA'. More importantly, the bold lettering – without any of the floral surrounds and coronal decoration common in such inscriptions – is of a piece with the image: a different, more brutal classicism. Below, even more oddly, is a musical inscription. The music represented is one of the best-known motifs from the *Elektra*, the theme which is repeatedly played from the second page of the score, and which is taken to represent Electra's 'unrelenting hatred'.[53] If the Greek inscription is poorly lettered, the music seems to expect a thoroughly proper level of literacy to be fully appreciated.

Plate 13 is a posed photograph of Edyth Walker (the one photo I have found of her in costume). Again, the black rags, dishevelled hair, distorted facial features, twisted fists, recall Charcot's asylum photographs or popular imagery of 'fallen women' rather than the conventions of classical opera. The photograph, however, posed though it is, also helps emphasize the careful rhetoric of Haviland's portrait, with its emphasis on Elektra's aggressive posture and with its directive captions and heading. The portrait, especially in juxtaposition to the photograph, demonstrates also how reports of *Elektra* constantly upped the ante of its shock value.

Plate 14 is – by way of contrast – one of very few photographic records of the performance I have been able to trace (all of which are of this same crowded scene).[54] This detail shows five women (hard to identify, but presumably the servant girls) with an inset of Edyth Walker. The set seems to show the wall against which the previous image is apparently meant to have been set, and the costumes are strikingly darkly coloured and boldly decorated in comparison with, say, the 'archaeologically accurate' costumes of 1890, or the poses of Viola Tree.

---

[52] The same misspelling occurs in a picture of Clytemnestra on the Covent Garden set in *The Sketch* 16 Feb. (1910), 193.

[53] On the motif, and further musical analysis, see e.g. del Mar (1962) 287–333; Carpenter (1989).

[54] This is a detail of a larger group scene. It is also reproduced in the *Daily Telegraph* and elsewhere.

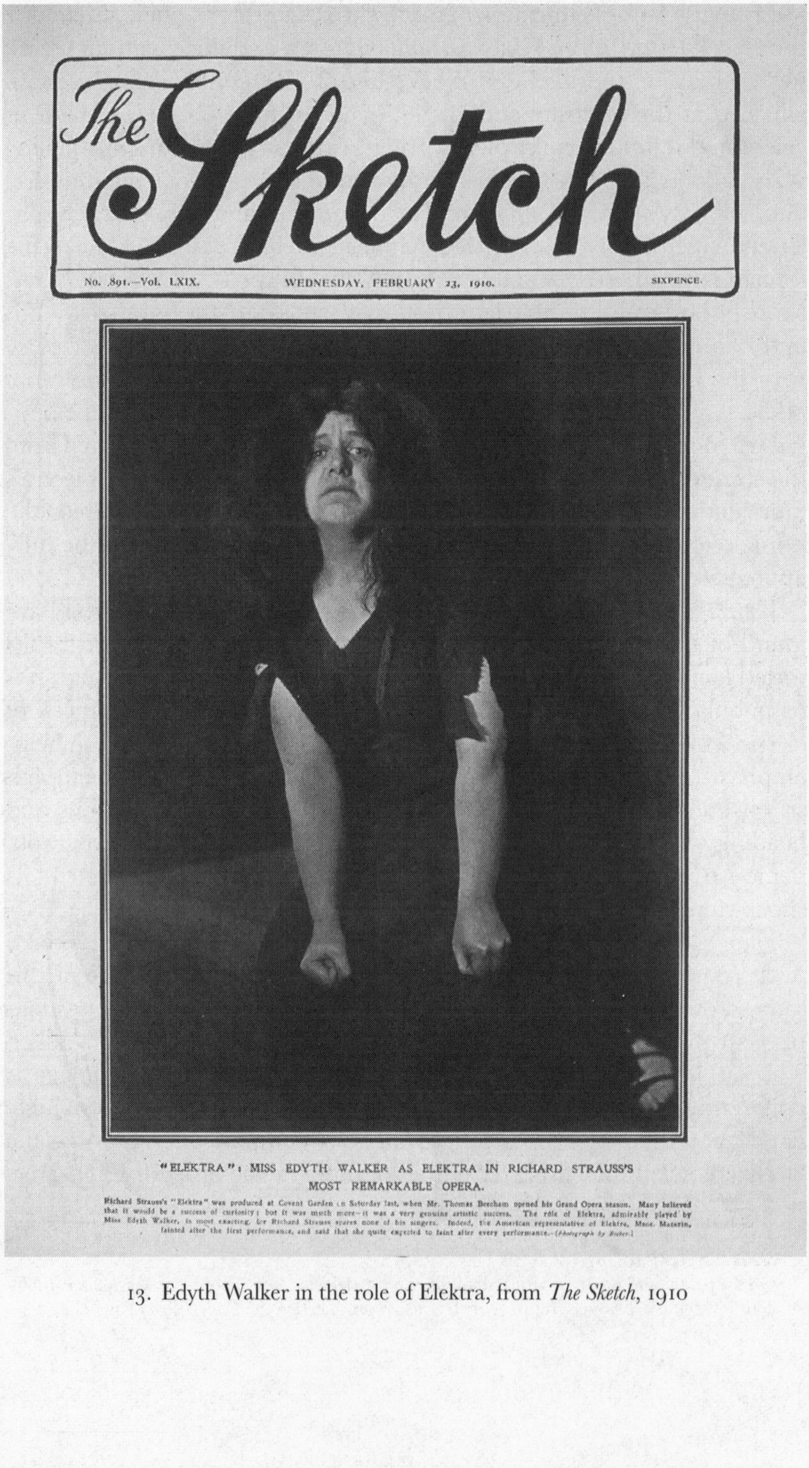

The Sketch

No. 891.—Vol. LXIX. WEDNESDAY, FEBRUARY 23, 1910. SIXPENCE.

"ELEKTRA": MISS EDYTH WALKER AS ELEKTRA IN RICHARD STRAUSS'S MOST REMARKABLE OPERA.

Richard Strauss's "Elektra" was produced at Covent Garden on Saturday last, when Mr. Thomas Beecham opened his Grand Opera season. Many believed that it would be a success of curiosity; but it was much more—it was a very genuine artistic success. The rôle of Elektra, admirably played by Miss Edyth Walker, is most exacting, for Richard Strauss spares none of his singers. Indeed, the American representative of Elektra, Mme. Mazarin, fainted after the first performance, and said that she quite expected to faint after every performance.—(*Photograph by Bieber.*)

13. Edyth Walker in the role of Elektra, from *The Sketch*, 1910

THE GREAT PRODUCTION OF "ELEKTRA": SOME OF THE PLAYERS.

Richard Strauss's "Elektra" had its first production in England on Saturday last, when Mr. Thomas Beecham began his season of Grand Opera at Covent Garden. Enormous interest in the occasion had been aroused by preliminary talk and paragraphs. That the interest was justified was everywhere apparent at the closing of the performance, and even those who were not in agreement with the composer's methods were bound to admit their value.—[*Photographs by the Dover Street Studios.*

14. The cast of *Elektra*, from *The Daily Telegraph*, 1910

(The portrait of Anna Bahr-Mildenberg as Clytemnestra shows a similar barbaric splendour.)[55] Together with the non-classical images on the pots and the archaic scenery, this indicates something of the Eastern exoticism which thrilled audiences. An interview with the designer, Attilio Comelli, in *The Standard*, reveals that these costumes were based explicitly on the recent Mycenean excavations of Schliemann and of Evans at Knossos (though he thought it right 'to reject the theory of the crinoline' adopted in Paris).[56] The costumes may strikingly differ from the floppy white robes of Viola Tree, but they are still supported by the scholarly claims of archaeological accuracy. Indeed, *The Daily Express* – plate 15 – ran a full-page spread setting the costumes against their proposed Mycenean originals.[57] The concern for 'authenticity', for finding a proper Greek paradigm – a *non-classical* repertoire – shows how carefully poised the production is in its Hellenism, and how concerned the media are to fit the opera into a recognisable model of Greekness. *The Daily Express*,

[55] Most easily seen in Puffett ed. (1989) pl. 4.
[56] *Standard* 12 February 1910. This interview again has not entered the literature on the opera.
[57] *Daily Express* 17 February 1910.

15. The costumes for *Elektra*, from *The Daily Express*, 1910

one would be justified in thinking, domesticates the imagery of the forthcoming production (which its reviewer certainly found really quite upsetting). It is rather Haviland's portrait which seems to me best to convey the passion and horror which *Elektra* provoked.

This juxtaposition of Viola Tree as Iphigeneia and Edyth Walker as Elektra expresses paradigmatically and in powerful visual terms how Strauss' opera was perceived to stand against the ideals of classicism. This was a new, violent, disturbing image of Greekness, of femininity expressed through classical models, and of the power of the past. It was this radical and aggressive reconceptualization of a Greek model that made *Elektra* so threatening.

The reviews of *Elektra* in London certainly reflect this sense of distaste and horror (as well as its powerful attraction). Even balanced reviewers reflected the immensely strong feelings for or against the opera, and the violent emotions on stage were matched by those of the critical audience. *The Spectator* attacks the work with exemplary force. The review is signed CLG, who is almost certainly the same CLG who favourably reviewed the Cambridge *Orpheus* for *The Guardian* back in 1890, which indicates sharply enough the pull towards conservatism in the London critical institutions. He writes: 'Electra is not merely the incarnation of hate but she is consumed body and soul by haematomania, with which it is her desire to inoculate her craven sister'.[58] This sense that Electra is mentally sick, as well as disturbed and violent, sets the tone for much of the criticism, which repeatedly rehearses the uneasily medical tone of 'haematomania', 'inoculates', and uncomfortably recognizes the sexual desire that seems to run through the character's unpleasantness. The production occurs at a fascinating point in the reception of psychoanalysis and the development of medical science: the 'diagnoses' of Elektra veer between self-conscious modern jargon 'neurasthenia', 'haematomania', and more long-lasting symptomologies, particularly 'epilepsy' (which was even for Charcot still part of the definition of madness).[59] This is equally marked in the more sophisticated reviews of Hofmannsthal's

---

[58] *Spectator* 104 (1910) 424–5.

[59] See e.g. Micale (1995), with very extensive further bibliography [from 1975 to 1995, over 400 works on the history of hysteria were produced; during the same period, medical diagnoses of hysteria almost disappeared – to the extent that the *DSM* (*Diagnostic and Statistical Manual*) – the standard American physicians guide – no longer lists 'hysteria': one of its replacements, rather nicely in view of the current chapter, is 'histrionic personality disorder']. I have learnt in particular from Oppenheim (1991); Goldstein (1987), Showalter (1985), and, more generally, the amusing essay of Heath (1982). For an example of the most modern(ist) work, see Bronfen (1998). On the continuing role of Greek ideas in modern psychology, especially female psychology, see the excellent King (1998).

play, as we will see shortly. So, *The New York Times* declares that in *Elektra* 'everybody is neurasthenic!', and the London *Times* calls the characters 'a company of raging monomaniacs', and, later, declared that it was not a real tragedy because Strauss 'bases the play upon the passions of self-willed individuals'.[60] The key note of shock here is 'decadence', that fin-de-siècle shibboleth.[61] Clytemnestra is a 'type of the most sophisticated decadence'. The opera is 'a work saturated with the spirit of decadence'. 'We have described it as decadent – it is worse than that: it is nauseous.' One critic found a crumb of comfort: Clytemnestra offers 'so vivid a picture of decadence that while she is on stage it is possible to forget all about the music'. *The Daily Express* summed it up with the memorable headline: 'DECADENT, NOT CLASSIC'.[62] We will see the roots of this charge in Hofmannsthal's Vienna shortly.

There was more, however, to reviewers' distaste than the typically late Victorian/Edwardian outrage at the explicitly sexual or self-professed psychological realism, an outrage which so dogged the performances of, say, Ibsen.[63] For Strauss was threatening Greekness – or his audience's intellectual investment in the glory that was Greece. Or at least critical reaction returned repeatedly to this challenged classicism to express its discomfort. 'This bestializing of the εὐκολία of Sophocles' shows how 'there is a world of difference between recasting a rough-hewn legend and barbarizing a consummate classic.'[64] The use of the untranslated and untransliterated Greek word – 'good temper' (Aristophanes' description of Sophocles in the *Frogs*) – performs, as ever, the reviewer's investment in 'true', 'unadulterated', Greekness (and the alienation or complicity of the reader, as with Erasmus' use of Greek). 'The classical personages are sicklied o'er with the pale cast of modern thought, and lovers of the classical tradition may resent its neuroticism and its realism.'[65] The connection of 'neuroticism' and 'realism' – charges famously thrown at Ibsen too – links worries about theatrical staging, psychological display, and propriety to warn lovers of the classical tradition (who will enjoy the reviewer's quotation of good, old English poetry) of the dangers of modernism. So: Hofmannsthal's 'originality lies in his ascribing to the

---

[60] *New York Times* 26 January 1910; London *Times* 21 February 1910; *Times* 24 February 1910. For 'neurasthenia', see Oppenheim (1991) 79–109, especially, 92–109. For 'monomania', see Goldstein (1987). 'Monomania' as a medical diagnosis was largely replaced by diagnoses of hysteria by 1890, which reveals also the datedness of the response of the critic of *The Times*.

[61] Standard here, despite its focus on France, is still Carter (1958).

[62] *Spectator* 104 (1910) 423; *Spectator* 104 (1910) 425; *Daily Express* 21 February 1910; *Times* 21 February 1910; *Daily Express* 21 February 1910.

[63] For reviews and reactions to Ibsen, see Meyer (1971).

[64] *Spectator* 104 (1910) 424.   [65] *Reynolds* 20 February 1910.

actors in pre-historic Mycenean tragedy, the decadent, hysterical emotion of twentieth-century Paris or Vienna. Whether it is right to take the gracious figures of Classical antiquity down from their pedestals and make them mingle with the crowd is a grave artistic question.'[66] There is a constant nationalism running through such critiques: 'the strident, bloodthirsty, German, Elektra . . . ';[67] 'Von Hoffmannsthal's [*sic*] transformation of the stately figures of Greek drama . . . [by] Teutonizing the tragedy, has also brutalized it.'[68] Making tragedy German is brutalizing it: the stately figures of Greece are made barbarians by Teutonic decadence.

This nationalism and the defence of Greekness are evidenced in the press not only in response to Strauss. It is fascinating that in each of the editions of *The Times* which carry reviews or commentary on the *Electra*, there is also a lengthy letter in the correspondence columns contributing to the long running debate on whether Greek should remain as a compulsory requirement for entrance to Oxford and Cambridge Universities.[69] The debate flared up in the early months of 1910. On 24 February a correspondent quotes Hazlitt, writing to his son, on why Greek is a necessary study: '"We feel the presence of that power which gives immortality to human thoughts and action, and catch the flame of enthusiasm from all nations and ages". The education which inspires such adequate expression of ardour', he concludes, 'can scarcely be reckoned at naught'. Why Greek matters and must be learnt properly is on the agenda of public debate. I will be looking in a later chapter at how the debate was already intense back in 1890, especially in Cambridge; and, as we saw in the previous chapter, it was still part of the heated discussion of the place of English in education in 1921. *The Times* letter columns help locate the tenor of its reviews of *Elektra*.

At the same time – by way of a single example of what should be an unpleasantly familiar mixture of late Victorian anthropology, science and imperialism[70] – *The Times* on the same day reports that the Hunterian lectures were given this year – 1910 – by Professor Arthur Keith on 'The Anatomy and Relationships of the Negro and Negroid Races', and the paper records with some care the conclusions of the third lecture: 'When

---

[66] *Leader* 21 February 1910. The general connection between nationalism and modernism is central to Jameson (1981).

[67] *New York Times* 26 January 1910.   [68] *Times* 21 February 1910.

[69] Discussed below, pp. 240–3. See Raphaely (1999) and Stray ed. (1998).

[70] See (for a selection from a vast field) Stocking (1987); Pratt (1992); David (1995) (whose chapter on Macaulay would be a lot more convincing if she looked at the Greek and Latin texts Macaulay was reading), Brantlinger (1988), Bolt (1971).

the shape of the Negro's brain was examined it showed features which might be called infantile... Those who knew negroes best described them as children.' (It was Hegel who called Africa 'a land of childhood').[71] Chamberlain's book, it will be recalled, was well-received in this cultural climate of Edwardian England. Nationalism, with its imperialism and racism, was deeply ingrained in English responses to the world – and to Strauss' *Elektra*.

I find the juxtaposition in this one copy of *The Times* of a review of *Elektra* to a letter supporting the compulsory study of Greek as a university entrance requirement, to a set of scientific lectures on the infantile nature of the negro races, a telling mix to help understand the impact of the first night of Strauss' opera (and a good demonstration of why scholars shouldn't read just the reviews). The passion of nationalism, the commitment to an image of Greekness, and the deeply expressed investment in propriety in public representation, coupled with the current concerns about degeneracy and the new psychological sciences, constitute an ideological weight which became quickly and integrally attached to Strauss' musical modernism (and which is the frame for the re-evaluation of Lucian and the success of Chamberlain's project). It was this brew of strongly felt convictions, supported by social convention, science, intellectual life, imperial power, that *Elektra* mobilized and provoked. Here, first of all, is what made the first performance of *Elektra* in London an event of such cultural impact.

II

In the German-speaking world, Hugo von Hofmannsthal's play, *Elektra*, which Strauss' opera so closely adapts, had already provoked an infuriated response and a fascinated scandal. From its first performance in Berlin in 1903, it became a *cause célèbre*. In the wake of an extraordinary burst of critical engagement, it was bought for twenty-two theatres in the first four days, and three impressions of the play sold out at once, with two more quickly following.[72] It is not strange that Strauss was attracted to it for a libretto, especially after the success of his self-consciously shocking *Salome*. More surprisingly, especially in the light of the later response to Strauss' opera, when Hofmannsthal's *Elektra* was

---

[71] Hegel (1956) 91: Hegel's writings on Africa are horrifying; but Bolt (1971) 137–8 produces many examples of the accusation of African 'childishness' by English anthropologists and explorers, including Richard Burton.

[72] See Hofmannsthal (1937) 132. Hofmannsthal himself later mentions five editions (1968) 164.

performed in London in an English translation in 1907, it provoked the briefest of notice, despite a fine cast (including Mrs Campbell in the title role). Hofmannstahl's play had an effect in Germany which could not be (re)produced in England, and which was significantly different from the impact of the later opera. Explaining why this is the case will un-cover a further story of the powerful forces of nationalism, of the threat of 'degeneracy' and of a contest over Greekness. For Hofmannsthal's *Elektra* both is a sign of a cultural crisis in German self-consciousness, and also changes the whole conception of Greek tragedy on stage for the twentieth century.

Hofmannsthal is an iconic figure for Freud's Vienna. He was closely as-sociated with the cast list of star literary figures of the city from Schnitzler to Kraus, George, Zweig, Bahr.[73] He spoke 'in an aristocratic Viennese German', a testimony to 'the poise of his patrician background'[74] – but his grandfather had been Jewish, and he became the victim of typical anti-Semitic slurs, particularly after his collaboration with Reinhardt in the early 1920s.[75] He was brought up a Catholic, and wrote powerfully in support of an idea(l) of an Austrian people and culture.[76] He could describe what he saw as the threat of cultural decline (like Chamberlain) as the coming of 'a great barbarism, a sensual, Slav and Jewish world'.[77] Yet his interests in psychoanalysis, aestheticism, literary experimenta-tion and the problem of the individual, set him firmly in the vanguard of modernism.[78] This awkward combination of both conforming to a nationalist literary and cultural tradition, and of alienation, discomfort and challenge – a 'conservative revolution'[79] – plays a continuing and formative role in his complex self-representation.

Apart from poems, essays, plays and short stories, Hofmannsthal left over 11,000 letters – nearly four times the voluminous output of Erasmus – and wrote continuously about his self, not merely in the long-running project entitled 'ad me ipsum', 'to me myself'. Berger cap-tures Hofmannsthal's interest in himslf in a fine phrase: he 'wallows in

---

[73] See Yates (1992); Renner and Schmid eds. (1991).

[74] Yates (1992).

[75] Cited by Yates (1992) 82–3. For his relation to Andrian, who was half-Jewish see Klienberger (1985); Hofmannsthal (1968).

[76] Ritter (1967).

[77] Cited by Yates (1992) 82 from *Reden und Aufsätze III (1925–1929), Buch der Freunde, Aufzeichnungen 1889–1925* ed. B. Schoeller and I. Beyer-Ahlert (Frankfurt am Main, 1980) 383.

[78] Ewans (1984); Worbs (1983); Urban (1978); Rey (1962).

[79] Rudolph (1971) (who discusses Hofmannsthal's interest in 'eine neue Antike', 'a new Antiquity' 131–5); the phrase, 'conservative revolution', is also adopted by Yates (1992) 20, and discussed well with extensive bibliography 157–217.

subjectivity'.[80] Indeed, Hofmannsthal was a child of the Vienna of his times in no way more 'than in [his] concern with "personality", with the integrity of individual identity'.[81] This fascination both with obsessive self-scrutiny, which culminates in the process of psychoanalysis, and with the integrity – or fragmentation – of the individual are central to the composition of the *Elektra* at all levels.

The story of the composition of the play inevitably unfolds through the mediation of Hofmannsthal's self-projections. Hofmannsthal first published poetry under the pseudonym of 'Loris' before he was eighteen, and he had been hailed as a prodigy and immediately accepted into Viennese literary society with acclaim (despite arriving to meet Bahr in short trousers).[82] Stefan Zweig wrote 'no other writer has at such an early age reached such a flawless mastery of speech, such elevation of ideals, or such saturation with the substance of poetry even in the least of his random lines, as this majestic genius who in his sixteenth or seventeenth year had inscribed himself upon the eternal rolls of the German language with poetry that will not die'.[83] (Poets used to get reviews like that . . .) Hofmannsthal himself described it thus: 'I was stepping out from the absolute solitude of my youth, precociously mature, but infinitely inexperienced.'[84] The extremism of his self-claimed 'absolute' solitude and 'infinitely' precocious state is typical of the late Romantic self-image of the artist at the limit.

Hofmannsthal moved away from his early lyrical verse, however, and he dramatized his shifting artistic aims in an influential prose work of 1901, the so-called 'Letter of Lord Chandos', a fictionalized letter addressed to Francis Bacon by a literary figure of early modern England, Lord Chandos, in which the turn away from poetry and the literary life – and even from language itself – is articulated. This is expressed in relation to the ancient world:

I wanted to decipher the fables, the mythical tales bequeathed to us by the Ancients, in which painters and sculptors found an endless and thoughtless pleasure – decipher them as the hieroglyphs of a secret inexhaustible wisdom whose breath I sometimes seemed to feel as though from behind a veil.[85]

---

[80] Cited by Yates (1992) 46.   [81] Yates (1992) 58.   [82] Zweig (1961 (1943)) 45–6.

[83] Zweig (1961 (1943)) 46, who discourses at length about the importance of the young genius Hofmannsthal for his (and his chums') world-picture. On Zweig in context see Robertson (1999) 112–29.

[84] Hugo von Hofmannsthal – Arthur Schnitzler *Briefwechsel* ed. T. Nickel and H. Schnitzler (Frankfurt am Main, 1983) 266.

[85] Hofmannsthal (1952) 131.

Hofmannsthal's attraction to ancient Greece is explicitly the lure of a mythic world which he desires to decipher – not just to appreciate or enjoy or experience, but, like a psychoanalyst, to read through their riddles to a secret, motivating world through which the breath of his art is moved. This need for decipherment, however, is also a search – a more Romantic ideal – for spiritual satisfaction in Greece:

I tried to rescue myself from this plight [the whirlpools which gave me vertigo, and reeling incessantly led me to the void] by seeking refuge in the spiritual world of the Ancients.[86]

The collapsing self, drawn into a vortex – a 'perilousness of the imagination', as he calls what he fears in Plato[87] – glosses the Romantic search for a spiritual Greece with the modernist fascination with disintegration of individuality and the 'crisis of language'. (This 'crisis of language' finds its most developed philosophical expression in the work of Martin Heidegger – who also turned back to an idealized Greek language to ground his pursuit of a new articulation of being and truth. Although many commentators have wished to separate Heidegger's unacceptable politics from his philosophy, it is easy to see at least how both are grounded in the same cultural tradition.) Right at the end of his life in 1928, Hofmannsthal spoke as the guest speaker at a school event (in which he rather struggles to reach the required feel-good level: 'we live in a critical moment of world history where there is no space for celebration').[88] He returned to the lure of the ancient world in a remarkable passage which recalls the language of the Chandos letter in even more lyrical and paradoxical expressiveness: 'The Ancient world of Greece' is 'a ghost world, pregnant with life, within us ourselves, our true, internal Orient, an open imperishable secret'.[89] Again, Greece is a secret, a secret within the self, awaiting decipherment, an Orient within even the anti-Eastern souls of the German-speaking audience, which seems to function almost as a subconscious, destabilizing as it is necessary, a world of ghosts paradoxically pregnant with life. With the *Elektra* too, as we will see, this willingness to find both the otherness of the Orient and the darkness of the modern self within the 'light' and 'purity' of Greece made Hofmannsthal's engagement with the past profoundly disturbing to his contemporaries.

---

[86] Hofmannsthal (1952) 135.   [87] *Ibid.*   [88] Hofmannsthal (1928) 99.
[89] Hofmannsthal (1928) 101: 'eine mit leben trächtige Geisterwelt in uns selber, unser wahrer innerer Orient, offenes unverwesliches Geheimnis'.

He dramatizes this uncanny engagement with the past most bizarrely in his little-read essay 'The Statues', in *Moments in Greece*. Hofmannsthal describes his visit to the Acropolis in Athens, which does not begin with a Winckelmann-like awe: 'This was Athens. Athens? So this was Greece, this antiquity. A sense of disappointment overwhelmed me...These Greeks, I asked within myself, where are they? I tried to remember, but I remembered only memories.'[90] Hofmannsthal cannot find any sublimity, any emotion of awe from sitting in the evening light by the Parthenon. ('Where do I surrender myself to it entirely? Here! Or nowhere. Here is the air, and here is the place. Does nothing penetrate me?')[91] Instead of the experience of the glory that was Greece, Hofmannsthal can retreat only to remembering memories within himself: there is no object for his reflections but his own internal life.

At this (paradigmatic) juncture of disappointed self-obsession, he sees a phantom of Plato walk past him, mocking his inability to participate in an experience of lost glory. This vision fills him with a dark sense of a double desecration – a desecration immanent both in the present architectural ruins and in the ruins of his mental guilt. 'It is your own weakness, I called to myself, you are unable to revive all this.'[92] Taking a text of Sophocles from his pocket, he strolls and reads. Though he feels 'the whole burden of his [Sophocles'] sorrow and at the same time the incomparable tenderness and purity of the Sophoclean line,'[93] even while reading tragedy above the theatre of Dionysus, he cannot decipher the ruins of the past to reveal its secrets: 'Impossible antiquity, I said to myself, aimless searching – the harshness of these words pleased me – Nothing of all this exists...A demonic irony hovers over these ruins which in their decay still retain their secret.'[94] He is still gnawing at this self-analytic failure to penetrate the secrets of the past (so typically put under the aegis of an uncanny irony, marked by impossibility, aimlessness, harshness) when he wanders into the museum, where – like a thunderclap – he sees five statues. 'At that moment something happened to me: an indescribable shock. It came not from outside, but from some immeasurable distance of an inner abyss.'[95] Hofmannsthal has his moment of total, ineffable artistic revelation ('indescribable', 'immeasurable', 'an abyss'), of discovering the secret, and it comes from within, for all that the statues are out there. This is the paradox Hofmannsthal struggles to express: 'They are there and are unattainable. So, too, am I.

[90] Hofmannsthal (1952) 180–1.   [91] Hofmannsthal (1952) 182.
[92] Hofmannsthal (1952) 183.   [93] *Ibid.*
[94] Hofmannsthal (1952) 184.   [95] Hofmannsthal (1952) 185.

By this we communicate.' He has found 'the secret of infinity in these garments' and it is 'from these statues that my soul received its direction'. Yet 'nothing about them alludes to the world in which I breathe and move'.[96] The 'secret' of Greece, for Hofmannsthal, thus becomes the paradox of communicating with the unattainable.

The revelation of 'The Statues' does not cancel the searching of his disappointed visit to the Acropolis, but re-values the 'demonic irony' of the secrets in ruined stone. As in the psychoanalytic process – never an empty parallel for Hofmannsthal – the journey of 'working through' is a necessary part of the recognition of the end point. For Hofmannsthal, communicating with the unattainable of Greece is an unending process – a constant process of self-dramatization, as Greece cannot be approached except through such self-exploratory narratives, a searching through that ghost-laden, secret-haunted, pregnant, inner world. A frightening and necessary Greece, within.

Some twenty years later, the ghosts are still re-appearing, albeit in a more domesticated fashion. In 1924, Hofmannsthal produced with Strauss *The Ruins of Athens*, a ballet spectacle, which involves a Wanderer seen 'as an idealized German artist of those half-forgotten days', to whom Hofmannsthal proposes giving 'the line: "His soul yearning for the land of the Greeks" as a kind of motto. I present him as he meditates on the ruins of the past in the deserted market place of Athens and is lighted, like Goethe, by a Promethean, productive, creative spark.'[97] (And the ballet is to end with 'a vision of the Panathenaic procession'.) The secret processes of his own inward re-writing of Greece informed Hofmannsthal throughout his creative life, even if in this late ballet the power to terrify, frustrate, and destabilize, seems somewhat dissipated.

Elektra, however, is undoubtedly Hofmannsthal's most powerful expression of his engagement with such a Greece of the (perilous) imagination,[98] and he writes in a customary, self-dramatizing way about its composition. In 1902 he wrote to the poet Schröder about the difficulty of finding a new literary direction (more Weltschmertz): 'It was my 28th birthday and I believe I can understand as follows the alarming paralysis of my productive powers which had been going on for nearly two years . . . it is the painful transition from the productions of

---

[96] Hofmannsthal (1952) 186–7.   [97] Strauss and Hofmannsthal (1961) 352.
[98] He also wrote several other specifically Greek and/or Sophocles-inspired works, most importantly an *Oedipus* and an *Alkestis*. With Strauss, he also produced, of course, *Ariadne auf Naxos* and *Die Ägyptische Helena*, and the ballet-spectacle *The Ruins of Athens*. See Esselborn (1969); Nauman (1967); Steingruber (1956) – and, by far the best of these, Jens (1955).

youth to that of manhood, a deep inward transformation, felt outwardly only through grief and dullness.'[99] (To his father he offers a more prosaic faffing: 'If only the weather would improve, and I could see the landscape . . . and my imagination lighten up in consequence, I would start.')[100] He met with Reinhardt, the producer and director, and the beautiful Eysoldt, the actress who would play Electra with such fervour, such intent aggression, (Hofmannsthal and she corresponded affectionately for some years[101]), and, with the stimulation of a commision, the play was completed in only three weeks.

Hofmannsthal had been reflecting on such a project at least since 1901. 'I was reading Sophocles' play in the garden and in the forest in the autumn of 1901. I remembered the line from *Iphigeneia*, "Electra with her tongue of fire", and as I walked I fantasized about the figure of Elektra, not without a certain pleasure in the contrast with the "devilishly humane" atmosphere of the *Iphigeneia*.'[102] This is no less careful a dramatic portrayal of the self than the picture of the poet desperately seeking Sophocles on the Acropolis. In the archetypal Germanic setting of 'garden and forest',[103] the artist, reading Greek, recalls Goethe, the greatest German of the German literary tradition, and his engagement with tragedy in his masterpiece, the *Iphigeneia*, where Elektra is described as having 'a tongue of fire' in a play depicted by its author as 'verteufelt humane', 'devilishly humane' (as opposed to 'demonic irony'). Rewriting Sophocles for Hofmannsthal is always rewriting himself into the tradition of German literature's engagement with Greek tragedy.

These deep concerns of Hofmannsthal with myth, with finding a new language of literary expression, and with the fragmented and searching self, required a new credo for his tragic writing. And he expressed his credo with lapidary directness: 'Let shadows emerge from the blood.'[104] It is this purusit of a new horror, the dark stain and uncertainty arising both from the violence of blood-letting and from the inheritance of the 'blood' of the past, which becomes the watchword of the *Elektra* – and the source of its powerful effect on the German public.

The shadows and blood which Hofmannsthal releases are conceptualized fully through the modernist intellectual world of Vienna.[105]

[99] Hofmannsthal (1937) 67.
[100] Hofmannsthal (1937) 56–7. This as early as 1901.
[101] Recently published: Eysoldt (1996).   [102] Hofmannsthal (1937) 383–4.
[103] See Schama (1995).
[104] *Reden und Aufsätze III (1925–1929), Buch der Freunde, Aufzeichnungen 1889–1925* ed. B. Schoeller and I. Beyer-Ahlert (Frankfurt am Main, 1980) 443, cited by Forsyth (1989) 22.
[105] The best introduction is still Schorske (1980); see also Le Rider (1993).

Hofmannsthal read widely in contemporary anthropology, myth studies, and particularly in psychoanalytic theory. Anthropology – a new field, then – made the scandalous discovery that the mythic tales of savage races and the mythic tales of Greece shared a violence and wilful nastiness.[106] The similarity between the early Greek tales and the tales from savage cultures upset the genealogical appropriation of a glorious Western past in Greece. The castration of Uranos, say, was not just an early and regrettable aberration in the repertoire of tales, but an easily paralleled model that linked mythic systems. An ancestry in glorious Greece and an ancestry in savage barbarism were less easy to tell apart. Similarly, anthropological theorists such as Maine, Morgan and Tylor, supported by scientists such as Darwin, constructed different evolutionary models for society, which proposed that all societies develop in similar ways: the privileged, honoured, unique descent from Greece was profoundly threatened as an ideal of Western self-definition.[107] The Swiss jurist J. J. Bachofen's great work *Das Mutterrecht* had a huge influence in these debates. He proposed – and explored at great length with an armoury of classical and literary scholarship – the claim that society was originally matriarchal, but was only slowly and violently turned to its current patriarchal condition. Bachofen's work provided a basis for Marx and Engel's theories of the family and the State, and was certainly one of the books which stimulated Hofmannsthal and his views of Greek tragedy – not to mention its violent, powerful young women.

At the same time, and overlapping with the inauguration of anthropology as a discipline, there was a broad intellectual exploration of the multiform ways of understanding myth.[108] Two particular strands of this intricate arena of debate need particular understanding for Hofmannsthal and the *Elektra*. Freud is only one of a series of scholars who sought to find an underlying 'key' to mythological tales (if rarely in a fully Cassaubon-like fashion). Max Müller's influential attempt in the middle of the nineteenth century to discover allegories of 'solar movement' (and other meteorological features) in (all) mythology was being rapidly replaced by more developed and developmental models, where, to take one of the most celebrated examples, Frazer extended Mannhardt's

---

[106] I have particularly learned from Detienne (1981); Stocking (1987); Olender (1989); Lincoln (1999). Anthropology has always loved its own scandalousness: Lévi-Strauss begins his seminal *La Structure élémentaire de la parenté* (Paris, 1949) with the scandal of incest as a universal – and thus apparently natural – cultural rule.

[107] See in general the amusingly written Burrow (1966); Leopold (1980); and, for further useful starting bibliography, Versnel (1990) 69.

[108] A nice overview in Versnel (1990), and Turner (1981) 77–134.

investigation of corn-spirits and vegetation demons into the huge edifice of *The Golden Bough*. Robertson Smith, Jane Ellen Harrison, Francis
Cornford and Gilbert Murray (whose work Hofmannsthal knew especially well,[109] and whose portrait was one of those that framed Viola Tree)
realigned myth back towards ritual.[110] Ritual – its gestures, performance,
and communicative power – was one way in which Hofmannsthal
sought to find a solution to what he called (his) 'Sprachkrise' – 'crisis
in/of language' – that runs throughout the 'Letter of Chandos' (where
words 'crumble in the mouth like mouldy fungi'). In his later essay
'On Pantomime' (1911), he writes 'a pure gesture is like a pure thought
from which also the intelligence of the moment, the limited individual,
the grotesque characteristic, are removed . . . True personality comes to
light in gesture.'[111] Dance itself, too, was a hot topic in German culture:
Isadora Duncan recalls 'How differently these German journalists listened than those to whom I explained my theories later in America.
They listened to me with the most reverent and interested contem-
plation, and the next day there appeared long articles in the German
newspapers treating my dance with grave and philosophical import!'
and 'My dances became a subject of heated even fiery debate':[112] she
became very close friends with several leading German intellectuals, including Herman Bahr, who wrote on Greek tragedy and modernism and
was one of Hofmannsthal's closest friends. Duncan's insistence on her
affinity to Nietzsche and Kant may look slightly less pretentious in such
company.

The physical, communicative powers of gesture in ritual, along with
its repressed memories of social forms and lost stories, play a large role in
Elektra. At one level, the drama with its sacrificial procession, mourning
songs, and final dance of death, makes the performance of ritual central
to its action. At another level, the language of the play, like Sophocles'
text, returns obsessively to an opposition of words and deeds, mere language and 'actual tokens which cannot be doubted' (as Elektra herself
puts it). What counts, what works – words, music, action? At the most
general level, drama itself, rather than lyric poetry, offers the possibility of
subordinating language to another spectacular regime of performance.

[109] See Hamburger (1963) 36.
[110] See in general Versnel (1990) and Calder ed. (1991); for more detailed background, see e.g. on
Harrison, Beard (2000); on Müller, Voigt (1976) – particularly on the political aspects of Müller;
on Frazer, Ackerman (1987). On Durkheim's role in this, see Humphreys (1978).
[111] Most easily found in *Gesammelte Werke in Einzelausgaben* ed. H. Steiner, 15 vols. (Frankfurt am
Main, 1953–70) *Prosa* III, 46–50.
[112] Duncan (1968) (1928) 125, 151.

Drama's expressiveness spotlights ritualized gesture. Hofmannsthal's turn to myth and ritual in an adaptation of ancient drama is thus to be seen as part of a modernist crisis of expressiveness. Stravinsky's *Rite of Spring* in 1913, or Diaghelev's 'Après-midi d'un faun' in 1911 – both performed in Paris to near hysterical audiences and active policing by the constabulary – show the threatening power of this spectacular new turn to violent and even sexualized ritual, and provide the context in which Elektra's dance of death should be viewed.[113] Like *Elektra*, the *Rite of Spring* (whose dancer also dies wordlessly) draws fully on contemporary anthropological research on ritual and violence to create through its modern – and threatening – experimentation a disturbing image of savagery and horror *within* the civilized world.

A second level of engagement with myth could perhaps be called, less anachronistically, 'history and archaeology' – and it is an area we have already seen with regard to Houston Stewart Chamberlain. I shall offer three ruthlessly cropped snapshots of major projects of the early nineteenth century, each of which constructed influential and highly productive general arguments in this field. Even these soundbites, however, will be enough to underline a crucial strand in the use of myth as an intellectual support for the cultural development of nationalism. Johann Gottfried von Herder's 'invention' of Das Volk – The People, The Race – developed the criteria of a shared myth, language, homeland and physiognomy for 'das Volk' – and his ideas functioned as a mobilization of group identity for a nascent nationalism (and as an argument for territorial claims). Myths were distinctive to a People and the People needs must have its Myths.[114] Sir William Jones (who died just before the beginning of the nineteenth century, but who was hugely influential throughout it) added to this a more precise and hugely influential idea of the 'Ursprache', the founding language: he not merely proposed the existence of Indo-European, a theorized, prime and master language, the basis of certain linguistically interlinked European and Indian languages, but also thus apparently offered philological proof of the dominant ancestry of the Aryan Volk (and with it a set of myths, and even a possible homeland in the past).[115] With even further specificity, Karl Otfried Müller's book *Die Dorier*, my third example, published back in

[113] For the contemporary responses to Stravinsky, see Lesire (1980).
[114] Useful discussion with further bibliography in Lincoln (1999) 47–75.
[115] Useful discussion with further bibliography of the linguistic background in Lincoln (1999) 47–75. Jones has a wider influence than is often admitted by those who were influenced by him: see Aarsleff (1967) 115–61.

1824, stressed the Dorian ancestry of the German Volk. It is a book which continued even into the late twentieth century to have an extraordinary (and depressing) influence, as Jonathan Hall has briefly and dispassionately outlined.[116] Müller's book presented an image of the Dorian race which fights for a sense of freedom, fights on land, putting faith in manpower and manliness; which values tradition; acts cautiously but wholeheartedly after deliberation; which predicates collective consciousness on ancestry and prefers autocratic forms of government. 'Above all else, the Dorian spirit was characterized by a tendency to subordinate individual elements to the whole and to preserve unity, from which obedience and self-restraint sprang.'[117] This image of the Dorian race – 'uncannily Protestant'[118] – ran throughout German constructions of Aryanism, to the extent that the blond Dorians, most Nordic of Greeks, racially most pure, became privileged ancestors of the German race. (The tyranny of Greece over the German imagination had its ancestor cult.) The 'New Dorians' were to be opposed, as in Chamberlain, to the degenerate East (which reversed and subverted the qualities of the Nordic Dorians). It is within this ideological world that Hofmannsthal's Clytemnestra will take on her full and precise power to shock.

It was, however, Freud and Breuer's *Studies in Hysteria* and Erwin Rohde's book *Psyche* which Hofmannsthal read while writing *Elektra*.[119] Hofmannsthal's absorption in psychoanalysis has fostered a small cottage industry, where Elektra has been seen not merely to suffer from a 'pathological fixation on her murdered father', but even to be based closely on the case of Anna O.![120] Certainly, early reviewers had no doubt that what distinguished Hofmannsthal's play was the portrayal of 'an *Elektra* which reflects our modern ideal of psychological art',[121] and the links between sex and violence, memory and suffering have been well explored by critics (although often deeply hated by the first reviewers). Yet in some way the fascination with Freud and Vienna and the status of Hofmannsthal as one of Freud's first literary converts has downplayed the importance of Erwin Rohde – classical scholar, friend and supporter of

---

[116] Hall (1997) 4–16.   [117] Hall (1997) 9.   [118] Hall (1997) 8.

[119] Hladny recalls that Hofmannsthal told him he had been looking at Freud/Breuer and Rohde before writing *Elektra*, but he also asked Bahr to lend him the *Studies in Hysteria* in 1904: see Forsyth (1989) 153 n.19 for the evidence.

[120] Butler (1938–9) (quotation: 168); Martens (1987); Urban (1978); Worbs (1983) (for the Anna O. parallel: 259–95); Bayerlein (1996).

[121] 'Eine "Elektra" im Spiegelbild unseres psycho-künstlerischen Zeitideals', *Wiener Mittagszeitung* 15 May 1903; see also Karl Federn (*Die Zukunft* 47 (1904) 234) who calls them 'Greeks viewed by modern psychology and modern cultural and social knowledge'.

Nietzsche – for Hofmannsthal.[122] For it was in Rohde that Hofmannsthal could read that the Furies – the demonic figures who dominate the final play of Aeschylus' *Oresteia*, which also tells of Orestes' revenge – were to be understood *psychologically*: 'In reality, these horrid figures only exist in the imagination of the mentally diseased.' What is more, divine purpose is fulfilled, wrote Rohde of tragedy, 'though human happiness may be destroyed in the process, and though pain, crime, agony, violent death may overwhelm the individual'. 'Only tragically extreme characters can have a tragic fate' – and Elektra above all is completely obedient to such old laws.[123] In Rohde, Hofmannsthal could discover the Furies comprehended as the violent psychological disruption of the mentally diseased, leading to the tragedy of an extreme character, led by unknown purpose to violent death through pain, suffering, crime – the 'crushing of the individual'. This picture of Elektra is integral to Hofmannsthal's reading of Sophocles.

Nor is it by chance that it is the psychology of women that Hofmannsthal so intently foregrounds. This is not merely because of the impact of Charcot's celebrated display of hysterical women in his clinical practice, and his influence on Freud (showmen, both) – which gives the spectacle of dangerous and damaged female psychology such a particular charge.[124] (Freud himself, by the way, only uses the phrase 'Electra complex' to dismiss it as someone else's new-fangled coinage, not to be adopted; but it is hard to believe that Strauss' *Elektra*, whose most beautiful erotic love song is sung to her dead father, and whose disturbed psychology becomes such a watchword of contemporary criticism, did not at least help the easy reception of this popular 'Freudian' idea.) Rather, it is the extensive contemporary debate commonly known as 'the woman question' which extends this psychological focus into a broader political sphere (much as Bachofen's anthropology led directly into the politics of the family and the state, or, say, Weininger's nasty but influential *Sex and Character* crystalized a connection between gender and race).[125] 'The nervous culture of Victorian England'[126] – and Europe's obsession with 'female malady' – meant that arguments about the education and the suffrage of women repeatedly turned on the (in)stability of female mental

---

[122] Brief comments, however, in Robertson (1986) 317–18; Rey (1962) 85; and Ewans (1984).

[123] Rohde (1925) 434, 427, 427.   [124] See the works cited above notes 51 and 59.

[125] Primary sources on 'the woman question' are usefully collected and edited in the three volumes of Helsinger, Sheets and Veeder (1983). On Weininger, an Austrian Jew who committed suicide at the age of twenty-three in 1903, see Robertson (1998); Radford (1998), who notes the influence of Chamberlain on him 92–5.

[126] The phrase is from Oppenheim (1991).

life,[127] and particularly during the bitterly contested election year of 1910, the Press often offers juxtapositions which now at least seem testimony to the interwoven discourse of gender and politics and art. The _Nation_, to take one good example, runs an article on the Strauss/Hofmannsthal _Elektra_ – 'a new reading of the black business of Clytemnestra's heart' – next to a piece by John Galsworthy arguing in favour of votes for women – 'a great and ever-increasing body of women [are] suffering from a bitter sense of injustice'.[128] The English turn to politics in response to Strauss, which I will be discussing shortly, is part of a cultural debate in which a contest about 'the female mind' is integral. The critics' fascination with the scientific – or sarcastically pseudo-scientific – diagnoses of Elektra's psychology, which testifies to this fascinating transitional moment in the popular reception of psychoanalytic theory, should not conceal the more general politics of gender embodied in the reaction to Strauss' opera.

There were also strong contemporary models for Hofmannsthal's composition of the wild and dancing Elektra which drew on similar intellectual concerns. Ibsen's Nora in _The Doll's House_ – one of the most powerful and most discussed stage heroines of the period – epitomizes the overlapping interests in psychoanalysis, the dance and gender (under the rubric of a shocking 'realism'). When Nora dances the Tarentella with increasing lack of control (to the increasing confusion and dismay of her husband), she is preparing the way for her outrageous desertion of her home and family. She 'dances what she cannot say'.[129] Dancing and female neurosis are inherently linked, as the physiologist, Harry Campbell explained in 1891: 'The movements of these wild dances imperceptibly shade off into the co-ordinate movements of the hysterical fit . . . Hence it is possible that the love of dancing, so peculiarly strong among women, is the outcome of a nervous organization affording a suitable soil for hysteria.'[130] The modern intellectual roots of the figuration of Elektra had theatrical predecessors too.

So anthropology, myth studies and psychology provide essential frames for Hofmannsthal's rewriting of tragedy. Nor is it hard to see why he turned to Sophocles' play rather than the version of Euripides or Aeschylus. Sophocles' play focuses on the conflict between mother and daughter, sister and sister, and sidelines the male plot of revenge to the first and last scenes of the play. (Hofmannsthal commented that the

[127] See in particular Showalter (1985); Oppenheim (1991) 181–232; Vrettos (1995).
[128] _The Nation_ 26 March, 1910; the review is signed by H .W. M.
[129] Robinson (1992) 15.   [130] Campbell (1891) 169.

libretto would follow its own logic better if Orestes played *no* part in the drama at all.) The consequent emphasis on the mental states of the female figures and the effects of the past on their actions and on their passionate exchanges, feeds directly into Hofmannsthal's concerns with psychological torment and the force of repressed memories. Above all, the absence of any staging of the gods – under the aegis of 'realism' – allows the privileging of human personality, disintegrating under pressure. (The versions of both Aeschylus and Euripides represent the gods in the action on stage.) But what is equally instructive for the scandal of Hofmannsthal is the contemporary reputation of Sophocles. Unlike the 'grandeur' of Aeschylus or the 'intellectualism' of Euripides (that Nietzsche in *The Birth of Tragedy* so disliked), the key adjective in the appreciation of Sophocles is 'pious'. Sophocles was a general, a civic leader, and also an official representative of religious cult; the 'good temper' for which Aristophanes (and the *Times'* reviewer of Strauss) praised him, contrasted with Aeschylus' sublime fierceness and Euripides' 'cleverness'. One example from the vast morass of the opinion makers will do, and here's Karl Otfried Müller again: Sophocles 'is, of all the Greeks, at once the most pious and the most enlightened'.[131] Indeed, although the *Elektra* concludes with brutal matricide, Jebb, the greatest of Sophoclean scholars in the Victorian pantheon, (and much influenced by German scholarship), writes that 'the vengeance [is] a deed of unalloyed merit' (however hard you may – should – find it to imagine a wholly praiseworthy matricide). 'It is the bright influence of Apollo that prevails from the first . . . light and purity.'[132] Jebb here closely follows August Schlegel in particular who paradigmatically saw in the *Elektra* of 'this pious and virtuous poet' a 'heavenly serenity . . . the fresh air of life and purity.'[133]

Hofmannsthal's *Elektra*, then, is written not merely against the calm purity of the white robes and columns of a Goethian tradition of classicism, nor merely against the conventions of contemporary classical stagings with its 'archaeologically correct' classicism and self-controlled propriety, but also specifically against – or through – Sophocles, the tragedian who, since Aristotle, had come to epitomize the acme of classicism itself. And wholly against the 'heavenly serenity' and 'fresh air and youth' – which his 'shadows from the blood' would smother. In a brilliant theatrical gesture (the precise thrill of which should by now be appreciated), Reinhardt maximized the shock for his audience at the first performance by starting the play with a rendition of the overture

[131] Müller (1858) 471.   [132] Jebb (1894) xxxix–xl; xlv–xlvi.   [133] Schlegel (1846) 96; 132.

of Gluck's *Iphigeneia*! Hofmannsthal was out to sacrifice a procession of sacred cows.

The stage direction, when Clytemnestra enters (much quoted even in the occasional early review), sums this up in the most direct and telling way:

In the broad window, Clytemnestra appears. Her sallow, bloated face in the glaring light of the torches, appears even paler over her scarlet robe. She leans on a confidante who is clothed in dark violet, and on an ivory staff decorated with precious stones. The train of her robe is carried by a jaundiced figure, with black hair, gathered together at the back like an Egyptian woman, with smooth face, resembling a rearing snake. The queen is completely covered with precious stones and talismans. Her arms are full of armlets, her fingers bristle with rings. The lids of her eyes appear unnaturally large and it seems to cost her an unspeakable effort to keep them open.

This wonderfully evocative passage offers so much more than a fragment of stagecraft. It is for the reader/director – and by extension the audience – the construction of a fully developed image of degeneracy. The flesh of the queen is sallow and bloated and her eyes are unnatural and over-heavy: the physiognomics of corruption and disease. She is surrounded by an Eastern-looking entourage, not only the insidious 'confidante' with its overtones of palace intrigue and treachery, but also the 'jaundiced' trainbearer, whose face – and notice how the simile takes us from the physicality of staging to the conceptualization of imaging – is 'like a rearing snake'. The queen's body is covered with jewellery, and specifically 'talismans' – savage ritual objects. Even the colours – pale sallowness, scarlet, dark violet, black, 'jaundiced' – are the palette of a voluptuous and sickening degeneracy.

Plate 16 begins to show the moments shortly after that staged entrance in the first production of the play in Berlin. The heavy stone walls and altar, reprised in the London production of the opera, summon up an archaic, brute, massiveness (to set against the lightness and purity of a colonnaded and columned temple), and plates 17, 18, 19 (selected from a remarkable and recently released set of portraits of Eysoldt[134]) show not only Elektra's ragged costume and dishevelled hair, but also something of the acclaimed physicality of Eysoldt's performance.[135] Again,

---

[134] Eysoldt (1996).

[135] Good selection of comments on Eysoldt's performance in McMullen (1985). The sets were strongly influenced by the work of Robert Craig, who was the lover of Isadora Duncan and who himself went on to design sets for a production of *Elektra* in 1913 (never realised) for Yeats in Ireland.

16. Hofmannsthal's *Elektra*, the entrance of Clytemnestra

17. Gertrude Eysoldt in the role of Elektra

18. Gertrude Eysoldt in the role of Elektra

the physiognomics of fear, torment and confusion are expressed through
a body language which finds its models in Charcot's asylum portraits
rather than in Lord Leighton's paintings. Even in these posed representations, the stark and tense arms and hands (notice the twisted fists in
plate 18) and the eyes, staring in fear (plate 17), rolling (plate 19), and
furrowed in confused introspection (plate 18), make a telling contrast
with the elegant langeur of Viola Tree's Greekness.

There has been surprisingly little informed critical discussion of
Hofmannsthal's adaptation of the Sophoclean text.[136] For although he
followed the plot lines of Sophocles closely, there are significant differences which strikingly highlight the modernist impact of his drama.
I shall indicate here just two of the most important of those moments.
Sophocles does not stage the gods, but it is integral to Jebb's view of
the matricide that 'the whole drama is pervaded by an undercurrent of
divine co-operation; the gods are silently at work'.[137] Central to this idea
is the moment of the false announcement of Orestes' death by the Tutor.

---

[136] As Ewans (1984) notes; Newiger (1969) is the most detailed and convincing, along with the more
general Jens (1955). Many of the others have a very precarious grip of the Greek texts and of
their nineteenth-century reception. Lloyd-Jones (1991) and, most recently, Davies (1999) show
clearly the dangers of a narrowly conceived textual analysis of Hofmannsthal.

[137] Jebb (1894) xlv.

19. Gertrude Eysoldt in the role of Elektra

Clytemnestra has come out of the palace to pray to Apollo: she offers up her prayer to the god for the happy outcome of her terrifying nightmares, for the secure possession of her power, and for the avoidance of the hostility of her children who oppose her. She ends by asking for fulfilment of what she cannot speak out loud – a sickening indirection that barely conceals her hope for the death of her son. It is at that point precisely that the Tutor enters with the news of – exactly – Orestes' death. For a reading like Jebb's, this must be treated as the ironic but certain answer of the queen's prayer by Apollo. The arrival of the Tutor is seen as a sign of god's hand at work. Orestes' matricidal act fulfils a divine wish and injunction.

How does Hofmannsthal allow the news of Orestes' death to be announced? It arrives as an unmotivated and unattributed rumour from town. We do not see Orestes and the Tutor plotting the false tale, nor do we hear, as we do in Sophocles, of Orestes' consultation of Apollo's oracle at Delphi. Hofmannsthal has removed not merely the divine machinery of the classical plot, but also and more importantly, the framework of moral authority which the gods provide. This world is one where human action is not anchored in the structured pattern of fulfilment and overseeing which the gods provide in Greek tragedy. In this godless scenario, dream, fantasy, hope, despair, lead action. It is just humans, locked into conflict, violence and psychological fragmentation.

The second moment which shows how deeply Hofmannsthal has drafted Sophocles according to his modernist agenda is the close of the play. In Sophocles, Clytemnestra is murdered first, and her body displayed, disguised as Orestes' own corpse, under a wrapping, in order to lure Aegisthus into the trap. The play ends with her brother leading the usurper into the palace to die where their father had been murdered, while the chorus sing the briefest of codas. This is a deliberately and pointedly condensed conclusion, restricted by Elektra's demand of Aegisthus' silence. It self-consciously avoids the grandeur of the closing procession of Aeschylus' *Oresteia*, or the wild *coup de théâtre* of the close of the *Choephori* (the second play of the *Oresteia*) where Orestes after the matricide goes mad, sees the Furies and rushes screaming from the stage. Hofmannsthal, however, has Elektra scrabbling in a futile and desperate search for the axe which killed Agamemnon, and which she has buried for the moment of revenge; and dancing, dancing in triumph, until she falls dead. It does not matter greatly whether you believe with Jebb that the Sophoclean *Elektra* ends in 'austere and solemn' calm, or, with many modern critics, that it ends in horrific, bitterly ironic misprision.

Hofmannsthal has in either case separated Elektra from the act of revenge and left her triumph undermined by her futile attempt at participation and her silent, solitary deathly dance. Both the loneliness and the destruction of the self, engaged in a ritualized gestural performance, scar Elektra's end with the marks of Hofmannsthal's modernism.

The contemporary responses to Hofmannsthal's *Elektra* in the German-speaking press – page after page of them – run the full gamut from enthusiastic appreciation, especially from his friends in literary Vienna, to furious opposition (especially in the more conservative press).[138] It undoubtedly touched a raw nerve in the German-speaking public: it spoke to the time. ('An imposing document of our own time ... spirit of our spirit, blood of our blood', proclaimed the critic, Siegfried Jacobsohn.)[139] But the majority of published reviews and articles assaulted Hofmannsthal's challenge to the Greekness from which the German spirit was descended. Even those who praised the play called it 'ungriechisch', 'unGreek'; and critics queued to censure the poet for having 'bestialized' antiquity, 'thrown it into chaos'. The 'noble', 'sublime', 'luminous character' ('Lichtgestalt') of Elektra had been turned into decadence and perversity; her light shadowed by 'sadism', 'hysteria', 'epilepsy' ... [140] And Hofmannsthal himself is – in one of the more poetical insults – 'a voluptuary of blood'.[141] After the first rush, Bekker may have asked – in his long article of 1909 – 'What does Sophocles matter to us?', but he asks this precisely (and vainly) to try to counter the continuing flow of committed comments claiming that Sophocles mattered a good deal, in order to pursue his own critical agenda.[142] The lead actress, Eysoldt, was singled out for being 'animalistic', 'primitive', 'erotically charged' and a 'slave to brutal reality', 'the insistent psychology of a lewd cruelty'.[143] My favourite is Wilhelm Schmid who fabulously combines his worry about psychoanalysis with his defence of the classical: 'That Elektra, who in the drama of the ancients is wholly untouched by eroticism, should finally be caught up in a whirlpool of psychoanalysis, as a model to demonstrate repressed sexual instincts, is perhaps the

---

[138] Selections of reviews are collected by Wunberg (1972) 76–144; Jens (1955) 152–4. Renner and Schmid eds. (1991)

[139] Cited by Nehring (1991) 131 from the *Wiener Sonntagszeitung* 1 November 1903.

[140] Remarks extracted from the reviews in the works cited in note 138 above.

[141] Alfred Kerr: 'Hofmannsthal ist ein Schwelger; oft ein zarter Schwelger; hier ein Blutschwelger'. *Neue Deutsche Rundschau*, December 1903, most easily found in Wunberg (1972) 79.

[142] Bekker's lengthy article (published in 1909) is translated by S. Gillespie in Gilliam (1992) 372–415. The quotation is from 378.

[143] Remarks taken from McMullen (1985) especially 645–9.

most miserable fate which could have overcome the unfortunate maiden. In this work [Hofmannsthal's *Elektra*] the noble, deeply suffering heroine is turned into a disgusting, hysterical mad woman for a public of instinct wallahs [Triebmenschen].'[144] The new ideas of psychoanalysis, here beyond the cusp of their incipient acceptance, threaten, it would seem, the very characters of the past, as if it were Elektra rather than Schmid who 'suffered' from the Freudian reading! It does not take a great psychoanalytic insight to suggest that something more than he cared to analyse bothered Schmid into such a confused and passionate paragraph. Hofmannsthal's *Elektra* threatened the construction of a German spirit through the inheritance and maintenance of a glorious Greek past. For all that Karl Federn could declare the project to be 'more Greek' than Sophocles himself, such a defence could only seem to be a rather desperate attempt to deflect the impact of Hofmannsthal's drama and the drama of the German response to it.[145] It changed Greek tragedy on stage for the century to come not merely in its dramaturgy of violence and psychological turmoil but also in the ideological weight that Greek tragedy could be made to bear. Hofmannsthal's act of creating myth *anew* was aimed surely at a grounding German myth of Greekness, and his staining of that myth with 'shadows from the blood' made this play a battleground in the crisis of *German* culture.

III

Despite (or because of) the intricate layers of cultural polemic which made this play such a scandalous success, Strauss – according to his correspondence with Hofmannsthal, which was published as early as 1925 – did not rush into committing himself to *Elektra* as his new libretto. When the news of the progressing collaboration was leaked to the Austrian press, however, it caused considerable excitement: Germany's greatest living composer (and the 'heir to Wagner' was a title whose possession was constantly being sought), bringing the scandal of his music (à la *Salome*) to the scandal of Hofmannsthal's masterpiece. The story of the collaboration has been often retold, directed by the poet's and composer's letters (and I shan't rehearse it here). I want rather to look in particular at

---

[144] Schmid (1940) 501. This was actually published in 1940, which adds a further layer to the insult of decadence. This is the same Schmid who offered one of the more dismissive and racist remarks on Lucian cited in the last chapter p. 98.

[145] 'Griechischer als die Griechen des Sophokles selbst', *Die Zukunft* 47 (1904) 234, cited by Jens (1955).

how Strauss' adaptation of Hofmannsthal also constructed a polemical positioning with regard to the inheritance of Wagner. It is not so much Strauss' attempt to find his own musical voice over and against Wagner that interests me – it has been the subject of much detailed musico-logical analysis, and a commonplace of criticism of the opera from the day it opened. Rather I want to trace how Strauss, in working through Hofmannsthal's Hellenism, is also cutting away at the very grounds of Wagner's self-representation. This will lead us into yet another struggle of a specifically German Hellenism.

For Wagner – and I hardly need emphasize the importance of Wagner and his cult for nineteenth-century Germany – not only had a lifelong engagement with ancient Greece but also made it fully integral to his idea of musical theatre.[146] Wagner indeed opens his first theoretical work with a direct statement of a Hellenizing ideal: 'In any serious investigation of the essence of our art today we cannot take a step forward without being brought face to face with its intimate connection with the art of ancient Greece.'[147] From that opening credo, both in his continual commentary on his music and in his constant self-promoting mythologizing, Wagner's passionate and public engagement with an ideal of Greece was such that 'confirmation of his own ideas by relating them to and deriving them from the Greeks became a way of thinking for him'.[148] Wagner in this way provides a paradigmatic model of a – the – German culture hero's self-formation through Greekness.

As with Hofmannsthal, the story of a life with Greek is a fundamental element in the many layers of Wagner's self-portrayal. 'No boy could have had greater enthusiasm for classical culture than myself', he recalls, although his schooling consisted in limping progress under pedantic teachers.[149] He tried several times with private tutors to learn Greek. On idealizing days, he claims that through translations 'again and again, amid the absorbing tasks of a life entirely removed from such studies, the only way I seemed able to gain a breath of freedom was to plunge into this ancient world, however much I was hampered by having almost completely forgotten the language'.[150] More bathetically, he recalls how the smell of a nearby tannery fills him with disgust both for Sophocles and

---

[146] There is no definitive study of this important aspect of Wagner: important articles and books include Schadewaldt (1999); Deathridge (1999); Ewans (1982) – each with further bibliography. The first lengthy study is the hagiographic Braschowanoff (1910). The importance of Nietzsche here is clear: see the fundamental study of Silk and Stern (1981), who may even underplay the interplay between the two men.

[147] *CWW* I. 32.   [148] Schadewaldt (1999).

[149] E. Foerster-Nietzsche ed. (1921) 125.   [150] E. Foerster-Nietzsche ed. (1921) 126.

for the Greek language, which he is once again failing to study.[151] None of this drawn-out story of not quite learning Greek stopped Wagner from being 'filled with such overwhelming enthusiasm for the subject that . . . I could only speak in terms of utmost enthusiasm'[152] for it. It is Aeschylus above all that attracts him, and here is how he finally portrays the impact of the great tragedian on his soul:

For the first time I now mastered Aeschylus with real feeling and understanding. Droysen's eloquent commentary in particular helped to bring before my imagination the intoxicating effect of the production of an Athenian tragedy, so that I could see the *Oresteia* with my mind's eye, as though it were already being performed, and its effect on me was indescribable. Nothing, however, could equal the sublime emotion with which the *Agamemnon* trilogy inspired me, and to the last word of the *Eumenides* I lived in an atmosphere so far removed from the present day that I have never since been really able to reconcile myself with modern literature. My ideas about the whole significance of the drama and of the theatre were, without a doubt, marked by these impressions.[153]

The contrast both with the story of Erasmus' heroic coming to Greek, and with that of Hofmannsthal's later longing to be penetrated by the power of a Hellenic past should help specify Wagner's high Romantic depiction of his encounter with Greek tragedy here. It reads like a textbook account of 'the sublime'.[154] The sphere of action is 'the imagination', and the impression made on it by powerful emotions. 'Real feeling' is an 'intoxicating effect' – which is (of course) 'indescribable'. The effect of 'the sublime' takes his self towards his true, authentic home, which is not the mundane and sordid world of the here and now. Wagner finds that 'I felt myself more truly at home in ancient Athens than in any conditions which the modern world has to offer',[155] just as Nietzsche can declare 'One is no longer at home anywhere; at last one longs for the only place in which one can be at home, because it is the only place one would want to be at home: the *Greek* world.'[156] The transport of the sublime is towards an ideal other place, an imagined Greece, which is the true home of the artist.

The composition of the *Ring* in particular encourages reflection on Wagner's Hellenism.[157] Aeschylus' *Oresteia* has indeed impressed the

---

[151] Wagner (1911) 46.   [152] Wagner (1911) 411.   [153] Wagner (1911) 415.

[154] My textbook here is de Bolla (1989).   [155] Wagner (1911) 412.

[156] F. Nietzsche, *Werke. Kritische Gesamtausgabe* ed. G. Colli and M. Montinari vol. VII. 3 *Nachgelassene Fragmente Herbst 1884 bis Herbst 1885*, 412–13 [August–September 1885 fr 41 [4]], translated by W. Kaufman in W. Kaufman and R. Holingdale, *The Will to Power*, New York (1968), 419.

[157] The fullest account is Ewans (1982).

whole concept of the drama. Like the *Ring*, the *Oresteia* is a themati-
cally linked sequence of three plays with a fourth more light-hearted
and shorter work (though the satyr play comes fourth, where *Rheingold* is
first). Like the *Ring*, Aeschylus' masterpiece is celebrated for constructing a 'divina commedia' with tragic human action in a massive cosmic
vision. Aeschylus' plays are linked too by repeated images (often now
called, somewhat awkwardly, 'leitmotifs'). The *Oresteia* focuses on a fa-
milial curse and concerns intrafamilial and intergenerational conflict.
The *Ring* in short breathes with Wagner's engagement with Aeschylus'
great trilogy.

Wagner's adaptive process, however, is never less than a complex activity of challenge and deep re-formation. It is never simple homage or
imitation. 'We do not try to revert to Greekness', he writes in *Art and
Revolution*, 'only *revolution*, not slavish *restoration* can give us back the highest art work.'[158] This revolutionary reworking of Greek principles is seen
at every level of composition. It is – at the most general level – not enough
to re-tell Greek myth: no Iphigeneias here; rather a rediscovered Nordic,
Teutonic set of stories must be revived to link his art with das Volk, The
People. As Herder argued, a distinctive Volk must have its distinctive
myths. At a different level, in the *Ring* there is no chorus (of the standard operatic type). The Greek chorus is so often said in contemporary
views of Greek tragedy to be the mediation of the judgement of the people, a directive guide from the poet for the people. The chorus, for
Wagner, is replaced by the music of the orchestra – a Dionysiac intoxication, rather than a verbal commentary. At the level of scenic composition,
the rewriting is similarly provocative. The *Oresteia* ends famously with a
torch-lit procession towards the Acropolis, home of Athene, goddess of
the city of Athens, a procession made up of the whole city, triumphantly
celebrating the possibilities of good rule and civilization which the order
of the city instantiates. (We have already seen how the grim ending of
Sophocles' *Elektra* plays off that ending.) *Götterdämmerung*, 'The Twilight
of the Gods', also ends with a torch-lit procession – but of a single girl,
the central focus amid the destruction of the home of the gods. Significantly, Wagner himself described this as 'the surrender of the gods'
direct influence, faced with the freedom of human consciousness'. This
Romantic sentiment – the pursuit of a freedom of consciousness, the
Freedom of the Purely Human – runs throughout Wagner's idealistic
claims. It stands contrary to all Greek ideas of theodicy, and ends the

[158] *CWW* I. 53.

Ring with a final image that – for all the backward pull of the trilogy – is profoundly unGreek.

The cult of Bayreuth's festival has also made it easy to see Wagner's work in its social context as an attempt to (re)create a version of the festival world of Greek drama, and, indeed, Wagner himself often encourages such a view. The 'Gesamtkunstwerk', 'total work of art', aimed at the state of Aeschylean tragedy in its combination of words, music, myth, action, and an audience of The People, imbued with authentic Spirit (although it was hard, even at the beginning, to see Bayreuth simply as The People's theatre). 'Greek tragedy denoted the culminating point of the Greek spirit', wrote Wagner;[159] indeed, Greek tragedy was 'the entry of the artwork of The People upon the public arena of political life';[160] tragedy 'flourished for just so long as it was inspired by the spirit of The People'.[161] The connection of the production of tragedy with a particular spirit (Geist) of The People (das Volk) was part and parcel of Wagner's own desire to produce a contemporary German nationalist art. In *German Art and Politics* and *What is German?*, the desired 'art of the future' can only be embedded in the art of of the German race, purified of all sullying influences (especially French and Jewish ones). This true art requires 'a purified and hence unified culture of the kind supposedly possessed by the Greeks; and it will underwrite the integration of the German race'.[162] The *Ring*, 'dedicated in trust to the German spirit' (as the inscription on the first printed scores has it), performed in a building dedicated in turn to its performance, will thus provide 'a reflection of unified nationhood and enduring spiritual vitality'.[163] Wagner's myth of Greece grounds his myth of a German nation.

Thus, in *German Art and Politics*, Wagner emotes: 'Hail Winckelmann and Lessing, ye who beyond the centuries of native German majesty, found the Germans' real ancestors [Urverwandten, 'Ur-kinsmen'] in the divine Hellenes!'[164] The descent from the divine Hellenes – Germans as the children of such gods – discovered by Winckelmann and Lessing, is the foundation of German majesty – the hoped-for glory of the nation. 'One may say', Wagner reflects, 'that the true idea of the Antique has existed only since the middle of the eighteenth century, since Winckelmann and Lessing'.[165] This claim – rather odd, at first sight – is justified on the following grounds: 'Through its inmost understanding of the Antique, the German spirit arrived at the capability of restoring the Purely

[159] *CWW* I. 43.   [160] *CWW* I. 135.   [161] *CWW* I. 136.   [162] Deathridge (1999) 136.
[163] Deathridge (1999) 137.   [164] *CWW* IV. 43.   [165] *CWW* IV. 156.

Human itself to pristine freedom'.[166] The German can restore essential, pure humanity to the freedom it needs to achieve its perfection (and remember his comments on the end of the *Ring* as the triumph of the freedom of human consciousness) – and such fulfilment comes through a comprehension of the past of antiquity – a comprehension articulated by Winckelmann and Lessing above all. Wagner's passionate recognition of 'Ur-kinsmen' in the Greeks is a structuring principle of his obsessive and racialist nationalism.

Much more could be said about Wagner, the Greeks and nationalism, though the prospect of spending more time with Wagner's prose is scarcely attractive: the issues of his nationalism and of his Hellenism are closely linked to his other political commitments, and his anti-Semitism in particular, and the critical debate around such issues shows no sign of calming down.[167] But what I have offered is enough to frame significantly Strauss' dramatic decisions. In much the same way that Sophocles' *Elektra* can only be fully understood through its intertextuality with Aeschylus' *Oresteia*, so Strauss' adoption of Hofmannsthal's adaptation of Sophocles needs to be set against Wagner's engagement with Aeschylus. Where Wagner offered a four-opera structure for an extended festival occasion, Strauss has but one act. (At least one contemporary British critic thought Strauss' failure to follow Aeschylus was his basic mistake . . .)[168] Where Wagner constructs a mythic narrative which stretches over time and space, involving gods, monsters, magic, dragons, and mystic fiery rings, Strauss offers a claustrophobic, real time, single space, domestic intensity. Where Wagner's use of the Nibelungen saga seeks to recover a myth for the German Volk, Strauss returns to the world of Greece – in such a way as to challenge the fundamental myths of contemporary Germanness. Where Wagner aims to construct a model of inspirational heroism – and could call his own son, 'Siegfried' – Elektra, and even Orestes in Strauss (Hofmannsthal, Sophocles . . .) were instantly perceived to pervert and distort any such models – in a squalid, psychoanalytically driven, dismaying image of humanity at its lowest ebb.

Think of the murder weapon. In the *Ring*, each weapon is invested with a magic power and symbolic force. Wotan's spear, Siegfried's sword, even the hammer of Mime play a role in the construction of a mythic universe, and are deeply expressive of the power of the gods and the performance of heroism. In Strauss' and Hofmannsthal's *Elektra*, the

[166] *CWW* IV. 155.   [167] See e.g. Weiner (1995) with large bibliography.
[168] *The Athenaeum* 4296, 26 February, 1910.

weapon is psychologically fetishisized by Elektra. Concealed, useless, desperately hunted for at the final moment, it takes on its force only through the disrupted imagination of Elektra. It is dirty, buried, a secret. It plays a part in the action only as such. In Aeschylus' *Oresteia*, Orestes as he appears over the bodies of his dead mother and her lover, displays the robes in which Agamemnon was entangled and murdered as part of the public symbolics of justification. Strauss' Elektra dies without being able to bring such a logic of revenge to light. Hofmannsthal introduced this scene and indeed its whole structure of ideas (there is no equivalent in Sophocles, or the other ancient tragedians); and the scene became one of the most celebrated of the opera. Elektra, scrabbling in the dirt, vainly searching for the unrecoverable weapon of past action shows in the most vivid and dramatic manner how Strauss is taking a polemical stance towards the symbolics of Wagner: Strauss has buried the weapon's associations of heroic action, and made even the search for it a sign of the corrupted human's precarious hold on significant action.

IV

The performance of Strauss' *Elektra* in England provoked one particular quarrel which seemed to contemporaries to put all others in the shade. It certainly brought the two heavyweights of operatic criticism head to head – in a way which is extraordinarily revealing of the *different* reception of the piece in England and in Germany, and, in particular, of the different *political* understanding of the import of the opera.

The first night was reviewed by Ernest Newman in the journal *The Nation* on 26 February. Newman was perhaps the most prolific and influential writer on music in Victorian London. I mentioned his book on Gluck which appeared shortly after the Cambridge performance of *Orpheus*, and apart from his constant journalism, his books on Wagner and opera in general were major factors in the construction of Victorian taste. Fascinatingly – and, for this book, after Erasmus and Lucian, perhaps inevitably! – he was a self-educated musician, who had been born William Roberts in a lower-class Welsh family: he invented the name 'Ernest Newman' for himself, and never spoke, even to his wife, of the first eighteen years of his life or had any contact with his family from that time. No better name for such self-invention than 'New Man', of course, and, after Wilde, how important it seems that he should have chosen 'Ernest' to mark the tone of his life to come. He began writing music criticism while working as a bank clerk in London, but by 1910 was well established as a professional critic.[169] Newman had strong and articulate objections to Strauss' writing, which he offers to counterbalance the timidity of other critics, who, he broadly hints, did not do their homework by studying the score and piano reduction of *Elektra* before the performance in order to appreciate the first night properly. 'All but the Strauss fanatics will admit that though he is undoubtedly the greatest living musician, there is a strong sense of foolishness and ugliness in him.'[170] If it were not for this 'strain of coarseness and thoughtlessness', he continues, Strauss 'would never have taken up so crude a perversion of the old Greek story as that of Hugo von Hofmannsthal'. It is not a modern view of ancient Greece that offends, 'but to make a play a study of human madness and then to lay such excessive stress upon the merely physical concomitants of madness, is to ask us to tune our notions of dramatic terror and horror down to too low a pitch'. For Newman, the physical signs of Elektra's mental anguish take the heights of Greek drama and make them low and squalid.

This has its nationalist component. Strauss has the 'besetting Teutonic sin of overstatement . . . all this blacking of his face and waving of his arms and howling "bolly-golly-blackman-boo!" at us leaves us quite unmoved'. Although it is primarily a musical failing that vexes Newman, it is – typically, as we have seen – expressed in terms of an English 'us' opposed to German 'overstatement', itself expressed in the chant of an infantile racist game. Newman allows the opera passages of beauty, but it is its 'violence' and 'ugliness' that he underscores repeatedly.

George Bernard Shaw replied on 12 March.[171] Disarmingly confessing that he had not yet himself seen the *Elektra*, he declares Newman – no holds barred – to be 'ridiculous and idiotic'. (Both reviewers in the debate talk much of manners while flinging personal and barbed insults: it is good to recall what 'old world courtesy' could actually involve.) But it is Newman as the avatar of Englishness that most upsets Shaw: 'he should by this time have been cured by experience and reflection of the trick that makes English criticism so dull and insolent'. (The trick is to assert that a work which does not please is 'ethically corrupt'.) Newman demonstrates the 'ridiculous and idiotic criticism as practised in England'. 'This lazy petulance which has disgraced English journalism in the form of anti-Wagnerism, anti-Ibsenism, this infatuated attempt of writers of modest local standing to talk *de haut en bas* to men of European

---

[169] Newman (1962) 1–41; Newman (1963), his wife's account; Cardus (1955).
[170] *The Nation* VI. 22, 26 February 1910: 843–4.   [171] *The Nation* VI. 24, 12 March 1910: 914–5.

reputation, and to dismiss them as intrusive lunatics, is an intolerable thing, an exploded thing, a foolish thing, a parochial boorish thing...' For Shaw, Newman's criticism of Strauss – which, remember, he has not yet heard: Shaw is never less than sure – is in a tradition of 'anti-Wagnerism, anti-Ibsenism' (those two patron saints of modernism in theatre and music), which betokens an English, small-island, parochial, vulgar rejection of the grandeur of European art.

It's worth recalling that the first full performance of the *Ring* in London was not until 1888, and the first British performance outside London was in Edinburgh the very weekend that *Elektra* opened.[172] Wagner was still a hot topic in cultural discussion, and only just an acceptable musical taste. The English resistance to Wagner was repeatedly articulated as a sensible British retreat from the excesses of Germany and the continent. And Shaw was already famous for his championing of the new music – and, as ever, is quick to live up to his reputation.

Shaw points in passing also to a further crucial frame for this outburst. Newman may, he explodes, 'diagnose the cases of Strauss and Hofmannsthal as psychopathic or neurasthenic, or whatever the appropriate scientific slang may be, and descant generally on the degeneracy of the age in the manner of Dr Nordau'. Shaw alludes here not merely to the by now familiar critical complaints against Strauss and Hofmannsthal of psychoanalytic influences, but also to another *cause célèbre* of these years, the work of Max Nordau, *Degeneration*. Published in German in 1892 and in English in 1895, this attack on modern culture and its modernist art as 'degenerate' provides the intellectual template for what becomes a catch-word of fin-de-siècle cultural thought, which we have seen swirling around Clytemnestra in particular in the reviews of Hofmannsthal and of Strauss.[173] Shaw wrote a huge rejoinder to Nordau, entitled winningly 'a degenerate's view of Nordau', which had been published in 1895 in *Liberty*, an American journal, and recently re-edited and republished in London.[174] He sarcastically attacked every aspect of Nordau's argument, but particularly his free use of a newly coined pseudo-scientific psychological vocabulary to denigrate the great Wagner's prose writings, and his equally offensive use of outmoded and deeply conservative musical

---

[172] See in general Sessa (1979); the Edinburgh performance also proved worthy of discussion in *The Nation*, as a cultural event of note.

[173] For the medical background to the idea of 'degeneration' see Harris (1989) 51–79; and in general see Pick (1989).

[174] 'A Degenerate's View of Nordau', *Liberty* (New York) XI. 6, 27 July 1895: 2–10 – with a retrospective and self-aggrandising preface, in Shaw (1908). For Nordau in context see Pick (1989) 24–7.

vocabulary to misunderstand the greatness of Wagner's musical compositions. Fifteen years on, Shaw detects a whiff of Nordau in Newman – and
once again feels the need to let fly.

Shaw's perception that resistance to Wagner first and now Strauss had
a fully nationalist basis is wholly in tune with much contemporary critical
comment on music (in a way which could easily find parallels in writing
on art and literature too) – and it was Shaw, it is less happy to recall, who
had so lavishly praised the nationalistic screed of Chamberlain. David
Irvine was a prolific and vocal supporter of Wagner and all Wagner
stood for. 'Nothing finer, more conclusive, profounder, and yet simpler
has appeared from any pen the whole century throughout', he gushes
about Wagner's essay 'On German Art and Policy' in 1899.[175] He wants
you to read it. 'We must leave this notable essay with a recommendation
to the English reader to master it, and then to ask himself, with his mixture
of Norman and Saxon blood, which of the two really lies at the root of
English greatness; which shall he cultivate, the spirit of conventionalism,
of artificiality, of ritualism, of pseudo-politeness, or of that blunt honesty
which dominates the Saxon spirit?'[176] It's not hard to see which side of the
opposition of nationalist stereotypes – the French or the German – is to
ground 'English greatness' here. So far, 'England has to depend on sport
and playing fields for its genuineness of character.'[177]   But affiliating
yourself to a Wagnerian commitment to the intellect offers a chance
of transcendence, to a new culture, a new society. If only, that is, 'the
learning and scholarship of English will permit of [Wagner's music]
being placed lucidly before the English public'.[178] What is at stake for
Irvine and Shaw in how you hear Wagner (and, later, Strauss) is your
national and cultural identity.

Newman replied with a sharp dismissal of Shaw and his bad manners,
concluding with acidly sarcastic thanks for such an educational letter 'so
rich in knowledge, so admirable in reasoning, so perfect in taste, so
urbane in style' – educative (in case you didn't get the sarcasm) 'in the
way that the language and antics of the drunken helots were held to
be useful for teaching Spartan youths the advantages of sobriety' (those
Greeks, again).[179] But Shaw continued, and now he had seen the opera.
He begins first with Gilbert Murray's *Electra* (a translation of Euripides),
the popularity of which means 'we know the poem as if it were an English
one', and he reflects on how difficult it is, despite the play's power, to

---

[175] Irvine (1899) 229.   [176] Irvine (1899) 245.   [177] Irvine (1899) 115.
[178] Irvine (1899) 245.   [179] *The Nation* VI. 24, 12 March 1910: 915.

sympathize with the matricides.[180] This is offered as a telling contrast with the Strauss/Hofmannsthal *Elektra*, which now receives the full flood of Shaw's appreciation. In the opera, he declares, Clytemnestra and Aegisthus are identified

> with everything that is evil and cruel, with all that needs must hate the highest when it sees it, with hideous domination and coercion of the higher by the baser, with the murderous rage in which the lust for a lifetime of orgiastic pleasure turns on its slaves in the torture of its disappointment and the sleepless horror and misery of its neurasthenia, to so rouse in us an overwhelming flood of wrath against it and ruthless resolution to destroy it.

What is more, so caught up in this emotion is Shaw (as we should be too, in Shaw's view) that 'even the gentlest of us could . . . twist our firm fingers in the black hair of Clytemnestra to drag back her head and leave her throat open to the stroke'. (No need for *surprise* at the undisguised glorying in this violence to the female in Victorian/Edwardian prose or in the operatic tradition.)[181] Yet even this emotional reaction to the opera is grounding for a more politicized reading (as one might expect from the leading Fabian intellectual). Shaw quickly refers to 'the European plutocracy', and in the same paragraph praises not just 'the atmosphere of malignant and cancerous evil' of the opera, but also 'the passion that must and finally can destroy that evil'. Indeed, not only is Strauss a single word weapon to cast 'against the fools and money changers who are trying to drive us into a war with Germany', but also the composer has spoken out 'with an utterly satisfying force . . . in protest against and defiance of the omnipresent villainies of our civilization'. For Shaw, Strauss' opera brilliantly and passionately exposes the corruption of contemporary civilization and the need for a forceful change in it. It's not just that Strauss' music is revolutionary. There is in the opera a clarion call to revolutionary politics.

Shaw continues with much celebration of the performance ('I owe it to Germany to profess my admiration of the noble beauty and power of Frau Fassbender's Elektra' – he was, of course, pilloried during and after the war for what were regarded as his treacherously pro-German views), and ends with a final slur against Newman, and an encouragement to all readers to join in 'the enthusiastic gratitude and admiration of the European republic, one and indivisible, of those who understand the highest art'. Once again, Europe (and Germany) is set against England,

---

[180] *The Nation* VI. 25, 19 March 1910: 969.
[181] See especially Bronfen (1992); Clément (1988).

as Shaw demands that you see the *Elektra* as a political comment on society, and your own reaction to the opera within such (European, national, cultural) politics. This was not a *wholly* odd intellectual reaction to Greek tragedy in Edwardian London: in 1907 Granville Barker had staged with Gilbert Murray Euripides' *Trojan Women* which had been seen by some as a very pointed comment on the Boer war; a production of *Medea* prompted responses led by the Suffragette question; even the tragedy of *Elektra* itself has a spare performance history which reveals a continual politicization in a less marked manner.[182] Shaw, however, was one of the country's most influential cultural critics holding forth in the most polemical way about a truly major theatrical and cultural event. It was making a very strong claim indeed for seeing *Elektra* as a political document.

Certainly, his piece prompted a reaction in precisely these terms. Newman wrote a further long, self-exculpatory letter in which he derided Shaw's 'enthusiastic fantasia' on Hofmannsthal, whose play 'to my mind, and the mind of many others, is . . . a most unpleasant example of that crudity and physical violence that a certain school of modern German artists mistakes for intellectual and emotional power'.[183] And he mocked Shaw's assumption that the audience's applause proved his own aesthetic and political contentions about the opera ('Oh, Bernard, Bernard, has it come to this?'). But, to my mind, more significant than this continuing bickering between grandees[184] are the other correspondents on the letters' pages, which comment on Shaw's politicized sense of the opera and its audience. One correspondent wonders: 'Was the recent furore on Strauss nights really informed by the spirit of social democracy?'[185] Another mocks the association of 'social democracy' and music; and produces a rather snappy *reductio ad absurdum* mocking what he imagines to be Shaw's political understanding of the opera, culminating with 'we [the audience] rejoiced when old Standard Oil went stupidly to his doom, ushered, appropriately, by Elektra, with a torch'. 'Seriously, I ask Mr Shaw to reconsider. What proportion of the boxes, stalls, circle and gallery are really so dissatisifed with things as they are? How many of them are Fabians, or even anti-Veto men?' The readers of *The Nation* recognized Shaw's political agenda, specified it through his well-known

---

[182] This sentence was made possible by the excellent work of Edith Hall: Hall (1999a), Hall (1999b), Hall (2000).

[183] *The Nation* VI. 26, 26 March, 1910: 1000–1001.

[184] The row blew up again in 1913, see Newman (1962) 139–62.

[185] This and following quotations from readers' letters are from the letters' column of *The Nation* VI. 28, 9 April 1910: 54–5.

left-wing stance, and rejected it. But the Editor – in a very rare gesture indeed – added an editorial comment to the letters' column: 'But when we see guilt and shame on the stage, do we not fit its exposition to our own most acute sense of what is wrong within – with ourselves – and without – with the world?' The editor published his reader's dissenting voices, but felt the need to reassert the inevitability – in his eyes – of a *political* reading of any staging of guilt and shame – for all that he does not follow necessarily Shaw's particular analysis. Shaw's strident opinion-making, in the wake of a general election, and in the midst of a long-running row about the English constitution (hence the correspondent's comment on 'anti-Veto men'), and in the highly politicized pages of *The Nation*, worked to put *Elektra* in a frame that went beyond artistic issues of degeneracy, in search of the broadest politics of revolution. In the force-field of Shaw, *Elektra* became an arena of political demonstration.

V

In November 1910, a further, less publicly heralded event also changed the course of Greek tragedy in England. The chancellor granted a licence for the first time for the performance of Sophocles' *Oedipus the King* – and on the same day he also allowed a licence for Beecham to produce Strauss' *Salome* with its script by Wilde. (Wilde's play in English had been banned in 1893 and would not get a licence until 1931.) As Fiona Mackintosh has observed, it is extraordinary to reflect that a classical text so familiar to generations of schoolboys should have been banned from production for so many years – especially on the grounds that it might 'prove injurious' and lead 'to a great number of plays being written . . . appealing to a vitiated public taste solely in the cause of indecency'.[186] It made little difference that the *Oedipus* had been performed in university productions or that the famous staging of Mounet-Sully had run in Paris for several years (where it had been seen by many of the major players of this chapter from Raymond Duncan to Sigmund Freud). Even so, it was a powerful public campaign rather than a change of heart which led to the licence being granted.

Salome was produced immediately. (The censor had required specific cuts in the text and attended the first performance at Covent Garden, but, as Beecham wickedly recalled, no cuts were actually made, and the censor – perhaps not quite up to the German – made no comment.)

---

[186] Mackintosh (1995): quotation of Sir John Howe from p.1.

Oedipus was not performed until 1912, however, when the celebrated production of Reinhardt came to England to be performed in Covent Garden with a translation into English by Gilbert Murray, rather than Hofmannsthal's German translation which Reinhardt had used in Berlin and throughout Europe. This production has been called 'the most influential production of Greek tragedy in the nineteenth century',[187] and its huge crowd scenes, strongly ritualized action and powerfully physical Oedipus indeed have proved a remarkably stimulating and much imitated conception of Greek drama. The English company toured the production for many years in Britain, as did the German company in Europe. Yet what strikes me most is the immense difference between the response to this production and the response to the *Elektra*.

Reinhardt's production opened on 15 January 1912. Once again, by chance, Viola Tree opened the week before (11 January) playing Eurydice in *Orpheus in the Underworld* – and the reviewer in *The Times* fondly recalled her Iphigeneia of previous years in praising her beauty and grace. The same night a dinner was held by the Albert Committee to honour Professor Reinhardt, at which Sir Herbert Beerbohm Tree proposed the toast to German Literature and Music. Throughout January, the letters pages of *The Times* are again taken up with another outburst of rowing over the compulsory Greek question. This time, following a report from the Classical Association published on 2 January, the focus of debate became the Average Boy and what he can and should learn at school. Many distinguished educationalists offered strongly voiced opinions; and two women even wrote on the subject, both commenting on the need for girls too to have a more varied education than just Greek and Latin. One letter is signed 'a woman', the other 'a dunce': no (grand) names or strutted titles for female correspondents . . . The major papers all carried long reviews of the play, almost exclusively full of praise for the effectiveness of the production.

The few dissenting notes largely concentrated on whether the emotional and physical force of the production was suitably Greek enough. (Not enough 'serenity'.) This prompted Gilbert Murray to write a long letter to *The Times* defending the production in fascinating terms.[188] Murray supports Reinhardt in a manner which shows strikingly his own intellectual commitments to anthropological study, ritual and even Nietzsche. 'By "Greeks"', he declares, 'we normally mean classical or

---

[187] Walton ed. (1987) 305. See also Styan (1982), though it is a rather thin account.
[188] *Times* 23 Jan. 1912 – from which the subsequent quotations come.

fifth-century Greek. Now the Oedipus story is not Greek in that sense. It is pre-Greek: it belongs to the dark region of pre-Hellenic barbarism.' Consequently, Reinhardt is intellectually justified in turning to the age of Oedipus rather than the age of Sophocles. 'Professor Reinhardt was frankly pre-Hellenic, partly Cretan, partly Mycenean, partly – to my great admiration – simply savage.' The very elements that so provoked with *Elektra* receive now the blessing of the maverick Regius Professor of Greek. He admits that he would himself have liked to see a bit 'more beauty, more depth, more religious mystery', but insists that Reinhardt's production 'has proved itself: it stands on its own feet, something vital, magnificent, unforgettable'.

In comparison with the scandal, heat and rowing over *Elektra*, Murray's quiet praise of the savage – which closes the debate – indicates how quickly cultural crisis can be diffused into other areas. It is not as though nationalism, gender, the representation of Greece, the imagery of the savage and ritual stop being deeply contested concerns. But a Greek play, banned by the censor only two years earlier, in a revolutionary German production (only two years before the war), now produced little fuss and much praise. Granville Barker even wrote to *The Times* to complain about how little hullabaloo there was, despite this victory over the fiendish censor . . .

Murray's translations were produced throughout the war years: the *Trojan Women* had particular political impact.[189] Strauss became the grand old man of German music living through both world wars. When he was finally cleared by the Allies in their Denazification programme, he was flown to London immediately after the war. At the BBC he conducted a performance of – of course – *Elektra* (a recording of which is still in the BBC archives). I do not know with what irony or with what political understandings *that* performance was heard.

VI

If theatrical perfomance is to be studied as an event, or performance history to be written, it is necessary, I think, to try to uncover the multiple frames that make an occasion a cultural moment (as I have been doing here): the full grammar of contemporary performances, the range of competing intellectual and social understandings, the varied media and genres of commentary and opinion formation. The excitement of that

[189] Mackintosh (1997).

first night was only very partially a question of what happened on stage, or of the composer's musical and dramatic development. The intricate way in which different elements of different cultures, different forms of representation and response, different life stories, interrelate and overlap to give the event of *Elektra* its particular significance is one generalizable point I hope will be taken from this chapter. There is so much more to understanding the staging of a play than a grammar of exits and entrances and gestures. But what concerns me more than any method-ological harangue is the specific way that Strauss' London opening also reveals how understanding the Greekness of this rewrite of Sophocles has been framed through – and by – modern national(ist) expression.

For the English debate about Strauss in London stages a crucial fracture in the response to *Elektra*. German-speaking audiences of Hofmannsthal and Strauss were challenged by a view of the Greek world which cut away at the myth of a Greek origin of German greatness. The resources of high culture were aimed against the postulates of a national, cultural identity. The tyranny of Greece over the German imagination was being turned against itself in this story of a degenerate tyranny, assaulted. Hofmannsthal's play and Strauss' opera – with their psycho-logical, intellectual, musical modernism – dismayed, thrilled, upset, and provoked an audience for whom education, elite education, depended on achievement in classical learning, as much as the genealogies of cul-ture required the glory that was Greece to epitomize the highest ideals of an idealistic nationalism.

The response in England, however, was different. Despite the power-ful role of classics in British education, and the wide circulation of the privileged images of an idealized classicism in Victorian and Edwardian media, none the less the engagement of Englishness in the Greek world lacked the genealogical lures of a German commitment. Greekness sim-ply could not engage the same level of nationalist fervour in England. Indeed, as we will see in the next chapter, it had become increasingly possible over the nineteenth century to argue that an Englishman's edu-cation had little need of Greek. Even the much earlier fervour for Greek independence which Shelley and others fostered, although it could claim famously 'We are all Greeks', also quickly added 'The modern Greek is the descendant of those glorious beings whom the imagination almost refuses to figure to itself as belonging to our kind.'[190] The formation

---

[190] Both quotations are from Shelley's preface to 'Hellas'. See below pp. 183–6 for discussion and bibliography on this issue.

of Englishness, the cultural agenda and work of which so dominates eighteenth- and nineteenth-century societies, discovers its foundation in an Anglo-Saxon heritage ('Kentish man'[191]) and does not seek to locate its particularity and strengths in the glory that was Greece. The Englishman who wished to find roots in Greece had to construct a genealogy via the Teutonic race (as Chamberlain had done), and thus claim close kinship with Germany. In 1910, under the pressure of the political situation which was to culminate in the war of 1914, this could no longer be a simple or popular gesture. Where Thomas Arnold, say, back in the 1840s could look to Germany as 'the land of our Saxon and Teutonic forefathers' in order to ground an integral English link with Greece[192] – even then a polemical gesture – for Newman and other reviewers 'Teutonic' is a term of insult. Although both German and English critics could abhor what was being done to Sophocles, it did not mean quite the same thing.

What is more, the English response to Strauss was constantly articulated as an English response to a German import – whether it is praise from Shaw for specifically German art, or Newman's recognition of 'Teutonic overstatement' (much as Isadora Duncan noted how much more seriously the German critics treated dance than did the American). English responses to the opera *rehearsed* the difference between Englishness and Germanness. A *performance* of cultural difference, cultural affiliation. (So, British critics began, in typical Empire mode, by rather sniffily observing the response of their American counterparts before the row turned more focusedly towards Europe.) Furthermore, Shaw and his correspondents were arguing about the degree to which the play engaged its audience in contemporary politics, even contemporary Fabian concerns. 'The politics of drama' here takes on a narrowly conceived focus (in a way which is not seen in Germany or America). As Matthew Arnold – a figure of great importance in the later Victorian construction of an ideal of Greekness[193] – wrote of his compatriots' intellectual practices (with his customary sting): 'The Englishman has been called a political animal and he values what is political and practical so much that ideas easily become objects of dislike in his eyes.'[194] Arnold would have turned the English political response to the artwork, the Intellect, of Strauss into grist for his mill. In responding to Strauss in a political manner, the English were, in Arnold's terms, being English.

---

[191] See Young (1995) for 'Kentish man'.
[192] CPW III. 268. We will see his son's admiration for Germany in the next chapter.
[193] See e.g. Baldick (1983) 18–58.
[194] Arnold (1962) 268.

The event of *Elektra* in London in 1910 shows not only how a Greek tragedy could become the expression of a crisis in cultural identity, but also how this crisis takes on different – and *interactive* – forms in Germany and England. Whether you start from the scandal of wearing sandals in New York or the heavyweight clashes of intellectual debate, from the trendiness of dance or the politics of national affiliation in the shadow of the first world war, the opera and its Greekness becomes a lightning-rod for intense issues of national and cultural essence. The fight over the image of Greece is also a fight about Englishness and Germanness. How you respond to Strauss' degenerate Elektra says a lot about who you are.

CHAPTER FOUR

Who knows Greek?

Hofmannsthal's modernism set out to attack an image of a pure and glorious Greece. Yet for a hundred years this image had already been the subject of contestation, qualification and debate (as well as idealization and fantasy). The dismissiveness of modernist rhetoric – or the ease with which 'Victorian' is still used as a catch-all term – conceals the far more difficult and interesting work that went into the construction of nineteenth-century Hellenism(s). In this chapter, I will take the question of what it means to say 'I know Greek' in order to see something of the polemical debates around Hellenism in the work of poets and politicians, journalists and academics, educationalists and scientists. Both Lucian and, as we will see in the next chapter, Plutarch were drastically re-evaluated in the years around the end of the nineteenth century. It was not only the modernist assault which caused this, but a longer and slower set of academic and political developments. It is these developments which this chapter is intended to explore.

I 1816, THE DRUG ADDICT AND THE PISS-A-BED POET

In 1816, Thomas De Quincey was already deeply addicted to opium. He was living in obsessive and solitary lethargy in Dove Cottage in the Lake District (with typical self-dramatization, in the very house where his poetic hero, Wordsworth had lived). In *Confessions of an English Opium Eater*, the publishing sensation of 1821, he recalls a terrifying encounter from that time. One day, he narrates, 'a Malay knocked at my door'.[1] (De Quincey duly notes that it was rather baffling to find a Malay in the English mountains, but conjectures he is on his way to a sea-port forty miles away.) The maid-servant who opened the door had 'never seen an Asiatic dress of any sort; his turban, therefore, confounded her

[1] De Quincey (1985) 55.

not a little'.[2] She ran to get the master, and De Quincey was faced by a tableau that fixated him, he says, more than any theatrical scene: the Malay's turban and dirty white trousers set against the dark panelling of the cottage kitchen; the English girl's expression of 'simple awe . . . as she gazed at the tiger-cat before her':

A more striking picture could not be imagined than the beautiful English face of the girl, and its exquisite fairness, together with her erect and independent attitude, contrasted with the sallow and bilious skin of the Malay, enamelled or veneered with mahogany, by marine air, his small, fierce restless eyes, thin lips, slavish gesture and adoration. Half-hidden by the ferocious looking Malay was a little child from a neighbouring cottage who . . . was . . . gazing upwards at the turban and the fiery eyes beneath it, while with one hand he caught at the dress of the young woman for protection.[3]

The 'racial, sexual and social paranoia'[4] of this tableau is acute. The girl whose face and attitude embody an Englishness which is 'exquisite', 'erect' and 'independent' – national characteristics, each, of course – is also the servant who with simple awe expects her master to be able to communicate with – to order – the outsider, the stranger, who is, to her, a 'tiger-cat' – a ferocious and exotic animal. The Malay's face is like wood (burnished in an Eastern style), with features not only thin, small, fierce, but also 'slavish' – thoroughly unEnglish. His appearance is not only bilious and sallow – the colours of Eastern corruption – but also fiery, ferocious and threatening. (There are no contradictions in paranoia.) The child – thus – needs protection from the turban and the tiger, the dehumanized danger from outside.

So how does De Quincey deal with the situation?

By quoting Homer.

I addressed him with some lines from the *Iliad*: considering that of such languages as I possessed, Greek, in point of longitude, came geographically nearest to an oriental one. He worshipped me in a most devout manner, and replied in what I supposed was Malay.[5]

Homer's epic tale of how the West first defeated the East saves the day for De Quincey. The Malay offers the Englishman the obeisance of devout worship: the *Iliad*, once again, is a cultural talisman that *works*. (It doesn't really matter which lines were recited: the Trojan war always tells of the defeat of the East.) When the Malay leaves, however, De Quincey, in order to lighten his long journey, gives him a guest-gift of

---

[2] De Quincey (1985) 56. [3] *Ibid.* [4] Leask (1992) 210. [5] De Quincey (1985) 57.

a large piece of opium, enough 'to kill three dragoons and their horses'[6] –
which the guest shockingly eats with delight in one gulp. Acute dismay
prompted by the thought of the Malay dying on the road – though no
corpse is ever found – feeds into De Quincey's later nightmares, a ghostly
and vengeful return. From the *Iliad*, then, to the *Odyssey*'s archetypal scene
of the false exchange of guest-gifts, of drugs that change you . . .

This truly strange scene of Homer-quoting has been well prepared for
already in *The Confessions*. (The literary affiliation to its great predecessor,
Augustine's *Confessions*, encourages you to see the child as father to the
man: the confessional mode structures tale-telling as self-formation.)
De Quincey begins his life-story by announcing how distinguished he
was for his 'classical attainments' at school, especially in Greek:

> At thirteen I wrote Greek with ease; at fifteen my command of the language
> was so great that I not only composed Greek verses in lyric metres but could
> converse in Greek fluently and without embarrassment – an accomplishment
> which I have not once met with in any scholar of my times.[7]

He explains that this fluency came from his (quite extraordinary) practice of *ex tempore* oral translation of the newspaper into classical Greek,
and he boasts that his teacher declared 'that boy could harangue an
Athenian mob, better than you or I could address an English one'.[8] The
star pupil, however, in turn despised his teachers' level of knowledge, and
resolved to run away from school – with a copy of Wordsworth in one
pocket, a volume of Euripides in the other. As he wanders, Odysseus-like,
in Wales, he took a room with a landlady who had been in service with a
bishop. A few days later, she pointedly tells De Quincey that the bishop
has just warned her against travelling 'swindlers'. De Quincey is moved
to an (epic) 'tumult of indignation' at this apparent imputation against
his character:

> I was, indeed, greatly irritated at the bishop's having suggested any grounds of
> suspicion, however remotely, against a person he had never seen: and I thought
> of letting him know my mind in Greek: which, at the same time that it would
> furnish some presumption that I was no swindler, would also (I hoped) compel
> the bishop to reply in the same language; in which case I doubted not to make
> it appear that if I were not so rich as his lordship I was a far better Grecian.[9]

A wonderful adolescent gesture of outrage, this, to write to the unsus-
pecting bishop in Greek! He really wants to let him know . . . At school

---

[6] De Quincey (1985) 57.   [7] De Quincey (1985) 6.
[8] De Quincey (1985) 7.   [9] De Quincey (1985) 13–14.

De Quincey defined himself and motivated his escape through his knowledge of Greek, and now when his character is threatened, he seeks to
prove himself by displaying his qualities as a Grecian – in order to show
the honesty of his nature (no swindlers know Greek), and, he hopes, to
humiliate the bishop in an imagined battle of Greek. The exchange may
display the pompous self-assertion of the adolescent, but it also shows
how De Quincey determines and defends his self through his knowledge of Greek. When he faces down the threat of the Malay with the
Iliad, De Quincey is again buttressing his social identity with his classical
attainments.

Not even the *Iliad*, however, could make the Malay leave De Quincey,
finally. Opium gives you strange dreams, and the Malay, returning in
the dark, opens in the Englishman a full flood of night monsters – night
monsters that reveal how De Quincey's Greek-quoting encounter with
foreignness must also be seen within a wider nationalist and imperialist
frame:

The Malay has been a fearful enemy for months. I have been every night,
through his means, transported into Asian scenes. The causes of my horror
lie deep . . . Southern Asia . . . is the seat of awful images and associations . . . No
man can pretend that the wild, barbarous and capricious superstitions of Africa,
or of savage tribes elsewhere affect him the way he is affected by the ancient,
monumental, cruel and elaborate religion of Indostan . . . I am terrified by the
modes of life, by the manners, and the barrier of utter abhorrence, and want
of sympathy, placed between us, by feelings deeper than I can analyse. I could
sooner live with lunatics or brute animals. All this and much more than I can say
or have time to say, the reader must enter into before he can comprehend the
unimaginable horror which these dreams of Oriental images and mythological
tortures impressed upon me.[10]

No stately pleasure domes of Kubla Khan for the 'furious jingoist'
De Quincey.[11] He knows the causes of these psychological torments
lie deep, too deep to analyse, but to modern readers at least his
dreams have a more historically specific socio-political frame than Freud
(or De Quincey) might lead you to expect. His geographical and anthropological horrors represent 'the fantasia of an imperial history characterized (at its worst) by the opium wars and the furious reaction to the
Indian Mutiny'[12] – a fantasia, that is, orchestrated by cruel commercial

---

[10] De Quincey (1985) 72–3. See the fine analyses of Leask (1992) 209–228; Barrell (1991) 74–6;
and also Clej (1995).
[11] Barrell (1991) 50.
[12] Leask (1992) 217, whose account I follow here. See also and more generally Makdishi (1998).

manipulation, dependent on the violent, vengeful, fearful control of subjected peoples.

The dream, like so much of De Quincey's writing, is funded by the language, images and uncertainties of British imperialist activity in the East.
The armchair imperialist asks you to tour the empire of savage threat
to prove the supreme dangers of Asia – dangers summed up in the expected categories of religion and social manners, and expressed in the
heightened language of the sublime – 'utter abhorrence', 'unimaginable
horror'. De Quincey is certainly not alone in this panicky view of the extreme nature of the Malay in particular. Edward Trelawny, Shelley's
friend, 'a flamboyant and mendacious adventurer', is typical when he
calls Malays 'the most fierce, treacherous, ignorant and inflexible of
barbarians':[13] the image of the 'frantic excesses' of the Malay's uncon-
trollable violence, screaming 'amuck' ('vengeance') and brutally slaugh-
tering his enemies was a special bogey-man of British imperialist anxiety.
The Malay is indeed running amuck in De Quincey's imagination.

What I find especially interesting, however, is that De Quincey's
rhetoric wants to draw the reader into sharing in his torments: you 'must
enter into' De Quincey's thought world, if you wish to comprehend
(what would otherwise be) his 'unimaginable horror'. Your sympathy is
in contrast with the 'barrier', the 'want of sympathy', 'placed between'
De Quincey and the East. This barrier, though, is a precarious divide.
The Malay is inside the writer (like the opium, imported from the East
and ingested). And the East lures the mind: 'the mere antiquity of Asiatic
things . . . is so impressive' that 'even Englishmen . . . cannot but shudder
at the mystic sublimity' of 'the cradle of the human race'.[14] It is not merely
abhorrence but sublime awe that underlies the power of the Orient
over the imagination of the English opium eater. 'I stood loathing and
fascinated.' That 'and', that 'fascination', undoes the barrier's protection. He can't just loathe . . . 'The great anxiety of De Quincey's dream
is . . . precisely one of *orientalization*'[15] – the threat of cultural miscegena-
tion or pollution that needs, but cannot fully maintain its boundaries, its
'barrier of utter abhorrence'. The rhetorical sympathies of the *English*
opium eater *performs* the uneasy construction of a national identity, and
wants to make you, the reader, complicit with it.

The quotation of Homer, then, marks a battleline between East and
West – a battleline defined by contemporary British imperialism. The

---

[13] Trelawny's comment is quoted by Leask (1992) 209; the description of Trelawny is Abrams ed.
(1979) 509. On Trelawny, the 'incurable romancer', see St Clair (1977).
[14] De Quincey (1985) 73.　　　[15] Leask (1992) 228.

encounter with the Malay provides a hinge between De Quincey's self-defining knowledge of Greek and his self-defining Englishness. There may be a certain sardonic distance of retrospection in De Quincey's tales of heroic Greek learning, but that self-awareness and humour should not prevent you from seeing how 'knowing Greek' is part of De Quincey's self-formation. (Opium's exposure of the vulnerability of the self makes De Quincey's self-buttressing acutely vivid.) De Quincey, not least by virtue of his impoverished wandering in Wales and his opium-fed solitude in Grasmere, is not exactly the typical writer engaged in a typical way in social life, but he is still articulating – defending, displaying – a social identity which threads a privileged knowledge of Greek into his cultural standing. 'Knowing Greek' is blazoned as a determining element of his self-representation – along with his connections to the literary lions of the day like Coleridge and Wordsworth, and his acute sense of a British imperial role. The self-proclaimed outsider and wanderer carries the identification tags of a solid citizen, and it is this tension between social propriety and transgression which helps give his story its scandalous attraction. (The story of a working-class De Quincey numbing poverty with laudanum would not have the same frisson.) 'Knowing Greek' is here fully imbricated with attitudes to class, gender, literary politics, national character, social roles and their transgression. Being Grecian is a fundamental element of De Quincey's cultural identity.

It is this which makes the far from typical De Quincey an exemplary figure for the question of this chapter: what does it mean to say 'I know Greek'?

It should not be surprising that a literary figure of the 1820s expresses a cultural identity through a self-conscious Hellenism. It is in this decade, after all, that Byron dies in Greece and becomes an immortal symbol of the fight for Greek freedom (despite the cynical manipulation of that image from the beginning by different Greek leaders and by Byron himself).[16] It is the decade in which Shelley, too, dies by water – after proclaiming his rallying cry to the Greek cause that 'we are all Greeks'.[17] With less sense of the grand political gesture of setting to sea, Thomas Love Peacock went down to the river – for a boat trip, taking with him

---

[16] See e.g. Butler (1981) (for general background); Webb ed. (1982); Constantine (1984); Clarke ed. (1989); Lambropoulos (1993); Webb (1993); Ferris (2000), all with further bibliography; also the earlier work of St Clair (1972); Buxton (1978); Spencer (1954); (1959); Spender (1924). For other materials see notes 25 and 35 below.

[17] See especially Wallace (1997).

to read his copy of Nonnus, the late Greek epic writer whose fame consists largely in not being read.[18] Leigh Hunt – to complete the troika of closest friends, Shelley, Peacock, Hunt – also spoke out for the cause of Greek freedom in 1821: 'If I know anything at all of the Greeks, we can hardly help being reminded of them at every turn of our lives. We can hardly open a book – we cannot look at a schoolboy – we cannot use a term of science but we read of the Greeks.'[19] A turn to an idealized image of Greece is a pervasive, life-long gesture of the dominant figures of the first quarter of the nineteenth century, and 'Romantic Hellenism' has rightly been seen as a central route through which a generation of English writers defined themselves aesthetically and politically in contrast to a previous generation of eighteenth-century neo-classical artists (who in turn defined themselves against the classicizing political theorists of the seventeenth century . . .).

It is probably worth stressing here – even if it can only be in the most general terms – just how varied and complex the symptoms of this 'Greekomania' (as Leigh Hunt called it) are. Despite the close links of friends like Shelley, Peacock, Hunt and Byron, there is no one group of Romantic Hellenists – it spreads across Europe and across different media – and despite a repeated idealism in the construction of the image of Greece, there is no one agenda for Romantic Hellenism. Classical antiquity itself, 'far from being a transparently available source of meaning . . . became, rather, a cluster of potentialities, a maze of fictions, a frame of reference whose edges (limits) remain unstable and blurred'.[20] So, at the level of political activism and revolutionary debate, Hellenism could signal – for a Shelley or a Byron – a 'conscious opposition to prevailing social and political moralities'[21] – an ideal of true freedom and of a society from which modern Britain could derive 'her admiration and her adoption of freedom of government, of liberality of sentiments and of patriotic enthusiasm'.[22] A (Greek) flag under which to march. In aesthetic terms, Hellenism discovered in Greece ideals of literary and artistic form, the models of excellence to inspire the striving artist: Greece became 'the reference point for all subsequent art and literature'.[23] Yet the unattainable perfection of the lost past repeatedly drives the artist to anguish over 'the ambivalent and opaque relation between ancient and

---

[18] Diary for 7 July – 26 August 1818 – with full list of his reading.
[19] *The Examiner* 7 October 1821.
[20] Aske (1985) 33. See also Webb (1993) 148–51, and, for good comments on the *opposition* to classics, 170–6.
[21] Aske (1985) 3.   [22] Leigh Hunt *The Examiner* 14 October 1821.   [23] Ferris (2000) 2.

modern, the difficulties encountered by [the artist] as he endeavours to retrieve the past':[24] the attempt to hear the silent voices on a Grecian urn, those sweeter unheard melodies. The aesthetic and the political can scarcely be kept separate, however, when Shelley writes 'Hellas' and 'Prometheus Unbound' as clarion calls to political action, or even when the renegade Byron becomes a famous poet – overnight, as he tells it – with the publication of 'Childe Harold's Pilgrimage', his poetic journey through Italy and Greece.

The purchase and display of the Elgin marbles in London (also in 1816) enshrines this fascination with the Hellenic ideal (for all that their decayed forms could not quite present the very perfection that Winckelmann's hugely influential account of ancient sculpture demanded).[25] The masterpiece of Greek art – and there was very little Greek art to be seen in Europe – was now for the English centrally sited in the capital of Empire. Shelley sums up one strand of response with his vividly polemical assertiveness: Greek sculptures, he declares, should not be taken as models for 'rules and canons of beauty' (as so many contemporary critics did), nor for 'proportions of anatomy' (as academic artists demanded), but rather they are models 'for illustration of the poetical expression of spirit and mind, light and thought'.[26] Shelley requires that what you see in Greek sculpture is a poetry of 'spirit and mind, light and thought': Greece is the inspirational model for the most profoundly held values of the intellectual idealist (whereas Byron sneered at Elgin's 'Misshapen monuments and maim'd antiques').[27] Shelley shows in exemplary fashion how the images of Greece could be turned to different and competing (aesthetic, political, social, moral) agendas. It is this that makes 'Romantic Hellenism' so pervasive and so complex a phenomenon. Yet for both Shelley and Byron – for all the cynical twists and misplaced hopes of their stories – it was something to die for.

Even from such a sketch of English Romantic Hellenism, it should be clear why it is a culturally charged moment when De Quincey represents himself as an ace Grecian. It is an image that has immediate literary and social purchase, and it is evidently significant that the intellectual who depicts his social and psychological descent so vividly should stress his formation as an educated and cultured individual in this way through

---

[24] Aske (1985) 33.
[25] The marbles arrived earlier, but there was much negotiation before they were bought in 1816 (St Clair (1996) 245–60) and displayed for the public in January 1817 (St Clair (1996) 261–80). See also Wallace (1997) 151–62, Webb (1993) 162–6; and Larrabee (1943).
[26] Shelley, quoted in Larrabee (1943) 193.   [27] See St Clair (1996) 180–200.

Greek studies. Yet what does strike a more particular and outlandish note is his insistence on his exceptional abilities with the ancient Greek language – his skill in turning the newspaper instantly and orally into classical Greek. It will need a little more argument to specify the import of *this* claim.

By way of contrast with De Quincey's Homeric performance, take a glance at the first great poem of Keats, his sonnet written also in 1816, 'On First Looking into Chapman's Homer'; a poem which dramatizes – and exposes – an engagement with Homer, by a poet who does not know Greek. The title is immediately provocative, especially in the light of the obsessive reading and re-reading of Greek and Latin texts that is such a common representation of cultured life through the nineteenth century. The provocation isn't merely that Keats is reading (just) a translation, but that he is just 'looking into' it, not reading or learning it: the glance and not the studied gaze. What form of attention is Keats holding up to your scrutiny?

> Much have I travell'd in the realms of gold
>> And many goodly states and kingdoms seen;
>> Round many western islands have I been
> Which bards in fealty to Apollo hold.

Keats came from a lower-class and poorly educated background, but 'even if we were ignorant of Keats' social disadvantages, his fulsome claim to literary ease would give us pause'[28] – not least for the obvious and disconcerting echoes of the beginning of the *Odyssey* itself in the triple repetition of 'much'/'many' and the language of travel. Keats is set up as the Odyssean man who knows, the master of words. The grand assertion of *much* travelling through *many* kingdoms of golden poetry, Apollo's realm, classical poetry – should the erudite poet boast of his erudition or just display it? – asserts a poetic authority in the richest of self-promoting terms. But this claim is a foil to a particular ignorance, and a moment of transformation:

> Oft of one wide expanse had I been told
>> That deep-brow'd Homer ruled as his demesne;
>> Yet did I never breathe its pure serene
> Till I heard Chapman speak out loud and bold.

Keats has – for all his journeys through poetry – only 'been told' about Homer, a basic schoolboy text. He has had no contact with the source of

---

[28] Levinson (1988) 12.

poetic grandeur, the origin of epic. He did not 'breathe' the air of Homer: there is no natural absorption, no lifegiving inspiration, no growing up with this poetry for Keats. This barest of second-hand experiences of that foundational text is now displaced by hearing Chapman 'speak out loud and bold'. Charles Clarke, a former schoolteacher of Keats, recalls one evening introducing Chapman to Keats by reading aloud the description of Odysseus shipwrecked on the coast of the Phaeacians, and he recalls Keats staring at him with awe-struck absorption. The sonnet was written that same night and sent to Clarke in the morning post.[29] Keats has not read Chapman, but only 'heard' him spoken out loud. 'Looking into' is itself a blind for a more passive enjoyment.

The experience is transformative, however, of Keats' emotional world:

> Then felt I like some watcher of the skies
> When a new planet swims into his ken;
> Or like stout Cortez when with eagle eyes
> He star'd at the Pacific – and all his men
> Look'd at each other with a wild surmise –
> Silent upon a peak in Darien.

Keats dramatizes his reaction before the discovery of Chapman as passive and silent wonder. Cortez – this story is actually of Balboa in the history books – keeps his men from the peak while he 'star'd' his fill with 'eagle eyes' – unlike the glance of the poet who only 'looks into' Chapman. Cortez can stare at the Pacific – the sea of poetry, as it were – but his men 'look'd at each other with wild surmise'. It was Keats, previously barred from 'the serene' of Homer, who stared at Clarke reading. Keats may liken himself to Cortez, but he has enacted the role of the men, silent before a figure who can open the way to the Pacific/the serene.

This poem, as Levinson puts it, '*signifies* [Keats'] alienation from his *materia poetica*'.[30] For all his reading, he has been kept from Homer; then Homer is discovered – except it is in Chapman's translation, a translation which he 'looks into' rather than studies or reads (and which was read to him). It produces, finally, an image of the silent poet – silenced by these pasts, newly seen – as his own position shifts between stout explorer and wildly surmising men, blocked from the place from which to stare. Keats, the traveller in golden realms, the explorer and discoverer, dramatizes his displacement.

[29] An often told story, see e.g. Lowell (1924) I, 176–9.
[30] Levinson (1988) 15.

Two years later, in 1818, Keats wrote to Reynolds 'I long to feast on old Homer . . . If you understood Greek and would read me passages, now and then, explaining their meaning, 'twould be, from its mustiness, perhaps a greater luxury than reading the thing one's self.'[31] Keats is still imagining an encounter with Homer and even luxuriating in the possibility of a fragmentary and indirect experience of the mustiness of antiquity (for his self). In the same year, he wrote a sonnet to Homer, that begins:

> Standing aloof in giant ignorance,
> Of thee I hear and of the Cyclades,
> As one who sits ashore and longs perchance
> To visit dolphin coral in deep seas.

His aloofness is an epic grandeur of not knowing, a 'giant ignorance' of Greek. He cannot make the sea-journey (of a Byron or Shelley) and can only sit ashore (a classic Greek image of uselessness and alienation) and long to visit the mysteries of those deep oceans. When he does visit that icon of the Greek spirit, the Elgin marbles, in 1817, he again dramatizes his own feelings of insufficiency in a sonnet. 'My spirit is too weak', it opens (a self-conscious aetiolation of the masterful response of a Shelley). He is reduced to 'a most dizzy pain' by the 'Grecian grandeur' wasted by time to a 'shadow of a magnitude', and heavily worries about his inevitably belated and incapable talents: 'I must die / Like a sick eagle looking at the sky.' Cortez's 'eagle eye' contrasts neatly with the sick eagle who can only look towards the unobtainable sky, failing, once again, to reach the serene. (Just looking.) Yet – and 'Yet . . . ' marks this transition in the poem – '. . . 'tis a gentle luxury to weep . . . ' The luxury of a poet's warm and wet emotion is still produced and performed, the poet's subjectivity, his desire and longing, anatomized intently. The idealism of Hellenism may leave all artists aspiring to an unobtainable perfection, but not knowing Greek becomes a special blockage and resource for the 'voluptuous feebleness'[32] of the Hellenizing Keats.

Keats is profoundly influenced by Hellenism, but it is a Hellenism without knowing Greek, which marks him out in terms of class and social standing, and which he himself dramatizes as a source of inspirational anxiety in his self-representing sonnets of poetic vocation. It is, however, also the response to this alienated poetry which is especially fascinating

---

[31] Keats *Letters* I, 239, Feb. 1818.
[32] Levinson (1988) 250. See also Aske (1985) 8–37.

to me, especially with regard to understanding De Quincey's boasts of Greek mastery.

Much contemporary criticism was hostile and explicitly so in terms of class and education – aggressively expressed as a failure of masculinity. Marjorie Levinson puts together some memorable remarks of Byron on Keats' work – 'a sort of mental masturbation – frigging his *imagination*'; 'Johnny Keats's *piss a bed* poetry'; 'the drivelling idiotism of the Manikin'; 'it is in their finery that the new under school are most *vulgar*' – which she sums up with: 'By his three way equation, linking self-reflection, masturbation and middle-class acquisition and display, Byron clarifies the social offensiveness of Keats's poetry.'[33] ('Clarify' is a delightfully dead-pan term for Byron's violent dismissiveness.) Keats' displays of his lack of Greek education easily fall under the rubric of 'social offensiveness'. Byron himself – *Lord* Byron, educated at Harrow and Cambridge – comfortably mocks the 'drill'd dull lesson, forced down word by word' of his own, proper school learning, and can wittily despise the college examination which rewards a student who 'Of Grecian dramas vaunts the deathless fame', while 'Of Avon's bard remembering scarce the name'.[34] At the same time, he prides himself on the special pleasure of reading Homer on the plain of Troy.[35] Byron's classy classical learning informs his verse and his life – but it is not so much scholarly skills as the learning and reading of ancient poetry which invests his Greek landscapes – landscapes of the mind – with associations and cultural significance. For all his transgressive behaviour and exile from England, Byron speaks from a position of cultural assurance that Keats can never reach. It is – of *course* – Byron who was immensely popular as a poet throughout Europe in his life and through the nineteenth century, and only gradually that Keats has gained an extended audience.

The biographical and critical tradition since Keats' romantically young death, however, has remained obsessed with Keats' Greekness. Keats 'saw divine visions and the pure Greek ideal because he had the essence in his soul'.[36] For Matthew Arnold, who will keep appearing in this chapter, and no lover of Keats' poetry, the images of the *Ode on a Grecian Urn* were 'as Greek as a thing from Homer or Theocritus'.[37]

---

[33] Levinson (1988) 18.
[34] *Childe Harold's Pilgrimage* IV, 75–6; 'Thoughts Suggested by a College Examination'.
[35] See Webb (1993) 158 for references. Makdishi (1998) sets Byron's philhellenism in the context of an orientalism, reminiscent of De Quincey.
[36] Horne (1844) II, 9.   [37] Arnold (1903) V. 137.

'Under the influence of the living spirit of Greece . . . the poet . . . sang, for a time, in full throated ease.'[38] Even less ecstatic judgements adopt a similar frame of evaluation. De Selincourt in 1905 recognized that Keats 'could know nothing . . . of the literature . . . in which the Greek spirit found true expression' – but still proclaims the poet to be 'innately Greek'.[39] Amy Lowell roundly declares 'Keats never had the slightest knowledge or comprehension of the true Greek spirit' – unlike herself, presumably.[40] Even recent critics who wish explicitly to escape from 'the problem of his ignorance of Greek' can claim that Keats 'desires to mediate or even displace his relation to antiquity . . . as though a naked encounter were too painful or importunate' – as if a 'naked encounter' could be simply a choice for a poet who did not even know the Greek alphabet.[41] There is a continuing and passionate investment in *how* Grecian Keats can be.

Byron can epitomize a classical learning – *Bildung* – for a generation of upper-class Englishmen, schooled in learning grammar and verse off by heart (though not necessarily with a total enthusiasm for the more technical aspects of scholarly endeavour). His dismissiveness of Keats, and the subsequent feverish critical attempts of others to invest him as the bearer of the true Greek spirit, also reveal a politics of class, education, gender, literary production. Keats can expose his emotional response to Greek art, address Homer and even write lengthy classicizing poems on mythological themes, yet his 'giant ignorance' of Greek means his expression of the Greek spirit can only become a source of exaggerated attack and defence: it cannot pass for knowledge, simply. He cannot 'breathe', like Byron, the Greek serene.

'Knowing Greek' always means more than an acquaintance with an ancient language. It can become part of a battle over what knowledge is, what knowledge should count (in making a man or a woman), what the institutions and practices of knowing should be, what the protocols and etiquette of cultured behaviour are. De Quincey's boasts of his classical attainments are striking because he does not simply show a gentleman's absorption and citation of the wise words of the classics, nor does he enter into the world of scholarship (where a Porson or a Bentley could lock swords). Like so much in De Quincey's *Confessions*, his knowledge – its style and expression of character – marks him out – like Keats – as not

---

[38] Larrabee (1943) 204.   [39] De Selincourt (1905) xliii, xlvi.   [40] Lowell (1924) 346.
[41] Aske (1985) 34–35. 'Naked' is presumably an echo of Keats' aspiration towards a 'more naked and grecian Manner' (*Letters* I. 207.)

fitting in. His self-exile from school and university enacts that alienation, as does his removal from polite society.

De Quincey, ever a figure of excess, knows *too much* Greek.

The revival of a passion for Greece in the first quarter of the nineteenth century had a long reach through Victorian England, Europe and America. Although this opening discussion of mine has been all too brief – there is so much more that could be said of the desires and devices of these texts and this era – it does provide a necessary starting point for the pages to come. For this chapter will be focused on what it means 'to know Greek' , especially in England, and how understanding such an issue changes through the later nineteenth century. Although Hofmannsthal may have been tempted to oversimplify Victorian Hellenism for his own rhetorical purposes into a single and looming project, it is fissured with conflicting debates, idealisms and projections. Romantic Hellenism is the ground from which the debates I shall be tracing developed. Trying to understand De Quincey's self-representation as a knower of Greek has required its framing by idea(l)s of Orientalism and Empire, gender and education, social etiquette and literary form, and – thus – De Quincey's text provides an exemplary demonstration of why 'knowing Greek' cannot be a simple or culturally neutral attainment. I will be looking not just at literary texts (like those of Keats and De Quincey), but, as in previous chapters, at a range of materials and interrelated questions: are there special qualities in the Greek language itself? How should schooling be organized? Is Science a better guide to living a good life? Is knowing Greek a question of spirit or scholarship? In short, what politics of knowledge are invoked by the claim to know Greek?

One overarching narrative for this period has been brilliantly explored in recent years by historians of education.[42] The story of the professionalization of Classics in the German-speaking world has been told both in pungent outline and in works of great detail.[43] It is sobering to recall that between 1608 and 1786 there was no edition of Sophocles produced in German (no Euripides between 1599 and 1778, no Homer between 1606 and 1759).[44] Yet despite what has been diagnosed as the 'almost

[42] Especially Stray (1998) (with excellent bibliography); Stray ed. (1998); Clarke (1959); Turner (1981); Dowling (1994); and, with less focus on classics but with important background, Ringer (1979); Engel (1983); Rothblatt (1968); (1976); Simon (1974); Roach (1991); Heyck (1982) ; Baldick (1987); Doyle (1989) and Collini (1991) 199–373.

[43] Albisetti (1983); Grafton (1983); Jens (1973); Ringer (1969); Butler (1935).

[44] Figures from Trevelyan (1934) x–xii.

complete collapse of humanistic studies at the beginning of the eighteenth century',[45] by the grand days of the nineteenth century, 'there was no one in any institution of higher education who was unable to read Plato or Homer'[46] (in Greek). Indeed, it has been claimed – with a certain wish-fulness, it might be thought – that in 1850 'the Utopia of the sixteenth century, a world of Latin-speaking dentists, Homer-reading lawyers, and Sophocles-quoting merchants, had become a reality'.[47] The huge influence of writers such as Goethe, Winckelmann, Lessing in linking classics to the formation of the German people found full institutional expression in the reforms of von Humboldt, who set Classics and in particular Greek as the privileged and central subject of the educational system in the German-speaking world. 'Knowledge of the Greeks is not merely pleasant, useful or necessary for us – no, in the Greeks alone we find the ideal of that which we ourselves should like to be and produce.'[48] The rapidity and force of the dominance of German 'Greekomania' gives a particular edge to the famous phrase 'the tyranny of Greece over the German imagination'. Greek study 'established the foundation of a new kind of national culture'.[49]

Schiller could be seen as a leading light of the revival of Hellenism in Germany, despite the fact that he knew no Greek, because of his passionate commitment (shared with his friend, Goethe, who did learn Greek) to promoting a Greek spirit (*Geist*) in the name of *Bildung* (culture, learning, civilization). Yet von Humboldt's educational reforms and the emphasis on language learning enshrined also a model of *Wissenschaft*, 'learning', or 'science', and the increasing demands of technical expertise fissured the claims of *Bildung* on the study of antiquity. 'Under Humboldt, indoctrination into research became mandatory', and a series of university seminars grew which 'trained speaker and audience alike never to assert anything without solid evidence'.[50] (Remember Shelley's response to sculpture ...) Squabbles – 'exhibitions of bad taste and ill-will'[51] – flared between scholars committed to 'pure philology' – language for language's sake – and scholars willing to entertain the interest of literature or history; the Humboldtian system was in danger of subverting itself: '*Wissenschaft* and *Bildung* could not easily fit into one curriculum.'[52] The demands of *Wissenschaft* increasingly separated scholarship from a

---

[45] Trevelyan (1934) 17. A more healthy picture is constructed for the earlier period by Ludwig (1998).
[46] Jens (1973) 69.
[47] Jens (1973) 69. Albisetti (1983) is more circumspect and more convincing.
[48] Von Humboldt (1963) 79.   [49] Wohlleben (1992) 170.   [50] Grafton (1983) 168.
[51] Grafton (1983) 173.   [52] Grafton (1983) 176.

more general cultural import: 'German scholars ceased to be able to communicate with ordinary educated men.'[53] Where at the beginning of the nineteenth century, 'Greekomania indirectly served the purpose of becoming conscious of one's own value and of advancing the ideals of national unity' – a project of cultural renewal – by the middle of the century, an education in *Bildung* was 'the characteristic quality of the ruling class', while the mandarins of the university world demanded ever more exacting requirements for knowledge.[54] By 1890, education was again a Question, and a new nationalism was called for, and in most ringing terms: the new Kaiser, Wilhelm II (the Kaiser, who, some years later, invited Chamberlain to his palace for discussions about Greece and race) delivered a battle cry to his army of educators: 'We should raise young Germans, not young Greeks and Romans.'[55] The professionalization of the discipline of classics increasingly made it a fenced and attacked ghetto of knowledge.

Christopher Stray's fine account of classical education in England (from 1830 onwards) focuses on the relation between schools and universities, but he also briefly underlines the difference of national context between Germany and England. He contrasts German nation-building Hellenism with a more 'domesticated Hellenism' in England, a Hellenism 'which was more at home in the world of ordinary appearances and social style'.[56] The continuation of an educational style and content between school and university produced an ordered world of shared knowledge and horizons of expectation – a discipline of acculturation: 'Education' – which here means education in Greek and Latin – 'became and remained a crucial status marker, the battleground of class identification'.[57] Yet in England too an increasing professionalization of the discipline can be traced alongside its decreasing role in the curriculum and its decreasing status as the privileged preserve of cultural capital (though such professionalization was never as rigorously policed as in Germany: England could keep 'cheerfully amateur classicists').[58] The close links between classical education and social performance make the battles which enable this sea-change especially complex – internecine, highly rhetorical, and conducted on different fields of endeavour – through to the casual and barely considered insults of elitism and irrelevance thrown at Classics in the modern debate. (This is not a history where I at least can maintain a distance.) The politics

---

[53] Grafton (1983) 184.   [54] Jens (1973) 72, 74.
[55] Quoted in the excellent discussion of Albisetti (1983) 3.
[56] Stray (1998) 26.   [57] Stray (1998) 27.   [58] Grafton (1983) 184.

of knowing Greek, especially in England, certainly cannot be disentangled from a history of class, social development, and two centuries of educational reform – a history in which you and I are still playing our roles.

The specific question of what it means to 'know Greek' is constantly framed – though not contained – by the history of education. While it is simply true that classical study at university became increasingly professionalized throughout the nineteenth century, and over the same period increasingly lost ground to the growing influence of science in particular, none the less I think it would be misleading to tell this tale as a neat teleological story (or – worse – simply as the triumph and tragedy of a discipline). There are many important figures who do not easily fit into such a developmental model: Gilbert Murray, Professor of Greek at Oxford, with his popular works for the English stage, and his role as a founding figure of the League of Nations; Gladstone, the Prime Minister, who published learned – and widely read – scholarship on Homer; or in Germany, Nietzsche, the Professor of Philology, who, led by Wagner and excoriated by his former high school colleague, Wilamowitz, went over to the dark side (as Wilamowitz would have it); or Hofmannsthal reworking Sophocles via the scholarship of Rohde for a large general audience . . . Nor do arguments for and against classical education over the century fall into a neat developmental pattern. This is a *messy* history, with high points of intense cultural conflict, and long continuities of repeated arguments or shared values.

The range of material that could be brought to bear on this subject is potentially vast, too vast for a chapter, and even for a single scholar to encompass. What I have chosen to do in each of the following three sections of this chapter is to select a particularly charged moment of disagreement, argument, debate in a specific year during the latter part of the nineteenth century, and to try to explore its significance in a world of shifting cultural priorities and political exigencies. I will be bringing on stage professional academics, politicians, literary figures, essayists, some of whom are major figures in the History of England (and beyond), some of whom are minor league (at best) – but exemplary too. After the prose of De Quincey and the verse of Keats, I am now going to look at the personal and institutional politics of education in England and America through the figures of Robert Lowe and Matthew Arnold; and, then, at the infighting of university academics at this time of change through the Cambridge dons, Walter Headlam and A. W. Verrall. My aim is to investigate through what I hope are paradigmatic moments and figures, the different perspectives that together created the social, intellectual and cultural impact of a long-running question, which is absolutely central to this book: what is at stake in knowing Greek?

II 1867, AND THE DETESTED MR LOWE SPEAKS OUT

On Monday, 6 May 1867 fully 200,000 people gathered in Hyde Park in London to hear speeches delivered by the leaders of the Reform League. This was – without microphones – a massive, symbolic gesture of support. The Government had rashly tried to stop the demonstration by threatening to close the gates of the park. All the previous week, heated speeches on the issue dominated the business of Parliament, the letters pages of the papers and the news itself. Some 16,000 people by Saturday had signed a petition to protest *against* the demonstration. *The Times* tried to argue that to hold such a meeting in a *Royal* park, 'not only without the the permission but avowedly in defiance of Government' constituted an act of *lèse-majesté* against the Crown itself, and ominously warned that 'unless the good sense of the public interfere to prevent it, next Monday may possibly be signalized by some act of folly'.[59] The Reformers worried with increasingly strident rhetoric with what legality the Government could attempt to stop a public gathering. Everyone knew that the previous year a demonstration had ended in a riot where the railings of the park had been torn down – an act of terrorism so shocking that even the patron saint of sweetness and light, Matthew Arnold, was moved to suggest that the rioters should suffer the death of a traitor to the homeland.

In the event, the Government backed down from confrontation, and, in a crackling atmosphere, the meeting took place without any of the 'tumult and disorder' which *The Times* had predicted. The Reform Act of 1867, passed shortly later, was perhaps the most significant step in the series of constitutional changes that fundamentally altered the political life of England in the nineteenth century, by widening the franchise to include even working-class householders. It was surrounded by a debate conducted in pamphlets, speeches, cartoons, marches, riots and the exchanges of personal power-broking from highest to lowest levels of the community. Politics writ large. Such constitutional reform directly affected the major educational reforms of the next decades. The connection between the change in franchise and the change in schooling

---

[59] *Times* Friday, 3 May 1867, p. 8.

was captured in a brilliantly striking slogan by Robert Lowe – that was (mis)quoted throughout the next years (and today): 'it will be absolutely necessary to compel our future masters to learn their letters'. (It is often brandished in the snappier but less pointed form 'We must educate our masters.')[60] Lowe had spearheaded the opposition to the Reform Act, but once it was passed, with his customary sardonic and precisely malevolent rhetoric he underlines for his colleagues that if the working classes now had the power to elect politicians, politicians had better teach the electorate their lessons.

Robert Lowe is one (anti)hero for this chapter, and a speech of his delivered in Edinburgh in November 1867 will be the centrepiece of this section. He was a hugely influential political figure, not least by being the equivalent of minister for education throughout the early years of major reform, a position coupled with responsibility for cattle plague (don't ask).[61] He also held the post of Chancellor under Gladstone's premiership, while, at the same time, writing leaders for *The Times*, delivering hundreds of speeches, and revelling with great public delight in the cut and thrust of the manipulation of the public perception of politics. He still wonderfully provokes and divides educational historians.[62] Through him, I wish to look at three issues in particular: first, the role of 'knowing Greek' in social reform; second – and this will involve several other major political figures and their speeches – I want to analyse the *range* of positions available in such debate about 'knowing Greek', a range that goes well beyond the obvious battle-lines of pro- or anti-classical study. Third, I want to stress the complex personal politics of educational debate: the interweavings of intimate ties, shared values, social venues which makes it difficult to associate a single figure simply with a single position within these debates, and which makes lines of causation and reasoning so much harder to trace. Personal politics is one thing that makes this story so messy. The 'us' and 'them' of battle keeps shifting and reforming, often in the same dining room...

Robert Lowe was an albino, with such short sight that he had to put his face against the page to read or write at all. It was joked in Oxford – typical Victorian university anecdote, this – that he would have done better in his exams if his nose had not wiped out half of what his pen

---

[60] Martin (1893) 323; 330–331. Most recent misquotation, Stray (1998) 167 who has 'teach' for 'compel'.

[61] Connell (1950) 92.

[62] Victorian biography: Martin (1893). Less hagiographic: Briggs (1955) 232–63; Winter (1976) (full-scale modern biography); and on educational policies, Sylvester (1974). Each reports extensive reactions to Lowe.

had written. Because of sensitivity to light, he rarely opened his eyes beyond a slit. I don't much like it when books insist on giving posed photographs to illustrate a character in a story, any character, as if the picture spoke for itself, or as if you could just read the personality from the portrait. The frontispieces of the two volumes of Lowe's thousand-page Victorian biography, however (plate 20), are not only a marvellous exercise in Victorian memorializing self-dramatization – this is how he is to be *pictured* by you, posterity – but also this physiognomics plays a significant role in his biography. All spectators agreed that whatever grim psychological damage you might like to imagine for a boy going through English public school of this period looking like that, Lowe the adult manipulated his own physicality to marvellous effect. His speech making was *seen* to match that appearance. The first picture is of the young Lowe at Oxford, scholar in the making, cap and gown as essential props, eyes fixed on a distant goal; the second is of the now Viscount Sherbrooke GCB, DCL – the successful public figure in his pomp, sashed and be-medalled. The patrician profile. The story of the transition between these two images is, in his biographer's hands, the story of his heroic triumph over physical deformity.

After teaching Greek and Latin at Oxford for some years without a position, he married into money, and under threat of blindness (which did not in fact come true until his final year) he moved to Australia in 1842, where, with what he had correctly predicted would be the opportunity of a swifter rise than in England, he soon became a very well paid lawyer and a political activist – with the batch of enemies you might expect from such a meteoric rise, and a dangerously divisive reputation, won not least by having brilliantly defended in the colonial court an upper-class English murderer who 'everyone knew' was guilty. It's a case that perfectly images his whole career: his carefully nourished reputation for obsessive integrity was in direct proportion to his relentless championship of unpopular causes and his constant exacerbation of class division.[63] No surprise when, during the Reform Bill debates, he became an object of unique vilification because he publicly characterized the (proposed) working-class voters as 'impulsive, unreflecting and violent people' full of 'ignorance', 'drunkenness' and 'a facility for intimidation'.[64]

He returned to England from Australia in 1850 to a life of politics and journalism. He was elected Member of Parliament for Kidderminster in

---

[63] He did – in the style of a Dickens' novel – pay for the upbringing of the child of the victim, however.

[64] Martin (1893) 273–4. His opponent, Bright, made havoc with these words.

20. Robert Lowe, (1836), and Lord Sherbrooke [Robert Lowe], (1889), from *Life and Letters of the Right Honourable Robert Lowe, Viscount Sherbrooke, G.C.B., D.C.L.,* by A. Patchett Martin (1893)

1852 amid such rancour that when the results were announced he was physically assaulted by the crowd, and his first act in his constituency was to run for his life. After 1867, he was MP for the University of London (the only constituency that could have him, sneered Disraeli). He made opponents more easily than friends in his professional life, though (it was said) he impressed many (and his biographer collects plenty of hagiographic testimonies). Lord Granville wrote with a friend's frankness (or is it understatement?) that 'His self-delusions about his own faults and merits were extraordinary'[65] – but there can be no doubting his status in the public imagination: 'No stranger goes there [to Parliament]', wrote *The Spectator*, 'without looking for the white gleam, or rather flash of his striking head, or listening anxiously for the cold, sardonic ring of his lucid voice, which vibrates like a glass ball throughout the House, penetrating it with a shiver of half-mocking intelligence'.[66] That's the voice you should hear when I quote from his speeches (and look back at the portraits ...)

Lowe was deeply influenced by his reading of Adam Smith at Oxford and was passionate about economic policy. Perhaps his most renowned – and reviled – policy as minister for education was to attempt not only to cut the rising education budget, but also, and more importantly, to tie school funding to results. It was he who first introduced performance related pay for teachers. 'Between 1861 and 1864 he managed to provoke the unanimous opposition of all parties interested in the question of education',[67] and the so-called Revised Code of 1862, the bill which contained these economic measures, caused a hullabaloo of protest. Matthew Arnold, who helped script the opposition to it (while working for Lowe's government department), called the policy 'the heaviest blow dealt at civilization and social improvement in my time'.[68] It has been argued that the Revised Code 'was above all an essay in the economics of education',[69] but it was widely perceived by contemporaries to be an assault on the culture of education and on the education into culture. Lowe, in short, is a starring figure in the virulent controversies which surround educational policy in this period, and the intense reactions he provokes – 'a Satan in the paradise of parliament', 'a treacherous friend, a bitter foe', 'fearless candour and independence'[70] – reveal most clearly the volcanic faultlines of debate.

[65] Quoted in Briggs (1955) 235.　　[66] *Spectator* 7 July 1866.　　[67] Briggs (1955) 235.
[68] Arnold's opposition is best described by Connell (1950) 203–42.
[69] Sylvester (1974) 59.
[70] There are literally hundreds of such extreme positive and negative remarks recorded in Martin (1893).

Through 1866 and 1867 Lowe was one of the most vocal opponents of
the Reform Bill, in reviews, essays and, above all, in a series of set piece
rhetorical displays especially in Parliament. Despite being a Liberal and
thus a colleague of Gladstone who sponsored the Bill, Lowe objected to
any move towards democracy which he, like many, associated with the
uncultured force of America. His friend, the Countess of Derby, agreed:
'For England . . . to make a step in the direction of democracy appears
to me the strangest and wildest proposition that was ever broached by
man.'[71] Here is the grand peroration to what was widely described as
one of the greatest parliamentary performances of a generation, Lowe's
defence of the English constitution against democracy: 'Surely the heroic
work of so many centuries, the matchless achievements of so many wise
heads and strong hands, deserve a nobler consummation than to be sacrificed at the shrine of revolutionary passion or the maudlin enthusiasm
of humanity . . . History may tell of other acts as signally disastrous, but
of none more wanton, none more disgraceful.'[72] Shoulder to shoulder
with the heroes and sages of past generations, Lowe depicts himself as a
noble fighter against the regiments of democratic revolutionaries – that
is, his own parliamentary party. His starry-eyed biographer takes up the
same rhetoric of heroic warfare: by autumn 1867, 'the battle with democracy had been fought and lost, but Robert Lowe, though defeated, was
in no way disgraced. With a handful of supporters he had withstood
the two greatest masters of the House of Commons of our time . . . It
is difficult in the whole of our parliamentary annals to point to a more
striking achievement.'[73] Even *Punch* wrote a long ballad honouring his
fight, which concludes with this awful stanza:

> They may look a long time ere they hit
>   On one who such muscle can show,
> One for truth's sturdy champion so fit,
>   As much-abused, honest Bob Lowe.[74]

It was shortly after this lost campaign, in November 1867, that Lowe
went to Edinburgh and delivered his speech, 'Primary and Classical
Education', which was headlined in *The Times* (for which Lowe worked)
and published as a pamphlet. (In the coming months, he delivered further
speeches in Liverpool and published further pamphlets on middle-class
education.) Despite – or because of – the fact that he had taught classics at
Oxford (and unsuccessfully applied for a chair in Greek in Glasgow), the

---

[71] Burchlere (1933) 128–9. For the background of Lowe's opposition see Harrie (1976).
[72] Martin (1893) 287–8.   [73] Martin (1893) 325.   [74] *Punch* 13 June 1867.

Edinburgh speech was an all-out attack on the role of classics in English education. 'My speech was one of the most successful I ever made', he wrote to his friend Mrs Billyard, 'It has indeed created a perfect furore' (one reasonable criterion of success) 'and is regarded with the utmost horror by schoolmasters and all who make their living by Latin and Greek' (another . . .)[75]

The speech is best known for its general claim that different disciplines should be evaluated by the (newly coined) science of 'ponderation' – a weighing by reflection: 'we shall put into the scales all the different objects of human knowledge and decide upon their relative importance'.[76] The politics behind this 'ponderation' of disciplines are clear enough: 'The question of education naturally divides itself into two branches – the education of the poor or primary education, and the education of the middle or upper classes.'[77] (That 'naturally' shows the work of ideology starkly – as if such divisive class-led definitions of the classroom were the work of nature.) It is 'the duty of the state . . . to test and ascertain the nature of the education given'[78] – though from his governmental office Lowe knew better than anyone that this 'duty' had been hard won through debate and legislation.[79] The poor electorate must now be given the knowledge to play a role in government, and 'the higher class of this country' must get a different education too, 'also for a political reason', if their position is not to be threatened. For them to continue to learn Greek is nothing less than 'suicide'. Education here is not for a job or profession but firmly to enable you to play the role of political citizen, voting, governing, evaluating.

Use value is, for Lowe, the overriding criterion of ponderation. He is happy – with lovely rhetorical flair – to allow that 'all knowedge, except heraldry, has some use'; but this is only a sop before brutally 'ponderating' the claims of knowing Greek. The man who walked as a boy with Darwin is clear about what counts: 'it is more important to know where the liver is situated and what are the principles that affect its healthy action than to know it is called *iecur* in Latin or ἧπαρ in Greek'.[80] 'Where there is a question between true and false it is more important to know what is true than what is false; it is more important to know the history of England than the mythology of Greece and Rome.'[81] And knowing

[75] Martin (1893) 330.   [76] Lowe (1867) 13.   [77] Lowe (1867) 3.   [78] Lowe (1867) 5.
[79] Particularly important here was the work of Sir James Kay-Shuttleworth, whose agenda is summed up in Kay-Shuttleworth (1862) and (1868).
[80] Lowe (1867) 14. (On 'walking and talking' as particular Victorian cultural model see Collini (1991) 189.)
[81] Lowe (1867) 14.

ancient geography is a positive bar to the proper practice of imperialism. Where Humboldt's idealism takes for granted that knowledge of Greek is 'useful', 'necessary', and 'pleasant', for Lowe, knowing Greek is either useless, false, or a block on national advancement.

The seductiveness and force of Lowe's rhetoric is caught best for me in this brief passage of selective reminiscence:

I thought how many irretrievable years of my life have I spent in reading the wars and intrigues and revolutions of these little towns, the whole of which . . . would not make a decently-sized English county . . . [82]

It is not just the stately cadence of this sentence, I think, which drives this rhetoric so well, nor even the slyly condescending contrast between the smallness of ancient towns and the majesty of the British Empire even in its home counties. It is rather the knowing echo of one of the most famous passages in the correspondence of the orator Cicero, which describes looking out over the small towns of Greece and reflecting on the decline of Empire and the instability of man's lot.[83] As Lowe considers the fall of the Empire of Greek study, it is the insidiously witty purloining of a classical image – with its weight, its ancestry, its associations for his classically trained listeners – that allows him to manipulate his audience's emotions so successfully. As Lowe boasted, it was a speech designed to 'create a perfect furore'.

It would be hard, however, to point to any immediate and direct institutional or narrowly defined political result of this speech, beyond a flurry of publicity for the politician. That's not the sort of cause and effect at stake here. It is at best one high-profile contribution to the long and slow process by which classics gave way in the curriculum to English and History in the humanities, and to Science in general. My thumbnail sketch of Lowe's political celebrity and the build up through the Reform debates should give a sense of why this was indeed a high-profile occasion and why the politics of Greek education are so charged. Yet its effect within the long and slow process of change can be further gauged also by setting it against a series of three other major political addresses delivered in Scotland that year, and by the response it provoked. For some complex affiliations and distances are being marked out within the politics of Liberal reform.

Earlier that year in Scotland at the University of St Andrew's John Stuart Mill had delivered his inaugural address as Rector on the same

---

[82] Lowe (1867) 22.
[83] Cicero *Ad Fam* IV v. It is in Sulpicius' consolation to Cicero for the death of his daughter.

subject, namely, 'the great controversy of the present day with regard to higher education . . . whether general education should be classical . . . or scientific'.[84] John Stuart Mill had been Lowe's most able opponent in the debate on the Reform Bill (as Lowe thought); he epitomized the 'sentimental Liberal' for the hard man of economics. Mill was also a distinguished writer (by now), and a leading Liberal ideologue, whose election to parliament had been seen as a turning point in the fortunes of the Liberal party,[85] and he was in the process of publishing texts that are still a watchword in democratic political thought, most notably his arguments for the education and enfranchisement of women. Mill and Lowe had worked together in the India office in the 1850s (under Thomas Love Peacock, bizarrely enough, the great parodist of economists and political philosophers, and lover of all things Greek), but they had never been intimate – and found disagreement easy. Mill, inevitably, did not take the same line as Lowe, but his drift is not, as one might expect, towards the apparently democratizing claims of English or history. He is happy to allow a place for science in the curriculum as well as Classics – 'Why not both?'[86] – but he sees the real problem in the system to be the poor teaching of Greek in schools. If Greek were only *well* taught, there would be room for science on the timetable. But he does stick firmly to the principle that the 'only language . . . and the only literature' acceptable are 'those of the Greeks and Romans'.[87] (Ancient) language study, for Mill, has a special place: it is only through language that a people's thoughts can be properly known, and without that knowledge of another people 'our intellects [are] only half expanded'.[88] Even from so celebrated a liberal, this general plea to learn from the Other is strik-ing – especially if you put it next to, say, De Quincey's furious jingoism. But it is ancient Greek and Latin, that particular other, which count above all . . . others. They are special languages. They have a 'peculiar value . . . on account of their regular and complicated structure':[89] 'The structure of every sentence is a lesson in logic.'[90] Knowing Greek, it seems, gives your intellect the chance of being wholly developed and rational. For the political philosopher, knowing the Greek language itself really matters.

Mill's argument here would be familiar to his audience. It was a commonplace in the defences of Greek that modern languages lacked the rigour of a proper grammar. James Harris, a widely read

---

[84] Cavenagh (1931) 138. Cavenagh is more accessible than Mill (1867).
[85] See e.g. Duff (1871) 76.   [86] Cavenagh (1931) 138.   [87] Cavenagh (1931) 145.
[88] Cavenagh (1931) 146.   [89] Cavenagh (1931) 145, 150.   [90] Cavenagh (1931) 150.

eighteenth-century grammarian, puts the case in as summary a form as possible when he argues that 'any language with less than five moods and twelve tenses is necessarily corrupt'.[91] (Even if you didn't know, you could probably guess that (the) one language with five moods and twelve tenses is Greek.) Indeed, Louth's standard grammar, reprinted forty-three times from the eighteenth into the nineteenth century, maintained that the 'only means to learn correct English were to be knowledgeable in the Classical languages, to frequent polite society, and to have read "ancient authors" extensively'.[92] Without knowledge of Greek and Latin, adds another dictionary preface, men will arise who 'not knowing the original import of words, will use them with colloquial licentiousness, confound distinction, and forget propriety'.[93] The normative slide from linguistic theory into language training into social formation is clear enough – distinction and propriety are at risk from such licentiousness in word formation – and this defence of the necessity of Greek for the English not only gets regularly repeated through the century, but also prompts many retorts in similar terms of social propriety. The sharp polemics of Cobbett in his *Political Register* of 1817 was influential among the young turks in particular: the so-called 'learned languages' aren't learned at all, he sniffs; studying them makes a student's mind 'frivolous and superficial'.[94] Particularly outrageous to him is the fee to join the Bar which is £100 for those without Greek but only £6 or £7 for those with it: the social cartel of Greek is also a direct economic benefit. The fear – or delightful hope – is that 'the contemptible, frivolous, lick-spittle animals' (he is referring to Etonians) 'will be pushed aside by Apprentices and Plough boys'.[95] Cobbett's view certainly did not go unchallenged. My opinions, he recalls, 'brought upon me such a torrent of *abuse* such as I hardly ever expected'.[96] You would no doubt be being rather naive if you thought that this pose of surprise was not part of Cobbett's wilfully outrageous opinion-making. By the time of Lowe, however, a challenge to Greek, to teaching the Greek language, no longer needed the armour of abusive satire.

Mill, the Liberal reformist, intellectual figurehead of the Liberal party, defends the traditional study of Greek as the only proper literary sphere, while Lowe, who resists social change, argues for a complete overhaul of the education system in the name of new democracy. Mill defends Greek

---

[91] Smith (1984) 23.   [92] Smith (1984) 6.

[93] Smith (1984) 6, citing S. Jackson's preface to his *Dictionary of the English Language*. Good background also in Mugglestone (1995).

[94] Cobbett (1817) 1077.   [95] Cobbett (1817) 1081.   [96] Cobbett (1817) 1061.

and Latin as uniquely privileged languages; Lowe (though he does 'not disparage Latin and Greek') thinks 'English has a prior claim' for 'what is most important'.

The tensions between these two positions are highlighted by a third speech in Scotland the same year by another leading Liberal politician. In March, Sir Mountstuart Elphinstone Grant Duff, MP for Elgin, new Rector of the University of Aberdeen, also delivered an inaugural address, also published as a pamphlet, also on education.[97] Grant Duff was another career politician – he became Under-Secretary of State for India under Gladstone and Governor of Madras. He was intimately intermeshed with just about everybody who features in this chapter. He was a close friend of both Thomas Huxley and Matthew Arnold (Arnold caught his first salmon on Duff's estate, an event apparently worthy of reaching the national press).[98] Duff had campaigned for Mill, whose election he regarded as 'the triumph of intellect over anti-intellect. Nay, it is hardly too much to say . . . the triumph of pure good over pure evil.'[99] Duff strolled to visit Darwin with Robert Lowe. Jowett had been his tutor at Balliol. He rode with Gladstone. He was passionate about dining clubs and the not-quite-public, not-quite-private world of the Victorian power breakfast. A full roll-call of the great and good of Victorian political life sat at his table. (His daughter, with what *we* would be tempted to see as bitterness, reminisced that he was 'not a family man', and adds that he was not good with children, and she thought him ugly, shy and no orator, though his writings were widely read.)[100]

Duff had supported the Reform Bill actively, but also had been involved in educational reform from the establishment of the commission of enquiry into the Public Schools in 1861. He depicted himself, with some justice, as a revolutionary in educational policy.[101] In his inaugural lecture in Aberdeen, he confesses that he had been 'stigmatized by the ignorant and prejudiced as an enemy of classical education' , but is quick to specify that 'an enemy of the present methods of classical education I certainly am, an enemy of classical education I certainly am not'. This, before declaring knowledge of the ancient world 'not a necessary but a luxury'.[102] Duff, the insiders' politician and Reformer, speaks out, like Lowe, against classical education. He distinguishes himself from his political ally Mill ('We have all read what Mr Mill lately said

[97] Duff (1867).
[98] Duff (1891) II, 14. See also Murray (1996) 223. The paper was the *Morning Star*.
[99] Duff (1871) 76.   [100] Duff (1930) v–xv, esp. v and ix.
[101] See Duff (1897) I 279.   [102] Duff (1867) 4–5, 7.

on the subject')[103] and implicitly from his friends Arnold, Jowett and
Gladstone, for whom commitment to following 'the example of Greece'
in 'our national life' was an imperative.[104] Rather, he aligns himself with
the most radical liberal tradition and its most recent proponents.

'"Things not words" is the very watchword of our best class of
educational reformers', he declares aggressively.[105] The phrase 'Things
not Words' in this educational context goes back, I think, to Thomas
Paine's *Age of Reason* (1794)[106] and, more than a 'watchword' of the 'best
class of reformers', it was the most buzzy of slogans from the most radical
figures in educational politics (which is why his sentence is self-consciously
so provocative). It was quoted – in different contexts and with different
valences – by Cobbett, Lowe, George Grote, William Godwin, William
Hazlitt, F. Farrar, and disparaged by Arnold amongst others.[107] It was
a banner for scientific and anti-classical revolution, which all too easily
after Darwin was seen as necessarily anti-Christian and anti-clerical. It is
a vivid gesture in the popularization – slow and contested – and educational institutionalization – even slower – of a new view of 'scientific
facts' (which has far-reaching implications for the understanding of political economy, say, in the work of Mill elsewhere).[108] For support, Grant
Duff cites the very recent 'book of Mr Farrar'. This was a stunning
collection of essays also published in 1867 (Grant Duff is really up to
date), with pieces by Henry Sidgwick, Lord Houghton, Professor Seeley
among other notables and young turks.[109] (These days Farrar, who wrote
a library of religious volumes, usually enters history as the author of
Eric, or Little by Little, a school novel with an evident agenda (and a rather
odd taste in corporal punishment). The education debate was conducted
at all levels of intellectual activity.)[110] Farrar's volume was a battle cry 'to
organize National Liberal Education',[111] and with shocking verve it supported the study of science and English, and, worse, attacked such sacred

---

[103] Duff (1867) 11.   [104] Arnold *CPW* XI. 314.   [105] Duff (1867) 15.

[106] Paine (1794) 31. The opposition of 'words' and 'things' is of course a commonplace of classical
languages, but its specific use in educational debate is marked. Paine opposed the dominance
of classical learning, see Aldridge (1967–8) for discussion.

[107] See e.g. Cobbett (1817) 1077; Grote (1856) 92; Lowe (1867); Godwin (1968) 438–9; Hazlitt (1902)
6; Farrar (1867) 239.

[108] See Poovey (1998) building on the work of Shapin and Schaffer (1985) and Dear (1995), for all
of whom the work of Bruno Latour is, of course, fundamental.

[109] Farrar ed. (1867). Farrar quotes Duff in return at 217.

[110] On Farrar and corporal punishment see Jenkyns (1981) 212–13, and on Swinburne (who prompts
Jenkyns' comments) in this connection see the wonderful analysis by Prins (1999) 112–73.

[111] Parker (1867) 80.

cows as Greek verse composition, teaching grammar, and even the place of Greek in the curriculum *tout court*.

The most fierce of its orators was Henry Sidgwick, guru of Cambridge reform, founder of Newnham College, a college for women, a college without a chapel. 'What', he asks, 'is this knowledge [of Greek] worth?'[112] The claim of classical literature to 'contain all knowledge' – which motivated Erasmus – is these days risible; even if Greek literature is good, so too is the literature of Germany and France. Who – he challenges his audience – even among those who had a classical education, actually reads classical texts after college? When did you last pick up Homer?[113] (This from Sidgwick who elsewhere recalls sitting in a Welsh pub with a friend eagerly competing to see who could quote the beginning of a stanza of Horace which the other could not complete!)[114] The only sop he allows the teachers of Greek is the brief concession that 'Greek is of use . . . to clergymen'[115] (a remark whose tone is hard to judge but whose dismissiveness is certainly provocative, as we will see). Otherwise, he proposes simply 'to exclude Greek from the regular curriculum'.[116] It is in the vanguard with such wild revolutionaries that Duff sets himself before his university audience: a radical new education for the radical new social order.

In demanding we ask what Greek is worth, Sidgwick, like Lowe, is attacking head on one of the standard defences of learning Greek, already marked as a cliché by another pamphleteer in Scotland in 1867, Professor W. Sellar, whose lecture 'Theories of Classical Learning' – my fourth speech – was also published in Edinburgh that year.[117] (The heavyweights I have been discussing rather upstaged this academic's contribution, though a few years later, you could find Sellar dining with Lowe in the residence of the Master of Balliol College, Oxford, Benjamin Jowett.)[118] Sellar notes '"It is not knowledge", they say, "but the exercise you are forced to incur in acquiring knowledge, that we care about".'[119] Greek, the cliché runs, is not in itself what counts most, but learning it is a special training, an exercise in a privileged style of knowing. Sidgwick dismisses this airily as 'mental gymnastics' (a self-reflexive phrase repeated throughout the century). For Sidgwick, Greek knowledge is without product, without *worth*.

---

[112] Sidgwick (1867) 89. [113] Sidgwick (1867) 106. [114] Stray (1998) 67–8.
[115] Sidgwick (1867) 91. [116] Sidgwick (1867) 141. [117] Sellar (1867).
[118] Martin (1893) 467. [119] Sellar (1867) 10.

Similarly, Sidgwick's comment that Greek is 'useful for clergymen' sounds provocatively off-hand, because attacks on classical study were repeatedly and heatedly reviled as anti-clerical, anti-Christian, anti-religious (in increasing order of general horror). So, Edward Thring, headmaster of Uppingham and former fellow of King's College, Cambridge, writing in 1864, sums up the matter with admirable brevity: 'The New Testament is written in Greek. No religious nation can give up Greek.'[120] We will see bus-loads of clergymen voting against the abolition of compulsory Greek for university entrance on exactly these grounds a quarter of a century later; but Thring's exemplary conservative defence of classics as the only possible school subject, despite his appeals to a religious nation, had already been overtaken by these political trendies and their pamphlets. Thring's biographer, less hagiographic than most, sadly reflects that 'People who nowadays attend educational conferences remember Edward Thring as an old-fashioned stickler for classics.'[121] One important effect of Sidgwick's and Lowe's all-out attacks on classics – excluding Greek as not a source of worthwhile knowledge – was to make the defence of the status quo of the total dominance of the curriculum by classics seem increasingly old-fashioned in an age of reform. Sellar, more circumspect, consequently observes that 'many of the sharpest advocates of classical studies acknowledge [the preponderance of Latin and Greek] to be excessive . . . No liberal mind will regret the abolition of this or any other monopoly'.[122] Sellar's argument is not just a poor man's Mill, but a (Liberal) working academic defending a position in the face of a Liberal political onslaught.

One particular element of Lowe's argument – also heard in Sidgwick and Duff – which is particularly hard to appreciate today is the strident claim that science constitutes a knowledge, a knowledge to set against Greek. This was a period, after all, when you still had to make an impassioned case for science to have *any* place in the school curriculum. And for many observers to suggest science lessons had a place in schools looked faintly ridiculous or dangerously modernizing. It is instructive – and now rather funny – to read one of the ground-breaking books in favour of scientific education, Herbert Spencer's *Education: Intellectual, Moral and Physical* (1861). Spencer is an important figure in the history of anthropology and political thought, who helped to popularize evolutionary models of social development. His work on education and the value of science comes to as blunt a conclusion as possible. 'Thus to

[120] Thring (1864) 82.   [121] Skrine (1889) 47.   [122] Sellar (1867) 7.

the question we set out with – What knowledge is the most worth? – the uniform reply is – Science.'[123] His phrasing – 'What knowledge is the most worth?' – finds obvious echoes in Sidgwick's and Lowe's arguments about the use value of knowing. The desire to establish science as the master of all knowledge – the answer to all questions of moral, social and intellectual taste – leads, however, to some really rather odd assertions. 'The swarms of worthless ballads that infest drawing rooms [are] compositions which science would forbid. They sin against science by setting to music ideas that are not emotional enough to prompt musical expression, and they sin against science by using musical phrases that have no relation to the ideas expressed'.[124] Science, it seems, will stop tasteless after-dinner songs, those ballads that sin(g) against science . . . I don't think Spencer is indulging in self-mocking irony here; and you can also read him putting poetry through the same scientific grinder: 'to be good . . . poetry must pay attention to the laws of nervous action which excited speech obeys'.[125] Physiology provides the rules for poetics, as Spencer strives to find his 'uniform answer' of Science.

The sheer extremism of the claims and counterclaims about education – all Greek, no Greek, scientists against singing – inevitably attracted satirists, which may in itself contribute to the biting tone of Lowe's speech. The most extended and celebrated parody of the absolute certainties of educationalists came out a few years before Spencer in Charles Dickens' *Hard Times* (1854), which gives another high literary perspective on the politics of education. This novel was eagerly awaited – Dickens was at the height of his fame – but it was largely panned by critics (though not, some years later, by Bernard Shaw, who found the social(ist) message perfectly judged).[126] To most, Dickens' parody was too blunt, especially in the opening scenes where the teacher Gradgrind runs his class according to the credo of 'In this life what we want is facts, nothing but facts'; and where – even more brutally – the Gentleman from the Government declares 'What is called Taste is only another name for Fact'. Mr M'Choakumchild – the names are not subtle – has studied a full curriculum including sciences, land-surveying and levelling, which leads the narrator to lament, 'If he had only learnt a little less, how infinitely better he might have taught much more.'[127] Dickens' savagery towards 'Facts' as the watchword of the new turn in education – echoed

---

[123] Spencer (1861) 53.   [124] Spencer (1861) 42.   [125] Spencer (1861) 42.
[126] See Collins ed. (1971) 300–55.
[127] The Newcastle Commission itself asked for 'schoolmasters with less knowledge and more education'. See Collins ed. (1971) 151.

in more *de haut en bas* fashion later by Arnold – did not persuade most of
his reviewers who found his caricatures unnuanced. Yet it is hard not to
hear at least distantly a note of Dickens' exaggerated prose when Farrar
in 1867 proclaims as his credo 'We require the knowledge of *things* and
not of *words*.'[128] The grossness of Dickens' satire becomes evident, however, as Farrar glosses such knowledge as 'something broader, deeper,
more human, more useful, less selfish, less exclusive'. This expression of
classic Liberal values makes knowing 'things', and (not) knowing Greek
an issue of Liberal policy.

Robert Lowe, then, in his Edinburgh speech of 1867 is establishing
a position, aggressively as ever, towards one pole of the bitter education debate. Although many of the detailed arguments – the uniqueness
of Greek, its use(lessness), its cultural value – were repeated from the
eighteenth to the twentieth centuries, the heady mix of constitutional
and educational reform at this juncture reframes the question of what
it means to know Greek and what the place of Greek in the curriculum is. Knowing Greek is fully part of a political agenda. Sidgwick and
Farrar published from within the centre of elite learning, and attacked
'knowing Greek' as the centre of elite learning; they find support in radical Liberal thinking and in the new claims of science, as they make their
assault on the tradition of university study and its corollary in the public schools. Lowe's arguments chime with theirs, but are aimed more at
the economics of education and, most importantly, at the social requirements of education within a class structure: his different stance on reform
shines through. This also distinguishes him from Grant Duff, the well-
connected reformer, who argues as ever for a continuum of educational
and social reform. Mill, however, who opposed Lowe on reform also
finds himself in opposition to Lowe on learning Greek (as does Sellar,
from within the university system). Lowe, who had the best access to the
press and to a wide audience, brought to bear the weight of his acknowledged (and hated) economic expertise and his governmental authority
against the 'usefulness' of learning Greek (a definition of the question
whose effects are still being felt). He made this 'usefulness' a *political* issue, not least by widening the debate away from the universities and
elite schools to a 'question of national importance' under the banner of
needing to educate a new electorate for their new role. Yet his opposition
to reform and to democracy in general also meant that in his eyes 'the elementary schools should not be organized to change the world but to
keep it exactly as it was'.[129] Lowe's institutional or political opposition to

[128] Farrar (1867) 239.   [129] Briggs (1955) 258.

Greek in schools is intricately intertwined with his own complex version of Liberalism.

Lowe's speech caused particular dismay to Gladstone, the Prime Minister, and to one of his oldest friends, Benjamin Jowett. Gladstone himself published extensively on Homer: *his* address before the University of Edinburgh, delivered in 1865, on the place of Classics in 'The Providential Order of the World' was published in its seventy page (*sic*) pomp, and went through four editions (to the bafflement of modern taste) the year before Lowe's less providential speech.[130] Lowe's speech couldn't be more pointedly opposed to the intellectual commitments of the leader of his party. Gladstone, however, went on to bring Lowe into his cabinet as Chancellor, and was regularly in social contact with him. Jowett was another public figure whom Lowe had met early in his political career; Lowe remained on close terms with him, and masterminded the necessary manoeuvres to get him appointed Master of Balliol (with Gladstone's Olympian support). Jowett 'would never have become master' without Lowe's efforts.[131] At Balliol, Jowett was instrumental in establishing a new ethos of university education, based on the study of classics, especially Greek, in the intimate setting of the tutorial, which came to epitomize the training of the young of England who would rule the Empire.[132] Jowett became synonymous with knowledge – knowledge that linked educational policy with a personal politics via a study of Greek – knowledge that *counted*. ('First come I. My name is J-w-tt. / There's no knowledge, but I know it. / I am the Master of this College. / What I don't know isn't knowledge.')[133] Jowett's teaching of Plato became an icon of the study of Greek as *useful*, even necessary education (hence the delight of the story of Swinburne, who, when he was reading the proofs of Jowett's celebrated translation of Plato, interrupted one of the Master's tutorials by joyfully crowing from the bedroom 'another howler, Master!').[134] One of the most regular visitors at the Master's Lodge was Robert Lowe (and Jowett regularly visited Lowe's London address). They discussed Greek together, at length. Lowe amused his friends by translating the press' barbs against him into Greek and Latin epigrams. Lowe could, and did, quote pages of Thucydides to make points of prose style.[135] Lowe also became a trustee of the British Museum where, like a Keats or a Shelley, he loved to stand before the Elgin Marbles: 'he loved to look again and

[130] Gladstone (1865).   [131] Faber (1957) 350.

[132] See Dowling (1994), and especially Symonds (1986). Larson (1999) gives an excellent overview of the issues with good further bibliography.

[133] Faber (1957) 21–2.   [134] Benson (1930) 151.

[135] Jowett wrote a memoir of Lowe printed in Martin (1893) 482–500.

again at the Greek statues and friezes, with an instinctive feeling for art which was very wonderful and acute. How he acquired such taste without eyesight and without special training seems inexplicable.'[136] In his final months of blindness, his solace was to have Homer read to him. Lowe remained a delighted and instrumental participant in Oxford's burgeoning Hellenism, and the artistic world of London's Greek displays.

'Knowing Greek' became a site of contention in social and educational reform, that came to a head in the debates of 1867. Those for and against constitutional reform could adopt different positions on educational reform – even though most (liberals at least) saw the necessity of a link between these areas of change. Yet extreme dismissals of classical education overlapped with an easy adoption of its ideals in the drawing room or between friends. Lowe happily writes a Greek epigram to deflect those who abused him for vilifying Greek learning. (It's not surprising that Jowett thought him 'so misunderstood', and said he spoke 'of his own subjects in a manner which, to the public, was puzzling and inconsistent' – privately, he . . .)[137] But the extreme assaults on classics had the effect of making total support for the status quo seem quickly out of date. Headmaster Thring could only seem a dinosaur. Mill and Sellar have to recognize the need to go beyond classics in the curriculum, for all that Greek and Latin possess for them such unique qualities. It was quickly and broadly *recognized* that 'In the times which are coming the classical languages will be less studied . . . Modern life tends more and more towards practical or scientific education . . . Mr Lowe and many other high authorities do not greatly deplore this change.'[138] Yet Jowett, whose powerful position as Master was engineered by Lowe, continued to keep Greek at the centre of his system of education at Oxford – with tentacles, it was boasted, throughout the corridors and caravans of Empire. Classics still dominated entrance requirements for government departments, the church, universities. The privilege of knowing Greek continued to link the reformers, their opponents and their pupils.

Lowe, along with his friends and colleagues, Mill, Jowett, Gladstone, Grant Duff, Sellar grew up studying Greek, and they shared a deep working knowledge of Greek, discussed Greek together, and revelled in their knowledge of the ancient world. It was a hard won and integral part of their lives. Yet the politics of reform and the politics of education were differently negotiated by each, with different ideals, policies and success.

[136] Mrs Chaworth Musters, in her memoir of her uncle, printed in Martin (1893) 519–20.
[137] Martin (1893) 497.
[138] Arnold (1869) xi – Matthew Arnold was annoyed (Raleigh (1961) 252) to be mistaken for this Arnold (no relation).

'Knowing Greek' was for them a political issue – an issue through which they could express concerns about class, social mobility, and the needs of society; about what *other* people should learn for the good of the state. They all *knew* Greek: they were arguing about what such knowledge could and should mean for England.

III 1883, AND SWEET MR ARNOLD GOES TO AMERICA

In 1883, the sixty-year-old Matthew Arnold went to America for the first time.

Arnold was by 1883 one of the grand old men of English intellectual society, and an extremely widely read essayist in post-bellum America. He had written about America in the development of his views on democracy and social reform, but it was only the invitation of Andrew Carnegie (whom he had met at dinner), along with the promotional skills of his manager, Richard D'Oyly Carte, which finally enabled him to make the trip across the Atlantic.[139] His son had run up considerable gambling debts at Oxford,[140] and Arnold, whose job as a school inspector never produced financial comfort for him, needed to make this tour and needed it to be successful.

'Lectures are to America what opera is to Italy and theatre to France', declared *The Daily News*[141] – that is, the archetypal form of popular intellectual entertainment and relaxation. Charles Dickens had visited earlier from England and his dramatic readings had been a fantastic critical and commercial success. Oscar Wilde would also be a great hit. At the same time as Arnold, Lily Langtry, the music-hall star, and Irving, the actor, were also crossing America (severally) for their different styles of multi-city tour. Media stars from England were big business. Arnold had steamed from England with a blaze of publicity from *The Times*, and his trip was eagerly anticipated in the American press. Arnold himself, writing home to family, describes with shocked fascination the constant demands of celebrity – the hand exhausted from autograph signing, the brain dulled from the constant round of receptions, the lack of privacy and time for writing and reading, the invasive press attention.[142]

---

[139] On Arnold and Carnegie see McBride (1988). On Arnold and America, see especially Raleigh (1961); Connell (1950) 68–83; Arnold's works on America are collected in *CPW* x; see also Coulling (1988); Mazzeno and Lefcowitz (1988).

[140] De Laura (1962) 277. The boy came good, and is one of the friends musically portrayed in Elgar's *Enigma Variations*.

[141] *Daily News* 22 October 1883.   [142] Arnold (1903) XV. 133–4.

An extraordinary number of lecture halls of a great size had been booked
for the coming three months. This tour was to crown Arnold's international repute in the English-speaking world.

Arnold delivered one particular lecture no fewer than twenty-nine
times in cities throughout the East, the Midwest and the South.[143] This
talk – 'Literature and Science' – with its wonderful Darwinian defence
of Greek will be my prime concern in this section of the chapter. It
had first been given as the Rede Lecture in Cambridge, England in
1882, and was slightly adapted for the American audience. When he
returned to Britain, he delivered it one last time in Dundee, a small
town in Scotland. The audience there was between 2,000 and 2,500
people, a staggering number for such a performance in such a place. He
regularly drew more than a thousand to halls in America, in the larger
cities, and 3,500 in Boston.[144] Coverage in the press was intense, and
the social whirl continuous. ('Then I dressed, found the students outside
the hall to escort me to the lecture hall, was cheered by them . . . At the
Hall I was again cheered, then I gave the lecture on Emerson, and was
cheered again . . . a reception was held, with all Andover in it . . . Then I
was driven to the station by Professor Churchill, introduced by him to a
"leading citizen", who talked to me all the way to Boston . . . Presently,
I shall be taken over a publishing house and a newspaper office, neither
of which I care to see, then I shall lunch with my agent and try my voice
in Tremont Temple; then I shall pay some calls of farewell . . . '[145] And
so on.) If you read Arnold's letters, Henry James' praise, or Carnegie's
awestruck admiration, you might easily fail to pick up that 'on the popular
or journalistic level . . . Arnold became a national joke'.[146] The tour was
certainly not the crowning success it had been planned to be.

Arnold's failure partly stemmed from an ambivalent response towards
elite English culture and *its* response to America, now after the Civil
War. James Lowell explained to Leslie Stephen that English support
for the Confederacy during the civil war more even than the status of
former colony rankled with him: 'I share with the great body of my
countrymen in a bitterness (half resentment and half regret) which I
cannot get over.'[147] In his published writing, Lowell is less apologetic.

[143] Dates and places listed in *CPW* x. 465–6.
[144] Arnold (1903) xv. 147.   [145] Arnold (1903) xv. 161–2.
[146] Raleigh (1961) 58 – see *Harper's Monthly Magazine* 77 (July 1888) 314 for William Howell's use of
the phrase.
[147] Lowell (1904) xv. 116–17.

In his lovely, if arch, essay 'On a Certain Condescension in Foreigners' (which Arnold read but didn't really get), Lowell comments 'Every foreigner is persuaded that, by doing this country the favor of coming to it, he has laid every native under an obligation, pecuniary or other . . .'[148] Arnold's reserved manner and talk of social nicety easily looked like 'a certain condescension', just as his generalizations about national identity proudly declared his foreignness – and he was also accused in the press of being merely in pursuit of 'filthy lucre' in his lecturing.[149]

You could indeed tell the story of the tour as a disaster.[150] Arnold's support of the grand cultural tradition, which led him to declare America simply 'uninteresting', because of its lack of cultural 'depth', was seen – unsurprisingly – as blatant old-world snobbery towards the new.[151] And there was plenty in Arnold's 'pompous and rather extravagant air . . . with a certain *hauteur* in his dismissiveness and sweeping judgements' to encourage an audience's dislike. The press mocked his 'harsh features, supercilious manners . . . and ill-fitting clothes', and his 'lecturing like an elderly bird pecking at grapes on a trellis'.[152] (The first is from the ever tough Chicago press, the second from Detroit.) What's more, his religious views dismayed the often deeply conventional Christianity of the towns he visited (and led to protests): Haverford College refused to let the heretic lecture, with the usual result of making the students even keener to hear him.[153] An elaborate newspaper hoax between rival papers led to the widespread circulation of disparaging views of Arnold and his views of America, and even when the hoax was revealed, the mud stuck.[154] The first lecture Arnold gave in New York before a distinguished audience of over a thousand spectacularly bombed because he was barely audible in the hall. General Grant, hero of the war, walked out. Even Mrs Andrew Carnegie thought Arnold's manner 'too ministeerial, Mr Arnold, too ministeerial', a remark which so tickled Arnold that he kept repeating it.[155] Even the stirring account of the success of the Emerson lecture in Massachusetts which I just quoted from Arnold's letters home, should have included the outraged response of Bostonians to his critical remarks on their hero, and the angry response to his talk in

---

[148] Lowell (1904) I. 298.   [149] Arnold (1903) XV. 139.
[150] Full range of responses recorded in Raleigh (1961) 47–87.
[151] Raleigh (1961) 78.
[152] Both remarks quoted (with others) Coulling (1974) 289. Arnold (1903) XV 176–7 himself quotes the Detroit description.
[153] Raleigh (1961) 73–6.   [154] Coulling (1974) 289–91.
[155] Whole story in Murray (1996) 303–30.

the papers (though other American cities rather enjoyed the discomfort of the Bostonians).

A disaster, then? Yet Arnold continued to fill halls, and his writing continued to maintain a hugely influential role. (Arnold's public reputation seems always to have lurched between strident dismissal and deep respect.)[156] *The Nation* in its obituary of him saw his power as offering a form of almost religious belief to a lost generation, unhinged by the new science of Mill, Darwin and Huxley: John Stuart Mill, Charles Darwin and Thomas Huxley had 'destroyed [young men's] interest in theological discussions which perturbed the previous generation . . . To tens of thousands who could not worship science . . . it seemed for a moment as if Arnold had hit on a way of proving something that could take the place of a creed and cultivate the faculty of reverence and keep alive the faith in the final triumph of righteousness'.[157] National joke, or guru to thousands of young men . . . Obituaries tend to be rather too committed to sad euphemisms, of course, and Arnold's engagement in religious debate, like his opposition to science, was far more complicated than *The Nation* suggests – and, as with Erasmus, shows how repeatedly and easily discussions of Greek become embroiled in *theological* controversy. But the journal does capture a central claim of 'Literature and Science' rather well. For with a religious sense of mission, Arnold's lecture was a crowning statement of his struggle against the claims of science and practical study and on behalf of classical literature.

'Science and Literature' provides the focus of the coming pages. I am interested, of course, in the arguments that Arnold delivered so many times to so many people. It is 'an essay which summed up in itself the essence of all his previous writing on an aspect of human thought . . . the epitome, the almost perfect statement of his doctrine'.[158] But I am also interested in seeing how this piece plays different polemical roles from its first delivery in Cambridge, England to its last performance in Dundee. Arnold's speech did not – could not – have the same impact in England and America, and the difference is testimony of the spread of arguments about 'knowing Greek' beyond the educationalist debates into the sphere of a broadly defined 'culture'. You do not have to agree with Arnold's biographer (who may have his own axe to grind) that Arnold is 'the Victorian who matters most'.[159] But it is certainly the case that

---

[156] Collini (1994) is good on this. See Wilkins (1959) for collection of comments.
[157] 'Matthew Arnold', *The Nation* 46, 19 April 1888, 316.
[158] *CPW* x. 462.   [159] Murray (1996).

Arnold's views of what is at stake in knowing Greek have had a long-lasting and profound effect on thinking about cultural value.

I need first to trace the line of the argument of the lecture itself. 'Practical men talk with a smile of Plato and of his absolute ideas...'[160] This is a wonderfully engaging and, to use an Arnoldian term, poised opening line to the talk. It is engaging – it engages you – because it inveigles you into a matrix of self-positionings: are you a practical man or not? One who smiles at Plato or not? Are you comfortable with such talk of Plato and his absolute ideas? It is poised because it enables Arnold to appear to develop a multiform and nuanced position, which will slide towards his own pre-ordained conclusion. 'Plato's ideas do often seem unpractical and impracticable', he confides, especially, perhaps, in 'a great work-a-day world like the United States',[161] his audience's world. Indeed, Plato's celebrated and snobby disdain for arts and trades is scarcely going to have much purchase in 'a great industrious community such as that of the United States'.[162] Education is often accused of being too influenced by the ideas of men like Plato: why should such a traditional education be 'inflict[ed] ... upon an industrious modern community': such a community 'must and will shape its education to suit its own needs'.[163] Indeed, 'the tyranny of the past, many think, weighs on us injuriously in the predominance given to letters and education'.[164] This evidently attractive account of old-style teaching is what Arnold sets out to counter. He aims to challenge 'the design of abasing what is called "mere literary instruction and education" and of exalting what is called "sound, extensive and scientific knowledge"'.[165] The opening word of the lecture, 'practical', now comes home to roost: it is the practical men, smiling at Plato, that Arnold is attacking. Which side of the fence were – are – you on? Is modern, workaday, industrious society enough for you?

The structure of Arnold's argument is articulated polemically as a self-defence. (Socratic ironies are never far from Arnold.) He begins by placing his case within a precise polemical context. Arnold's celebrated definition of 'culture' – 'to know the best which has been thought and said in the world' – had been publicly criticized by the great scientist and reformer, T. H. Huxley, as if Arnold were the prince of *belle lettres*, of 'ornamental' education. (Arnold's brilliance at coining catch-phrases such as 'sweetness and light' means that his ideas – still – are recognisable

[160] *CPW* x. 53.   [161] *CPW* x. 53.   [162] *CPW* x. 54.
[163] *CPW* x. 55.   [164] *CPW* x. 55.   [165] *CPW* x. 55.

and trivialisable in equal measure.) Arnold carefully distances himself from Huxley's attack: 'when we talk of knowing Greek and Roman antiquity . . . I for my part mean a knowledge which is something more than a superficial humanism, mainly decorative.'[166] Rather, he means a 'scientific' knowledge of Greek antiquity, a full picture: 'When I speak of knowing Greek and Roman antiquity . . . as a help to knowing ourselves and the world, I mean more than a knowledge of so much vocabulary, so much grammar, so many portions of authors in the Greek and Latin language; I mean knowing the Greeks and Romans, and their life and genius, and what they were and did in the world, what we get from them, and what is its value.'[167] Robert Lowe's exemplary critique of the study of vocabulary, grammar and learning ancient texts off by heart are sidestepped by Arnold's broad sense of knowing Greek. Arnold's defence will not be of the *form* of traditional education. He wants you to know something else.

Arnold, however, also agrees promptly and disarmingly with Huxley that science undoubtedly has a place in 'the best that has been thought and said in the world', and concedes that 'the habit gained of dealing with facts is a most valuable discipline' (he will not challenge science's innovative comprehension of the physical world).[168] Science, too, he declares, must have a place (no extreme dismissiveness here).[169] This carefully polite polemical nicety, however, is all introduction to the more aggressive central case of the essay. Arnold aims totally to dismantle Huxley's own central claim that 'an exclusively scientific education is at least as effectual as an exclusively literary education'. For Arnold, rather, an education in literary knowing is wholly necessary if science is to have an adequate, proper and long-lasting role in human life. Science is to be subordinate to literary knowing. Arnold – enacting 'sweetness and light' – introduces his slashing arguments as an exercise in 'tentative inquiry' (as opposed to the 'ability and pugnacity of the partisans of natural science [which] make them formidable persons to contradict').[170] Such rhetorical self-deprecation – typical of Arnold and straight from the classical handbook on rhetoric – certainly does not prevent the boldest of phrase-making and a most passionate defence.

Arnold immediately and starkly declares that 'the constitution of human nature' will be the weapon to shoot down the partisans of 'natural

---

[166] *CPW* x. 57.   [167] *CPW* x. 57–8.   [168] *CPW* x. 61.
[169] For more general discussion of the issue of science in Arnold see Connell (1950) 170–202; Dudley (1942).
[170] *CPW* x. 61.

science'. By adding the adjective 'human' to 'nature', Arnold wants to wrestle 'nature' back from the (natural) scientists. He wants 'facts' on his side too: 'Deny the facts altogether, I think he scarcely can. He can hardly deny that the powers which go to the building of human life . . . are the power of conduct, the power of intellect and knowledge, the power of beauty, and the power of social life and manners.'[171] Knowledge, all knowledge, is interesting; items of knowledge are integral to any intellectual pursuit; instrumental knowledge requires experts – yet it is relating such knowledge to a wider 'sense of human life' that is essential. Natural sciences, like the study of Greek accents or metre, are limited because it 'will be *knowledge* only which they give us; knowledge not put for us into relation with our sense for conduct, our sense for beauty, and touched with emotion by being so put'.[172] And such limited knowledge will be 'for the majority of mankind, after a certain while, unsatisfying, wearying'.[173] Without a full contextualization within human society, defined by conduct, intellect, beauty, manners, any fact, any account of the natural world, will be ultimately without satisfaction. Science without ethics or aesthetics is just boring.

The qualification Arnold slips in – 'to the majority of mankind' – is an important strategic hinge. He is happy to allow the expert mathematician, like his friend Professor Sylvester, or the 'born naturalist' his – always 'his' – special gifts, talents and obsessions. Education, general education, however, must have different criteria. (It is the middle ground Arnold is fighting for, just as classical study had been attacked as useless 'for most people'.) The rhetorical diffidence of Arnold's 'tentative inquiry' *enables* him to move to one side the extremes of research or of attainment in the name of a more general human requirement of relating even such facts of science to behaviour, aesthetics, ethics – and thus of proving that it is the educative power of literature, especially ancient literature, which makes it possible to connect, only connect. (Whenever a rhetorician pleads diffidence, we should be on the look out for the aggressive strategy such diffidence embodies.) If you were to ask *how* 'poetry and excellence [are] to exercise the power of relating the modern results of science to man's instinct for conduct, his instinct for beauty', Arnold, I am afraid, confesses 'I answer that I do not know *how* they will exercise it', before adding, 'but that they can and will exercise it I am sure'.[174] And once again it is Homer who will be the test-case. Homer's 'conceptions of the physical world were, I imagine, grotesque, but his

---

[171] *CPW* x. 61–2.   [172] *CPW* x. 65.   [173] *CPW* x. 65.   [174] *CPW* x. 68.

words 'have a fortifying and elevating and suggestive power, capable of wonderfully helping us to relate the results of modern science to our own need for conduct, our need for beauty.'[175] Homer's power is to make science of true human value. As Arnold's piece is a lecture, perhaps it is not worth pausing over the fact that he evidently just restates rather than proves his claim here. For the case of Homer leads to a grand peroration in support of knowing Greek.

Greek has been the object of particular assault by practical men of science. ('Greek is the grand offender in the eyes of these gentlemen.') Yet 'the instinct for beauty is served by Greek literature and art as it is by no other literature and art'. The human 'instinct for self-preservation' should therefore inevitably keep 'Greek as part of our culture'. Arnold – as before with his remarks on grammar – hopes that 'Greek will come . . . some day to be studied more rationally than at present'[176] – a clear enough statement against current school practice. But he ringingly declares that Greek 'will be increasingly studied as men increasingly feel the need in them for beauty, and how powerfully Greek art and Greek literature can serve this need'.[177] He includes women in his vision of Greek studies of the future – his example from the past is Lady Jane Grey – and, for the American audience, he singles out Smith and Vassar for pioneering such work. Indeed, the need for Greek – its 'antique symmetry' – is so great in humans that Arnold wants it to be instinctual and natural – the final revenge of the classicists on the natural scientist. And he makes the point with a brilliant and funny purloining of Victorian science's most celebrated new discovery, the origin of the species:

The 'hairy quadruped furnished with a tail and pointed ears, probably arboreal in his habits', this good fellow carried hidden in his nature, apparently, something destined to develop into a necessity for humane letters. Nay, more; we seem finally to be even led to the further conclusion that our hairy ancestor carried in his nature, also, a necessity for Greek.[178]

A necessity for Greek, it seems, is natural, and determined from our hairy days hanging from the branches . . . Where the scientists made learning Greek an institutional and intellectual barrier to comprehending the facts of the natural world, Arnold's ironic delight in turning the origin of the species to his own purposes makes learning Greek the very

---

[175] *CPW* x. 68.   [176] *CPW* x. 70–1.   [177] *CPW* x. 71.   [178] *CPW* x. 72.

fulfilment of Nature's plan. Knowing Greek is an instinctual necessity inside us all, hairy or smooth.

This wonderfully unexpected conclusion epitomizes years of opinion making, in tone and in sentiment. His irony often greatly disturbed his starchy Victorian readers, and the turn to the Greeks in his poetry was repeatedly criticized as too great a withdrawal from contemporary life – a negative, if integral, side of his celebrated pose of disinterested critical observation.[179] His support for Greek in the public sphere is matched by a more private account. 'I read five pages of the Greek anthology every day, looking out the words I do not know; this is what I shall always understand by *education* and it does me good and gives me great pleasure.'[180] A private letter offering a no doubt selective and creative image of the public man at leisure; but both the emphasis on the word '*education*' (from a school inspector and polemicist on educational theory) and the echo of the standard ancient rhetorical criteria of educational purpose ('profit' and 'pleasure') provide the frame of public debate against which his reading habits (are to) echo. To the boys of Eton he more simply glosses his definition of culture again with 'Of the *best*, the classics of Greece and Rome form a very chief portion.'[181] Diligently, he sent a copy of the speech to Gladstone, as he thought the Prime Minister would enjoy its views. Supporters of Greek, together in high places . . .

In his role as Inspector of Schools, however, he took a more pointedly political and reforming line. The aspirations of some to have Greek learnt at the new state schools 'are dangerous', he wrote in a departmental report, because 'they tend to make us lose sight of the actual present condition of our problems of popular education, and so far they do harm'.[182] Even to *want* to have Greek on the curriculum is destructive since such idealism can distract from the real and more pressing needs of the schools he visited. Similarly, Latin should be the second language after English, a subsidiary topic. 'But it should by no means be taught as in our classical schools; far less time should be spent on the grammatical framework, and classical literature should be kept quite out of view.'[183] The practical concerns of school teaching run through these reports in a way scarcely evident in the speech-making of Lowe, Duff and Mill. He wrote to Duff: 'what is the good of for ever talking about the Greeks and Hellenism, if nine people out of ten

[179] Collini (1994).   [180] Arnold (1903) XV. 368.   [181] *CPW* IX. 21.
[182] Arnold (1908) 207.   [183] Arnold (1908) 149.

can have no notion, from practical experience, what they are like and wherein their power'.[184] Arnold, it seems, can also manipulate the criterion of 'practical experience' as a criterion for teaching and learning Greek.

Pivotal to the connection between Arnold's work as a Government Inspector of Schools and his role as public intellectual is his report, published as a volume (in 1868), called *Schools and Universities on the Continent*. This was the product of a lengthy fact-finding trip through Switzerland, Italy, France and Germany. (Arnold was always fiercely in favour of French literary culture and deeply imbued with a Goethean sense of self-fulfilment through art.) His report was written in 1867, at the height of the debate about reform and education. It contains lengthy descriptions of the educational systems of those countries, and observes that, although the debate between classical and modern education is not yet resolved, none the less these foreign systems have many lessons for England, which, in his eyes, lags lamentably far behind the continent in educational reform.

Humboldt is quoted on the frontispiece of this book, and its passionate conclusion calls for a full overhaul of the English system in favour of a true (Prussian) '*Altertumswissenschaft*', 'Science of Antiquity'. He pillories current teaching methods in England and their obsession with philology. Too few students can pass into the hallowed halls of knowing Greek because the entrance ticket is set too high: 'a student must be of the force of Wolf who used to sit up the whole night with his feet in a tub of cold water and one of his eyes bound up to rest while he read with the other'. 'Such students', he adds laconically, 'are rare.'[185] *Altertumswissenschaft*, however, provides 'an unsurpassed source of light and stimulus'. 'The Greek spirit' gives a 'precious lesson'.[186] Some may claim that it is 'only through philological studies' that '*Altertumswissenschaft* itself [is] truly revealed', but 'for all practical purposes this proposition is untrue'.[187] Knowing Greek should not mean suffering under grammar books and composition exercises, but finding the light, the stimulus, the lesson. What is needed for schools is a more general education, he proposes. In the name of the 'Modern Spirit', cut out so much Latin and Greek verse composition and grammar (it is not an 'intelligent tradition', but mere 'routine'); find a place for moden literature, for the mother tongue, and even for foreign languages. Natural science too has

[184] Arnold (1903) XIV. 396.   [185] Arnold (1868) 262.   [186] Arnold (1868) 258, 259.
[187] Arnold (1868) 263. I have silently corrected spelling/printing errors in this and following citations from this work.

its role ('it is also a vital and formative knowledge to know . . . the laws which govern nature'.)[188] 'Every man is born with aptitudes which give him access to vital and formative knowledge . . . The business of instruction is to seize and develop these aptitudes.'[189] Greek is to be the queen of the disciplines in the new world of schools and universities, where each person's aptitudes lead to fulfilled knowledge, in order, as the frontispiece proclaims in Humboldt's voice, 'to raise the culture of the nation ever higher and higher'.

This report was not widely reviewed (though the liberal Farrar praised it lavishly, and, at great length, Oscar Browning of Eton and King's, took umbrage at its anti-English stance), nor is it much discussed today.[190] But it sets out in Arnold's more technical prose three central ideas which will recur throughout the next years' writing right up to 'Literature and Science'. First, and most in tune with the late 1860s, education needs radical reform. The final sentence of the book is 'I cannot help presenting myself once more to my countrymen with an increased demand: *organize your secondary and superior instruction*.'[191] Arnold, so often put down as a grandmaster of elitism and tradition, is active right at the centre of liberal reform. Second, the issue of education is a national concern, and one to be evaluated by international comparison. Fulfilment through education – culture as (self-)cultivation – is for Arnold not just or primarily the task of an individual in a Goethean artistic quest, but the social duty of at least a group and ideally a nation. His commitment to Hellenism is fully part of a nationalism that necessarily embraces strong and often disturbing notions of class and race in pursuit of an Englishness for the English.[192] This inevitably affects his reception in America. Third, and of most direct relevance here, his maintenance of Greek as the pinnacle of educational achievement, although he calls what he requires '*Altertumswissenschaft*', is a promotion of Greek as *Bildung* – that is, the promotion of a sense of a specifically Greek spirit, of ideals of 'dignity and a high spirit . . . the love of things of the mind, the flexibility, the spiritual moderation' of 'an antique symmetry'.[193] Scholarship is secondary to spirit. Arnold doesn't mind admitting that he has to look up words when he reads the Greek anthology.

[188] Arnold (1868) 258.   [189] Arnold (1868) 258–9.
[190] Though see the good remarks of Court (1992) esp. 108–11. Browning's review is in *Quarterly Review* 125 (October 1868) 473–90; Farrar's in *Fortnightly Review* (June 1868) 709–11; see also W. Bagheot *Fortnightly Review* (June 1868) 639–47.
[191] Arnold (1868) 296.
[192] See Court (1992); Faverty (1951); Young (1995) 55–89.
[193] Arnold (1868) 265; *CPW* x. 71.

Arnold made his name as a polemicist through his savagely sardonic critique of translations of Homer while he was Professor of Poetry at Oxford; he worked as a professional within the educational system throughout his life; unlike Mill in particular, he called repeatedly for increased centralized control of education. Yet his ideal remained a Hellenism which could illumine and improve the present emotionally, intellectually, morally – 'an instrument of intellectual deliverance from the confusion of contemporary life'.[194] Far from expressing a backward-looking traditionalism, this form of 'knowing Greek' was a challenging model for 'young men': it filled lecture halls with a message about modern culture. 'Knowing Greek' was a cultural promise.

Culture and Anarchy was the book which made Arnold's idea of Hellenism a cultural icon. The volume, a collection of previously published essays, was published in 1869, and set its agenda in response to the education debates of the previous years (and, as ever, in particularly hostile opposition to Robert Lowe's imposition of 'mechanical' tests of reading, writing and arithmetic). Its frame, however, is much wider than the education system *per se*, as the subtitle, 'an essay in political and social criticism' indicates. '*Culture and Anarchy* is a sustained protest against what [Arnold] saw as the intellectual, asthetic and emotional narrowness of English society – against its puritan moralism, its provincialism, its smugness and complacency, its lack of interest in ideas or feelings for style, its pinched and cramped ideals of human excellence; against, in short, its "philistinism".'[195] This is the prose work of Arnold's which has received most attention from modern critics, and here I need make only the barest of comments by way of leading back towards 'Science and Literature' and its American reception.

Culture and Anarchy's catchy anatomy of the English class system – he divides the English into barbarians, philistines, and populace, that is, the upper, middle and lower classes – and the cultural matrix of 'Hebraism and Hellenism' (borrowed from Heine), quickly became instantly recognisable slogans, repeated, brandished, parodied (as did 'sweetness and light', with which his Hellenism is imbued). The reader (thus) is invited to place himself or herself as a barbarian, philistine or even among the uneducated masses – or to take up the possibility of being an 'alien'. You are invited to judge your culture according to the 'governing idea of Hellenism', which is '*spontaneity of consciousness*' and/or 'that of Hebraism', which is '*Strictness of conscience*'.[196] Hebraism focuses on the ideals of

[194] Faverty (19) 31.   [195] Collini (1994) 78.   [196] *CPW* v. 165.

'duty, of moral will, of subjugation of the self'. Hellenism, by contrast, 'concerns itself more with knowledge and beauty, with the play of ideas and charm of form'.[197] And England, especially middle-class England, he made plain, infected all its citizens with an excess of Hebraism. The discomforting that Arnold aims at – 'it is very animating to think that one at last has a chance of *getting at* the English public'[198] – was effective, in that there is no happy position beyond Arnold's dismissive and ironic description of England and Englishness for his English audience. Readers often responded angrily to what they saw as his snootiness – a 'Greeker-than-thou tone'[199] – and his *de haut en bas* dislike of contemporary achievement and value ('shuddering aloof from the rank exhalation of vulgar enthusiasm and holding up the pouncet-box of culture betwixt the wind and his nobility': Henry Sidgwick in full cry again).[200] It is no surprise that the book was received both with anger and with delight, as a beacon and a sneer, both as a radical call and – more often – as an anti-liberal polemic. *Culture and Anarchy* made Hellenism a sign of the state of the nation and a symbolic term in the contestation of English cultural life.

The phrases by which Hellenism was identified in *Culture and Anarchy* – 'a kind of aerial ease, clearness and radiancy', 'full of what we call sweetness and light', 'simple and attractive ideal', 'a delicate discrimination', 'to see things as they really are' – constantly emphasize control, balance, serenity, clarity – terms adapted from an earlier period of German Greekomania. ('Serenity' in particular was a watchword of post-Winckelmann art appreciation, as it was of post-Goethean literary criticism.)[201] They might seem to evoke a certain distance, or even other worldliness, though they are no doubt cousins of his famous praise of the perfect Sophocles who could 'see life steadily and see life whole'. Yet the religious polemic which runs through *Culture and Anarchy* (especially his criticism of the Dissenters which so dominates its opening pages) coupled with his specific political jibes against the political leaders of the day, and the highly provocative description of current social and intellectual vapidities, give Arnold's criticism a biting contemporary edge. (The aims of steadiness and poise were striven for with some self-consciously exaggerated and mocking poses.) An engagement with a Greek ideal –especially in contrast with Hebraism – demanded a

[197] Collini (1994) 82. Best discussion of this is still de Laura (1969).
[198] Arnold (1904) II 186.   [199] Jenkyns (1981) 265.
[200] Sidgwick, H. 'The Prophet of Culture', *Macmillan's Magazine* 16 (Aug. 1867) 271–80. Arnold echoed this criticism *CPW* v. 116.
[201] Morrison (1994).

religious self-assessment and a stance on national culture, and thus, inevitably, controversy. To talk of Greekness directly embroiled the reader
in critical self-evaluation (and led to personalized criticism of Arnold by
his opponents).

In 1883 in America, Arnold is returning to these arguments to re-
state his position. Cheered by students, mocked by the press, lionized or
snubbed by intellectuals, and constantly 'getting at' his audience, Arnold
cannot just talk of 'Greek versus Science' as if it were an issue of the school
curriculum. He is at the very least doing so in the role of the figurehead
of a new Hellenism as a means of cultural and political criticism. What's
more, his most widely circulated book, *Literature and Dogma* had made
Arnold anathema in orthodox religious circles. (Published in 1873 it
ran to five editions and sixteen further 'popular editions' in his lifetime.
Reviewers' key notes: 'ignorance', 'insolence', 'imbecility', 'wild imagination and hopeless conclusions'.)[202] It also made him a major player
in non-ecclesiastical discussion of religion ('rare moral and intellectual
force', 'powerfully conceived').[203] For many in America Arnold was a
threateningly unorthodox religious figure, someone to keep your children from hearing. How snide, then, how rhetorically loaded is Arnold
being when he casually notes that Darwin 'once owned to a friend that he
did not experience the necessity for two things that most men find so necessary to them – religion and poetry'?[204] Arnold – the poet and religious
writer – rhetorically *sidelines* the extreme figure of the 'born naturalist'
because he lacks what most men (should) require – poetry and religion.
Arnold delivers 'Literature and Science', in short, freighted with a public history of intellectual controversy. Arnold proclaims the necessity of
knowing Greek, and such a proclamation is mapped by the lines of his
years of public argument about education, religion and the politics of
culture.

There is, however, also a more specific polemical context in play here.
At the end of 1880 Thomas Huxley had delivered a lecture at the opening of Sir Josiah Mason's new Science College in Birmingham, England,
which had been published in 1881. Huxley, his biographer proudly declares, 'did as much as any man to determine the shape of English elementary education for the next three quarters of a century'.[205] Certainly
his science textbooks made the advancement of science in school possible, and he helped establish the London Board of Education. At the same

[202] Coulling (1974) 235–68; Collini (1994).
[203] Also taken from Coulling (1974) 236.   [204] *CPW* x 65.
[205] Bibby (1972) 85; see also Bibby (1959) and Bibby ed. (1971).

time, his victory in open debate over the Bishop of Oxford was a celebrated symbolic turning point in the public perception of Darwinism,
and (thus) the advance of modern science over and against a religious
understanding of the world. As a largely self-taught and brilliantly innovative naturalist from the most undistinguished of backgrounds he
was himself a marvellous icon of the new educational opportunities of a
non-classical system. He too became an English media intellectual star.
('America seems to have gone wild with excitement. The whole nation
is electrified by the announcement that Professor Huxley is coming to
visit.')[206] Back in 1868 he had published 'A Liberal Education and Where
to Find it' (originally a speech delivered – pointedly enough – in a new
working man's college in South London). This contains a brilliant and
sarcastic assault on current teaching practice, a comparison of the sorry
state of English education in comparison with German, and a highly
politicized account of 'useful' education. In 1879, he started an abortive
campaign to abolish compulsory Greek as an entrance requirement at
Cambridge. His unique combination of top-flight scientific research and
high profile political activism continued into the 1880s when he delivered
his opening address to the new science college at Birmingham.

This speech, like Arnold's reply a year or so later, sums up many
years of opinion making and comes freighted with a history of polemics.
Huxley defends at length two propositions: the first is that 'neither the
discipline nor the subject matter of classical education is of such direct
value to the student of physical science as to justify the expenditure of
valuable time upon either'.[207] The precision of this should be clear by
now. He carefully cuts off both standard defences of classics: neither the
way Greek is learnt – 'mental gymnastics' – nor what is taught, 'peerless
literature', has value – that is, use – for the student of science. It is a waste
of time (that Victorian industrial bugbear). The second proposition is a
necessary buttress to the first: 'for the purposes of attaining real culture,
an exclusively scientific education is at least as effectual as an exclusively
literary education'.[208] (We have already seen Arnold's come-back to this.)
Huxley, note, is claiming 'real culture' for science: 'perfect culture should
supply a complete theory of life based upon a clear knowledge alike of its
possibilities and its limitations'.[209] And that means science is necessary
in order to comprehend the world of nature. Indeed, it is even necessary
for knowing Greek: he reproaches those who teach the humanities for
lacking 'the spirit of ancient Greece', by which he means not a lack of

---

[206] Letter to Huxley, quoted, Bibby (1972) 96.   [207] Huxley (1881) 7.
[208] *Ibid.*   [209] Huxley (1881) 9.

Arnoldian 'sweetness and light', but rather the failure to see that to 'know all the best thoughts and sayings of the Greeks' means we should study Greek *science*. Huxley turns Arnold's definition to make science the proper subject of even the Greek lesson! So, finally, if you want to improve society, what is needed is not classics, but a scientific appreciation of the 'common principles of social action' – sociology not Hellenism.

Huxley does not name Arnold as his opponent, but he has no need to: his audience and Arnold knew against whom he was speaking (and if they missed it, *The Times* pointed it out anyway). Indeed, Huxley and Arnold were close friends, who exchanged unpublished and published work, corresponded frequently, dined together, met at the club, and expressed 'such affectionate liking and regard' for one another that their disagreement has been seen as 'nothing more than an amicable clarification, the shoring up of a basic agreement'.[210] Certainly Huxley is keen not just to disparage classical education, and Arnold saw his speech as 'playful sarcasm' rather than scornful insult: 'What you write of me', writes Arnold to Huxley, 'is extraordinarily kind and fair: forbid that I should make such a bad return as to enter into controversy with you.'[211] Arnold, too, carefully praises Huxley in his speech and sees the advance of science as inexorable. Yet the differences between their positions, for all the outbreaks of politeness, are fundamental and irreconcilable. The personal politics are again difficult to discriminate with sufficient rigour. Arnold fishes with Duff, has dinner with Huxley, drops a pamphlet off with Gladstone – and argues publicly with all of them on matters of deep importance to them all. It would seem that the discussion of classical education, like the even more anguished discussion of religion and the self, elided the boundaries between public and private, and extended the personal debate within a body of friends into the public arena of national policy making. The coherence, the intermeshing, of the intellectual, social and political world is a feature of the later Victorian scene.[212] Shared values, a shared education and shared social venues construct a specific and rather comfortable forum for turning society's inevitable hostilities, insults and malice into a more stately performance.

The effects of this gentlemanly agreement to disagree, however, are more longlasting. Arnold's Hellenism – its view of the Greek spirit – downplayed knowledge of the Greek language itself; indeed he called for the complete revision of Greek teaching and was even happy to

---

[210] See Coulling (1974) 281–6; Murray (1996) 253; quotation from Walcott (1970) 104.
[211] Armytage (1953) 352.   [212] See Collini (1991).

see Greek minimized in the national curriculum. He spoke of Homer's Greek with a new and influential vocabulary when he was Professor of Poetry in Oxford in the 1860s, but he did not revert in his later polemics to defending the specialness of the Greek language nor did he subscribe to the value of the 'mental gymnastics' of learning it. The ease with which Arnold's defence of Hellenism became seen as an elitist, traditionalist, or plain snooty removal of the self from everyday life, coupled with his own critical stance on the education system, and with his recognition of the inevitable and necessary rise of science, meant that his promotion of Hellenism, unintentionally, contained within it also the seeds of the decline of Greek studies.

When Arnold gave 'Literature and Science' as the Rede Lecture in Cambridge, England, or when he gave it in Dundee a year later, he spoke very much to the specifics of this later Victorian, English debate. Not all the Cambridge audience could be alive to the allusions and the freight (and, ominously for the American tour, those at the back couldn't really hear anyway![213]); nor could they all be aware of the specifics of the controversy with Huxley: yet the talk is given and received as if that knowledge were shared. In the hotbed, as it were, of university reform, Arnold's speech is part of an ongoing controversy in a decade of controversial speeches, pamphlets, journals. At the centre of an intellectual world, speaking from and to that centre, this speech is a wonderful symbol of how Victorian debate proceeded – complete with its commentary, from student notes to *The Times*, from personal letters to counter-speeches.

When Arnold speaks in America, however, he speaks as the emissary. For all that the debates over modes of education were keen in the United States, and for all the transatlantic intellectual traffic between, say, Lowell, Emerson, Carnegie *et al.*, 'Literature and Science' was inevitably received as a broadside from the elite centres of old education to the new world – with both the deference and the scorn you might expect of such an exchange. It had, simply, a different political purchase. Arnold's criticism of England in the name of Englishness – which inevitably brought his Hellenism into intricate and integral relation with his nationalism – was triangulated in America by the fierce self-consciousness of a post-civil war, nascent social order.[214] His Hellenism's critical superiority was

[213] *Cambridge Review* 21 June 1882, 391–2.
[214] It is interesting to note that at an important conference at Princeton in 1917 on the role of Classics in the curriculum, in all the talks and in the (more than 100) collected statements of support (including one from the President of the United States and three former Presidents), there is no explicit reference to Arnold or to Arnoldian Hellenism. See *Value of Classics*, Princeton, 1917, edited by A. West *et al.*.

quickly – though, of course, not by all – seen as *anti-American* – opposing a set of exclusive, old values to the new hopes of the United States. Walt Whitman is telling, if extreme (as ever). In an essay ironically entitled 'Our Eminent Visitors', he attacked Arnold's failure to understand America;[215] for years after, he mocked Arnold's desire to come and tell Americans about their own country. ('What a hell of a fellow . . . to come across here and tell us about America!')[216] He described Arnold's version of the world as 'rich, hefted, lousy, reeking, with delicacy, refinement, elegance, propriety, criticism, analysis: all of them things which threaten to overwhelm us'.[217] Arnold's proselytizing for the 'sweetness and light' of Hellenism became a moment to rally round a new nation's values against the insidious pull of the old world. Arnold in America cannot be one of Whitman's 'us'. Knowing Greek is subsumed within being American.

Arnold's promotion of Hellenism, then, in England and America intertwined his version of knowing Greek with the burgeoning concerns of nationalism, of science, of education, of taking a critical stance towards society and politics. In his most ironic vein, he could make knowing Greek a Darwinian necessity of the race of man. But the humour should not detract from the seriousness with which Arnold makes Hellenism an integral factor in the constitution of the cultured self. Yet his 'Greeker-than-thou' manner and dismissive argumentation also worked to associate 'knowing Greek' with an exclusivity and elitism which its denigrators played on (and still do). What's more, his professionally authorized criticism of the educational system together with his insistence on the *Geist* or *Bildung* of Hellenism eased apart knowing the Greek language from what counted for him in Hellenism, 'sweetness and light'. The fuzziness and inaccuracy of his depiction of the ancient world – which critics and supporters have equally noted – have a strategic role in his argument, too. What he wanted for *Altertumswissenschaft* is not what the contemporary German professoriate would have recognized by the term.

One-time fellow of Oriel College, Oxford, former Professor of Poetry at Oxford, professional Inspector of Schools for the Government, Arnold none the less speaks up for a far from academic sense of knowing Greek (although he is often despised for his intellectual elitism). *Bildung* is all. 'Self-culture is the ideal of man', as Oscar Wilde succinctly put it in homage to Arnold, and in the name of Goethe and the Greeks.[218]

[215] Whitman (1964) 541–5.   [216] Traubel (1906–64) II. 497.
[217] Traubel (1906–64) III. 400.   [218] Quoted Jenkyns (1981) 264.

It would be hard to select a more emblematic or more centrally active figure in the Victorian struggles over education and culture than Matthew Arnold, yet what Arnold reveals is how difficult it is adequately to place such a central figure within the matrices of professionalism/amateurism, academic life/cultural world, *Altertumswissenschaft/Bildung*, or even pro-Greek study/anti-Greek study. Arnold shows just how many different intellectual concerns, historical trajectories, political agendas transect the cultural promise of knowing Greek.

When Arnold concludes 'Literature and Science' with a hope that man's 'need for conduct', and 'need for beauty' will always make the 'attraction' of Greek 'irresistible', he is not expressing a 'simple trust'[219] in the future. Rather, he is constructing a highly nuanced rhetorical stance, in terms of his own intellectual history and in terms of the current arenas of controversy, a stance which aims to perform its own ideals of poise and genial humour on the reader, while setting his own sense of Hellenism against the pugnacious forces of science. It means to have an effect on you. He wants you, too, to join him in cultivation of the values of knowing Greek. Arnold, in England and America, is fighting to set Greek as a central value in his promotion of culture, yet the very terms in which he constructs his arguments, for all his social and cultural centrality, produce exactly the type of image which made possible the assaults of modernism and its sciences. The paradox of Arnold is that (like one of his heroic, doomed figures from Homer) his noble resistance turns out not just to delay but to guarantee the fall of the citadel.

IV 1891, AND MR HEADLAM STARTS A ROW

For the final section of this chapter, I shall be going parochial – back to Cambridge, to King's College, and to the very building I work in and the committees I sit on. The key players in this story are not likely to set the pulse of a non-classicist racing these days (though both are still names to conjure with in the history of studying Greek tragedy). But I do hope from the previous discussion that it will be appreciated why, even if some defensiveness may be in order, 'parochial' can't be a suitable term for arguments about knowing Greek (which engaged so many major figures of Victorian government and culture), especially when set in Cambridge, which is not only one of the centres of liberal reform but also, with Oxford, counts as the leading intellectual institution of the

[219] Jenkyns (1981) 274.

English-speaking world during the nineteenth century. The power and influence of Cambridge and Oxford in this era can scarcely be overestimated – Jowett's boasts of his students' elevated positions throughout the Empire were not without foundation – and yet the universities were also constantly embroiled in reform, both institutional and in terms of the ethos of study. After the political manoeuvring of Robert Lowe and the cultural politics of Matthew Arnold, it is time to look at the more narrowly academic world of the teachers of Greek.

My story concerns the publication of Walter Headlam's pamphlet 'On Editing Aeschylus'. It is a violent attack by Headlam – a 162-page review – of A. W. Verrall's recently published commentaries on Aeschylus' *Agamemnon* (1889) and *Seven Against Thebes* (1885). It is an extraordinary and vitriolic piece that brings intercollegiate rivalry, odium philologicum, and Housmanesque dismissal to a new boiling point. The row is about 'knowing Greek'. Headlam has a repeated rhetorical strategy of asking what an editor of Aeschylus should know, what knowledge he should possess, and then expressing shock at Verrall's ignorance.

There is no Greek of any period that is not useful . . . It is only by knowledge of prose that we can know what is poetical in any language; it is only by knowledge of late prose that we can judge what may or may not be glosses . . . No one will be hardy enough to deny that a competent editor of Aeschylus must possess knowledge at least of Homer, Hesiod, Solon, Theognis, Pindar and the lyric poets, Sophocles, Euripides, Herodotus. No one will aver that an editor is competent if ignorant of ordinary scholastic phrases.[220]

To edit Aeschylus you must *really* 'know Greek'. This general case is supported with a battery of detailed and often abstruse linguistic points, made in similarly strident tones: 'to be unacquainted with this matter of αὐδᾶσθαι, in connexion with which these passages are well known, is a strange thing in an editor of Aeschylus'.[221] 'Dr Verrall, like little boys learning Greek, seems to think that δέ is always adversative . . . '[222] Headlam aims to flatten Verrall with what he knows.

Headlam was twenty-five and only recently (1890) appointed a fellow at King's College, Cambridge.[223] Verrall, a fellow of Trinity College, Cambridge, who was to become the first Professor of English at Cambridge, was already a very well-known scholar, who had, as one

---

[220] Headlam (1891a) 1–2.   [221] Headlam (1891a) 41.   [222] Headlam (1891a) 123.
[223] Walter Headlam and his cousin James Headlam (with whom he is sometimes confused) were appointed to fellowships at King's on the same day; James became a distinguished civil servant in the same department as Matthew Arnold.

shocked reviewer pointed out, examined the Cambridge tripos before Headlam had become an undergraduate.[224] For Headlam (and his supporters) his broadside was a statement of principle that aligned him with the masters of *Altertumswissenschaft* in Germany. 'He stood for the highest ideals of Greek scholarship; and that ideal, he thought, was sometimes best served by personal criticism.'[225] That highest ideal should include 'his own marvellous knowledge of tragic diction', 'knowledge of the latest and worst authors', 'knowledge of anthropology', 'some acquaintance with the ideas of the East' – all in service of understanding the historical norms of Greek usage, its 'ideas'.[226]

Indeed, surpassing 'knowledge of Greek' became a repeated, central trope in descriptions of Headlam. 'There was an amusing phrase frequently on his lips when he dealt with the common tribe of modern emendators – "The man doesn't know Greek"' and 'he would fall into peals of cackling laughter'.[227] The image is rehearsed most amusingly and at greatest length by E. F. Benson:

> Their [the other classical fellows of King's] knowledge of Greek ended just about where Walter Headlam's began: his mind was Greek . . . Though he was of a rich and boyish humanity he had also that queer aloof quality which develops in those whose life is centred on research, and he passed into regions where no calls or needs of the flesh could penetrate.[228]

The life of research (that ideal of Germanic *Altertumswissenschaft*) in Benson's lightly ironic and elegant description of Headlam's denial of the flesh is allowed to look back towards some very distant ancestors in Jerome and the Fathers – scholarship as a higher calling. But Headlam's is no self-lacerating asceticism. Rather, it is an archetype of the 'absent-minded professor'. Benson gives a marvellous portrait of Headlam in his book-lined and crazily messy study, hunting a word, forgetting his shaving water, losing his lunch under a pile of papers:

> Then he found the passage he had originally started to hunt up. Awfully interesting: it was a slang word, not very polite, in use among the daughters of joy in Corinth during the fifth century BC. These intelligent ladies seemed to have an argot of their own: there were several other words of the sort he had come across. He became lost in this pursuit, his pipe had to be relit several times, and presently a smell of roasting metal brought him back for a brief moment to the

[224] A.B.C [Cook] (1892a) 317.   [225] Headlam, C. (1910) 78.
[226] Quotations from Headlam (1910) 48.
[227] [Shane Leslie] 'Walter Headlam', *The Academy* 8 October 1910, 351.
[228] Benson (1930) 134.

surface of life. His shaving water had all boiled away, and so he put out the the spirit lamp.[229]

And so on, unshaved and unfed, prey to serendipity and to obsession, Headlam works late into the night. That's what it means 'to know Greek'.

This image of Headlam speaks to a Victorian delight in eccentricity of character and 'brilliance' (which always justifies the eccentricity) – a delight typically encapsulated in the dinner-table squib or the anecdote in one's volume of memoirs. Indeed, Headlam's 'knowledge of Greek' and 'academic' manner drift into a host of stories about him. Headlam used his brilliant Greek to write brilliant thank-you poems to girls of Newnham College (their response is not recorded); he had a brief flirtation with Virginia Woolf,[230] who was busy learning Greek and trying to translate the *Agamemnon* which Headlam was writing a commentary on. (Her famous essay 'On not knowing Greek' implicitly raises the gender issues of such knowledge.[231] It is not by chance that all the dominant figures of this chapter – as of the others in this book – are male, since Greek study was so much perceived and practised as a male preserve, challenged only by a few heroines. Public figures like Jane Harrison or George Eliot (with whom the next chapter will end) inspired a string of less celebrated poets and scholars – and suffered for the public recognition of their scholarship.)[232] *Using* Greek is always charged, and could become, it seems, part of a particularly elaborate form of lightly eroticized exchange in the rarified Cambridge scene (with the swapping of billet-doux in Greek). Woolf describes Headlam as 'flirtatious', but also writes after a brief disagreement 'But we made it up – a subtle phrase secret and ambiguous. How d'you think we made it up?'[233] Woolf likes flirting with her sister about who knows what . . . Headlam's Greek knowledge made him an attractively knowing figure for her.

---

[229] Benson (1930) 135.   [230] Nicholson ed. (1975) *index s. v.* Headlam.

[231] Woolf (1925): unlike George Eliot's Maggie Tulliver, knowing Greek is not an explicitly gendered issue for Woolf's essay, though she undoubtedly experienced the strictly gendered lines of teaching Classics. It was for the contemporary English press, however: when Agnetta Ramsay was the only person in 1887 to get a top division first class honours degree in classics (beating Headlam), it prompted articles in the London newspapers and cartoons in *Punch*: a fine account of this in Mitchell (1995). The year 1890 was a watershed, remembered for what the *Engliswoman's Review* of 15 July 1890, called a 'record absolutely without precedent' of female success in the Cambridge Tripos – including Philippa Fawcett coming top in mathematics. Virginia Woolf's study of Greek and specifically the issue of gender is about to be discussed by Yopie Prins at length.

[232] See Beard (2000); Prins (1999) – who is preparing a study of Virginia Woolf's Greek learning; Gregory (1997); and for a basic collection of primary sources on women and classical education Kersey (1981). On Eliot see below pp. 286–8.

[233] Nicholson (1975) 294.

None the less, for all his Greek brilliance, even his hagiographic biographer (and nephew) notes that Headlam in his attack on Verrall 'had not yet learned to write English prose with ease as well as point, nor had he mastered the still more difficult art of presenting his material in such a manner as to produce the utmost effect'.[234] Indeed, while most reviewers noted Headlam's brilliance, all (except perhaps Wecklein in Germany[235]) spoke extensively and with distaste for the 'personal criticism' included in the book. 'He has produced a criticism, remarkable indeed for wide reading but far more remarkable for its arrogance. Were he Bentley and Porson, Kennedy and Jebb, rolled into one, he could not assume a more lordly air of superiority . . . simply a bêtise, a piece of condescending arrogance.'[236] 'To publish such a reckless calumny on the character of an eminent scholar . . . is a proceeding that cries aloud for some decisive token of public disapprobation.'[237] Arnold's and Huxley's disagreements have already shown us how gentlemen should conduct such arguments.

Verrall was moved to print a pamphlet by way of rejoinder, a twenty-eight-page document which not only expresses his intellectual differences in a general manner, but also decries the personal tone of the attack (which he repeatedly calls a libel). Verrall (according to his biographers) was unpolemical and rather cheerful about the varied reception of his speculations (as well as being a popular teacher and colleague). It is unwise, he suggested, in his poised counter-rhetoric, to get too heated over 'matters of opinion'. (This effectively genial tactic was duly picked up by columnists: 'on many points discussed by Mr Headlam there is ample room for diversity of opinion'.)[238] But for all that he stresses the difference between knowledge and 'matters of opinion', Verrall concludes ringingly 'It is untrue altogether that I do not know my subject, that I have neglected the means of information, or that I practise any other method than the one only scientific method which Mr Headlam, truly if somewhat ostentatiously, himself professes.'[239]

The means and matter of knowing (as well as academic authority) are what is at stake here, but the personal voices of Headlam and Verrall – the manner and manners of knowing – are intimately intertwined with the problem. Headlam, earlier in 1891, had published a brief review of Jebb's edition of *Philoctetes*, which within the frame of praise for Jebb's life work, suggested that Jebb had not made sufficient use of lyric and gnomic poets, nor paid enough attention to the 'causes tending to ms.

---

[234] C. Headlam (1910) 78–79.   [235] Wecklein (1893).   [236] Anon. *The Academy* (1892) 595.
[237] A.B.C [Cook] (1892a) 317.   [238] A.B.C. [Cook] (1892a) 316.   [239] Verrall (1892) 28.

corruption'.[240] Professor Jebb, then the most renowned and publicly celebrated classicist in Britain, elected MP later that year and soon to be offered a knighthood, responded quickly to the tyro with a bitter rebuttal on points of detail concluding: 'In the present instance I can only regret that having decided to publish an article which relies so much on the authority of the writer, the editors did not invite "W.H." to sign his name.'[241] The year before in the same journal Headlam had published a satirical oration in the style of Demosthenes (in English) put into the mouth of Professor Jebb opposing the City Council's proposal to convert a portion of Jebb's garden into Sidgwick Avenue (the street on which the present Classics Faculty stands).[242] It was a mocking piece that made some impact (and was reprinted in a collection of pieces from the journal in 1898).[243] Headlam had also – uniquely – won seven William Browne medals for composition and the Porson prize (a noted achievement in a system which so rewarded composition). What is more, in 1889, when Headlam had visited Florence to work on manuscripts of Aeschylus, Jebb had written letters of introduction for him.[244] So, since it is the case that all pieces in the *Cambridge Review* are signed only by initials, it is not clear whether Jebb's remark about signatures is disingenuous, ironic, or simply insulting. It clearly had an effect, however, as Headlam, sticking precariously to his guns, adds further examples in the following edition of the *Review* and ends:[245]

Professor Jebb considers that I might have been invited to sign my name. I should have been quite ready to do so since I approve the principle of signing criticisms. By giving only my initials, however, I was going as far as was consistent with the custom of this *Review*. Thereby I acknowledged authorship; but I did not wish to make my name conspicuous.

WALTER HEADLAM

Verrall, referring to this incident, notes 'From what I had seen of Mr Headlam in another case, I did not expect to find him in my own case a very ceremonious critic.'[246] In 1891, the young Walter Headlam had indeed made a conspicuous name for himself in Cambridge – and else-where. As his biographer sadly notes, his subsequent work was 'received by the scholars of his own university with chilling silence'; he was not invited to lecture or give papers; 'he was not even placed on the Greek

---

[240] Headlam (1891b) 288.   [241] Jebb (1891) 306.
[242] Headlam (1890). On the fondness of Jebb for this house and garden, see C. Jebb (1907) 230–1.
[243] The impact is recalled briefly in C. Headlam (1910) 29.
[244] See C. Headlam (1910) 35.   [245] Headlam (1891c) 324.   [246] Verrall (1892) 5; cf 17.

Play Committee at Cambridge'.[247] Virginia Woolf comments after his death: 'I think there was something very charming about him, but he was difficult, and I think he had quarrelled with most of the people at Cambridge.'[248]

Headlam himself gives a further insight into the politics of knowledge – and signatures – in an unpublished letter to his sister of February 1892.[249] I quote it at some length since it gives such a precise and rare picture of academic insider dealing, the behind-the-scene politics of the construction of a persona through the published word.

The other book ['On Editing Aeschylus'] isn't so agreeable to talk about. There is really no answer to it; but I expect most of the papers that review it will be reluctant to acknowledge its justice. You see they have in almost all cases praised the books I expose, sometimes extravagantly, and it is natural that they should be unwilling to admit that their opinion was totally wrong. I have had a good confirmation of what I knew to be the case from a Dr of Letters to whom I sent my book. He wrote to me 'I think I have censured V. as much as anyone, but have been in the habit of saying pretty things about his scholarship. I now see that where I gave then credit... I ought to have detected and exposed ignorance and utter lack of scholarship'. Some little time afterwards I went to see him and he said 'I am in a fix. I have got your book to review, and, you see, I reviewed V.'s book before in the same paper. It isn't easy to know what to say, and I want to do you justice.' That review will be anonymous; but you see that the reviewers whom I do not know and who are less scrupulous are hardly likely to do me quite justice –

Public status depends on public voices each of which is interwoven, for Headlam, with private affiliations and dependencies. (Writing for his sister, he avoids naming the future anonymous reviewer whose identity I have been unable to trace...) As the letter makes plain, it is not only what you know but whom you know which structures how you are... known. Headlam ruefully shows his unsuccessful playing of this political game.

Nor was Verrall a simple target for criticism. His work was very widely known and influential. 'His contemporaries were partly enthralled, partly amused and partly revolted', wrote Fraenkel nicely, 'but no one could disregard or whittle away the force of his influence'.[250] ('When all is said and done', concludes Fraenkel, 'we are here in the presence of a first-rate mind and a real artist's soul... [who] knew a great deal of

---

[247] C. Headlam (1910) 80. An exclusion made more biting by the fact that the committee was stacked with his colleagues at King's itself including Oscar Browning, Waldstein, Austen-Leigh, M. R. James (a long-term correspondent and friend).

[248] Nicholson ed. (1975) 386.   [249] In King's College Library.   [250] Fraenkel (1950) 57.

things Greek and – despite the long catalogue of his linguistic sins drawn up by Headlam – he knew the language exceedingly well.')[251] Fraenkel, the great German scholar in exile in Oxford – a prince of *Altertumswissenschaft* – *knows* how to talk about what knowledge counts, and delivers a magisterial judgement on whether Verrall really 'knows Greek'.

It is striking that A.B.C. (A. B. Cook, the future Professor of Archaeology), who published the outraged rebuttal of Headlam's 'charge' on 19 May, from which I quoted above, on 9 June in the same journal published a satirical piece parodying Verrall's (and Mayor's) styles of commentary, and the whole institution of classical commentary, applied to the text of a (spoof) whaling ballad.[252] The 'text and apparatus' of stanzas 11 and 12 rehearse Headlam's and Verrall's distinctive interests:

> Still on the Siren whistles
> Her sombre song and sad;
> He looked around for missiles:
> **Headlam says "Metre bad!"**

> Out spoke that savage sailor,
> "Your wailing's quite outshone,
> For I too am a whaler":
> **Verrallian etymon**

"Verrall's" commentary begins: 'The common misinterpretations of this ode are too notorious to call for detailed refutation. As mangled by most critics and commentators, it is a mere agglomeration of meaningless verbiage, or – if we credit one savant – replete with vegetarian vagaries. The fact is that they all (like the Siren before them) have "missed the point" entirely . . . ' It proceeds with mock emendations and sophistries of an acutely observed Verrallian type. Similarly, ten years earlier (9 May 1881), H. R. Tottenham published a lengthy prose parody of Verrall by glossing a Punch and Judy show as if it were a Greek tragedy; Tottenham also published an open 'Letter to Verrall' in 1889 (both pieces were reprinted in 1895).[253] It is typical of Verrall's position in the public eye that the *Cambridge Review* happily glossed the account of one of his lectures (on the *Birds* as a parody of Judaism (*sic*)) with 'se non è vero, è Verrall' ('maybe not veracious, but certainly Verrall').[254]

Verrall, unlike many of his classicist colleagues, was a figure who provoked public recognition and strong response. Headlam had evidently

---

[251] *Ibid.*
[252] A.B.C. [Cook] (1892b). The whole is reprinted and discussed in Henderson (1998), who directed me to this gem.
[253] Tottenham (1895).
[254] Quoted with reminiscence of the lecture by Glover (1943).

misjudged the line between acceptable satire and unacceptable abuse. Too personal. Not insignificantly, Headlam later is reported to have declared Housman's prefaces to his Manilius and Juvenal to be some of his favourite prose . . . [255] Housman, the Professor, has been avidly defended (and privately enjoyed) for his personal invective (on the grounds, in one of the most recent and desperate apologies, that such abuse makes the world safer for another Porson!).[256] Headlam with less personal authority, found himself ostracized even from the Greek Play Committee.

And the argument rumbled on. In 1902, Headlam lambasted Tucker's edition of the *Choephoroi* – his *Supplices* had been crushingly received by Housman in 1901 – not merely in similarly distinctive tone ('I mention it because it is the way schoolboys are now taught to think') but also with an unrepentant glance backwards: Tucker 'has come under the influence of Dr Verrall . . . . [and] Dr Verrall's method is well known'.[257] Tucker, however, unlike Verrall, responded with a matching violence, complaining of Headlam's 'pretensions to dictatorship' (as opposed to his own 'more intelligent and more modest conception of the function of an editor', stating that 'in several important departments of Greek scholarship . . . Mr Headlam betrays very defective qualifications'; that his 'method is unscientific, behind the times, and that his criteria . . . are too purely subjective', claims which need 'little illustration to those *che sanno* [in the know] (as he might put it)'.[258] Who knows Greek, who *knows*, is the taunt and claim. Moreover, Tucker bitterly resented the 'unpleasant temper' of the review, which 'renders it impossible for him to make a fair, much less a generous statement, or even to quote correctly'.[259] Nor was the personal basis of the review left implicit: 'In my preface I pay to Dr Verrall the tribute which courtesy and conscientiousness demanded . . . I can readily understand that such a tribute is disagreeable to the writer of a certain pamphlet "On Editing Aeschylus".'[260] And with a remark precisely designed to hurt the underproducing Headlam (which also marks the infighting of the politics of reviewing again), Tucker concludes: 'I trust no reviewer will behave in this way to Mr Headlam when that gentleman finds the energy and courage to publish a complete edition of some classical work.'[261] George Thomson, who completed Headlam's indeed unfinished work for publication, looking back at this personal politics from his rather different

---

[255] Headlam, C. (1910) 32. Wilkinson (1980) 33 notes 'His familiarity with the world of ribald journalism . . . was surprising even in a Harrovian.'
[256] Naiditch (1996).
[257] Headlam (1902a), quotations from 348, 353.
[258] Tucker (1903), quotations from 125, 126.
[259] Tucker (1903) 127.   [260] Tucker (1903) 127.   [261] Tucker (1903) 128.

perspective, saw these wrangles in quite other political terms: 'it was not to be expected that such a comprehensive and exacting approach to the subject should commend itself to bourgeois empiricists . . . it will be carried forward by Marxists'.[262] Fraenkel, as we have seen, also replays the debate in his great edition of Aeschylus' *Agamemnon*. Headlam's attempt to dismiss Verrall's knowledge – even in Tucker's work – becomes embroiled not merely in the complex politics of his own positioning as a critic, but also in the continuing process of critical glossing, with which his violent knowledge has been received.

Between polemic and satire, public debate and private manoeuvring, personal voice and educational policy, boundaries and markers in the politics of knowledge are being staked out. Headlam, 'greatly superior in seriousness and devotion to the truth'[263] is struggling for a scientific method with a disciplinary fervour; Verrall, who had, for Fraenkel, a 'seductive glamour' that meant 'to the young student Verrall may become a danger',[264] brought a quite different sense of the subject and its audience to bear in his trajectory towards the chair of English. How to comment on a Greek text, with what knowledge (and at what cost) are questions embroiled here in the changing status of Classics and the changing status of the don.[265] The irruption of the personal tone (along with satire and invective) marks the level of engagement in this stasis.

Yet there is another debate taking place in 1891 in Cambridge which provides a further relevant frame. The argument about whether Greek should remain compulsory for Cambridge admission had been rumbling for some time and although it would not be resolved for some years yet, 1891 was a turning point.[266] The university proposed establishing a syndicate to consider whether Greek could be replaced and if so by what. A hastily convened meeting at Professor Jebb's house announced by a fly-sheet that it had met and intended to oppose such a syndicate and called for support.[267] A series of fly-sheets with long lists of names were circulated. The arguments spread rapidly to the national press, and several distinguished luminaries pitched in to contest what knowing Greek might mean. Henry Sidgwick, one of Jebb's closest friends, declared in blunt terms which you will recognize, that 'elementary acquaintance

---

[262] Quoted in Varcl and Willetts eds. (1963) 17.
[263] Fraenkel (1950) 58–9.
[264] Fraenkel (1950) 57. His comparison of Headlam and Verrall re-plays their row in Fraenkel's own terms.
[265] Rothblatt (1968); Engel (1983); Stray (1998).
[266] See Raphaely (1999).
[267] Flysheet of 12 August 1891. See also the flysheet of 14 August 1891.

with Greek, now required by the Previous Examination [entrance ex-
amination] is useless as a means of acquiring knowledge, and valueless as
a source of literary culture'.[268] J. K. Stephen, one of Headlam's closest
friends and also a fellow at King's, privately published a long booklet
whose aim, he declared, was 'to estimate the value of a knowledge of
Greek as part of the intellectual equipment of a well-educated man'.[269]
It is a curious and fascinating document.

Stephen, cousin to Virginia Woolf, was a charismatic but odd man
who, the year after this publication, went mad and starved himself to
death (at one point previously he had a document printed, whose background and effect is hard to reconstruct, in which he listed doctors' opinions proving his sanity and ability to play a role in society).[270] Briefly, he
was a chief suspect for being Jack the Ripper, which makes his performance as the mad murderer, Ajax, in the first Cambridge Greek Play,
seem particularly apt. His lengthy defence of Greek is in many ways a
compendium of arguments culled from over the previous hundred years.
The Greek language is the most perfect of languages ('it is the very best
language', 'a masterpiece of the human intellect')[271] which he proves by
the effect of Greek on the audience of the Cambridge Greek Play, who
are so moved by 'the power and sweetness of Greek words'.[272] Ancient
Athens was the era 'when highly sensitive and intellectually brilliant people were, and knew themselves to be, at their very best'.[273] It is good to
teach Greek precisely because 'it is a difficult [language] to learn'.[274] He
even adds the social benefit of learning Greek which is 'indispensable to a
properly educated man'.[275] But what I find particularly interesting is that
he represents himself as a very amateurish classic indeed: 'I do not read
Greek easily, nor write it at all, though I dare say I could hammer out a
score of iambics if my life depended on it'[276] (bravado? false modesty?).
Stephen argues indeed not for a value in *knowing* Greek, but rather for
'the value . . . of *having known Greek*'.[277] It is the trace of 'knowing Greek'
that counts. Stephen tries to construct a theory for the practice of forcing
all students to learn some Greek before they can come to the university:
he suggests that the process of learning but then not using or even forgetting Greek – a process which the opponents of compulsory Greek singled
out as a waste of time – is of positive value. Greek is capable of informing

[268] Flysheet of 19 October 1891. This Henry is the brother of the twelve-year-old Minnie engaged
to E. F. Benson's father, the archbishop.
[269] Stephen (1891).
[270] A copy is preserved in King's College Library.   [271] Stephen (1891) 13, 14.
[272] Stephen (1891) 16.   [273] Stephen (1891) 18.   [274] Stephen (1891) 23.
[275] Stephen (1891) 6.   [276] Stephen (1891) 11.   [277] Stephen (1891) 13.

a person – in the sense of self-formation within, rather than providing information. As the ruins of Greece construct the perfect Romanticized landscape, so, it seems, the educated man should carry the fragments of a lost knowledge in his mind. (Our) culture, for Stephen, depends on this ghostly Greek within. A bizarre final twist of the argument, then, a strange nostalgia, that demands that Greek must continue to be taught so that it can continue to be forgotten, and continue to be the lost world on which each man founds his cultured self.

Headlam, as one might expect by now, neither attended Jebb's meeting nor signed the fly-sheet. Nonetheless, granted his close friend's special involvement, and his many colleagues' passionate arguments (supported by trainloads of clergymen who travelled to vote the proposal down), Headlam's commitment to a highly technical and laboriously acquired Greek knowledge must be seen in the light of this national debate about 'knowing Greek'. The internal wrangle between the young don of King's and the older don of Trinity about glossing Aeschylus and knowing Greek may have become secondary to this wider debate. It was not publicly recalled, for example, as far as I can discover, when, with some piquancy, Verrall and Headlam lectured back to back in the Senate House in competition for Jebb's chair; neither got the job. 'Of the raptured audience . . . few can have realised that it was the first and last time [Headlam] was allowed to speak to his university',[278] wrote an obituarist – though the wonderfully named Mr Image, of Trinity, in a personal letter gives a different view: 'Headlam I thought a wee bit too *gracious* . . . Had I been nearer, I should have expected to sniff a *perfumed* elegance . . . Vexatious too, every now and then, to have analogies (lightly worn like a flower) to Beethoven and Wagner. How superior!'[279] But both debates are sign and symptom of the tensions around the disciplinary formation of classics.

Even within the hallowed halls of academia what 'knowing Greek' meant could become a source of anguished and vitriolic debate. Although the argument between Headlam and Verrall is explicitly about linguistic

---

[278] [Shane Leslie] 'Walter Headlam' *The Academy* 8 Oct. 1910, 351. The lectures can be read in *Praelectiones Delivered Before the Senate of the University of Cambridge 25, 26, 27 January 1906* (Cambridge, 1906). Verrall spoke at 2.30, Headlam at 5.00 on the Friday.

[279] Letters of J. M. Image to W. F. Smith 1906–13 (Trinity College Library, Cambridge). Thanks to Chris Stray who brought this letter to my attention. It includes the information that Headlam gave everyone a sixteen-quarto-page handout! Image's other letters show him to be passionate about all sorts of university competitions, including verse composition prizes, as befits a very undistinguished classical tutor.

competence, it is also a story about how privileged knowledge circulates, about how status and social performance are part of the constitution of a discipline, about how a discipline regulates itself. Such academic in-fighting is also framed by the wider debates about compulsory Greek and the reform of the universities, not least as the image of the don's brilliance and eccentricity is constructed and disseminated as part of the myth of knowledge. Headlam and Verrall never have had the influence of Arnold or the power of Lowe, but they are an integral element in the cultural history of what it means 'to know Greek'.

V

In the middle part of the eighteenth century, Lord Chesterfield wrote to his son, suggesting some career options: 'What do you think of being Greek professor in one of our Universities? It is a very pretty sinecure, and requires little knowledge (much less than, I hope, you have already) of that language.'[280] I suspect that the collusive encouragement of father to son is designed primarily to praise and reinforce the boy's learning rather than to denigrate university scholarship. But it does contrast neatly, and, I think, tellingly with Fraenkel's magisterial evaluation of his predecessors' linguistic knowledge from the most stringent of academic standards. The journey of this very long chapter has been from the scriptoire of Chesterfield's drawing-room to the desk in Fraenkel's college study – a story of 'the perpetual revolution that was the nineteenth century's contact with Greek'.[281] I could, I am well aware, have chosen to add more characters and more details to my account. Whoever works on Victorian culture has to make selections, often pretty drastic ones, even in the most compendious of volumes. (For a classicist, used, like Headlam, to trying to know the evidence exhaustively and to reading it all minutely, it is particularly frightening to be faced by such a wealth of materials.) Further discussion, however, would not alter the simple point of the chapter, however, which has, I hope, emerged with sufficient clarity and sufficient complexity: to ask 'Do you know Greek?' is rarely, if ever, a question simply of linguistic competence.

Indeed, even claims of linguistic competence become embroiled in intricate cultural and personal politics, whether it is De Quincey's druggy boasts of brilliance or the *parti-pris* anecdotes of Lowe's skill at Greek

---

[280] Stanhope (1932) III. 1084 (no. 1518). Cf. 604, 725, 728, 731–2, 752, 1057, 1066, 1107, 1180 for the continuing story of the boy's classical education.
[281] Grafton (1992) 243.

epigrams, or the technical and intercollegiate disputes of Verrall and Headlam. Above all, the question of knowing Greek becomes repeatedly entwined with issues of nationalism and Empire, with issues of educational policy (which cannot avoid notions of citizenship and constitutional reform), and with cultural politics (which sets at stake the very construction of the cultured – acculturated – self). Because of this, the personal politics which always vein academic, intellectual and governmental exchange, become particularly charged and particularly destabilizing when we try to trace the contests over knowing Greek. The project of finding what it means to know Greek constantly has to manoeuvre through the *knowingness* of its participants, the shared and tacit exchange of expectation and of social formation. The history of the question 'Do you know Greek?' is a messy history because there are so many competing and challenging concerns which cross it, and so many implicating arenas which catch you, like the Victorians, in your own personal and cultural politics. Which is one reason why it is worth pursuing. It certainly is also a continuing history. The echoes of the Victorian debate should be loud and clear when T. S. Eliot defends tradition with 'It is only upon readers who wish to see a Christian civilization survive . . . that I am urging the importance of the study of Latin and Greek',[282] or when, more recently, Allan Bloom declares that 'Greece provides the assurance that there was something better than what is' in order to keep the American mind from closing.[283]

So can I ask you if you know Greek? You *will* have a story in reply to that question even if now is not the time or place that you want to be prompted into answering. It is worth pondering, however. I would imagine that, for all its complexity and for all its emotional upheavals, your story cannot have quite the same political and social purchase of the powerfully felt conflicts of the nineteenth century. I know my story doesn't. The difference between then and now is, at one level, the inevitable consequence of the declining privilege of classical studies, and is thus perhaps not so surprising. But one *cost* of this history is the difficulty that many modern readers demonstrate in comprehending the Victorians' engagement with Greek. (I can't see how it can be seriously argued that *not* to know Greek is *not* a significant barrier to appreciating Arnold, or Mill or Pater.) For the Victorian elite, shared education,

---

[282] Eliot (1936). The specifically Arnoldian debt of Eliot is discussed by e.g. Raleigh (1961); Baldick (1987) 109–33; Honan (1988).
[283] Bloom (1987) 304. As every chapter of this book shows, the turn to Greece need not be conservative.

including the absorption of Greek through extensive memorization, and shared expectations that ground even the altercations over Greek, made 'knowing Greek' part of cultural knowingness, and such knowingness is an essential aspect of any cultural history worth the name.

As Hardy's Jude or Eliot's Maggie Tulliver shows, there's no knowing Greek – no knowing – without desire. A desire that is not just a wish for social or intellectual achievement, but a self-consuming, self-forming interest, informed by the exchanges of status, power, cultural regulation and social expectation. That's why the simple question 'Do you know Greek?' can never have a simple answer.

CHAPTER FIVE

The value of Greek. Why save Plutarch?

I

When the monster of Mary Shelley's *Frankenstein* arrives in the hut of the poor old man, cultural education is the novel's evident agenda, both for the monster and for us, the readers. The old man has only three books, saved in a 'leathern portmanteau'; but how many books do you need to civilize a brute? For religious understanding – a necessary foundation, just as in De Quincey's view of the uncivilized East – there is Milton's *Paradise Lost*. This is a pointed Romantic and Radical gesture, to turn to the high peaks of poetic expression rather than the more obvious choice of the Bible (which is the usual requirement of any desert-island list of books). For sentimental education – for the monster is to be educated into feelings – there is Goethe's *Sorrows of Young Werther*. For anyone in Shelley's circle, and especially for the eloped wife of the dissolute poet, Goethe is a flag-waving selection. This is not just because he is a pioneer of Romantic Hellenism (*Frankenstein*'s subtitle is *The New Prometheus* – for the Shelleys, Prometheus is the iconic figure who links radicalism and Hellenism); but also it is because Goethe is the anatomizer of the nature of feelings, and of the relation of feelings to nature.[1] The unnatural monster's education into natural feelings needs Goethe's guide: all of this monster's 'affinities' must be, in one sense, 'elective'. But for an education into politics and history there is Plutarch's *Lives*. Plutarch, like Milton or Goethe, can sum up a whole world of Western knowing, a stupendous body of work which has the power to make a monster transcend himself.

The description of the monster's reading of this curriculum is wonderful, and dramatically enacts the anthropological agenda suggested by the title of *The New Prometheus*: these are books to make a man. *Young Werther* – read first – has a powerful effect because of its description of 'gentle and

---

[1] The most recent and fullest biography of Mary Shelley is Seymour (2000); on Shelley's Hellenism see especially Wallace (1997).

domestic manners . . . combined with lofty sentiments and feelings'.[2] The monster wept, he sympathized, he was led to wonder, speculation, astonishment – and to ask 'Who was I? What was I? Whence did I come? What was my destination?'[3] Goethe stimulates not just the proper and privileged human emotions, but also the (proper and privileged) Romantic *questions* of identity. *Paradise Lost* is the culminating reading experience, which excites the most profound sentiments of awe: from Adam's relation to God, and Satan's fallen state, the monster begins to articulate an answer to those questions of who he is.[4] Now he is ready for his increasingly horrified reading of the laboratory notes which reveal the full story of his creation. Between the suicidal Werther and the creation of Adam stands Plutarch, an education into 'high thoughts'. Plutarch 'elevated me above the wretched sphere of my own reflections, to admire and love the heroes of past ages.'[5] Plutarch gives a sense of the past, and raises miserable self-reflection towards paradigms of greatness, towards models of moral excellence: 'I felt the greatest ardour for virtue rise within me, and abhorrence for vice, as far as I understood the signification of those terms, relative as they were, as I applied them, to pleasure and pain alone.'[6] Plutarch claims that his *Lives* have the power to cultivate a reader in virtue through imitation, and the monster fulfils that programme – though Shelley with her usual intellectualizing precision insists that the genesis of moral feeling without further experience is limited to the fields of pleasure and pain. Plutarch is a source and resource of moral feeling, of history, of models of virtue. He is a storehouse of the value of Greek culture. Plutarch, for Shelley, is a necessary read in the self-formation of a civilized being.

Plutarch's value is the central concern of this chapter – both how Plutarch himself constructs a sense of the value of his own Greek culture, and how his body of work becomes a battleground for understanding the value of the past and of past knowing. For as with Lucian, not only does Plutarch write extensively about what it means to be Greek, but also his critical evaluation undergoes an extraordinary sea-change, which strikingly underlines modernity's new comprehension of antiquity. Plutarch could act as a summation of Greek culture and one of the three fundamental educative manuals of the West for Mary Shelley, but his stock has fallen so low through the twentieth century that when the comedy

---

[2] Shelley (1974) 123. All quotations are taken from this, the 1818 text.
[3] Shelley (1974) 123.
[4] Milton is a most important source for *Frankenstein*, see Baldick (1987) 40–2.
[5] Shelley (1974) 124.   [6] Shelley (1974) 124–5.

team of *Monty Python's Flying Circus* briefly mocks him as one of the great masturbators of history what is surprising is not that such an authority figure should be the butt of irreverence, but that Plutarch could still possibly play such a role for a popular comedy show (even when the comedians are showing off their Cambridge education).[7] In all our contemporary discussions of a core curriculum, who, these days, would put Plutarch in their top three books?

In her selection of the *Lives* for the monster's education, however, Mary Shelley is drawing on a significant and deep-rooted contemporary comprehension of Plutarch (in her construction of what would prove to be an immensely popular and long-lasting mythic image of monstrosity).[8] This comprehension has a long history. For as with Lucian and his self-inventions, Plutarch was perceived as the very epitome of Greek culture and its value for Erasmus and the Renaissance rediscovery of Greek (to mark the circle of this book's narrative). Erasmus found inspiration (as well as information) in Plutarch, and Plutarch became fully part of the educational curriculum. Shelley, however, was engaging in particular with the contemporary radical intellectual project, integral to her family background.[9] Plutarch was 'claimed as an apostle of liberty by the revolutionaries in France, by the Radicals in England, and by the Founding Fathers in America'.[10] Icon and inspiration for these Romantic rebellions was Jean-Jacques Rousseau, who made Plutarch the very source of his Republican virtues: 'When I was six years old, Plutarch fell into my hands: at eight I knew him by heart . . . ' (Plutarch by heart?).[11] 'From these interesting readings, from the discussions they occasioned between my father and myself was formed that free and republican spirit, that indomitable and proud character, impatient with the yoke and servitude.'[12] Plutarch and Rousseau's father together – through discussion and imitation – made him the man he is: 'Ceaselessly occupied with Rome and Athens, I lived, so to speak, with these great men, myself born the citizen of a Republic and son of a father whose love of the fatherland was his strongest passion, I caught fire with it from his example . . . I became the character whose life I read.'[13] This torch of liberty was passed on. In the midst of the Revolution, Madame Roland writes from prison in Paris to request the books she needs most: 'first of all Plutarch's *Lives*

---

[7] On the poster accompanying the record of the Philosophers' Song.

[8] See especially Baldick (1987). Also Levine and Knoepflmacher (1979).

[9] For the nature of Shelley's reaction to her political background see Sterrenberg (1979). *Frankenstein* is dedicated to William Godwin.

[10] Berry (1961) 25.　　[11] Rousseau (1995) 574.

[12] Rousseau (1995) 8.　　[13] Rousseau (1995) 8.

which at the age of eight I used to take to church instead of my prayer book'.[14] 'It was from this moment that date the impressions and ideas which made me a Republican.'[15] 'The Greek biographer's incisive portraits of the great men of antiquity, his narrative skill, and the loftiness of his moral judgement awakened the precocious reader to the heroic potentialities of the human spirit.'[16] And lest you miss the genealogy, she draws the line explicitly: 'Rousseau then made the same impression on me as had Plutarch when I was eight . . . Plutarch had disposed me to be a Republican, he had inspired in me true enthusiasm for the public virtues and liberty. Rousseau showed me domestic happiness . . . '[17] The revolutionary genealogy continued to be asserted. Charlotte Corday, the assassin of Marat in the name of the Republic, also records reading Plutarch and Rousseau as a young girl; and in one of the many lurid attempts to flesh out the scanty fragments of her life-story into a biography, it is even claimed that she read Plutarch all the day before killing Marat.[18] It is this tradition which leads George Bernard Shaw – ever keen on the catch phrase – to call Plutarch a 'revolutionists' handbook'.[19] It is this, the revolutionary inspiration, that establishes Plutarch with Goethe and Milton as a mainstay of Shelley's educational pantheon.

Yet Plutarch courses through the reading of conservative and rebel alike throughout the last half of the eighteenth century. Montesquieu – to go to a body of political writings which were anathema to the leaders of the French revolution – repeatedly alludes to Plutarch, to his stories and to his rhetorical figures.[20] Plutarch appears in list after list of childhood reading and of adult political reflection, most commonly in an offhand way, with an easy expectation of shared recognition of a corpus of heroic narratives. Plutarch was very much part of a classical – which is to say cultured – training – which both enables Rousseau's passion and makes it remarkable.

This familiarity with Plutarch runs on well into the nineteenth century too. The true origin of this chapter was the moment when as a child I read Captain Marryat's novel of 1841, *Masterman Ready*, an adventure about a family shipwrecked and surviving on a desert island. (Few children these days, I suspect, read Marryat, but Joseph Conrad and Virginia Woolf

---

[14] Roland (1989) 47.

[15] *Mémoires* II. 22 cited by May (1964) 36 [my translation].

[16] May (1970) 15: cf. for her more general Hellenism, 'je soupirais en songeant à Athènes . . . je me promenais en ésprit dans la Grèce', *Lettres* II.1.375, cited May (1964) 39.

[17] *Lettres* II. 185, cited and translated May (1970) 58.

[18] Reinhold (1984) 255. See van Alstine (1890) 37.

[19] Cited Jones (1974) 136.   [20] Howard (1970) 48–52.

wrote essays in praise of him, and, more worryingly, both Carlyle and Strindberg were fans.[21]) In *Masterman Ready*, the family Seagrave (the names are rather clunkingly significant) survive their shipwreck thanks to the practical knowledge of Masterman Ready, an old and trusty sailor who stays with the family when all the others leave them to their fate. Marryat himself was an extraordinary man of 'violent passion' who had done heroic deeds of derring-do in the Napoleonic wars (including diving into a raging sea to save the life of William Cobbett's son, leading a fire-ship attack, and invading Borneo in a manner to drive De Quincey over the edge). He retired to a bizarre life as a former sea-captain and lionized novelist (friend of Dickens, he also toured America, becoming the enemy of all true Americans when his sarcastic and dismissive diary of the trip was published). Inveterate gambler, street brawler, he ended up on a failing estate in Norfolk, deserted by his wife, but surrounded by his many children and a menagerie of animals (which he jumped out of his bedroom window to feed in the morning...)[22] Both Woolf and Conrad observe how Marryat's own naval experience and knowledge (along with the 'glamour of his temperament'[23]) produce a convincing sense of the real in his adventure stories, but it is the moral vision of his narrative which now makes him seem such a transparent purveyor of imperial and national values. Masterman Ready, the trusty salt, the epitome of British yeoman stock, teaches the family (and us) the tricks of survival; Mr Seagrave teaches his family; they all quote from the Bible repeatedly to justify their actions; they conquer nature; they defeat violently a horde of natives; the children start a directed path to manhood. Only one box of books is washed up to aid the process of ensuring the family's survival in the Englishness. It contains Plutarch's *Lives*. '"I am glad to have them"', comments Mr. Seagrave, '"they are excellent reading for young and old...perhaps the best case which could have been saved."'[24] What I recall vividly from my childhood reading is the surprise, that if you could have only one box of books, Plutarch would seem an excellent choice. I did not then, of course, know that Emerson had also wanted to save Plutarch from a fiery fate: 'If the whole world's library were burning

---

[21] Woolf (1950) 39–48; Conrad (1898). For Strindberg's and Carlyle's reactions see Warner (1953).

[22] Pocock (2000) is a very readable life in the form of a yarn, but does not include much material that is not already available in Warner (1953), Marryat (1872), Hannay (1889). Gautier (1973) links the biography and the novels. The detail of the leap from the bedroom window is taken from a wonderful (anonymous) article on a visit to his estate, published in the *Cornhill Magazine* of July 1867, 152.

[23] The phrase is Conrad's (1898) 73: 'his greatness is undeniable' (75).

[24] Marryat (1970) 261.

I should as soon fly to rescue [Plutarch], as Shakespeare or Plato, or next afterwards.'[25] Or that Montaigne had written 'I can hardly do without Plutarch.'[26] My thought was just 'Why (save) Plutarch?'

Particularly in the English-speaking world the retreat from Plutarch has been drastic and sudden. By the beginning of the twentieth century, it is a commonplace that 'few today read Plutarch'. Despite the rapid growth of scholarly books and articles on so many ancient authors and on so many aspects of classical culture, during the fifty years of 1918–68, there was scarcely any year in which more than a couple of brief pieces on Plutarch were published in English – and these are almost always short articles in dry and technical style. There was no New Critical Plutarch, no symbolist Plutarch, no Marxist Plutarch, no structuralist Plutarch, no narratological Plutarch . . . Plutarch not only shows how the belief in a constant canon of great books – the classical tradition – has to ignore major shifts in cultural evaluation and expectation both in the scholarly community and in society in general. He also provides the perfect example of the process of cultural forgetting which is one of this book's dominant concerns. When Plutarch becomes a closed book, what is being forgotten? What is at stake in saving Plutarch?

II

Plutarch was born in Chaeroneia near Delphi in the 40s and died probably around 120. He performed as a priest at Delphi – the traditional centre of the world in Greek conceptual geography – and although he visited Rome and travelled in the Mediterranean (as one would expect of a well-heeled intellectual), he proudly spent most of his life in the small town of Chaeroneia. The known details of his life are few, however, and almost entirely gleaned from his own writing: he represents himself as closely linked to several important Roman political personages; as the centre of a self-consciously intellectual community; as an active and important political and social figure at the local level, with the expected range of not hugely impressive activity on a broader national and international stage.[27] From Homer onwards, the Greek heroic ideal could be expressed as the aim of being 'a speaker of speeches and a doer of

---

[25] Berry (1961) 35. 'I must think we are more deeply indebted to him than to all ancient writers', *The Early Lectures of Emerson* ed. S. Whicher *et al.* (Cambridge, Mass, 1966–72) II. 329–30.

[26] Konstankinovic (1989) details borrowing and the scholarly tradition; for earlier studies see especially Villey (1908) and the brief remarks of Hirzel (1912) 123–6.

[27] The material is still best presented in Jones (1971). See also Russell (1973).

deeds': Plutarch's *Lives* and other writings represent and commemorate the actions of great men, and collect and celebrate the sayings of the wise, the royal, the famous. Plutarch's own doing of deeds, however, is the speaking of speeches – or rather the production of texts (*logoi*). It is Plutarch the creator of a world picture with whom I am concerned here – or, more precisely, with Plutarch as the model and modeller of what it means to be Greek. Saving Plutarch is saving a figure engaged in the preservation of a cultural tradition – a preservation which is also a creative act of formation.

Plutarch is well aware of the politics of the 'nowadays': all his *Lives* are of figures of the distant past, stretching back to Theseus, the legendary founder of Athens. These biographies are models for today to live and learn by. But these great political and military leaders lived in a different world of opportunity: 'Nowadays', he writes, 'when the affairs of cities no longer involve leadership in war nor the overthrow of tyrannies nor the forming of alliances, what foundation for a famous and brilliant career could a man have?'[28] This nostalgic longing for past grandeur comes from Plutarch's treatise on statecraft, *Political Precepts*, his advice to a young man from Sardis who wishes to start a career in public life. This work marks more clearly than any other of Plutarch's his role as an elite but subordinate citizen of Empire. Greece had been part of the Empire for nigh on 200 years; 'Both Greek and foreign war has been banished for us and disappeared', he declares, 'and the people have as much freedom as those in authority deal out, and more is perhaps no better'.[29] The blessings of peace are real enough to Plutarch who repeatedly regrets the sapping wars of previous generations between Greek cities; yet a freedom which is granted by those who maintain unbroken power over you is veined with a certain paradox, and the 'perhaps' in 'more is perhaps no better' allows for a variety of assertive or regretful readings of this recognition of slipping autonomy. Indeed, whereas Pericles, whenever he put on his general's cloak, reminded himself 'Watch yourself, Pericles, you rule free men, you rule Greeks, Athenian citizens', the statesman of nowadays must declare 'You rule as a subject [*archomenos archeis*] you rule a city instructed by the proconsuls, the Emperor's representatives':

You should not pride yourself, nor trust in crowns, when there is always a senator's boot above your head.[30]

---

[28] *Mor* 805a; *Prae. Ger. Rei.* 10. See especially Swain (1996) 161–82 for discussion of this treatise; also Jones (1971) 110–21; Desideri (1986).

[29] *Mor.* 824c; *Prae. Ger. Rei.* 32.

[30] *Mor.* 813e; *Prae. Ger. Rei.* 17. For the translation as 'senator's boot', see Oliver (1953) 958 n.27.

The Roman senator's boot defines and delimits the sphere of the political, now. The politician of today is more like an actor – and remember Lucian's care with the destabilizing *mimesis* of public life – who 'for all the passion of performance cannot step beyond the permission of those who rule over him' – his scriptwriter, the prompter, the rhythm of the verse, the poet . . . [31] The modern Greek politician must march to another, Roman tune. He cannot have his own lines.

This tension between subordination and achievement is precisely and sharply articulated:

> In private and public discussion the politician must educate others in the weakness of Greek affairs. Under these conditions, wise people take the one advantage on offer, to live in calm and harmony: fortune has left no prize to compete for. What authority, what reputation is there for those who win? What power is there when the small order of a proconsul can destroy it or transfer it to someone else?[32]

To have understanding – to be a wise man – means recognizing political impotence; the politician must keep teaching weakness to the citizens; and the fate [*tuche*[33]] which has left no prize to compete for – that is, the fate of Roman conquest, the 'fortune of the Romans' – is instantiated in the the arbitrary reversals of a proconsul's word, which undermines any pretensions to power in a Greek leader. Even the celebrated examples of the grandeur of Greece – the battle of Marathon and so forth – should be left nowadays to the schools of the sophists who use such stories to puff up the vanity of the common people.[34] Seeing a Greek of nowadays trying to emulate his noble ancestors is ridiculous – it's like 'watching a little boy trying on his daddy's boots and putting on his daddy's garlands'.[35] The crown of laurel, that symbol of achievement, nowadays makes a man a child – it performs his inferiority, however charmingly. If the great examples [*paradeigmata*] of the past serve to underline the laughably impotent pursuit of power today, what price the project of Plutarch's *Lives*?

Yet despite this thread of acute and authoritative self-denigrating analysis, the *Political Precepts* does offer lengthy advice on how to succeed in public, how to go on embassies, how to become a political somebody (and Plutarch himself had a statue erected in Chaeroneia which proclaimed and celebrated his Roman citizenship). What's more, although

[31] *Mor.* 813f; *Prae. Ger. Rei.* 17.   [32] *Mor.* 824e-f; *Prae. Ger. Rei.* 32.
[33] On Plutarch's view of the divine influence on Roman rule, see Swain (1996) 151–61.
[34] *Mor.* 814c; *Prae. Ger. Rei.* 17. See Swain (1996) 167–69.
[35] *Mor.* 814a; *Prae. Ger. Rei.* 17.

the first paragraph quotes Homer's line 'to be a speaker of speeches and a doer of deeds', and the text repeatedly harks back to the days of Pericles (and the writing of Thucydides), it's not long before Plutarch's political examples include Cato, Scipio, Pompey, the great Roman leaders. The work's opening discussion of different audiences for political activity contrasts different communities: the Athenians (easily moved, fond of clever speeches and of praise), the Carthaginians (stubborn, opposed to playfulness), the Thebans, the Spartans and so forth.[36] These international ethnic snapshots make the point that the statesman should be sensitive to the specificity of an audience, but also take it for granted that there is an *empire* of communities which provide the contemporary context for politics. The biting indictments of contemporary Greek powerlessness are framed by the acceptance and expectations of Empire. The constitutive tension of Plutarch's *Political Precepts* is between the recognition of the limitations of the power of a Greek within the Roman Empire and the acceptance of the new social conditions within which any achievement is now calibrated. Being Greek means being Greek within – or under – the Roman Empire.

This ambivalence of Greek self-assertion within the power-plays of Empire also runs through the *Lives*. The choice to establish a repeated comparison of Greek and Roman biographies (rather than Greek and Greek, say, or Roman and Roman) inevitably puts cultural difference on the agenda.[37] Yet, as with the *Political Precepts*, much of Plutarch's writing smoothly assimilates Greek and Roman aspiration, expectation and moral precept. The very structure of parallelism which sets Roman life against Greek, and the procedures of judgement and evaluation, which the formal passages of comparison [*synkrisis*] enact, are turned to create a single frame, a shared perspective, rather than any revolutionary fervour of an opposition between 'us' and 'them'.[38] That single frame, however, is distinctively Greek. Its language is Greek (of course), and it translates or transliterates Roman political terms into Greek versions; and, most importantly, its perspective is formed through a Greek tradition. The figures who populate its gallery are both Greek and Roman, but its intellectual stance stems from a traditional *paideia*: Plato in his Platonist guise, the classic poets – Homer, the tragedians, the lyric masters, especially Pindar. Its moralism draws on the long tradition of ethical

---

[36] *Mor.* 799c–800b; *Prae. Ger. Rei.* 3–4.

[37] See Duff (1999) especially 243–309; Jones (1971); Pelling (1986a); (1989); Swain (1990a), (1990b); Boulogne (1994).

[38] Pelling (1986b); Larmour (1992); Duff (1999) 243–286 (with good further bibliography).

writing formalized in the Hellenistic schools. That educated perspective is Greek – and adopted by many cultivated Romans. Plutarch's works are repeatedly addressed directly to Romans. They engage Romans. They heroize Romans. The genial austerity of his moral judgement – which makes him so readily attractive to Christian readers – presents a Greek face to an educated Roman readership. Plutarch never refers to the world of Roman politics or the war machine of Empire as 'we': Lucian is the first Greek writer to slide himself into that collusiveness. The assimilation of Plutarch's Greekness to Rome has its limits and resistances, and it is the articulation and exploration of those limits and resistances which this chapter sets out to investigate. What does – can – Greekness now mean to Plutarch? How is his Greekness implicated in the Roman world?

[handwritten note: Thesis]

There are moments when Plutarch's texts flare into a more disruptive expressiveness. The *Life of Cimon*, for example, begins with a story set in Chaeroneia, Plutarch's home town, about a handsome but dodgy Greek youth called Damon and the Roman commander who fell in love with him. The violent outcome of the Roman's lust and Damon's murderous response put the whole town under threat of Roman reprisals, and it is saved only by the intervention of Lucullus – the Roman general whose biography is paired with the life of Cimon. It is this conclusion with Lucullus that at the most direct level motivates the inclusion of the novelistic tale of sex and banditry. But the tale is also more pointed about Roman power. The Roman commander, Plutarch comments, when his attempts at seduction failed, was clearly bent on rape, 'on the grounds that our home territory was at that point in a sorry state and ignored because of its smallness and poverty'.[39] Chaeroneia, which Plutarch represents with pride elsewhere, is depicted as politically insignificant and socially run down in those days: and this is offered as the grounds for the Roman's archetypally tyrannical behaviour. (The rape of a well-born youth as an abuse of superior power is one of the clearest markers of the stereotype of the tyrant in Greek tradition.)[40] The precariousness of Greek security stems both from the arbitrariness of Roman force and from Greece's own sorry incapacity to rise above smallness and insignificance. Vulnerability to rape and reprisal forms an uneasy element of Greek self-representation.

[handwritten note: Colonial mentality]

This uneasiness is most evident in the biographies of the three Romans most directly involved in the conquest of Greece, Sulla, Flamininus and Cato. Each gives a strikingly different sense of Greek and Roman

[39] *Cim.* 1.2.   [40] See e.g. Fisher (1992) 27–31; 128–9.

interaction, and together they provide a complex matrix of potential evaluation. Sulla's activities are described in an irredeemably negative manner. He suffers from a 'terrible and unassuageable passion to capture Athens', he corrupts and destroys the lands he wins; stimulates his soldiers to debauchery and pillage – and, inevitably, himself lives in 'lewdness and adultery'.[41] With the customary overlap of military and sexual language, Sulla rapes Greece. Greek culture here is the victim of the Roman's uncontrolled violence. So, too, the savage and passionate end of a figure like Marius could have been avoided, Plutarch smugly explains, 'if anyone had persuaded him to sacrifice to the Greek Muses and Graces'.[42] Yet Flamininus, whose earlier campaigns brought Greece under Roman authority, is hagiographically celebrated as a liberator – a term he himself promoted when he proclaimed Greek liberty at the Isthmian games of 196 BCE – a proclamation received with such a volume of grateful applause, enthuses Plutarch, that crows fell dead from the sky.[43] Had Flamininus not been so fine a man, Plutarch lauds, 'Greece would not have so easily been happy with foreign rule'.[44] Not only is it taken for granted that Greece is happy with foreign rule, but also it is the very virtue of the foreign commander that makes this possible.

Flamininus fought and defeated Philip V of Macedon who at that time dominated Greece: hence the language of 'liberation'.[45] Plutarch develops this idea, however, at length in an extraordinary picture (that comes straight after the image of the crows falling dead from the skies). He imagines the Greeks, tired from their celebratory banquets, weary from embracing each other and shouting out in joy, now sitting and discussing the idea of Greece itself.[46] Their discussion is a bizarre history lesson, a history lesson which makes Roman domination a wondrous salvation and turns inside out the standard language of triumph. 'Greece', they would say, 'has fought many wars for freedom but none as secure and sweet as this'. Indeed, in the great wars of the heroes of the past, if you exclude Marathon, Salamis and a few others, actually 'Greece has fought all her battles to enslave herself. Every trophy is set up as a memorial of our own disaster and shame.' In this new history lesson, with its careful exclusions and wholehearted rhetoric, every former and famous victory is a self-inflicted calamity, every triumphant memorial a sign of shame. But now foreigners, 'from whom it is remarkable to receive anything of

---

[41] *Sulla* 13.1–2.
[42] *Marius* 2. 2–4. 'Greek education, παιδεία, is for Plutarch man's most valuable possession', Swain (1990b) 192. Cf *Cor.* 1. 3–5 with Pelling (1989).
[43] *Flamininus* 10. 6.   [44] *Flamininus* 2.4.
[45] See Swain (1988); (1996) 146–50; Jones (1971) 94–9; Pelling (1986b) 85–8.
[46] *Flamininus* 11.1–4.

use in word or policy', have risked the greatest dangers and undertaken the greatest tasks in order 'to rescue Greece and set her free from harsh masters and tyrants'. It is a commonplace to assert that it is better for Greeks to fight barbarians than other Greeks: but the ideological force of this passage makes every action between Greek states self-destructive mutilation, stopped only by the liberating intervention of foreigners (who should be welcomed, not fought). These are represented as the views of the celebrating Greeks, and not simply Plutarch's. But nor does he distance himself further from this stunning example of how victors write history, even in the words of the defeated. Greece is saved by Rome.

Perhaps most remarkable, however, is the pairing of the biography of Flamininus with the biography of Philopoimen. For Philopoimen, who is celebrated for his nobility and military prowess, is not only the Greek who led campaign after campaign of war between different Greek communities, but also who came into direct conflict with Flamininus (resisting the Romans in a differently conceived project of Greek freedom). Philopoimen was consequently threatened even after death with a full-scale *damnatio memoriae* by the Romans; but Plutarch is more impressed by the Roman who admiringly declared Philopoimen to be 'the last of the Greeks', implying, writes Plutarch from his century, 'that Greece produced no great man after him, nor anyone worthy of herself'.[47] A hero who fights to save Greece, then, and whose death means there are no more (real) Greeks. Something died with Philopoimen . . .

The formal comparison [*synkrisis*] between Flamininus and Philopoimen needs all of Plutarch's poise. This is the only pair of lives where the two heroes meet (and fight) and hence judgement between them is intricately bound up with a whole set of conflicts, institutional, political, military. He begins his *synkrisis* by declaring that no Greek, not even Philopoimen, could compare with Flamininus in benefactions to Greece, since *they* all fought Greek against Greek, whereas *he* fought on behalf of the Greeks. This reprise of the stirring prose of Flamininus' biography is tempered, however, by a recognition of the moral shortcomings of the ambitiousness of both men, which leads into an evaluation of their respective military skills, which clearly asserts the superiority of Philopoimen. The decisive factor here is that Flamininus had the support of the constantly growing power of Rome, whereas Philopoimen's victories are in the context of a Greece in decline – a frame of reference that their encounter instantiates rather than merely

[47] *Philopoimen* 1.4.

illuminates. Philopoimen proved himself an exemplary leader of men
in and out of office. Consequently, and despite the opening declaration that no Greek could compare with Flamininus in benefactions to
Greece, the final paragraph declares: 'the generosity and humaneness
that Flamininus displayed to the Greeks was noble; but more noble was
the firmness and love of freedom that Philopoimen displayed to the
Romans'. The reason offered for this calibration is the generalization
'for it is easier to bestow favours on those that ask than to disturb those
more powerful with opposition'. These boldly different and juxtaposed
opinions prompt this fascinating final sentence:

Since after such an examination, the difference between them is hard to evaluate,
you judge whether we will seem to arbitrate not poorly, if we grant the crown
for military expertise and leadership to the Greek, but the crown for justice and
goodness to the Roman.

The confession of difficulty – perhaps not surprising in view of the
different judgements juxtaposed in the *synkrisis* – is one of a range of self-
conscious concluding remarks that Plutarch uses to mark the work of
evaluation and summation. What is more striking (and unparalleled) is,
first of all, that the heroes are called 'the Greek' and 'the Roman' (rather
than by name). After the paired stories of fighting to save or to set free
Greece, there is at least the invitation to read the narrative as expressive
of a national conflict. Who is saving Greece? And the reader must be
engaged in a process of self-positioning by the act of evaluation. *Skopei*,
he instructs, 'you judge', 'look and see'. The direct address to the reader
is extremely rare in the rather impersonal format of the *synkrisis*, and thus
marked. It echoes the language of the classical orators who often ask the
voting audience to see and judge a speaker's performance, a case.[48] Its
full force is seen perhaps most clearly at the conclusion of the *synkrisis* of
Agis, Cleomenes and the Gracchi, where Plutarch states: 'from what
has been said, you can now perceive for yourself the difference between
the heroes'. The second-person address places your judgement on the
line. Your evaluation, your position on the values involved in fighting to
save Greece is what the performance of the *synkrisis* provokes. It is not
just that Plutarch uses his structure of 'compare and contrast' to explore
virtue and vice, but also and crucially that the reader is to share in that
exploration, that performance. You decide . . . The *synkrisis* invites you to
join in the *krisis* of judgement.

[48] See Goldhill (2000a).

Plutarch himself indicates this function of his writing in an extraordinary programmatic sentence in the prologue to his *Life of Pericles*. He is explaining how his exemplary figures work for you, the reader: he comments that such exemplification 'forms the character of the spectator not by imitation but by providing him with critical judgement by analysis of the work'. This sentence is extremely dense and needs careful unpacking. The reader is depicted as a spectator at a drama [*theatês*], whose character is formed [*êthopoiein*] by the experience of observation. This Platonic or Aristotelian notion of drama as a character-building activity is carefully distinguished from a Platonic theory of art, however. It is not *mimêsis*, 'imitation', which produces the man. Rather, it is the 'analysis of the work' – *historia tou ergou* – a process of intellectual inquiry focused on *Plutarch*'s work, his historical studies, as much as on the 'deeds' he celebrates. And what this process of analysis provides for you is *prohaeresis*, a mode of decision making, 'critical judgement'. Reading the work of Plutarch makes your intellectual character by critical exercise. Reading *Pericles* is to make you imitate not so much Pericles as Plutarch . . .

The sense that a reader's cultural self-positioning can be set at stake by Plutarch's biographical writing is seen in a different and tellingly intricate way in the *Life of Cato the Elder*, the third of the conquerors of Greece. Cato, Plutarch narrates, spent much time in Athens and made a speech in which, the story goes, he 'spoke to the people in Greek, stating that he admired the virtue of the ancient Athenians and that he was happy to view so large and beautiful a city'.[49] In fact, Plutarch corrects, he spoke in Latin and used a translator who used many phrases to fill out Cato's brevity; and, more to the point, Cato 'mocked people who admired Greekness'; 'in general he thought the words of Greeks came from the lips, the words of Romans from the heart'.[50] Cato is so often represented as a figure of old and true Romanness – austere, hard, patriotic and so forth (even when teased for it by an Ovid). The suggestion that he could have uttered the standard rhetorician's (and tourist's) praise of Athens is dismissed by Plutarch, the critical historian. It was probably an interpreter's added cliché – not least because Cato thought Greeks' language to be necessarily superficial (unlike his own). How should a Greek reader approach this? Or a Roman reader? Cato was desperate to keep his son away from Greek influence and proclaimed that 'Rome would lose its Empire if it became infected with Greek learning.'[51] (The threat of Greek, as in the Talmudic passage with which this book opened, is

[49] *Cato* 12. 4   [50] *Cato* 12. 5.   [51] *Cato* 23. 2–3.

the destruction of one's city and culture. (Greek) books infect the self.) Plutarch adds his direct authorial comment here: Cato spoke 'too rashly for his years' – and 'history reveals the emptiness of his insult: as the city has risen to its greatest, so it has made Greek education and culture its own!'[52] Each reader – reading in Greek – is to distance himself from the model of Cato, whose Romanness cannot assimilate the Hellenization of Roman culture. Not only is the Roman reader offered the image of a 'too Roman' Roman, but also has before him the Greek correction of the great Roman's rejection of Greekness. (And the Greek reader thus reads of the folly of a Roman resistance to Hellenic culture.) Not only is there a range of possible positions for any reader to take on such a cultural tension, but also as an integral part of that range is the imagining of other readers' different takes. So Plutarch says that Cato would not let his son go to a Greek doctor, because he had heard, Plutarch suggests, the assertion of Hippocrates that he would never serve a barbarian. That is, Cato sees himself, the Greek text indicates, as a potential barbarian in Greek eyes, and thus he rejects Greek science in favour of his own herbal remedies – which results, Plutarch drily notes finally, in him losing his wife and son to a fatally mistreated disease.[53] In the process of cultural self-assertion, there is a real danger in mis-recognizing the value of Greek culture. Between Greek and Roman cultures – as between two mirrors – seeing oneself being seen and internalizing the perspective of the other – these are integral transactions in the processes of assimilation. Plutarch's *Cato* dramatizes the dangerous boundary of cultural resistance and acceptance.

It is necessary to detail these shifting (self-)positionings at work in the intricate interplays of assimilation and resistance partly because modern criticism has repeatedly posed the question 'Is Plutarch anti-Rome?' This question is simply not nuanced enough to account for Plutarch's writing (and even the best attempts to answer it cannot escape the straitjacketing of the question).[54] Plutarch's *Lives* may have inspired revolutionary Republican feeling in the eighteenth century, and the model of an intellectual leading a revolt against Empire (Gandhi or Lenin, say) may well have helped to frame the issue of Plutarch's politics in terms of revolutionary resistance to (or collaboration with) imperial power. But these models are distorting for Plutarch, who certainly did not lead military or political opposition to Rome – as is made strikingly plain by contrasting

---

[52] *Cato* 23. 3.   [53] *Cato* 23. 3–4.
[54] I have learnt most from Jones (1971); Pelling (1989); Boulogne (1994); Swain (1996); Duff (1999).

the intellectual at Delphi with, say, the Jewish revolts of the first century, or even with a radical Christian like Tertullian (who raged against just about everything Rome stood for in his Rome-educated rhetoric).[55] Plutarch is intimately *engaged* with a Roman cultural (and political) world, which itself is engaged with Greek cultural value. These sinuous lines of interchange make 'pro-' or 'anti-Rome' far too simple a matrix within which to explore Plutarch's writing. With the *Life of Cato* we have just seen how Plutarch's Greek version of a Roman version of what a Greek would think about barbarians serves to show up the Roman's excessive resistance to Greek cultural value in the name of a true Romanness. Plutarch mobilizes different levels of pleasure and instruction in his narrative, and it is hard to turn this layered complex of positions into an 'anti-Roman' perspective – without at least a drastic oversimplification of Plutarch's writing.

What is equally important, however, is that such an oversimplification would also distort the cultural work that Plutarch is doing, the performativity of his prose. The multiple perspectives of Plutarch's tale of Cato place the reader between the mirrors of Greekness and Romanness, and stimulate an awareness of the precarious work of cultural self-definition. Being Roman and being Greek – the values of Romanness and Greekness – are intertwined and mutually implicative – and it is not only the parallel Greek and Roman Lives which show this. Nor is it only in explicit statements about Rome or Romans that a cultural self-definition is being articulated. Plutarch's most expressly political writing may show most clearly how his assertion of Greek cultural authority can never escape the insecurity of its subordination to Roman power, but this work of reinventing and promoting a Greek culture is an all-consuming project that runs throughout his writing. Reading Plutarch is to share in the precarious project of saving Greek culture.

III

Consider, for example, the Greek way with naked bodies. Which is, as we saw with Lucian's *Anacharsis* and his games with the oddity of the gymnasium, an area of social intercourse where it is particularly pertinent (and funny) to dramatize the outsider's view of the glories of Greek life.

---

55 Especially relevant for my understanding of ancient assimilation and resistance have been: Momigliano (1975); MacMullen (1984); (1990); Gruen (1984); (1998); Bickerman (1988); Bowersock (1990); Millar (1993); Frankfurter (1998); Hopkins (1999); Woolf (1994); (1999).

Cato the Elder was a 'good father', Plutarch tells us;[56] and in line with his interest in *paideia*, the biographer outlines the Roman's constant concern and care for his boy's education, to the extent of his writing out his own History of Rome in large letters so that the child should always have in his own home a proper guide and aid to ancestral virtue.[57] 'Cato declared that he was no less careful about indecency of speech in the presence of his son than in the presence of those holy maidens which the Romans call the Vestals, and they never bathed together.'[58] The praiseworthy decorousness of speech is parallel to decorousness with naked bodies. (Corrupt language and corrupt sexual behaviour often go together in classical representation. Mouths should not be misused.) The slight distancing that Plutarch introduces by specifying the foreignness of the term 'Vestals' ('what the Romans call') serves to prepare us for the cultural oddity of Cato refusing to bathe with his son, which needs explanation:

For this seems to have been a common custom of the Romans: for even fathers-in-law and sons-in-law avoid bathing together, taking a dim view of uncovering themselves and nakedness. However, when they had learnt about naked exercise from the Greeks, they themselves in turn infected Greeks with the practice of doing it even with women.[59]

This is a fascinating account of a process of cultural assimilation. The Romans – the good old Romans, like Cato – were so suspicious of being naked together that even the least sexualized relations, son-in-law and father-in-law, were not expected to bathe together. This – to the Greek outsider – seems to have been the common, specifically Roman and quite unGreek, practice in the past. But contact with Greeks – the culture Cato said would bring down the Empire – means learning *gymnousthai* – 'how to be naked', 'to go naked', 'to exercise in the nude' (the *gym*). Contact with the Greeks means an education into the practice of Greek civilization. But the Romans in turn 'infect', 'defile' the Greek practice by encouraging the most suspicious of naked contact, namely, between men and women. (The extent to which Romans did promote mixed bathing at bath-houses still produces quite a lather amongst academics.)[60] The accuracy of Plutarch's historical reconstruction of Roman bathing is not the issue: what is important here is his need to see a dynamic interaction between Greek and Roman cultures, which gently allows misunderstanding and misperception a role in the process – especially

---

[56] *Cato* 20. 1.   [57] *Cato* 20. 5.   [58] *Cato* 20. 5.   [59] *Cato* 20. 5–6.   [60] See Fagan (1999).

from the Romans, who, bizarrely to Greek ideas, veer between proscribing naked exposure for all and allowing men and women to mix naked. Romans thus 'learn' from Greeks and 'infect' Greeks: the reciprocity of cultural contact is skewed towards the Greekness of the writer.

Nakedness is again the issue in *Roman Questions* 40. The question asked is 'Why is it not permissible for the priest of Jupiter to oil himself in the open air?' As usual, more than one answer is canvassed. The first is that in the old days, it was neither holy nor good for sons to bathe with a father, or sons-in-law with fathers-in-law; and so, since Zeus is 'father Zeus', anything in the open air is in Zeus' sight and should be seemly. This takes for granted, again, the old Roman custom of men avoiding bathing together. The second suggestion is that just as you wouldn't strip off in a temple, so you shouldn't strip off before the gods in the sky. The third answer is that it is just a local and specific ritual taboo such as all societies have. But this is expanded – anthropologically, as it were – to reveal a more general social cause for the specific prohibition:

For the Romans used to be extremely suspicious of oiling, and they are of the opinion that nothing is the cause of the enslavement and effeminacy of the Greeks so much as the gym and the wrestling schools. These institutions produce in the cities much listlessness and inactivity and indolence and pederasty and corruption of the bodies of young men by sleep and walking and rhythmic movement and precise diet. This led them unawares to give up military training and to delight in being called well-honed and beautiful athletes rather than noble warriors and horsemen.

Plutarch sharply represents one strand of Roman thought. Paradigmatically, Cicero (who puffs to his friend Atticus, 'You know what I think of Greek games!') in *Tusculan Disputations* quotes Ennius, the granddaddy of Roman poetry: 'to bare one's body around citizens is the beginning of outrageous behaviour', *flagiti principium est nudare inter cives*.[61] Indeed, from the fifth-century BCE onwards, even Greek writers reverse the claim that the gymnasium is a good preparation for war by insulting the uselessness of the overtrained athlete.[62] Plato himself contrasts the necessity of a good citizen's good physical training with the precarious overdevelopment of the specialist athlete.[63] In the second and third centuries in particular, doctors, athletic trainers and philosophers compete over who gives better instruction in health. Yet Plutarch here

---

[61] *ad Att.* 16.5; *Tusc. Disp.* 4. 33. 70.
[62] See Jason König (2000), from whom I have learnt for the following paragraphs.
[63] E.g. *Rep* 403d ff.

represents the Roman view in stridently extreme language: the gym is not only a school in idleness and listlessness, but also in slavery and effeminacy (a Greek self-representation?) The regimen of the body – the standard categories of regulated sleep, walking, rhythmic movement, diet – is mocked as a (Socratic) 'corruption of the young'. This may seem a strident Roman assault on the Greek culture of the gym, but Plutarch does not easily distance himself from it. He concludes the discussion with this accommodating mitigation: 'it is indeed quite a task to escape from such charges if you strip off in public; but if you oil yourself and care for yourself at home there is no error'. Plutarch resists the public role of the gymnasium in the *polis*, and the continuing popularity of athletics as a sign of masculine achievement. It's not merely that he dismisses athletics, a common enough intellectual posture, but rather that he suggests that doing such exercises at home would be acceptable – an odd compromise for standard Greek mores at least. Plutarch's Greekness is no simple idealism.

This resistance to what might be thought to be a paradigmatic sign of Greekness is in line with his own short work on exercise, training and diet, *Health Precepts*. This is a polemical work, nominally in the form of a dialogue, though it is mainly one long speech. It establishes its polemics by the dramatic device of recalling and rejecting a doctor's comments on philosophy. *Health Precepts* will be a philosopher's take on health, which repeatedly rejects the precise diet regimes of the doctors and trainers in favour of a more holistic, philosophically led regime. It is a unique – and curiously engaging – document in that it specifies itself to be a health handbook for scholars and politicians (and thus puts reading aloud as one of its key exercises for the body!) Baths, in the treatise, are a normal and regulated part of both pre-dinner and post-exercise activity. So 'to take a cold bath after exercise is ostentatious and adolescent rather than healthy' (a precept defended with Plutarch's almost obsessive interest in the flow of heat and cold); cold baths always lead to overprescriptive regimes.[64] But 'warm baths have a lot in their favour', and, if you are already comfortable, 'a warm massage with oil by the fire' is also desirable.[65] The academic or politician is encouraged by Plutarch towards a restricted and more private training: a walk, a discussion, a rub down with warm oil, all in the pursuit of a philosophically trained and balanced life within the small *équipe* of friends. In the *Roman Questions* too, Plutarch's ease with private exercise and oiling shows how his image of Greekness stems from a particular Greco-Roman elite intellectual background, which can

---

[64] *Mor* 131b; *de Tu. San. Prae.* 17   [65] *Mor* 131 c-d; *de Tu. San. Prae.* 17.

be contrasted, say, with the world of intense public athletic competition throughout the cities of the Greek East. Plutarch has his own particular perspective on that central sign of Greek life, athletic exercise. Plutarch is projecting a specific, poised and carefully constructed image of Greek cultural life.

Indeed, the *Roman Questions* as a whole is a work which goes to the heart of Plutarch's cultural politics. It is paired with *Greek Questions*, and there was also a now lost third work, *Barbarian Questions*. This trilogy provides an immediate matrix of categorization – and a question. If Greek is traditionally and normatively opposed to barbarian, how is the Roman to be triangulated into the schema? Both the *Roman Questions* and *Greek Questions* have a similar structure. Each poses a technical and often abstruse question of cultural practice in the form 'Why does . . . ?' (*dia ti*) and offers one or more answers in the form 'Because . . . ' (*hoti*) or 'Is it because . . . ?' (*ê hoti*). This format draws on a long and varied intellectual tradition. On the one hand, Aristotle's *Problems* (a spurious work which none the less is taken as the headstone of a prose, philosophical tradition) poses and answers a series of scientific and other questions on exactly this same linguistic style. On the other hand, the term I have translated in the traditional way as 'questions' is in Greek *aitia* – 'causes', 'origins', 'reasons' – and it is a term which alludes also to the tradition of 'aetiological' poetry, epitomized by Callimachus, the greatest of the Hellenistic poets, whose masterpiece, called precisely *Aitia*, used the structure of asking questions about religious and other practices to put together a long, highly intricate narrative poem about the origin or causes of things – and this aetiological project had many children, most notably Ovid's *Fasti*, which also uses the question and answer format to explore and tell the tale(s) of the Roman calendar – its myths and festivals. Plutarch's mix of traditions in his *Aitia* is self-consciously adopting and adapting the pose of the *sophos*, the educated authority. He is making a question of Romanness, of Greekness – and of cultural difference itself.

Plutarch's strategy of pairing the *Greek* and *Roman Questions* establishes an asymmetry in a more developed and manipulative way than the parallelism of the *Parallel Lives*. First, the reader of both works is assumed to be Greek (or, at its least marked, a Greek-educated person). That is, the first person is reserved for Greek behaviour ('Why do we . . . ?'), and the Roman practices are most often described in a rather vague third person: 'Why do they . . . ?' Roman characters are introduced, Roman language translated, transliterated and explained. There are, of course, generalizations which include all human life: but the subject position of writer and projected reader is that of an educated Greek faced by the question of cultural difference or oddity.

This asymmetry has been superbly analysed by Rebecca Preston.[66] Like other scholars, she notes that the *Roman Questions* in the majority of cases offer a choice of more than one possible reason for a question 'Why does . . . ?' (unlike the Aristotelian *Problems*), whereas the *Greek Questions* more commonly asks 'Who . . . ?', or 'What . . . ?' questions, and offers single explanatory answers. 'The difference in the style of answers in the *Greek Questions* and the *Roman Questions* seems to suggest that Plutarch positioned himself quite differently in relation to Roman culture than he did in relation to Greek culture.'[67] Greek culture can be seen as fissured and conflictual: different Greek cities have different vocabularies, practices and beliefs which need explanation. Greece is imaged as a collection of autonomous states – but the perspective of that image is also a general Greek *paideia*, assumed to be curious about such local differences, and fully informed about the shared treasure of Panhellenic myth and history. There is almost a timeless quality about this image of Greek cities – there is scarcely any indication of the institution of the Roman Empire in the *Greek Questions*. So – to take one short but not wholly bland example – question 55 of the *Greek Questions* asks 'Why is it, when the Samians sacrifice to Hermes the Joy-Giver, it is permitted for anyone who wants to steal and to take clothes?' And answers: 'Because according to an oracle they left the island of Samos for Mycale and survived for ten years by piracy. After this, they sailed to the island again and defeated their enemies.' A particular, odd ritual – allowed clothes stealing at a festival of Hermes – provokes a question. The framework is familiar and needs no glossing: a well-known island, an Olympian god, and an activity which is in some sense easily paralleled from, say, Spartan rituals of initiation, which also famously required its future noble warriors to steal.[68] And the answer gives a brief, decontextualized narrative with an expected moral force. The ritual has divine authority, and, as with so many aetiological stories of ceremonial, the story concerns the possession of territory and war. There is no need to explain (for us) Hermes' evident connection as the god of thieves and found objects.[69] The question and answer establishes a horizon of expectation which is fully informed by Greek culture. Local difference serves to reinforce Greek cultural identity.

[66] Preston (2001) from which I have learnt much. See also the less nuanced Boulogne (1987); (1992).
[67] Preston (2001) 97.
[68] Jeanmaire (1939); Vidal-Naquet (1981) 151–74; Cartledge (1987) 30–2.
[69] Kahn (1978).

Roman Questions, however, not only regularly multiplies explanations – as if Roman culture is far harder to pin down – but also repeatedly subsumes Roman culture within Plutarch's own Greek world-view. Preston stresses three dominant strategies of Plutarch, each of which privileges the perspective of the Greek *sophos*. First, Plutarch regularly offers a Greek source to explain Roman activity and supports that source over and above other explanations. Second, Plutarch uses an analogy or model from the Greek world to justify an explanation – even when there is no causal link. Third, Plutarch adopts a moralizing or ethical explanation which makes his own Greek, educated perspective seem natural, necessary and correct ('It's only natural that . . . '). Preston articulates each of these strategies at length with some finely detailed examples. Here is one neat case, not fully explored by Preston, which captures each of Plutarch's manipulations in one lengthy answer.

The question (25) is 'Why do they reckon the day that follows the Kalends, the Nones or the Ides to be unsuitable for leaving home or for travel?' Plutarch offers *us* at least six possible answers for what *they* do. The first answer is ascribed to what 'the majority think and Livy writes in his *History*' – that is, it cites Roman tradition and a Roman intellectual authority. Livy's explanation is that it is a memorial to a disastrous battle with the Gauls at the river Allia, which took place on the day after the Ides of July. This, however, is explicitly dismissed by Plutarch for its 'many illogicalities' – not least that the battle could be shown to have taken place on a different day. The Roman intellectual and what is generally thought to be the case by Romans are both subject to Plutarch's superior analysis. He secondly offers an analogy with Greek customs ('Consider the following analogy . . . '[70]): the Greeks sacrifice to the Olympian gods on the day of the new moon, but on the next day to the heroes and spirits. Thus, the second day here too is inferior, and, accordingly, regarded as ill-omened. Such an analogy is not a cause, so much as a way of establishing a dominant Greek perspective. This leads, thirdly, to a Pythagorean reflection on number theory: the first number is a monad and divine, the second is a dyad and opposed to the first – which would also explain why 'the day after' is imperfect and thus ill-omened. Fourth, a Greek story is told: unlike Livy's *alogia* ('illogicality'), this story of Themistocles 'has some foundation in reason' [*ekhei logon*]. It is a little fable about how the relaxation of The Day After could not be there without the work of The Feast Day (a fable designed to show

---

[70] The nice translation of Babbitt in the *Loeb*: ὅρα δὴ μή, καθάπερ . . . .

the generals who followed Themistocles would be nothing without their illustrious predecessor). A nice anecdote – but a quip of Themistocles from classical Athens is scarcely capable of explaining why the Romans don't go out on the day after the Ides! The fifth and sixth reasons appeal to what's natural. You can't do business without preparation, so the day after a festival is a bad day for such activity, when you can't properly prepare on a holiday. And, finally, Plutarch asks, isn't it just natural even today? Don't we like to have a gap after the delight of a festival before we have the unpleasantness of work?

My selection of examples has, of course, maximized the contrast between the style of the *Greek* and *Roman Questions* in order to make my point as strongly as possible. None the less, this case does provide a remarkable collection of potential answers and cultural positions, and shows just how extraordinary Plutarch's answers to the question of Roman culture can be. We are asked to move from criticizing the explicit Roman accounts (both general and of a named intellectual), to trying a Greek religious analogy, to proposing a Pythagorean scientific hypothesis, to telling a fable from the storehouse of classical Athens, to, finally, offering what is likely and customary for us as reasonable men. There is no conclusion or judgement between reasons (except the slur on Livy). The reader is invited to take any, all or none of the suggested reasons. ('From what has been said, you can perceive for yourself...') Each part of its multifaceted inventiveness, however, offers a Greek perspective and draws on Greek knowingness to explain Roman social activity. You are being asked to share in Plutarch's intellectualizing gaze at another's culture, to approach Roman culture through Plutarch, gatekeeper of knowledge.

Yet it would be too simple to see this just as Plutarch the Greek outsider objectifying and trying to explain the otherness of Roman culture. For Plutarch is also happy in the *Roman Questions* as elsewhere to flaunt his deep insider knowledge of Roman institutions and ceremonials – much as the *Lives* fluently trace the narratives of Roman greatness as exemplary and much as he represents himself as an active participant in elite Roman political and cultural life. Indeed, the *Lives* twice explicitly direct the reader to the *Roman Questions* for more extended treatments of particular social niceties of Roman practices.[71] (The cross-referencing between his different texts by Plutarch encourages you to treat his productions as a connected body of work.) What's more, as Preston carefully draws out, both the emphasis on the great Greek past and the difficulty of fully

---

[71] *Rom.* 15.5; *Cam.* 19. 8.

explaining Roman culture, even or especially in Greek terms, undermine the (contemporary) cultural confidence of the *Questions*. 'The tentativeness of answering' shows how the 'Romans cannot be assimilated into the Greek world view so easily. The explanatory power of Greek culture has limits.'[72] Explaining cultural difference inevitably embroils the explainer in a complex and self-implicating process of accommodation and resistance, comprehension and appropriation, knowingness and misunderstanding. Why does Plutarch multiply explanations of cultural practice? Is it because he is asserting the power and authority of his knowledge, the value of Greek education to express the truth of things? Or is it because as an outsider he can never fully and surely comprehend the otherness of Rome? Or is it because he can – through his elite and privileged understanding of Roman culture – explain Romanness in an accommodating manner to a primarily Greek audience?

My favourite *Roman Question* sets at stake the origin of Roman culture itself. It is question 22, which asks 'Why do they think that Janus is two-faced and represent him thus in paintings and sculpture?' Ovid points out that Janus is a Roman god without a Greek equivalent – a specifically Roman figure – a remark which makes particular sense within the fruitful tradition in ancient polytheistic writing of explaining foreign gods in terms of one's own pantheon.[73] (As Lucian's *de Dea Syria* showed, encountering another religion is an especially charged moment for the interplay of accommodating appropriation and resistant incomprehension in cultural contact.) As befits the figure of Janus, Plutarch gives two answers which face in opposite directions, but which both pose the question of the origin of Romanness itself.

Is it because, as they tell the story, he was by birth a Greek from Perrhaibia and he crossed to Italy, and lived with the barbarians there and changed his language and way of life?

Or is it rather because he changed and reorganized the people of Italy to another form of life: they had used wild plants and lawlessness, he persuaded them to grow crops and to have government?

The first answer – attributed to an anonymous 'they' – claims that Janus, the most specifically Roman of gods, was by birth actually Greek, but when he came to Italy, because he lived with barbarians – the local inhabitants – he himself changed his tongue and life-style, and thus

---

[72] Preston (2001) 117.

[73] *Fasti* 1.89–90; cf Macrobius *Saturnalia* 1.7.19. See Preston (2001) 98–99, and Boulogne (1987) and (1994) for further discussion.

became barbarian rather than Greek. Hence the 'two faces'. This slyly suggests that the uniquely Roman figure has a Greek origin, but his oddity is explicable because of his corruption by local Italian barbarians. Janus, the Greek, is barbarized by his transfer to the Italian landscape. The second answer, however, suggests a different pattern of acculturation. In this account, Janus makes the Italians civilized – via the classic Greek expressions of civilization, namely, agriculture and civic polity. Here Janus is not changed but changes. (Hence, the 'two faces'.) This second answer may be preferable ('or is it *rather* . . . '?) and indeed this version seems to find echoes elsewhere in the *Roman Questions* and the *Lives*. Yet both answers find the origin of a key Roman figure in Greece and make the Greekness of this Janus either barbarized by contact with Italy or the force necessary to give the barbarous Italians a beginning of civilization. There is no civilization in this mythical nexus without Greekness.

Rebecca Preston sensitively sets this lovely passage of cultural one-upmanship against an intricate intellectual background.[74] Roman writers too debated the varied origins of their religious and social practices; their mythic narratives placed various Greek heroes as early inhabitants of Italy; Roman writers were also capable – like Cato – of denying violently any such beneficial interaction with Greek culture. *Explaining* Rome was a pervasive Roman concern. Greek writers too took different positions – from the total silence on the Roman Empire in the ancient novels, to the encyclopedic history of Dionysius of Halicarnassus whose *Roman Antiquities* so assimilates Roman culture to Greek that 'for Dionysius, there is no Roman culture'.[75] Plutarch is, then, taking his own stance on the question of the cultural origins of Rome. But what is more important for my purposes here is the self-articulation of Plutarch between the faces of Greece and Rome – turned towards Rome, returning to Greece, and finding a purity of cultural identity impossible to maintain. It's not just that he is constantly mired in the embracing power of Empire (its governing institutions, the lure of its narratives, its delimitation of authority). It's rather that the boundaries of Greekness and Romanness – as with all myths of cultural origin at the site of cultural conflict – prove all too permeable, all too intertwined. Establishing and preserving the value of Greekness becomes not just the assertion of an identity but a set of questions about cultural self-positioning.

---

[74] Preston (2001) 98ff.   [75] Preston (2001) 100.

In short, you can see in *Greek* and *Roman Questions* Plutarch doing the *cultural work* of trying to maintain and authorize a Greek cultural perspective in the face of Roman power. This is the *negotiation* of cultural difference *in process*.

IV

What is most remarkable about Plutarch, however, is the sheer range of his output. So far I have looked – selectively, for sure – at the *Lives*, with their parallel accounts of Greek and Roman military and political heroes; at his political theory, with its articulation of Greek potential and impotence within Roman power structures; and at some of his writing on cultural anthropology, as it were, tracing the interfaces of cultural difference between Greek and Roman societies. Yet Plutarch also writes on religion, on science, on education, on philosophy, on erotics, on historiography, on literary criticism – and so on. Over seventy treatises survive, collected in what is known as the *Moralia*. This Latin title is a translation of the Greek *Ethica*, which means not merely writing on ethical or moral issues, but more generally on the conglomeration of concerns which make up a way of life.[76] Plutarch's encyclopedic intellectual production is a cycle of education that produces and promotes the knowledge to live a life, a life informed by Greek knowing (even, or especially, when addressed to Roman patrons). This is a programme to understand the world, to make it the known world.

How are the co-ordinates of this world map of Greek knowing formulated? What is (Greek) learning? There are, first of all, explicit educational texts, that begin with the education of children, and move through *How a Young Man should Study Poetry*, to *On Correct Listening to Lectures*, to *Advice to an Uneducated Prince* (a text which Erasmus translated for Henry VIII and which provides an instructive model for the Renaissance obsession with the correct advice and education of young rulers). These 'how to' texts show in exemplary fashion the constant move in Plutarch from an apparently narrow intellectual topic to the broad issues of proper living. *On Correct Listening to Lectures* is a fascinating and paradigmatic case.[77] The treatise manipulates a central tension that runs through its advice. On the one hand, no young man can be properly educated unless he listens and learns from his elders and betters (like the author), and so he must learn to pay proper attention to a speaker, not rustling, coughing

[76] On the difficulty of the translation of *êthos* by *mos*, see Quintilian 6.2.8–9.
[77] Goldhill (1999).

or giggling. Education depends on the deep absorption of the lesson:

Sit in an upright position without lounging or sprawling; look directly at the speaker; maintain a pose of active attention, with a clear expression on the face, without a sign of insolence or bad temper . . . Not only are frowning, a sour face, a roving glance, twisting the body, crossing the legs, unseemly behaviour, but also nodding, whispering to another, smiling, sleepy yawns, lowering the head. Everything like this is reprehensible and needs a good deal of care to avoid.[78]

A full physiognomics of the face and body is itemized and regulated in the name of propriety. Your body shows how you have been and are being educated. The lecture room is a place for scrutinizing the bodily practice of an audience. If you manage to 'listen with self-control and respect', however, you 'learn and absorb the useful lecture'.[79]

On the other hand, the aim of rhetoric is the persuasive seduction of the listener, and to be won over is to be mastered, to be emasculated, to lose control. The young must indeed be immensely careful about their ears: 'virtue's only hold on the young is their ears, if they are guarded, pure, unpolluted and untouched by base language'.[80] So Plutarch cites Xenocrates warmly, who ordered 'ear-guards to be worn by children rather than athletes', as 'children have their characters distorted by words'.[81]

Until philosophy has given you the necessary internal critical protection, Plutarch recommends 'ear protectors' – like old football gear – because of the dangers of 'influence and persuasion'. When you listen, do not give yourself over. The self-controlled and respectful listener absorbs useful speech, but must also 'see through and detect lying or useless discourse' – a critical listening that does just assimilate but also resists.[82] ('From what has been already said, you yourself will be able to judge . . . ') Subject and object of language's power, the citizen is always engaged in an uneasy dialectic between being the master and the victim of words. How words enter and leave your body needs training, control and submission to the regulation of propriety, informed by the regime of philosophy. Listening is a formative element in the askesis of the critical subject. Or as Plutarch concludes in the last words of the treatise: 'Right Listening is the beginning of Right Living.'[83] Advice on how to sit in lectures turns out to be an issue of how to live. A lesson for life : . . .

---

[78] *Mor.* 45c; *de Rect. Rat. Aud.* 13.   [79] *Mor.* 39c; *de Rect. Rat. Aud.* 4.
[80] *Mor.* 38b; *de Rect. Rat. Aud.* 2.   [81] *Mor.* 38b; *de Rect. Rat. Aud.* 2.
[82] *Mor.* 39c; *de Rect. Rat. Aud.* 4.   [83] *Mor.* 48d; *de Rect. Rat. Aud.* 18.

On Garrulousness takes a different and more oblique didactic stance on the use of language and its role in society. 'Philosophy takes upon itself an awkward and difficult task of therapy with garrulousness', it begins.[84] Philosophy, from the Hellenistic period onwards, claimed itself to be a therapy of desire, a therapy for the buffeting of life.[85] Here, with mock grandeur, Plutarch aims philosophy's medicine at excessive talkativeness. The foundational problem for philosophy, Plutarch goes on archly, is that its talking cure can't have an impact on the garrulous, because they never listen – and, playing with the medical language, 'lack of silence syndrome has as its first symptom lack of listening syndrome'.[86] *On Garrulousness* – amusingly enough one of the longest of his treatises on social and emotional issues – runs together story after story from Greece and Rome about the dangers of language, the benefits of silence, the error of misplaced words, and the awfulness of the chatty. (Where Theophrastus in his *Characters* described the horrors of the Garrulous Man in barely a page, Plutarch has more than thirty pages of anecdotes, in his most disorganized style.) So, Anacharsis, when he slept at Solon's house, 'was seen to put his left hand on his genitals but his right hand on his mouth'. That was because 'he thought, and thought rightly, that the tongue needed the stronger restraint'.[87] (Sexual and linguistic propriety, again, are linked.) Or, the race of barbers is infected with talkativeness by their customers: cue string of stories about barber shop gossip.[88] After some sixteen chapters of these tales, Plutarch comments that what has been offered is not an *accusation* of garrulousness, but a *medical procedure* – because what's required for emotions or conditions [*pathê*], is 'diagnosis and treatment' – *krisis* and *askêsis*.[89] *Krisis* is also the standard word for 'judgement', and *askêsis* for the habituated practice which is the expression of a regulated life in Greek ethical writing. Indeed, the only cure for garrulousness, Plutarch finally suggests, is not restraint, but 'habituation' [*êthos*].[90] If one habitually provides examples of propriety and habitually answers in a terse and directive manner, there is hope that the garrulous man can learn self-control. *Askêsis*, concludes Plutarch, 'controls all things and is stronger than anything'.[91] *On Garrulousness*, then, also finally

[84] *Mor.* 502b; *de Garr.* 1.
[85] See especially Nussbaum (1994); Foucault (1986); also Annas (1992) 103–22, 189–200.
[86] *Mor.* 502c; *de Garr.* 1: καὶ τοῦτον ἔχει πρῶτον κακὸν ἡ ἀσιγησία, τὴν ἀνηκοΐαν.
[87] *Mor.* 505a; *de Garr.* 7.   [88] *Mor.* 509a; *de Garr.* 12.
[89] *Mor.* 510c; *de Garr.* 16. See Ingenkamp (1971).
[90] *Mor.* 511e-f; *de Garr.* 19. Plutarch links *êthos* ['habituation'] etymologically and semantically to *êthos* at *de Virt Moral.* 443c.
[91] *Mor.* 515a; *de Garr.* 23.

suggests a way of life, a full training in daily experience, is the endpoint of its advice.

This treatise enjoys its anecdotes: it piles up a storehouse of clever tales of misplaced words and broken silences for you to enjoy and use; its own length is a (long-running) game. ('He is garrulous', confesses Mahaffy.[92]) It both jokes with the language of philosophical cure, and yet, at the same time, has an underlying normative message. Through its charms and fragmentary pleasures, it still projects an ideal: an ideal that links *krisis* and *askesis*, judgement and training, to the picture of culture (*paideia*) embodied in the tradition of *logoi* from which his anecdotes are plucked. When the final paragraph proclaims with portentous emphasis, 'above all else and alongside all these cases, one must keep to hand and remember this saying of Simonides . . . ', it is not only the specific wisdom of Simonides that is being enjoined, but the whole process of evaluating, selecting, preserving, recalling the wise words of the past: saving Greek culture.

Plutarch also plays the role of professional *sophos* at its most austere level. He writes extensively on philosophy and on scientific problems. A philosophical understanding of the world runs throughout his output, and he is always happy to 'digress' into scientific explanations of phenomena. Philosophy and science are two master discourses to divide, explain and control the world (as experienced). Plutarch is never happier than when he can use his philosophy to promote a way of living, which includes bodily *askesis* explained and controlled by physical science. His *Health Precepts* is thus an archetypal Plutarchan text, as are the 'digressions' on heat and cold, say. He also takes on philosophical problems in a more playful manner. His *Gryllus*, for example, a discussion of whether animals are rational, is a dialogue between Odysseus and one of his sailors, who has been transformed into a pig by Circe – but who wants to remain a beast, since the pigs' attitude to the world seems more philosophically justifiable than the humans around him.[93] Plutarch's longest single work, the *Sympotic Questions*, has the setting of a symposium, that archetypal Greek institution, and poses and debates a set of questions, related both to the performance of the symposium and to a whole range of trivial and grand issues (from the production of truffles to the epidemiology of new diseases). What is at stake here is not merely the circulation of the *sophia* of the Greek and Roman world, but also the proper way to conduct a symposium. The image of the small

[92] Mahaffy (1890) 291.   [93] Goldhill (1995) 64–6.

group of highly intellectual, elite, Greek educated men, discussing academic points with all due propriety and bonhomie is a model for social interaction. The educated man (or *pepaideumenos*) in action. The world becoming the known world by the performance of Greek learning – and the reader learning Greek learning. But – Plutarch requires you to be selective and judgemental – I want to end this section by looking at two works which have perhaps a less obvious contribution to the tradition of Greek culture, namely, *On the Malice of Herodotus*, and *On Isis and Osiris*.

On the Malice of Herodotus often embarrasses Plutarchan scholars: it seems 'rather an oddity...hard to read in its original spirit and it is not amiable'.[94] The word translated 'malice' is *kakoêtheia* which means a 'nasty prejudicial disposition', and it is Plutarch as much as Herodotus who seems tainted by that slur. How could Plutarch attack so vitriolically such a cultural icon as the Father of History? Plutarch offers an explicit motivation in the first paragraph: 'Since he has employed his malice particularly against the Boeotians and Corinthians (although he spares no one else), I think it is my duty to come to the rescue both of my ancestors and of the truth'.[95] It would seem that Plutarch's polemic is motivated by local honour and defended in the name of truth. There is, however, much more at stake than this evident parochialism.

The general principles of what constitutes 'malice' are outlined in the extensive preface. They include a delight in abuse, in preserving the worst versions of stories, in selecting the most aggressive evaluative vocabulary, in omitting good stories, and in manipulative and ungenerous accounts of motivation. These criteria are then applied to various sections of Herodotus' *History* at length and often with rhetorical violence, misrepresentation (to the point of misquotation), and strongly worded disapproval, including outraged second person addresses to the historian himself. ('What are you saying?!....') In particular, by far the greatest emphasis is laid upon Herodotus' account of the critical battles of the Persian wars, especially Thermopylae and Salamis. Plutarch's first example, however, is also telling: he takes his start from the beginning of Herodotus' text. Herodotus famously founds his history of East–West conflict on a relentlessly rationalistic account of the mythic repertoire. Where mythology has Europa carried off by Zeus in the shape of a bull, and Io changed into a cow and pursued by a gadfly, Herodotus tells us a set of rapes and seductions on trade routes between mainland Greece and the seaboard of Asia Minor. This brilliantly disruptive history is attributed

---

94 Bowen (1992) 2.   95 *Mor.* 854e–f; *de Mal. Her.* 1.

slyly to 'Persian intellectuals'.[96] Plutarch wants none of this:

All Greeks believe that Io is considered divine and worshipped with religious honours by the barbarians and that her name has been given to many seas and to the most important straits because of that repute [*doxa*].[97]

The story of Io is a foundational myth of East–West conflict, of the origin of cultural and political difference. Herodotus wants to make the myth into an account of expected and predictable human exchange ('no woman allows herself to be raped if she doesn't want to', he declares notoriously, appealing to common knowledge in order to ground his narrative patterning in the normal).[98] Plutarch sees this not merely as an undermining of the theology of Greek supremacy but also as a denigration of 'the greatest and most noble act of Greece', namely the Trojan War.[99] Herodotus' intellectualism threatens the glory that was Greece.

Indeed, Plutarch links this opening salvo to his next complaint with 'Herodotus is such a barbarian-lover...'[100] This second complaint focuses on the attribution of human sacrifice to the Greeks rather than to Busiris, the Egyptian. How could Herodotus 'turn that pollution back on to Greece?!' This accusation of 'philo-barbarism' is followed by a sarcastic rebuttal of Herodotus' claim that the Persians learnt how to sleep with boys from the Greeks (the wrong sort of cultural education): 'How can the Persians owe this lesson to the Greeks when almost everyone agrees they castrated boys before they ever saw the Greek sea?'[101] What is at stake here again is not only the origin of (unacceptable) cultural practices – cultural value – but also the flow of education. In the same way that he himself suggested that the civilizing force of Janus must have come from Greek origins, so here he denies that 'vice' could have been taught to the East by Greeks. In the same breath, he ridicules a Persian genealogy that makes Hercules, conqueror of monsters, an Assyrian by descent. Herodotus' history, for Plutarch, sets at risk the foundational and originary value of Greece.

This anxiety courses through Plutarch's detailed critique of Herodotus' account of the battles of the Persian wars. As Plutarch himself

---

[96] See Nagy (1987), reworked in Nagy (1990), and more generally Gould (1989).
[97] *Mor.* 856d–e; *de Mal. Her.* 11.   [98] *Mor.* 856f; *de Mal. Her.* 11.
[99] *Mor.* 856e; *de Mal. Her.* 11.
[100] *Mor.* 857a; *de Mal. Her.* 12: οὕτω δὲ φιλοβάρβαρός ἐστι....
[101] *Mor.* 857b–c; *de Mal. Her.* 13.

made plain in his *Political Precepts*, these battles remained a staple of the rhetoric of the history of Greece. From the great Funeral Speeches over the War Dead in classical Athens, to the contemporary rhetoric schools of the Empire, the glorious defeat of the mass of Persia by the mighty handful of the hardy Greeks is the model of military achievement, of the winning of glory. In the *Political Precepts* Plutarch may have sniffed against such rhetorical memorials in contrast with present impotence, but he also loves to record the telling moments of that campaign himself: it is part of the shared knowing of his cultural milieu. Hence, the danger of Herodotus' smooth and beguiling prose is that as the beautiful rose conceals the destructive beetle, so the very attractiveness of Herodotus' writing 'conceals the divisiveness and misrepresentation of its malice'.[102] So, concludes Plutarch in the last words of the treatise, we must watch out lest we 'accept unknowingly opinions [*doxai*] which are out of place and false about the greatest cities and men of Greece'.[103] This is not a re-statement of the parochialism of the opening paragraph. *Doxa* – 'fame', 'repute', 'opinion' – is what makes the greatest men and cities great, and if this *doxa* is false or 'out of place' [*atopos*], then the foundational history of greatness becomes fissured with rivalry and doubt. Plutarch's contentiousness is aimed at removing contentiousness from the histori-cal foundation of Greece's greatness. He aims to preserve the *doxa* of a glorious past. Saving the story of the saving of Greece . . .

Plutarch is unsurprisingly quick to scorn Herodotus' well-known (barbarian-loving) claim that the Greeks learnt about religious proces-sions and festivals from the Egyptians. *On Isis and Osiris*, however, is Plutarch's full-scale engagement with Egyptian religion from a quite dif-ferent rhetorical standpoint. This lengthy treatise is addressed to Clea, a priestess at Delphi – the very centre of Greek religion – who has been initiated into the mysteries of Osiris by her mother and father.[104] She is described by Plutarch as the perfect recipient for his disquisition, and as a devotee who straddles the religious boundaries of East and West she is indeed a carefully chosen figure for the rhetorical strategies of this, Plutarch's longest religious work. For Plutarch in *On Isis and Osiris* sets out to bring Egyptian religion, its tales, practices and allure, under the aegis of a Greek, philosophically informed, theological comprehension. The famous second book of Herodotus' *History* which focuses on Egypt,

---

[102] *Mor.* 874b; *de Mal. Her.* 43. [103] *Mor.* 874c; *de Mal. Her.* 43.
[104] *Mor* 364e; *de Is. et Os.* 35.

uses the antiquity of Egypt and the power of its religious narratives to un-
dercut Greek claims of an authoritative antiquity; he also uses Egyptian
knowledge to show up claims of a privileged Greek knowledge; he uses
the exoticism of Egypt to reflect on the constructedness, the convention-
ality of Greek ideas of the natural. Herodotus – from Halicarnassus, the
boundary city between the Eastern Persian Empire and the Greek world
of Ionia – has, he declares, been to Egypt and claims for himself the first-
hand knowledge of autopsy. He uses that knowledge in his exploration
of the fragility and power of Greekness, as his story of the war between
East and West becomes a kaleidoscopic journey of cultural conflict and
cultural self-definition.[105] Plutarch, however, in *On Isis and Osiris* makes
no claim to first-hand knowledge of Egypt (even though elsewhere in his
writings he says he has visited it); his is a journey through the scholarly
traditions of Egypt. And far from allowing the antiquity, knowledge or
exoticism of Egypt to ruffle his Greekness, Plutarch – firmly resisting the
sly manipulations of Herodotus – evaluates, dismisses and organizes this
Egyptian other from a perspective centred on Delphi. Plutarch suggests
that the divine in all its manifestations is open to the same (Greek) understanding, and plays the same role in men's lives. Plutarch, looking at
the vast array of weird mythologies and religious practices from around
the Mediterranean, fully enacts the *bon mot* of Philostratus: 'To the wise
man everything is Greece.'[106]

The three rhetorical manoeuvres that were so evident in the *Roman
Questions* are also extensively deployed in *On Isis and Osiris*. First and fore-
most, he repeatedly sets Greek authorities over and against Egyptian
sources. Most commonly, he simply cites Greeks as authoritative (Homer,
Hesiod, Plato, Euripides, Eudoxus in particular – all figures whom
Herodotus and others especially associated with Egyptian wisdom or
Egyptian travels). He also sets Greek against Greek: he criticizes Eudoxus
for scepticism, Euhemerus for 'quackeries', and others for 'slick evasion
of the true explanation'.[107] He evaluates traditions, enacts the process of
critical judgement – and always in such a way as to define the authoritative horizon of intellectual expectation as Greek. He finds Greek origins
for rituals and names, especially when others had claimed Egyptian priority. Let me give one typical example of this self-assertive Hellenocentric
scholarship. He explains that Osiris' name comes from two Greek words

---

[105] See Gould (1989); Hall (1989); Hartog (1988); Lloyd (1990); Redfield (1985).
[106] *VA* 1.35. For further extension of this phrase see Whitmarsh (2001). See also Alston (1996).
[107] *Mor.* 377a; *de Is. et Os.* 64; *Mor.* 360a; *de Is. et Os.* 23; *Mor.* 359e; *de Is. et Os.* 22 – Griffiths' zippy
translation of ῥᾴστῃ ἀποδράσει τοῦ λόγου χρῶνται.

hosios, 'holy', and *hieros*, 'sacred'. (He earlier derived 'Isis' from the root *oida* 'to know': the Greek roots of sacred knowledge are means and matter of this debate!) He comments:

there is no need to be surprised at the re-modelling [*anaplasis*] of these words into Greek. The fact is that a huge number of other words which went out with those who migrated from Greece, persist even till today – living as strangers in foreign lands. Some who gloss such terms when they occur in poetry, falsely accuse them of being barbarisms.[108]

The Greek etymologies of the Egyptian names of Egyptian gods can be traced to Greek migrations – as if Egyptian religion, like Janus, really came from Greece, and finds its roots in an incoming Greek population. Thus, if such 'Egyptian' words appear in poetry, they should not be glossed as 'barbarisms', but welcomed back as Greeks who have been living abroad. The history of migrating words and people may be hard to reconstruct here, but the ideological dominance of Greek cultural value is clear enough. The logic of explanation is in service of the promotion of a cultural privileging. You shouldn't be surprised at this . . . .

In the so-called Books of Hermes, continues Plutarch, Greek and Egyptian names are given for gods and so 'there is no need to be competitive over names. But I would rather concede Serapis to the Egyptians than Osiris. Serapis is foreign. Osiris is Greek. But both I regard as part of one god and one power.'[109] Here is the process of *krisis* in action – the stance of reasoned intellectual judgement; aimed, however, at the assertion of a single, dominant point of view. Serapis can be conceded as foreign, but at the price not merely of securing Osiris firmly for Greece, but also of seeing both as the emanation of a single divine principle – which, as Plutarch goes on to explain, is comprehensible in and through Greek philosophy. The apparent discrimination between Serapis and Osiris, his intellectual care, also works towards the general assertion of the 'one power'.

The use of analogy, secondly, is also strongly marked. How, asks Plutarch, should the Egyptians' solemn and mournful sacrifices be explained? 'Also among the Greeks many similar things are done, and at about the same time . . .'[110] As in the *Roman Questions*, the ethical stance of Plutarch's view of the world has an uncontested authority (the third major strategy of self-authorization). Here in *On Isis and Osiris* not only is the stance of the author a theologically and philosophically informed

[108] *Mor.* 375e–f; *de Is. et Os.* 61.   [109] *Mor.* 376a; *de Is. et Os.* 61.
[110] *Mor.* 378d; *de Is. et Os.* 68; cf *Mor.* 381d–e; *de Is. et Os.* 75; *Mor.* 379c–d; *de Is. et Os.* 70.

positioning, but also it is a fully articulated and considered perspective. Clea, the priestess and addressee, is instructed to read '*piously* and *philosophically*' to avoid 'superstition which is no worse than atheism'.[111] When the Egyptians tell myths, 'you must not think that any of these tales actually happened or took place like that'.[112] As a general principle in religious matters, 'it is necessary to take the reason [*logos*] that philosophy provides, as our initiator into the mysteries, and to reflect in a pious way on each thing that is said and done'.[113] Myth and ritual need a philosophical evaluation. From Plato (at least) onwards, taking up philosophy is expressed in terms of an initiation into a mystery religion; in philosophy's encounter with religion this language has a special charge. Yet, unlike so much modern philosophy, this reason is also in service of a sense of reverence and the holy – pious philosphy. Thus Plutarch – in some of his most often quoted lines – talks of the precarious and risky journey of the intellectual towards the divine: 'some go completely astray and fall into superstition; and others in turn who flee from superstition as from a quagmire, unwittingly have fallen over the precipice of atheism'.[114] Firmly avoiding the Scylla and Charybdis of religious and philosophical error, the reader's power of *synkritic* judgement, guided by reading Plutarch, leads to the grail of an educated, cultural self-control – the achievement of being Greek, with Plutarch.

Plutarch's encounter with Egypt is not a Herodotean tale of awe and autopsy. The book-lined study, the scholarly disagreement, the philosophical comprehension, the instructions on how to read – to process – Egyptian religion as an integral element of a precarious journey between the quagmire of superstition and the precipice of atheism construct an image of the educated man's succesful struggle for an understanding of the world, an image which proved particularly attractive to the Victorian readers who bothered with this text. Plutarch's recognition of a single divine principle which he calls God [*ho theos*] and which is to be approached through *Logos*, made Mahaffy wonder how Plutarch could have come so close to Christianity and not even mention it. 'Had Plutarch been at Athens when S. Paul came there, he would have been the first to give the Apostle a respectful hearing.'[115] Archbishop Trench not only acquits

---

[111] *Mor.* 355d; *de Is. et Os.* 11: ὁσίως καὶ φιλοσόφως.

[112] *Mor.* 355b; *de Is. et Os.* 11.   [113] *Mor.* 378a–b; *de Is. et Os.* 68.

[114] *Mor.* 378a; *de Is. et Os.* 68.

[115] Mahaffy (1890) 349. Mahaffy, a professor from Dublin, Ireland, and a widely selling, popular author on Greece, had, like Headlam, a vitriolic and long-lasting row with Jebb, because of his bad review of a book of Jebb. I have gratefully learnt from an unpublished essay by Aude Doody on this.

Plutarch 'of any conscious attempt to fight against that truth which was higher than any he had', but also wonders 'how far he and his fellow workers may have served as heralds of the Gospel'.[116] Oakesmith – a civil servant in the post-office who wrote in an Arnoldian tradition on Plutarch – enthused, 'Among the best and purest adherents of that faith [Christianity] his teachings would be regarded as efficacious for the sincerest goodness.'[117] What is being struggled over in *On Isis and Osiris* is not just religious difference; nor is it merely a struggle over the Egypt of the imagination – integral though that is to the self-determining discourse of Rome and Greece. Rather, the didactic arguments of this text are aimed at promoting the cultural privilege of a philosophically educated Greekness. This is – as Mahaffy and Trench and Oakesmith differently recognize – a text that sets at stake what it means to view the world properly: a text of self-formation. In Plutarch's religious writing, as in his other texts, there is an ongoing cultural polemic. Where Lucian in *de Dea Syria* uses the interaction of religious differences to play so ironically with the categories of insider and outsider, Plutarch – writing from the centre of the Greek world – looks at Egypt to find Greece, to lay the foundations of his Greece, to assert once more the power of Greek *paideia* in the face of the multiplicity of the world.

It does not much matter precisely where you enter the circle of Plutarch's *enkuklios paideia*, his cycle of education/culture. This section began with explicitly didactic texts on listening to lectures and ended with grand theoretical and scholarly expositions of Egyptian religion. It would have been possible to reverse this order, or to take a different selection of subjects and treatises altogether. This is not just because there are cross-references between the treatises which encourage such a movement between works (nor because stories and examples are repeated from treatise to treatise). Nor is it that each treatise says the same thing or adopts exactly the same stance – far from it. Rather, Plutarch's project is to make the world the known world, a world viewed from the perspective of an educated Greek, a viewing which is itself an integral performance in the process of becoming that educated Greek. Hence what matters is the cycle of *paideia* itself, its potentially synoptic gaze (and not where you enter the circle). 'To the wise man everything is Greece': for Plutarch it is essential that the object of knowing is, precisely, *everything*; that the starting and ending point of knowing is Greece; and that the

---

[116] Trench (1873) 13.   [117] Oakesmith (1902) 227.

subject and product of knowing is the wise man – the authority. Plutarch *enshrines* the value of Greek knowing.

Sympotic Questions, Plutarch's longest work, has many characters who take part in dialogues about cultural matters over the dinner table. In particular and in contrast with Plato, Plutarch depicts himself as a character in these exchanges along with his father and grandfather (and son and brother). As in the *Odyssey*, the display of the patriarchal line (in action) is a normative image, but for Plutarch what counts is not so much the establishment and maintenance of the household, as the establishment and maintenance of an intellectual tradition, a tradition of Greek intellectuals passing on the value of Greek knowledge. The conversation enacts the construction of that tradition, and, in reading it, the line is extended by each reader. The *Sympotic Questions* is a dialogue that articulates tradition as a conversation with and about the Greek past. It is this conversation which Plutarch invites you to join and continue.

V

When a silence fell in a conversation in Greece, you would say 'Hermes is passing.'[118] Hermes passed over Plutarch in approximately 1850. A shockingly abrupt silence engulfed what had been one of the most active intellectual exchanges between present and past. With grim irony, the *Encyclopedia Britannica*, a project which owes so much to Plutarch's intellectual, imperial gaze, notes at the end of the nineteenth century that Plutarch's *Moralia* is 'practically almost unknown to most persons in Britain, even to those who call themselves scholars'.[119] And even the *Lives* which so motivated the childhood passions of the French Revolution were so ignored that Mahaffy could write in 1890, 'it is only recently and timidly that modern scholarship is re-introducing the *Lives* into the Grecian studies of the young'.[120] No doubt some people still read Plutarch, but these extreme statements testify to his perceived drastic loss of status. What could have produced so rapid a turnaround in the intellectual attractiveness of an ancient author? How could so complete a cultural forgetting take place, so suddenly?

In the last main section of this chapter, I want to explore how this sudden silence came about. The most bizarre suggestion for such a reversal of fortune comes from an American writing in the multivolume German encylcopedia *Aufstieg und Niedergang der römische Welt*. In one of

[118] Kahn (1978).   [119] Words penned by Paley.   [120] Mahaffy (1890) 291.

the articles on Plutarch, it is noted that Plutarch became deeply unfashionable in the latter part of the nineteenth century, and gives a single and clear reason: the appendix of Karl Marx's Jena dissertation, in which Plutarch is strongly criticized as a historian.[121] When I read this claim, I was excited because it seemed to offer a wonderful turning point in the handbook for revolutionaries: the text that fired the thinkers of the French Revolution dismissed by the thinker who fired the revolutions of the twentieth century. A nineteenth-century synoptic view of the world rejecting an earlier synoptic knowledge. It was with some surprise that I (gradually) discovered that not only was Marx's dissertation not published until extremely late in the hagiographic tradition, but also the appendix survives only in a single fragment of less than a page in longhand written by someone other than Marx himself. It takes a remarkable act of faith to suggest that an unread and unsurviving manuscript could have such power over intellectual history, and could create such a rupture.

I have not found one, single, clear reason for the loss of Plutarch, but rather a set of causes which together and from different angles produced this reversal. As we will see, academic evaluation played an important role in Plutarch's collapse in status, but this evaluation draws on and is bolstered by the wider circulation of dismissive images of the author and, perhaps most importantly, by a broad shift in ideas of heroism and the past, which is more far-reaching than the disdain of scholars.

The academic criticism of Plutarch as a historian, which Marx is said to rehearse, is certainly one crucial element in his changing status.[122] The development of German scholarship (which has played such a large role in the argument of the previous chapters also) depended, as we have seen, on a heavy investment in a model of scientific research and in a (Romantic) commitment to the authority of originality. Plutarch was a much mauled victim of this investment. Scholars queued up to dismiss violently the historical methodology of the *Lives* in particular. Not only was Plutarch repeatedly shown to be inaccurate in his versions of the past, but also he was easily shown to have stitched together his narrative from fragments of earlier and greater minds. Where Thucydides was an active participant in the war he narrated, and from the outset of his history set accuracy as the prime criterion for his writing, and made evaluation of first-hand sources his methodological credo – an image of

---

[121] Harrison (1992).

[122] Noted by Russell (1973) 161; Reinhold (1984) 259. Self-consciously against this trend stands the remarkable book of Hirzel (1912), who has to ask, none the less, 'Was ist Plutarch für uns, was kann er noch sein?' (200 – the title of his last chapter).

the historian which German classical historians found all too easy to take as an icon of their own work – Plutarch wrote about a glorified past by collecting snippets of other texts, which he barely understood, let alone evaluated, and which he put together in a barely consistent manner. He was the epigonal historian *par excellence*. Like Lucian, Plutarch was just not classical. The gentle Gilbert Murray sums up this assault succinctly: 'he was no scientific historian and the value of his statements depends entirely on the authorities he happens to follow'.[123] (Or, more dismissively, Niebuhr trashes the *Lives* as 'a collection of silly anecdotes' and Arthur Hugh Clough declares that England 'thinks Plutarch an old fool'.[124]) So pervasive and alluring is this image that Perrin, the leading American Plutarchan scholar, a writer unquenchably optimistic about Plutarch's status in the public eye, puts as the frontispiece of her edition of the *Lives* of Cimon and Pericles the lapidary evaluation of Wilamowitz, authority of German authorities: 'Plutarch is a man who is stylistically exceptional, historically without judgement, and unconcerned with chronology.'[125] It is under such an aegis – the historian without historical judgement or sense of chronology! – that Perrin publishes the author on whom she spent her working life.

For Rousseau and the other revolutionaries with which this chapter began – who probably encountered Plutarch in the immensely influential French translation of Amyot[126] – Plutarch's writing gave access to the noble Greek and Roman republican heroes. He helped provide the Roman dress in which the French Revolution was played out. An honorary Roman, as it were. The more intently German scholarship focused on Greekness itself, however, the more Plutarch's 'lateness' became an issue on a par with his dodginess as a historian. It is ironic in the light of Plutarch's deep engagement with questions of cultural identity and of authoritative knowledge that his staus as non-classical Greek should now be seen to undermine his claims to knowledge, and that his style of knowing should now appear to embody his uncertain claims to cultural and racial privilege. Quite simply, Plutarch became an exemplar which proved that the post-classical was second-rate. At best, Plutarch might be the 'last of the Greeks'; but more commonly, in the words of Nietzsche no less, he was a 'trivial Johnny-Come-Lately' ('abgelaßte Epigone'), saved only and barely by meagre traces of a true – classical – 'Greek instinct'.[127]

---

[123] Murray (1917) 396.
[124] Cited in Gould (1930) 2, and Garrod (1931) 111–12.
[125] Perrin (1901).   [126] Aulotte (1965).
[127] F. Nietzsche *Kritische Gesamtausgabe der Werke* ed. G. Colli and M. Montinari (Berlin and New York, 1967–) vol. III., 352, discussed by Ingenkamp (1988).

The rapid development of science and scientific education in universities and schools through the nineteenth century also contributed tellingly to this rupture in reading Plutarch, the collapse of his *doxa*. Plutarch's account of the physical world (like Galen's of the human body) rapidly became seen as insufficient and could not yet be interesting as 'the history of science'. The claim of authoritative, encylopedic knowledge was no longer supportable. There is nothing so out-of-date as an out-of-date encylopedia. Caught between the accusation of unscientific historical writing and unscientific science, Plutarch now embodied the second-rate, and needed to be expelled from the Pantheon of Hellenism.

Where Plutarch had been for the eighteenth century a source and resource, a treasurehouse of Greek value and knowledge, for the later nineteenth century he became a corrupt and misleading collector of other sources, and an unreliable and inaccurate warehouseman of historical knowledge. This scholarly critique no doubt had a lasting effect on syllabuses (Plutarch has played almost no significant part in the curricula of schools and universities in the twentieth century), and through syllabuses on a public perception of Plutarch. German-led scholarly disdain, motivated by the claims of scientific history, contributed significantly to the silencing of Plutarch in the Western intellectual tradition.

But beyond this dismissive academic criticism, Plutarch also developed a more widely dispersed 'image problem'. Even the passion of Rousseau and the didacticism of a Marryat could be turned against him. Plutarch was a text that was first met as a child and could easily be associated with childish reading. Erasmus may have translated Plutarch for young Prince Henry, but collections of 'tales from Plutarch' for children begin to circulate, and change Plutarch's role in nineteenth- and twentieth-century pedagogy.[128] Where an explicit aim of such collections may have been to lure children towards models of virtue and the glories of the past ('our country may demand from us ... service as unselfish and self-sacrificing as that which the noblest heroes of ancient Greece and Rome rendered ... '[129]), or even to help produce Christian family life ('omitting some digressions, which would be neither profitable nor interesting for the reader, and substituting for them such reflections as Plutarch may have made if he had been a Christian'[130] – an extraordinary editorial credo whose smugness is far from the religious controversies of

---

[128] See e.g. Weston (1911?); Ratcliff (1928); Gould (1930).
[129] Weston (1911?) preface.
[130] Quotation from the preface of *Lives of Illustrious Greeks. For Schools and Families*, published by the Religious Tract Society in London in 1849 [no author].

an Erasmus or even an Arnold), the effect was to diminish Plutarch in comparison with Aeschylus or Plato, say, the greats of classical Athens – always texts for grown ups. Homer was made into a particularly cloying version for children by Charles Kingsley ('My dear Children, some of you have heard already of the old Greeks . . . Those of you who are boys will, perhaps, spend a great deal of time in reading Greek books; and the girls, though they may not learn Greek, will be sure to come across a great many stories taken from Greek history . . . ').[131] But Homer – from the childhood of Greece ('for nations begin at first by being children like you'[132]) – also maintained his role as the founder of the genre of epic, and re-appeared throughout a person's education. Plutarch could not, any more, reach for the exalted status of a Greek master. Fascinatingly, every children's edition of Plutarch I have seen does away with the structure of *parallel* lives, offering only a series of single, exemplary tales, and, consequently, there is also a repression of Plutarch's *synkriseis* – that is, the work of critical and cultural evaluation. Plutarch's young readers are not, it seems, to be placed between cultures, at least in the Plutarchan manner. Greek stories, Roman stories are in support of a more direct national heritage.[133]

This shift in Plutarch's image, and, in particular, his sliding from moral and scientific authority to children's didactic manual, is brilliantly reflected in one of the greatest of nineteenth-century novels, George Eliot's *Middlemarch* (from the 1870s). Now, Eliot knew and read almost everyone mentioned in my previous chapter (Will Ladislaw in *Middlemarch* even takes opium and dispiritedly compares his physiological response to De Quincey's[134]); and in her commitment to women's education, the new science, and classics, she is centrally placed in many of the debates I have been tracing (it was not by chance that she was the last author I cited in that chapter).[135] While writing *Middlemarch* she read several works of Plutarch, both from the *Lives* and the *Moralia*: she read them with Emerson's edition (and lavish preface) and, of course, shared this reading with G. H. Lewes.[136] (It is typical of Eliot's voluminous – and

---

[131] Kingsley (1868) [1855] preface. See Jenkyns (1991) 1. J. Church who produced *Stories from Virgil, Stories from Homer, Stories from Livy* – all advertised as perfect books for prizes – interestingly does not seem to have produced a *Stories from Plutarch*.

[132] Kingsley (1868) [1855] preface xii.

[133] Ratcliff (1928) has questions at the end for study: no 236: 'Which of the five figures of this book would you rather have been? Account for your choice.'

[134] Eliot (1988) 68.

[135] On Eliot and the new learning, see Beer (1983), Shuttleworth (1984).

[136] See Pratt and Neufeldt (1979).

obsessively obscure – reading that she both reads the highly unfashionable *Moralia* and does so in the edition of Emerson, an intellectual guide
who shares so many of her concerns. Emerson was distinctly unusual in
his devotion to Plutarch.)[137] Her primary interest in reading Plutarch is
hard to determine. She was certainly fascinated with the possibilities of
heroic action; but she also spent some time researching materials for a
long epic poem on Timoleon, one of the most 'revolutionary' of the *Lives*
of Plutarch. She also read Plutarch on religion, however, and other less
obvious pieces, which are harder to locate except in terms of her general and consuming interest with both religious and scientific thought.
(That Casaubon publishes pamphlets on Egyptian mystery cults reflects
a wider reading than Plutarch, however.)[138] It is in the final chapter of
this epic novel that Plutarch makes his named entrance, as Eliot ties up
the loose ends of her narrative's life-stories with her customary irony and
layered knowingness. Mary Garth, a character whose amused and solid
judgemental observations of the action have made her seem to many
readers to be a figure for the author herself,[139] is said to have become an
author herself:

When Mary wrote a little book for her boys, called 'Stories of Great Men,
taken from Plutarch' and had it printed and published by Gripp and Co.,
Middlemarch, everyone in the town was willing to give the credit of this work
to Fred [her husband], observing that he had been to the University, 'where the
ancients were studied' . . .[140]

George Eliot, whose own writing skills were snidely attributed to
Lewes, and who knew that she studied the ancients more avidly than
many University Men,[141] ironically imagines another female writer –
published with the aptly named Gripp and Co. – producing Plutarch
for children. The irony of this subject – of how heroic examples are
produced and circulated – is brought home in the final paragraph of
the book where 'we insignificant people with our daily words and acts'
are compared to the lost world of a heroic past: no more will 'a new
Antigone . . . spend her heroic piety in daring all for the sake of a brother's
burial: the medium in which their ardent deeds took shape is for ever

---

[137] See Berry (1961) *passim*.　　[138] See e.g. Travis (1999).
[139] Karl (1995) 512, typically: 'there is little question Mary Garth is a persona for Eliot herself'.
[140] Eliot (1988) 677–8.
[141] Dorothea's attempts to learn Greek and the men's reaction to it are described painfully in ch. 7
of *Middlemarch*. Eliot was herself friends with e.g. Jowett and Jebb: Karl (1995) 469. On the
Woman Question specifically see also Beer (1986) 147–99. On Lewes' actual contribution to
editing *Middlemarch* see e.g. Karl (1995) 489.

gone'.[142] It is because the medium for heroic, ardent deeds is passed, and there is now only the heroism of the everyday (for which Dorothea has striven) that Plutarch can become a comforting and uplifting children's book. For all of Eliot's intellectual framing and destabilizing ironies, the final image is of Plutarch as pious tales for children.

The image of Plutarch the historian and scholar also became damagingly caught up in the Victorian era's own self-definition against the immediate past (which particularly in the latter part of the century is an obsessive and public interest of intellectuals). His popularity in the eighteenth century and his own life-style – the small town antiquarian, as it were – tainted Plutarch by association, as if he were himself one of the eighteenth-century amateur intellectuals who so liked him. Mahaffy, for example, in 1890 calls Plutarch 'thoroughly parochial', with an 'absence of calm and dignity', even to the point of 'garrulous unreserve'; 'a man who abhorred extremes', 'loved compromises', and showed an 'amiable vanity' – all in all, attributes which he sums up tellingly as a 'small and shabby gentility'.[143] Later, we find the image explicitly drawn out: 'Plutarch himself must have been something like the highly cultivated 'squire-parson' found here and there in the eighteenth century'.[144] It is as if Plutarch represents the learning of the country squire rather than the metropolitan intellectual – a fitting icon of eighteenth-century values and behaviour, but not of the forward-looking scientist of London, Paris or New York, the self-image of the late nineteenth-century fashionable intellectual.

These problems of 'image' could beset even classical Greek authors, however, and the specific negative picture of the country squire also helped damn Xenophon, who provides a remarkably insightful parallel life to Plutarch here. For Xenophon, and especially the *Cyropaedia* (his education of a prince, with its romantic tales of love and adventure) was immensely influential throughout the Renaissance and eighteenth century, particularly in the development of the novel.[145] Yet he too became derided in the nineteenth and twentieth centuries as non-scientific and even anti-intellectual. It became a commonplace, still repeated today, that unlike Plato, Xenophon simply didn't understand Socrates and his discussions: he was on the outside of the Socratic circle, nose pressed

[142] Eliot (1988) 682.
[143] Mahaffy (1890) 347–51. Mahaffy was well aware that he himself came from Trinity College, Dublin in Ireland and not from Oxford, Cambridge or even London.
[144] Barrow (1967) 19 – an heir of these Victorian and Edwardian views.
[145] See e.g. Tatum (1989); Cooper (1998), and the sensible brief comments in Nehamas (1998).

to the distorting glass of the window. Xenophon, like Plutarch, was an unreliable source for history and learning. Xenophon, too, through the *Anabasis*, became a school author *par excellence*. Boys could read the easy Greek as an adventure story (without any sex, philosophy, or tragedy); everyone was to know how the Greeks of the March of the 400 shouted '*Thalassa, Thalassa*', 'the sea! the sea!'. And then move on to adult reading. The image of the country squire became so fixed that as late as 1974 a well-respected philosopher could trot out this description: 'Xenophon quite closely resembles a familiar British figure – the retired general, staunch Tory and Anglican, firm defender of the Establishment in Church and State, and at the same time a reflective man with ambitions to write edifying literature. (American Xenophons do not seem to be so common).'[146] These amusingly sniffy remarks, for all the easy seductiveness of their literary and national stereotyping, spectacularly miss the mark. 'Firm defender of the Establishment in Church and State' scarcely represents a man exiled from his democratic city to live in the community of its worst military and political enemies, and who fought (and wrote about fighting) for a charismatic barbarian revolutionary. Nor does 'staunch Tory and Anglican' – to which ancient Greek could such terms ever be applied?! – help us get close to the man who boldly developed literary forms, wrote a founding text of erotic fiction, and who passionately defended and memorialized a trendy and shocking philosopher, put to death for religious and political crimes. Xenophon provided for previous generations a privileged representation of Greece; he was, like Plutarch, a repository of the knowledge of Greece, and a writer whose strategies of representation defined the way Greece was conceptualized. As with Plutarch, the redefinition of Greece through the nineteenth century constructed a new portrait of the figure of Xenophon – out of contemporary stereotypes, contemporary ideological needs. The status of Xenophon and Plutarch is deeply affected by the circulation of such images in the classroom, public debate, the novel: and both slipped from a position of authority via the schoolroom to an obscure and shabby gentility.

Both academic criticism (which is easy to trace) and the dissemination of dismissive images (which is harder to pin down) worked, then, to silence Plutarch. But there is also a more general frame which must be considered, and which is, to my mind, the most significant element of this discussion. For Plutarch's sense of the heroic and his sense of

---

[146] Irwin (1974) 410. The fact that he is reviewing Leo Strauss might be relevant.

the heroic self in particular seem to be profoundly out of kilter with Victorian preoccupations (as Eliot's irony has already indicated). The popularity and sophistication of the novel in the nineteenth century, with its narratives of inwardness and psychological growth (at the head of which could be placed George Eliot); and the very development of a science of psychology and its impact on the popular conceptualization of the self (which we saw with the response to Strauss' *Elektra*) contrast in the most striking way with Plutarch's external evaluation of public behaviour and his lack of interest in psychological development. It is by now a commonplace of modern scholarship that Greek notions of character [*ēthos*] are significantly different from modern interest in personality, the inward and unique construction of a self.[147] But without tragedy's poetic grandeur and profoundly dramatic monologues and dialogues of doubt and self-awareness, Plutarch's sense of character – an absolutely central aspect of the power and success of the *Lives* – could not but appear thin and superficial to the readers of Victorian novels and Victorian psychological sciences.

This is, however, part and parcel of an explicit and profound shift in the political and historical idea(l) of the heroic self. Perhaps the most importantly paradigmatic figure in this self-conscious development is Thomas Carlyle. Both in *On Heroes and Hero Worship* and in his biographies of Cromwell and others (to say nothing of his own self-fashioning as prophet), Carlyle is 'peculiarly modern' in that he makes a 'concern with the unconscious' central to his view of the world, along with 'an exploration of alienation in self and society'[148] – neither of which can be said to be consuming interests of Plutarch. Whether *On Heroes and Hero Worship* is seen now as a searching 'attempt to substitute a new "hero-archy" for a vanishing secular and religious hierarchy',[149] or whether it is seen as a more pernicious proto-fascist document in its 'emphasis on master morality versus slave morality, command and obedience, militarism and strength, even cruelty as virtues',[150] it is clear that Carlyle spoke with extraordinary allure to his contemporaries. 'His influence upon the rising intellectual generation was so extraordinary that it has never been approached in modern British history by any other single intellectual figure.'[151] *On Heroes and Hero Worship* may be testimony to the confusion and alienation of Carlyle's own mind – even Carlyle hated these turbulent and inconsistent essays, he said, as his worst work – but

---

[147] See Pelling ed (1990); Gill (1996), each with further bibliographies.
[148] LaValley (1968) 3, 5, 7 (with further discussion 236–52).
[149] Rosenberg (1985) 115–6.   [150] LaValley (1968) 271.   [151] Le Quesne (1982) 61.

it sold an extraordinary number of copies. (Gosse calculates that the popular edition alone sold 100,000 copies in the last twenty-five years of the century –that is, thirty-five years after its first publication, and many years after the zenith of Carlyle's fame in England.) *On Heroes and Hero Worship* aimed to produce 'a new selfhood' and 'a new society', which are 'to emerge from the increased loneliness and alienation of the artist'.[152] Carlyle himself is testimony to what he hoped to see: 'a new epoch is born like a phoenix from the ashes of the old'.[153]

Carlyle was self-consciously aware of his claim to modernity, and specifically his distance from the immediate past ('a sense of the wickedness of the eighteenth century dominates Carlyle'[154]). It's not so much the political clarion calls that concern me ('We want a superior race'), terrifying though their resonances are today (Goebbels read Carlyle to Hitler in the bunker and noted a tear in the Fuhrer's eye . . .) Rather, it's the way in which Carlyle repeatedly shows that his era is – as his friend Emerson put it – distinguished by 'a tendency to introversion, self-dissection, anatomizing of motives'.[155] The inward-looking heroes of Carlyle rely on *intuition* – with no sign of the *paideia* that is such a criterion in Plutarch's writing. For all Carlyle's commitment to social change (which in part explains why Dickens dedicated *Hard Times* to him), his heroes are increasingly lonely and alienated figures (with none of the emphasis on an embedded social and cultural life that is typical of Plutarchan narrative). The superiority of the hero for Carlyle invokes worship and not the cultivated evaluation of *synkrisis*. The immense influence and passionate sense of rupture that Carlyle sets in motion, prompts an equal (and mutually implicative) reaction in the forgetting of Plutarch's value(s).

What is perhaps most surprising about Carlyle is the way in which he performs that forgetting. Carlyle's output is voluminous, repetitive and off-puttingly bombastic. Yet I have not found one significant engagement with Plutarch in his work. This is, I think, a telling, rather than a casual silence. His education, his subject matter and his friendship with Emerson would all lead one to expect him to have read and thought about Plutarch's heroes. Yet I have not been able to trace any explicit sign of this. Arguments from silence are always difficult to maintain, but it is perhaps both Carlyle's seductive modern approach to heroism and his all too easy sidestepping of Plutarch that help consign Plutarch to the shadows.

The lines which link Carlyle to Nietzsche, to Wagner, to Shaw (with his *Man and Superman*) are never less than intricate and complex. Nor, of

---

[152] LaValley (1968) 271.   [153] Bentley (1957) 74–5.
[154] Bentley (1957) 43.   [155] See Harris (1978) 1 – and *passim*.

course, is it Carlyle (any more than Marx or any other individual) who is directly or solely responsible for the re-evaluation of Plutarch. What is crucial, however, is that the values, strategies, intellectual perspectives that link Carlyle, Wagner, Nietzsche, Shaw (say), and the cultural forces which made heroes of those intellectuals for an era, form the context in which Plutarch had to be redefined. The silencing of Plutarch, *our* forgetting of his value, is an integral element in the bloody history of modernity, and of nationalism and its heroes.

Cultural forgetting, then, is part of cultural complicity. Not knowing Plutarch is fully part of *our* modern values – of what makes up the intellectual, political, psychological, narratives of the modern self. A modern reader *must* be bored by Plutarch. That boredom, however, is more than a token of taste or sophistication. It is a sign of an unquestioning complicity with the ideological commitments of modern culture.

An agenda of saving Plutarch, then, could now only be a heroic or doomed quest to resist the prison of the contemporary. And yet, for me at least, resisting the prison of the contemporary – recognizing the limits of the now in knowing – is the very lure and promise of intellectual inquiry. Plutarch opens – and re-opens – the question of the historical and cultural construction of knowledge.

VI

'Who needs Plutarch?' is a question which interrogates the space between past passions and present forgetting, a space mapped by contemporary commitments and the present's reorganization or recognition of the past. It is a question which reveals the complicities of cultural memory and cultural silencing, of how forms of knowledge are privileged or denigrated. Plutarch – in *my* reading – is himself a saviour, a preserver of the culture of Greece. His encyclopedic project of making the world into the known world through the power of Greek knowledge; his construction of Greek value over and against Roman authority and Egyptian mystery and antiquity; his narratives of past heroes as defining exemplars for the desires of the present; the dynamic of assimilation and resistance he enacts; together construct a new sense of Greekness. Plutarch re-invents Greece. It is a project defined by the power of the Roman Empire, which requires this new construction of tradition (encyclopedias make great imperial projects). What we have seen in Plutarch's varied and interconnected productions is a new tradition of knowing, under construction. Plutarch's encyclopedia is his Empire of Knowledge.

In the context of the shared education of eighteenth-century radical and conservative thinkers, Plutarch functioned not merely as a repository of the knowledge of antiquity, but also as a store of privileged heroic narratives of human achievement. Plutarch was an essential part of the antique dress in which revolution and restoration were enacted. The cultural revolutions of the nineteenth century silenced Plutarch. Both the silence and the passion for Plutarch are formulated within deeply rooted ideological commitments. Plutarch thus exemplifies the major concern of this book: how modern, self-interested and self-implicating pursuit of the value of ancient Greece becomes embroiled with the Greek world's self-interested, self-implicating construction of the value of Greekness. It is within this matrix of appropriation and self-concern, misrecognition and idealism, polemic and projection, that reading Plutarch takes place. Our appropriation or recognition of the past value of Plutarch's Greekness is constantly being re-engaged with Plutarch's construction and promotion of the value of Greekness and of the past.

The title of this chapter posed the question 'Why Save Plutarch?' not so that I can answer simply 'because he is a good and interesting writer whose huge influence in pre-nineteenth-century Europe and America requires attention rather than ignoring, especially if writers of the stature of Rousseau, Shakespeare, Emerson are to be fully appreciated'. Rather, it is because this question opens up the issue of cultural value itself, and our inevitable complicity with its construction. Reading Plutarch should make you acutely aware of your placing in and by modern culture. And such self-awareness about the historical construction of knowledge (and knowingness) is, surely, a value that needs preserving.

Conclusion: rainbow bridges

And so, finally – and with a certain inevitability – to a figure whose fervent particularity has not prevented him becoming exemplary both for modernist thought and for an engagement with the Greek past:

One is no longer at home anywhere; at last one longs for that only place in which one can be at home, because it is the only place one would want to be at home: the *Greek* world. But it is in precisely that direction that all bridges are broken – *save* the rainbow bridges of concepts! And these lead everywhere, into all the homes and 'fatherlands' that existed for Greek souls. To be sure, one must be very subtle, very light, very thin, to step across these bridges![1]

Writing in 1885 in the notebooks that would become *The Will to Power*, Nietzsche is expounding his own assertion that 'German philosophy is the most fundamental form of Romanticism and Homesickness.' Nietzsche, with an exile's nostalgia, wants to go home, he wants *back*: 'man will *züruck*'.[2] Since he no longer can feel at home anywhere – what better expression for the grounding alienation of the artist which Carlyle demanded? – his journey must be to the past, the foreign country where one would desire to be at home, namely, the Greek world.[3] This longing to journey back, however, can only serve to emphasize the *distance* of his exile in the here and now: 'all bridges are broken' in that direction back. What is left? Just – in his marvellous phrase – 'die Regenbogen der Begriffe', 'the rainbow bridges of concepts'. These rhetorical colours lead into all 'the "fatherlands" of the Greek souls'. His inverted commas around the term 'fatherlands' underline, I suppose, its especially

---

[1] F. Nietzsche *Werke. Kritische Gesamtsausgabe* eds. G. Colli and M. Montinari vol. VII, 3, *Nachgelassene Fragmente Herbst 1884 bis Herbst 1885*, pp. 412–3 (August–Sptember 1885 fr. 41 (4)): 'Man ist nirgends mehr heimisch, man verlangt zuletzt nach dem zurück, wo man irgendwie heimisch sein kann, weil man dort allein heimisch sein möchte: und das ist die griechische Welt! Aber gerade dorthin sind alle Brücken abgebrochen, – *ausgenommen* die Regenbogen der Begriffe! Und die führen überall hin, in alle Heimaten und "Vaterländer", die es für Griechen-Seelen gegeben hat! Freilich man muß sehr fein sein, sehr leicht, sehr dünn, üm diese Brücken zu schreiten!'
[2] *Ibid.*   [3] See Goldhill (2000b) for further exposition.

extended metaphorical usage. These are the fatherlands 'of the Greek souls', the intellectual space mapped and illuminated by 'the rainbow bridges of concepts'. A Greek world of the Mind. Hence, no heavy-booted marching: 'one must be very subtle, very light, very thin to step across these bridges'.[4]

Nietzsche's search for another 'Heimat', another homeland, proceeds by travelling back in history through the Renaissance, through early Christianity, through the Stoics, to the Pre-Socratic philosophers of archaic Greece. He concludes:

A few centuries hence, perhaps, one will judge that all German philosophy derives its real dignity from being a gradual reclamation of the soil of antiquity, and that all claims to 'originality' must sound petty and ludicrous in relation to that higher claim of the Germans to have joined anew the bond with the Greeks, the hitherto highest type of man. Today we are again getting close to all those fundamental forms of world interpretation devised by the Greek spirit through Anaximander, Heraclitus, Parmenides, Empedocles, Democritus and Anaxagoras – we are growing *more Greek* by the day; at first, as is only fair, in concepts and evaluations, as Hellenizing ghosts, as it were; but one day, let us hope, in our *bodies* too! Herein lies (and has always lain) my hope for the German character![5]

Nietzsche's pursuit of another country is also the celebration of the *German* character. German philosophy will be judged according to to how it will have – imperialistically – reclaimed the soil of antiquity: it will have annexed the ancient world. This will prove (to be) a tie of race and blood: the highest claim Germans will be able to make is 'to have joined anew the bond with the Greeks, the hitherto highest form of man'. We have already seen with Chamberlain and others how deep-rooted is this nineteenth- and twentieth-century German assertion of a privileged national and cultural identity based on descent from the idealized purity and majesty of Greece. Nietzsche (for all his radicalism) stands in a line with Herder, von Humboldt, Karl-Ottfried

---

[4] 'Fein, leicht, dünn' – or just *leptos*, as a Hellenistic poet would have it.
[5] Nietzsche *Werke*, 'Vielleicht, daß man einige Jahrhunderte später urtheilen wird, daß alles deutsche Philosophiren darin seine eigentliche Würde habe, ein schrittweises Widergewinnen des antiken Bodens zu sein, und daß jeder Anspruch auf "Originalität" kleinlich und lächerlich klinge in Verhältnisse zu jenen höheren Anspruche der Deutschen, das Band, das zerrissen schien, neu gebunden zu haben, das Band mit der Griechen, dem bisher höchst gearteten Typus "Mensch". Wir nähern uns heute allen jenen grundsätzlichen Formen der Weltauslegung wieder, welche der griechische Geist, in Anaximander, Heraklit, Parmenides, Empedokles, Demokrit und Anaxagoras, erfunden hat – wir werden von Tag zu Tag *griechischer*, zuerst, wie billig, in Begriffen und Werthschätzungen, gleichsam als gräcisirende Gespenster: aber dereinst, hoffentlich auch mit unserem *Leibe*! Hierin liegt (und lag von jeher) meine Hoffnung für das deutsche Wesen!'

Müller who so passionately developed the idea of the Dorians as the founding ancestors of the German *Volk*. Nietzsche's alienation is fully imbricated with a fierce *nationalism* also. So, he boasts for the Germans that 'we are growing *more Greek* by the day'. (That 'we' is a rhetorical encouragement to join in Nietzsche's programme as much as a boast of Nietzsche's own Hellenization.) This 'growing Greek', as one might expect from a philosopher and his rainbow bridges, is firstly an issue of 'concepts and evaluations'. Light of foot and subtle, we *think* ourselves (in) Greek, 'like Hellenizing ghosts'. This is an image which, in its paradoxical conjunction of foundation and insubstantiality, grounding and lack, is strikingly echoed in the 'ghost world, pregnant with life' of Hofmannsthal's Greece of the mind.[6] Yet Nietzsche – even more bizarrely – aims further for a total physical metamorphosis, a change 'in our *bodies*' (as if by reading Heraclitus we will all get great muscle definition and iliac crests). Such is his hope for the German character. Becoming Greek, with Nietzsche.

Nietzsche's longing summarizes vividly a three stage structure of thought that I have been exploring throughout this book. First, Greece, ever a country of the imagination, is (re)discovered as a special, privileged locus of artistic and intellectual worth and authority, and proclaimed to be a foundation and origin of Western ideals: 'the highest form of man'. Each chapter has shown this in different ways: Erasmus' theological discovery of Greek letters, Lucian's self-fashioning as Greek, Hofmannsthal's insistence on a modernist Greece within us all, Arnold's proclamation of the 'sweetness and light' of Greece, Plutarch's encylopedic celebration of Greek knowledge. Greece is reinvented as a source and model of cultural value. Second, this rediscovery necessarily expresses and seeks to span the distance between Greece and the here-and-now of 'us': 'all bridges are broken in that direction'. So Lucian and Plutarch look back to a lost Greece of a glorious past; Erasmus' renaissance redraws lines of affiliation to the past of the Church and beyond to a different world of understanding; Hofmannsthal, Lowe, Arnold, and their opponents are embroiled in a battle about progress towards modernity and the foundational status of the ancient world. The image of Greece thus becomes bolstered by idealism and fissured by lack and absence – a site of contention and difference as well as value and authority. A place to fantasize and argue over. Third, this rediscovery of an idealized and contested

---

[6] Above, pp. 143–5.

Greece is a deeply self-implicating activity – an act of self-fashioning. Nietzsche's homesick self is being constructed in and by his engagement with ancient Greece: he is, he demands, becoming '*more Greek*' in his mind and body, day by day. So too with the figures of my narrative, from Erasmus to Arnold, from Plutarch and Lucian to Hofmannsthal – all of whom make becoming Greek, being Greek, promoting Greek, essential and integral elements of a cultural identity. The work of remaking Greece is an act of self-formation.

This three-stage argument, in short, shows how the rediscovery and redeployment of the value of knowing Greek(ness) have repeatedly played a formative role in the construction of the self. This recognition fully informs the strategies and rhetoric of this book. This book has not aimed to be just about learning Greek or just about the image of Greece in artistic or literary production. Rather, its concern has also always been with how such struggles over the past engage and help form their participants. How the past is recognized and evaluated is a function of the viewer's self-positioning. What is called 'the Classical Tradition' is a debate under constant and active reconstruction by *participation*. It is a process you and I are engaging in, now.

This sense of constant and active reconstruction is central to both the structure and style of my argument. I have repeatedly moved between ancient texts (and their construction of Greekness) and modern readings (and their sense of Greekness), trying to trace as sinuously as possible how the reader of the past is constantly caught between two mirrors, as it were, caught between self-reflections. Hence, Lucian's slippery project of 'becoming Greek' is framed by Erasmus' delight and Chamberlain's despair with him – and by modern criticism's continuing inheritance of such readings (much as Plutarch's authoritative knowingness is still being silenced by the concerns of modernism). 'Reception' is too blunt, too *passive* a term for the dynamics of resistance and appropriation, recognition and self-aggrandisment that make up this drama of cultural identity. Learning Greek is itself caught up in such ideological battling. The value of learning Greek provokes passionate educational debate in the Renaissance and Victorian Europe (and America), with quite different personal and theological agendas. Learning Greek becomes an issue of cultural self-assertion (and not just educational policy); hence my focus on the self-presentation – the personal as well as institutional politics – of Erasmus, Lowe, Arnold and their opponents. So too Strauss' *Elektra*, as a reworking of Sophocles, becomes caught up in the self-defining war of national identity, and its performance becomes a lightning-rod for arguments about changing ideas of Hellenism within changing ideas of Englishness and Germanness. It seems to me that such a historical perspective, working *between* past(s) and present, and such an interdisciplinary approach (with its *range* of questions and materials) are both absolutely necessary, if the active debate of 'the Classical Tradition' is to be adequately appreciated. Reading the past and engaging in the present are constantly and actively intermeshed.

This recognition that an engagement with the ancient world has proved a self-implicating and self-formulating activity must have worrying consequences for my own self-positioning, however. The trivialization and marginalization of Plutarch and Lucian at the end of the nineteenth century may show clearly enough the damaging ideological biases that fully and integrally ground German scientific scholarship. But even that recognition, with its inherent criticism of nationalism and racism, must be a function of my own intellectual and political stance. And beyond such self-scrutiny, it seems likely that my participating in a tradition, a debate, involves me in a host of misrecognitions and uncontested assumptions, where self-scrutiny has failed. Readings can never be innocent (however naive). I have tried to work as self-awarely and as carefully as possible with and within the constraints of such a Chinese box of self-implication. One casualty has been the pose of the disinterested and objective scholar with a steady gaze across the centuries at the past. I find the rhetoric of this pose profoundly distorting of the stakes of modern intellectual activity, especially for the types of question broached in this book. It will, I hope, by now, be appreciated why it is hard to find the pose of disinterestedness and objectivity acceptable when the frame of discussion includes the issues of racism, nationalism, gender, your whole relation to society and position within it.

Nor is it by chance that this conclusion began with Nietzsche, and the interface of his German nationalism and his nostalgia for Greece. One overarching narrative of this book has been the profound shift in conceptualization of Greek and Greekness between the Renaissance and eighteenth century, on the one hand, and the post-Enlightenment world of the nineteenth and twentieth centuries, on the other. Hence, my two accounts of an education in Greek significantly centred first around Erasmus and second around Matthew Arnold; hence my mobilization of Lucian's Renaissance and Victorian judges, and my opposition of Plutarch's eighteenth-century enthusiasts to his Victorian detractors; hence the detailed look at a shocking new, modernist version of a Greek tragedy, which aims to dismantle a nineteenth-century classicism. These far-reaching shifts cannot be reduced to a story of 'changes in taste'. I have used the phrase 'cultural forgetting' – the opposite of 'cultural memory', as it were – to sum up how a nexus of social, intellectual, personal and institutional interests work to refashion and to silence the authors and passions and comprehensions of the past. I hope that this book not only puts some hugely significant, but now largely neglected crises of the past back into view, but also lays the process of 'cultural forgetting' itself open to new understanding.

So, who needs Greek? The needs, cares, obsessions about Greek and Greekness which I have been tracing from the ancient world to today, certainly show how impoverished a perspective it would be to turn to the paradigmatic figures of Erasmus, Hofmannsthal, Wagner, Keats, Shelley, Arnold, Lowe, Mill, Rousseau, Emerson (let alone Lucian and Plutarch) *without* (their) Greek. Greek and Greekness mattered profoundly for these and most intellectuals of their age(s) – and, it might seem, Greek and Greekness have *always* been a problem to care about and to argue over. Only the most blinkered presentist would claim it is adequate to read Erasmus without (his) Greek learning, Arnold without (his) Homer, Derrida without (his) Plato. The costs of such forgetting of Greek are the miscomprehension and trivialization of the past and our stake in it (and it is a pity how much academic work seems happily complicit with such a process). Yet it would be an unthinking and ridiculous conservatism which demanded a constant rehearsal of the concerns of the past. It is both impossible and – equally important – undesirable to remain subject to the ideological and intellectual dictates of a former regime. The question 'who needs Greek?' is not a classicist's triumphalism or despair, but rather an injunction towards a self-aware and informed exploration of one's own place in history and in culture – one's own stake in cultural value. As far as I am concerned, it's the *question* 'who needs Greek?' that we can't do without.

Works cited

Aarsleff, H. (1967)   *The Study of Language in England 1780–1860*, Princeton.

Abrams, M. H. ed. (1979)   *The Norton Anthology of English Literature*, New York and London.

Ackerman, R. (1987)   *J. G. Frazer: His Life and Work*, Cambridge.

Ackroyd, P. (1998)   *The Life of Thomas More*, London and New York.

Albisetti, J. (1983)   *Secondary School Reform in Imperial Germany*, Princeton.

Aldridge, A. O. (1967–8)   'Thomas Paine and the Classics', *Eighteenth-Century Studies* 1: 370–80.

Allen, P. S. (1934)   *Erasmus*, Oxford.

Alstine, Mrs R. van (1890)   *Charlotte Corday*, London.

Alston, J. (1996)   'Conquest by Text: Juvenal and Plutarch on Egypt', in Webster and Cooper eds. (1996).

Anderson, G. (1978)   'Lucian's *Nigrinus*: the Problem of Form', *GRBS* 19: 367–74.

   (1989)   'The Pepaideumenos in Action: Sophists and their Outlook in the Early Empire', *ANRW* II. 33.1: 80–208.

   (1993)   *The Second Sophistic: A Cultural Phenomenon in the Roman Empire*, London and New York.

Anderson, W. (1965)   *Matthew Arnold and the Classical Tradition*, Ann Arbor.

Annas, J. (1992)   *Hellenistic Philosophy of Mind*, Berkeley.

Armytage, W. (1953)   'Matthew Arnold and Thomas Huxley: Some New Letters 1870–1880', *Review of English Studies* 4: 346–53.

Arnold, E. (1869)   *The Poets of Greece*, London.

Arnold, M. (1868)   *Schools and Universities on the Continent*, London.

   (1903)   *The Works of Matthew Arnold*, 15 vols., London.

   (1908)   *Reports on Elementary Schools 1852–1882*, London.

   (1962)   *Lectures and Essays in Criticism*, ed R. H. Super, Ann Arbor.

   (1993)   *Culture and Anarchy, and other writings*, ed. S Collini, Cambridge.

Aske, M. (1985)   *Keats and Hellenism*, Cambridge.

Aulotte, R. (1965)   *Amyot et Plutarque: La tradition des Moralia au XVIème siècle*, Geneva.

Bainton, R. (1969)   *Erasmus of Christendom*, New York.

Baldick, C. (1983)   *The Social Mission of English Criticism 1848–1932*, Oxford.

(1987) *In Frankenstein's Shadow: Myth, Monstrosity and Nineteenth-Century Writing*, Oxford.

Baldwin, B. (1973) *Studies in Lucian*, Toronto.

Baldwin, T. (1944) *William Shakespere's Small Latine and Lesse Greeke*, 2 vols., Urbana.

Barrell, J. (1991) *The Infection of Thomas De Quincey: A Psychopathology Of Imperialism*, New Haven.

Barrow, R. (1967) *Plutarch and his Times*, London.

Baslez, M-F., Hoffman, P., and Pernot, L. eds. (1993) *L'Invention d'Autobiographie: d'Hésiode à Saint Augustin*, Paris.

Baumgarten, M. (1996) 'Seeing Double: Jews in the Fiction of F. Scott Fitzgerald, Charles Dickens, Anthony Trollope and George Eliot', in Cheyette ed. (1996).

Bayerlein, S. (1996) *Musikalische Psychologie der drei Frauengestaltenin der Oper Elektra von Richard Strauss*, Tutzing.

Beard, W. M. (2000) *Jane Ellen Harrison*, Cambridge, Mass.

Beecham, T. (1944) *A Mingled Chime*, London.

Beer, G. (1983) *Darwin's Plots: Evolutionary Narrative in Darwin, George Eliot and Nineteenth-Century Fiction*, London.

(1986) *George Eliot*, London.

Benson, E. (1930) *As We Were: A Victorian Peepshow*, London.

Bentley, E. (1957) *A Century of Hero Worship: a study of the Idea of Heroism in Carlyle and Niezsche, with notes on Wagner, Spengler, Stefan George and D. H. Lawrence*, 2nd edn, New York.

Bentley, J. (1983) *Humanists and Holy Writ: New Testament Scholarship In the Renaissance*, Princeton.

Bernheimer, C. (1989) *Figures of Ill Repute: Representing Prostitution in Nineteenth-Century France*, Cambridge, Mass.

Berry, E. (1961) *Emerson's Plutarch*, Cambridge, Mass.

Bibby, C. (1959) *T. H. Huxley: Scientist, Humanist, Educator*, London and New York.

(1972) *Scientist Extrordinary: The Life and Scientific Work of Thomas Henry Huxley 1825–1895*, Oxford.

Bibby, C. ed. (1971) *T. H. Huxley on Education*, Cambridge.

Bickerman, E. (1988) *The Jews in the Greek Age*, Cambridge, Mass.

Billault, A. ed. (1994) *Lucien de Samosate. Actes du colloque international de Lyon organisé au Centre d'Études romaines et hello-romaines, les 30 Septembre-1er Octobre 1993*, Lyon and Paris.

Bingham, M. (1978) 'The Great Lover': The Life of Herbert Beerbohm Tree*, London.

Black, E. (1988) *The Social Politics of Anglo-Jewry 1880–1920*, Oxford.

Bloom, A. (1987) *The Closing of the American Mind*, New York.

Bolgar, R. (1954) *The Classical Heritage and its Beneficiaries*, Cambridge.

Bolt, C. (1971) *Victorian Attitudes to Race*, London and Toronto.

Bompaire, J. (1958) *Lucien Écrivain: imitation et creation*, Paris.

Boulogne, J. (1987) 'Le sens des "Questions Romaines"', *REG* 100: 471–6.

(1992) 'Les *Questions Romaines* de Plutarque', *ANRW* II. 33.6: 4682–708.

(1994) *Plutarch: un aristocrate Grec sous l'occupation Romaine*, Lille.

Bourneville, D.-M. and Régnard, P. (1878) *Iconographie photographique de la Salpêtrière*, Paris.

Bowen, A. (1992) *Plutarch: on the Malice of Herodotus*, Warminster.

Bowersock, G. (1969) *Greek Sophists in the Roman Empire*, Oxford.

(1990) *Hellenism in Late Antiquity*, Cambridge.

(1995) *Martyrdom and Rome*, Cambridge.

Bowie, E. (1970) 'The Greeks and their Past in the Second Sophistic', *P&P* 46: 3–41.

Boyle, M. (1977) *Erasmus on Language and Method in Theology*, Toronto.

(1981) *Christening Pagan Mysteries. Erasmus in Pursuit of Wisdom*, Toronto.

Branham, R. B. (1989) *Unruly Laughter: Lucian and the Comedy of Traditions*, Cambridge, Mass.

Brantlinger, P. (1988) *Rule of Darkness: British Literature and Imperialism 1830–1914*, Ithaca.

Braschowanoff, G. (1910) *Richard Wagner und die Antike*, Leipzig.

Bremer, J. M. (1992) 'A Daughter Fatally Blocked: von Hofmannsthal's *Elektra*', in Hillenaar and Schönau eds. (1992).

Brenk, F. and Gallo, I. eds. (1986) *Miscellanea Plutarchea*, Ferrara.

Brewer, J., Gardner, J. and Brodie, R. (1862–1910) *Letters and Papers, Foreign and Domestic of the Reign of Henry VIII*, 21 vols., London.

Briggs, A. (1955) *Victorian People*, Chicago.

Brirley, A. (1987) *Marcus Aurelius*, London.

Bronfen, E. (1992) *Over Her Dead Body: Death, Femininity and the Aesthetic*, Manchester.

(1998) *The Knotted Subject: Hysteria and its Discontents*, Princeton.

Brown, P. (1978) *The Making of Late Antiquity*, Cambridge, Mass.

(1988) *The Body and Society*, New York.

Burchlere, Lady Winifred Anne Henrietta Gardner (1933) *A Great Lady's Friendships: Letters to Mary, Marchioness of Salisbury, Countess of Derby 1862–1890*, London.

Burke, P. (1992) 'The Renaissance', in Dover ed. (1992).

Burnett, S. (1996) *From Christian Hebraism to Jewish Studies: Johannes Buxtorf (1564–1629) and Hebrew Learning in the Seventeenth Century*, Leiden.

Burrow, T. (1966) *Evolution and Society: a Study in Victorian Social Theory*, Cambridge.

Bury, E. (1994) 'Lucien, honnête homme', in Billault ed. (1994).

Butler, E. M. (1935) *The Tyranny of Greece over the German Imagination*, Cambridge.

(1938–9) 'Hofmannstahl's *Elektra*. A Greco-Freudian Myth', *Journal of the Warburg Institute* 2: 164–75.

Butler, M. (1981) *Romantics, Rebels and Reactionaries*, Oxford.

Buxton, J. (1978) *The Grecian Taste: Literature in the Age of Neo-Classicism*, London.

Caccia, N. (1907)   *Luciano nel Quatrocentro in Italia: le rappresentazione e le figurazioni*, Florence.

Calder, W. M. III ed. (1991)   *The Cambridge Ritualists Reconsidered*, Atlanta.

Campbell, H. (1891)   *Differences in the Nervous Organization of Man and Woman: Physiological and Pathological*, London.

Campbell, L., Phillips, M., Herbrüggen, H. S. and Trapp, J. (1978)   'Quentin Matsys, Desiderius Erasmus, Pieter Gillis and Thomas More', *Burlington Magazine* Nov. (1978): 716–26.

Cardus, N. (1955)   'Ernest Newman', in Van Thal ed. (1955).

Cargill-Thompson, W. (1980)   *Studies in the Reformation*, London.

Carpenter, T. (1989)   'The Musical Language of *Elektra*', in Puffett ed. (1989).

Carter, A. (1958)   *The Idea of Decadence in French Literature 1830–1900*, Toronto.

Cartledge, P. (1987)   *Agesilaus and the Crisis of Sparta*, Baltimore.

Cassin, B. (1995)   *L' effet sophistique*, Paris.

Cavenagh, F. ed. (1931)   *James and John Stuart Mill on Education*, Cambridge.

Ceserani, D. ed. (1990)   *The Making of Modern Anglo-Jewry*, Oxford.

Chamberlain, H. S.(1899)   *Die Grundlagen des Neunzehnten Jahrhunderts*, Munich.

  (1910)   *The Foundations of the Nineteenth Century*, trans. J. Lees, with the assistance of Lord Redesdale, London and New York.

  (1916?)[not dated]   *The Ravings of a Renegade: being the War Essays of Houston Stewart Chamberlain*, trans. C. Clarke with an introduction by L. Melville, London.

  (1921)   *The Foundations of the Nineteenth Century*, trans. J. Lees, with the assistance of Lord Redesdale, with an introduction by Lord Redesdale, London and New York; 2nd edn.

Chambers, R. (1935)   *T. More*, London.

Chase, J. (2000)   *Inciting Laughter: the Development of 'Jewish Humor' in 19th century German Culture*, Berlin and New York.

Cheyette, B. (1993)   *Constructions of 'The Jew' in English Literature and Society: Racial Representations 1875–1945*, Cambridge.

Cheyette, B. ed. (1996)   *Between 'Race' and Culture: Representations of 'The Jew' in English and American Literature*, Stanford.

Cheyette. B. and Marcus, L. eds. (1998)   *Modernity, Culture and the Jew*, Cambridge.

Christ, W. von (1924)   *Geschichte der griechischen Litteratur*, revised by W. Schmid and O. Stählin, 6th edn, Munich.

Christie, R. (1899)   *Etienne Dolet, The Martyr of the Renaissance*, 2nd edn, London.

Clark, G. (1992)   *Women in Late Antiquity: Pagan and Christian Lifestyles*, Oxford.

Clarke, G. ed. (1989)   *Rediscovering Hellenism: The Hellenic Inheritance and the English Imagination*, Cambridge.

Clarke, M. (1959)   *Classical Education in Britain 1500–1900*, Cambridge.

Clebsch, W. (1964)   *England's Earliest Protestants*, New Haven.

Clej, A. (1995)   *A Genealogy of the Modern Self: Thomas De Quincey and The Intoxication of Writing*, Stanford.

Clément, C. (1988)   *Opera or The Undoing of Women*, Minneapolis.

Cobbett, W. (1817)   *The Political Register 32*, London.

Collini, S. (1991)   *Public Moralists: Political Thought and Intellectual Life in Britain 1850–1930*, Oxford.

(1994)   *Matthew Arnold: a Critical Portrait*, Oxford.

Collins, P. ed. (1971)   *Dickens: the Critical Heritage*, London.

Connell, W. (1950)   *The Educational Thought and Influence of Matthew Arnold*, London.

Conrad, J. (1898)   'Tales of the Sea', in Conrad (1921).

(1921)   *Notes on Life and Letters*, London and Toronto.

Constantine, D. (1984)   *Early Greek Travellers and the Hellenic Ideal*, Cambridge.

Coogan, R. (1992)   *Erasmus, Lee and the Correction of the Vulgate: the Shaking of the Foundations*, Geneva.

C[ook], A. B. (1892a)   'Mr Headlam's Charge', *Cambridge Review* 13: 316–17.

(1892b)   'Criticism Criticised', *Cambridge Review* 13: 364.

Cooper, J. (1998)   'Notes on Xenophon's Socrates', in *Reason and Emotion: Essays on Ancient Moral Psychology and Ethical Theory*, Princeton.

Cooper, K. (1996)   *The Virgin and The Bride: Idealised Womanhood in Late Antiquity*, Cambridge, Mass.

Coulling, S. (1974)   *Matthew Arnold and His Critics: A Study of Arnold's Controversies*, Athens, Ohio.

(1988)   'Matthew Arnold and the American South', in MacHann and Burt eds. (1988).

Coulton, G. (1934)   'H. W. Fowler', *The Society for Pure English*, Tract 43, Oxford.

Court, F. (1992)   *Institutionalizing English Literature: the Culture and Politics of Literary Study 1750–1900*, Stanford.

Cowen, A. and Cowen, R. (1998)   *Victorian Jews Through British Eyes*, London and Portland.

Croiset, M. (1882)   *Essai sur la vie et les oeuvres de Lucien*, Paris.

Curran, S. ed. (1993)   *The Cambridge Companion to British Romanticism*, Cambridge.

Daly, A. (1995)   *Done Into Dance: Isadora Duncan in America*, Bloomington.

Daniell, D. (1994)   *William Tyndale: A Biography*, New Haven.

David, D. (1995)   *Rule Britannia: Women, Empire and Victorian Writing*, Ithaca and London.

Davies, M. (1999)   'The Three Electras: Hofmannsthal, Sophocles and the Tragic Vision', *Antike und Abendland* 45: 36–65.

Dear, P. (1995)   *Discipline and Experience: The Mathematical Way in the Scientific Revolution*, Chicago.

Deathridge, J. (1999)   'Wagner, the Greeks, and Wolfgang Schadewaldt', *Dialogos* 6: 133–40.

De Bolla, P. (1989)   *The Discourse of the Sublime: History, Aesthetics and the Subject*, Oxford.

De Laura, D. (1962)   'Four Arnold Letters', *Texas Studies in Literature and Language* 4: 276–84.

(1969)   *Hebrew and Hellene in Victorian England*, Austin.

Del Mar, N. (1962)   *Richard Strauss*, 2 vols., London.

DeMolen, R. ed. (1978) *Essays on the Works of Erasmus*, New Haven.
De Quincey, T. (1985) *Confessions of an English Opium-Eater*, ed. G. Lindop, Oxford.
De Selincourt, E. (1905) *John Keats: Poems*, London.
Desideri, P. (1986) 'La vita politica e cittadina nell' imperio: lettura dei *Praecepta Gerendae Rei Publicae* e dell' *An seni Res Publica Gerenda Sit*', *Athenaeum* 64: 371–81.
Detienne, M. (1981) *L'Invention de la mythologie*, Paris.
Dewar, M. (1964) *Sir Thomas Smith: a Tudor Intellectual in Office*, London.
Didi-Huberman, G. (1982) *Invention de l'hysterie: Charcot et l'Iconographie photographique de la Salpêtrière*, Paris.
Dijkstra, B. (1986) *Idols of Perversity: Fantasies of Feminine Evil in Fin-de-Siècle Culture*, New York.
Dionisotti, A., Grafton, A. and Kraye, J. eds. (1988) *The Uses of Greek and Latin: Historical Essays*, London.
Dover, K. ed. (1992) *Perceptions of the Ancient Greeks*, Oxford.
Dowling, L. (1994) *Hellenism and Homosexuality in Victorian Oxford*, Ithaca.
Doyle, B. (1989) *English and Englishness*, London and New York.
Dudley, F. (1942) 'Matthew Arnold and Science', *PMLA* 57: 275–94.
Duff, G. M. (1867) 'Inaugural Address – On his Installation as Rector of the University of Aberdeen, March 22nd, 1867', Edinburgh.
   (1871) *Elgin Speeches*, Edinburgh.
   (1891) *Notes from a Diary 1851–1872*, 2 vols., London.
   (1930) *A Victorian Vintage*, ed. A. Bassett, London.
Duff, T. (1999) *Plutarch's Lives: Exploring Virtue and Vice*, Oxford.
Duncan, D. (1979) *Ben Jonson and the Lucianic Tradition*, Cambridge.
Duncan, Irma (1965) *Duncan Dancer*, Middletown.
Duncan, I. (1968) *My Life*, London. (First published 1928.)
Eade, J. ed. (1976) *Classical Traditions in Early America*, Ann Arbor.
Easterling, P. (1999) 'The Early Years of the Cambridge Greek Play: 1882–1912', in Stray ed. (1999).
Easterling, P. ed. (1997) *Cambridge Companion to Greek Tragedy*, Cambridge.
Edmunds, L. ed. (1990) *Approaches to Greek Myth*, Baltimore.
Edwards, M. and Swain, S. eds. (1988) *Portraits: Biographical Representation in the Greek and Latin Literature of the Roman Empire*, Oxford.
Eliot, G. (1988) *Middlemarch*, ed. D. Carroll, Oxford.
Eliot, T. S. (1927) Review of H. W. Fowler (1926), *The New Criterion* 5: 121–4.
   (1936) *Essays Ancient and Modern*, London.
Ellmann, R. (1987) *Oscar Wilde*, London.
Elsner, J. (2001) 'Describing Self in the Language of the Other: Pseudo(?)-Lucian at the Temple of Hierapolis', in Goldhill ed. (2001).
Endelman, T. (1979) *The Jews of Georgian England 1714–1830: Tradition and Change in Liberal Society*, Philadelphia.
Engel, A. (1983) *From Clergyman to Don: the Rise of the Academic Profession in Nineteenth-Century Oxford*, Oxford.
Esselborn, K. G. (1969) *Hofmannsthal und die antike Mythos*, Munich.

Ewans, M. (1982)   *Wagner and Aeschylus: The Ring and the Oresteia*, London.
   (1984)   'Electra: Sophocles, von Hofmannsthal, Strauss', *Ramus* 13: 135–54.
Eysoldt, G. (1996)   *Der Sturm Elektra*, ed. L. Fiedler, Salzburg and Vienna.
Faber, G. (1957)   *Jowett*, London.
Fagan, G. (1999)   *Bathing in Public in the Roman World*, Ann Arbor.
Falkner, T., Felson, N. and Konstan, D. eds. (1999)   *Contextualizing Classics: Ideology, Performance, Dialogue*, Lanham.
Farrar, F. (1867)   'Of Greek and Latin Verse Composition as a General Branch of Education', in Farrar ed. (1867).
Farrar, F. ed. (1867)   *Essays on a Liberal Education*, London.
Faverty, F. (1951)   *Matthew Arnold the Ethnologist*, Evanston.
Feldman, D. (1994)   *Englishness and the Jews: Social Relations and Political Culture*, New Haven.
Ferguson, W. (1933)   *Erasmi Opuscula*, The Hague.
Ferris, D. (2000)   *Silent Urns: Romanticism, Hellenism, Modernity*, Cambridge.
Feuchtwanger, E. ed. (1973)   *Upheaval and Continuity: A Century of German History*, London.
Field, G. G. (1981)   *Evangelist of Race: The Germanic Vision of Houston Stewart Chamberlain*, New York.
Fisher, N. (1992)   *Hybris*, Warminster.
Flashar, H. (1991)   *Inszenierung der Antike: das griechische Drama auf der Bühne der Neuzeit*, Munich.
Flintermann, J.-J. (1995)   *Power, Paideia and Pythagoreanism: Greek Identity, Conceptions of the Relationship between Philosopher and Monarch and Political Life in Philostratus' 'Life of Apollonius'*, Amsterdam.
Foerster-Nietzsche, E. ed. (1921)   *The Nietzsche-Wagner Correspondence*, New York.
Förster, R. (1886)   'Lukian in der Renaissance', *Archiv für Litteraturgesichte* 14: 337–63.
Forsyth, K. (1989)   'Hofmannsthal's *Elektra*: from Sophocles to Strauss', in Puffett ed. (1989).
Foucault, M. (1986)   *The Care of the Self*, London and New York.
Fowler, H. W. (1907)   *'Si mihi – !'*, London.
   (1922)   'On Grammatical Inversion', *Society for Pure English* Tract 10.
   (1926)   *Dictionary of Modern English Usage*, Oxford.
   (1929)   *If Wishes Were Horses*, London.
Fowler, H. W. and Fowler, F. G. (1905)   *The Works of Lucian of Samosata*, 4 vols., Oxford.
Fox, A. (1982)   *Thomas More: History and Providence*, Oxford.
Foxe, J. (1837–41)   *Acts and Monuments*, ed. S. Cattley and G. Townsend 8 vols., London.
Fraenkel, E. (1950)   *Aeschylus. Agamemnon*, 3 vols., Oxford.
Francis, J. (1995)   *Subversive Virtue: Asceticism and Authority in the Second-Century Pagan World*, University Park.
Frankfurter, D. (1998)   *Religion in Roman Egypt: Assimilation and Resistance*, Princeton.

Garrett, C. (1966)   *The Marian Exiles*, 2nd edn, Cambridge.

Garrod, H. (1931)   *Poetry and the Criticism of Life*, Cambridge, Mass.

Gautier, M. (1973)   *Captain Frederick Marryat*, Paris.

Gay, P. (1970)   *The Bridge Of Criticism: Dialogues among Lucian, Erasmus and Voltaire on the Enlightenment*, New York.

Geffcken, J. (1907)   *Zwei griechische Apologeten*, Leipzig.

Gerlo, A. (1969)   *Erasme et ses portraitistes*, Nieukoop.

Gibbon, E. (1994)   *Memoirs of My Life and Writings*, ed., A. Cockshut and S. Constantine, Bodmin.

Gill, C. (1996)   *Personality in Greek Epic, Tragedy and Philosophy*, Oxford.

Gilliam, B. (1991)   *Richard Strauss's Elektra*, Oxford.

Gilliam, B. ed. (1992)   *Richard Strauss and His World*, Princeton.

Gilman, S. (1986)   *Jewish Self-Hatred: Anti-Semitism and the Hidden Language Of The Jews*, Baltimore and London.

(1991)   *The Jew's Body*, New York and London.

(1993)   'The Image of the Hysteric', in Gilman *et al.* (1993).

(1996)   *Smart Jews: The Construction of the Image of Jewish Superior Intelligence*, Lincoln and London.

Gilman, S., King, H., Porter, R., Rousseau, G., and Showalter, E. (1993)   *Hysteria Beyond Freud*, Berkeley.

Gilman, S. and Chamberlin, J. E. eds. (1985)   *Degeneration: The Dark Side of Progress*, New York.

Gilmore, M. (1978)   '*Apologiae: Erasmus' Defences of Folly*', in DeMolen ed. (1978).

Gladstone, W. (1865)   'Address on the Place of Ancient Greece in the Providential Order of the World, Delivered before the University of Edinburgh on the third of November, 1865', London.

Gleason, M. (1994)   *Making Men: Sophists and Self-Presentation in Ancient Rome*, Princeton.

(2001)   'Mutilated Messages: The Semiotic Body in Josephus, in Goldhill ed. (2001).

Glover, T. R. (1943)   *Cambridge Retrospect*, Cambridge.

Godwin, W. (1968)   *Uncollected Writings 1785–1822: Articles in Periodicals and 6 Pamphlets*, eds. J. Marken and B. Pollini, Florida.

Goldhill, S. (1991)   *The Poet's Voice*, Cambridge.

(1994)   'The Naïve and Knowing Eye: Ecphrasis and the Culture of Viewing in the Hellenistic Word', in S. Goldhill and R. Osborne eds., *Art and Text in Ancient Greek Culture*, Cambridge.

(1995)   *Foucault's Virginity*, Cambridge.

(1999)   'Body/Politics: Is There a History of Reading?' in Falkner, Felson, and Konstan eds. (1999).

(2000a)   Placing Theatre in the History of Vision', in N. K. Rutter and B. Sparkes eds. *Word and Image* in *Ancient Greece*, Edinburgh.

(2000b)   'Whose Antiquity? Whose Modernity? The "Rainbow Bridges" of Exile', *Antike und Abendland* 46: 1–20.

(2001a) 'The Erotic Eye: Visual Stimulation and Cultural Conflict', in Goldhill ed. (2001).

(2001b) 'Setting an Agenda: "Everything is Greece to the Wise"', in Goldhill ed. (2001).

Goldhill, S. ed. (2001) *Being Greek Under Rome: Cultural Identity, the Second Sophistic, and the Development of Empire*, Cambridge.

Goldstein, J. (1987) *Console and Classify: The French Psychiatric Profession in the Nineteenth Century*, Cambridge.

Gordon, W. (1990) *Humanist Play and Belief: the Serio-comic Art of Desiderius Erasmus*, Toronto.

Gould, F. J. (1930) *Great Sons of Greece*, London.

Gould, J. (1989) *Herodotus*, London.

Gourgouris, S. (1996) *Dream Nation: Enlightenment, Colonization and the Institution of Modern Greece*, Stanford.

Gowers, E. Sir (1957) 'H. W. Fowler: the Man and His Teaching', The English Association Presidential Address, London.

Grafton, A. (1983) '*Polyhistor* into *Philolog*: Notes on the transformation of German Scholarship 1780–1850', *History of Universities* 3: 159–92.

(1992) 'Germany and the West 1830–1900', in Dover ed. (1992).

Grafton, A. and Jardine, L. (1984) *From Humanism to the Humanities: Education and the Liberal Arts in Fifteenth- and Sixteenth-Century England*, Cambridge, Mass.

Graziosi, B. (1999) 'Inventing the Poet: A Study of the Early Reception of the Homeric Poems', PhD Cambridge.

(forthcoming) *Inventing Homer*, Cambridge.

Gregory, E. (1997) *H. D. and Hellenism: Classic Lines*, Cambridge.

Griffin, J. ed. (1999) *Sophocles Revisited: Essays presented to Sir Hugh Lloyd-Jones*, Oxford.

Grote, J. (1856) 'Old Studies and New', *Cambridge Essays*: 74–114.

Gruen, E. (1984) *The Hellenistic World and the Coming of Rome*, Berkeley.

(1998) *Heritage and Hellenism*, Berkeley.

Halkin, L.-E. (1993) *Erasmus: a Critical Biography*, trans. Tonkin, A., Oxford.

Hall. E. (1989) *Inventing the Barbarian*, Oxford.

(1999a) 'Sophocles' *Electra* in Britain', in Griffin ed. (1999).

(1999b) '1845 and all that: singing Greek tragedy on the London stage', in Wyke and Biddiss eds. (1999).

(2000) 'Medea on the Eighteenth-Century London Stage', in Hall, Macintosh and Taplin eds. (2000).

Hall, E., Macintosh, F. and Taplin, O. eds. (2000) *Medea in Performance 1500–2000*, Oxford.

Hall, J. (1981) *Lucian's Satire*, New York.

Hall, J. (1997) *Ethnic Identity in Greek Antiquity*, Cambridge.

Hamburger, M. (1963) 'Hofmannsthal and England', in Norman ed. (1963).

Hannay, D. (1889) *The Life of Frederick Marryat*, London.

Harrie, C. (1976) *The Lights of Liberalism: University Liberals and the Challenge of Democracy 1860–86*, London.

Harris, K. (1978)   *Carlyle and Emerson: Their Long Debate*, Cambridge, Mass.

Harris, R. (1989)   *Murders and Madness: Medicine, Law and Society in the Fin de Siècle*, Oxford.

Harrison, G. (1992)   'The Critical Trends in Scholarship on the non-philosophical works in Plutarch's *Moralia*', *ANRW* II. 33.6: 4646–81.

Hartog, F. (1988)   *The Mirror of Herodotus*, trans. J. Lloyd, Berkeley.

Havercamp, S. (1736–40)   *Sylloge Scriptorum qui de Linguae Graecae Vera et Recta pronuntiatione Commentarios Reliquerunt*, 2 vols.

Hayum, A. (1985)   'Dürer's portrait of Erasmus and the Ars Typographorum', *Renaissance Quarterly* 38: 650–87.

Hazlitt, W. (1902)   'On Classical Education', in *Collected Works of William Hazlitt*, ed. A. Glover, vol. I, London.

Headlam, C. (1910)   *Walter Headlam: His Letters and Poems, with a memoir by Cecil Headlam*, London.

Headlam, W. (1890)   'A Private Oration', *Cambridge Review* 11: 228–9.

(1891a)   *On Editing Aeschylus: a Criticism*, London.

(1891b)   'Jebb's *Philoctetes*', *Cambridge Review* 12: 288.

(1891c)   Jebb's *Philoctetes*', *Cambridge Review* 12: 324.

(1902a)   'Tucker's *Choephoroi* of Aeschylus', *Classical Review* 16: 347–54.

(1902b)   'Metaphor, with a note on the transference of epithets', *Classical Review* 16: 434–42.

(1910)   *Aeschylus' 'Agamemnon'*, Cambridge.

Heath, S. (1982)   *The Sexual Fix*, London.

Hegel, G. W. F. (1956)   *The Philosophy of History*, trans J. Sibree, New York.

Helm, R. (1906)   *Lucian und Menipp*, Leipzig.

(1927)   'Lukianos' in Pauly-Wissowa *RE* 13.2 cols. 1725–77, Stuttgart.

Helsinger, E., Sheets, R. and Veeder, W. (1983)   *The Woman Question: Society and Literature in Britain and America 1837–1883*, 3 vols., Chicago.

Henderson, J. G. (1998)   *Juvenal's Mayor: the Professor who Lived on 2^d a Day*, Cambridge.

Heyck, T. (1982)   *The Transformation of Intellectual Life in Victorian England*, London.

Hillenaar, H. and Schönau, W. eds. (1992)   *Fathers and Mothers in Literature*, Amsterdam and Atlanta.

Hirzel, R. (1912)   *Plutarch*, Leipzig.

Hoffmann, M. (1994)   *Rhetoric and Theology: the Hermeneutics of Erasmus*, Toronto.

Hofmannsthal, H. von (1928)   'Vermächtnis der Antike', *Die Antike* 4: 99–102.

(1937)   *Briefe 1900–1909*, Vienna.

(1952)   *Selected Prose*, trans. M. Holtinger, T. and J. Stern, New York.

(1968)   *Hugo von Hofmannsthal – Leopold von Andrian: Briechwechsel*, ed W. Perl, Frankfurt am Main.

Holzberg, N. (1988)   'Lucian and the Germans', in Dionisotti, Grafton and Kraye eds. (1988).

Honan, P. (1981)   *Matthew Arnold: a Life*, New York.

(1988)   'Arnold, Eliot and Trilling', in MacHann and Burt eds. (1988).

Hopkins, K. (1999)   *A World Full of Gods*, London.

Horne, A (1844)   *A New Spirit of the Age*, 2 vols., London.

Howard, M. (1970)   *The Influence of Plutarch in the Major European Literatures of the Eighteenth Century*, Chapel Hill.

Hudson, W. (1980)   *The Cambridge Connection and the Elizabethan Settlement of 1559*, Durham.

Hughes, P. (1956)   *The Reformation in England*, 4th edn, 3 vols., London.

Huizinga, J. (1952)   *Erasmus of Rotterdam*, London.

Humboldt von, H. (1963)   *Humanist without Portfolio*, ed. and trans. M. Cowlan, Detroit.

Humphreys, S. (1978)   *Anthropology and the Greeks*, London.

Hunt, E. (1940)   *Iohannis Dominici Luculla Noctis*, Notre Dame.

Huxley, T. H. (1868)   'A Liberal Education and Where to Find It', reprinted in Bibby ed. (1971).

   (1881)   *Science and Culture, and other Essays*, London.

Ingenkamp, H. (1971)   *Plutarchs Schriften über die Heilung der Seele*, Leiden.

   (1988)   'Der Höhepunkt der deutschen Plutarchrezeption: Plutarch bei Nietzsche', *ICS* 13: 505–29.

Irvine, D. (1899)   *Parsifal and Wagner's Christianity*, London.

Irwin, T. (1974)   Review of L. Strauss *Xenophon's Socrates*, *Phil. Rev.* 83: 409–13.

Jameson, F. (1981)   *The Political Unconscious: Narrative as a Socially Symbolic Act*, Ithaca.

Jardine, L. (1993)   *Erasmus Man of Letters: the Construction of Charisma in Print*, Princeton.

Jarrott, C. (1964)   'Erasmus' *In principio erat sermo*: a controversial translation', *Studies in Philology* 61: 35–40.

Jeanmaire, H. (1939)   *Kouroi et Kouretes*, Lille.

Jebb, C. (1907)   *Life and Letters of Sir Richard Claverhouse Jebb*, Cambridge.

Jebb, Sir R. (1891)   'Jebb's *Philoctetes*', *Cambridge Review* 12: 306.

   (1894)   *Sophocles. Electra*, Cambridge.

   (1900)   *The Antigone*. Cambridge.

Jedin, H. (1961)   *A History of the Council of Trent*, 2 vols., trans. E. Graf, London.

Jefferson, A. (1963)   *The Operas of Richard Strauss in Britain*, London.

Jenkyns, R. (1981)   *The Victorians and Ancient Greece*, Oxford.

   (1991)   *Dignity and Decadence*, London.

Jens, W. (1955)   *Hofmannsthal und die Griechen*, Tübingen.

   (1973)   'The Classical Tradition in Germany: Grandeur and Decay', in Feuchtwanger ed. (1973).

Jocelyn, H. ed. (1996)   *Aspects of Nineteenth-Century British Classical Scholarship*, Liverpool.

Jones, C. (1971)   *Plutarch and Rome*, Oxford.

   (1972)   'Two Enemies of Lucian', *GRBS* 13: 475–87.

   (1986)   *Culture and Society in Lucian*, Cambridge, Mass.

Jones, H. (1974)   *Revolution and Romanticism*, Cambridge, Mass.

Jones-Davies, M. ed. (1984)   *Le Dialogue au temps de la Renaissance*, Paris.

Jonghe, H. de (1980)   'Erasmus and the *comma Johanneum*', *Ephemerides Theologicae Lovanienses* 56: 381–9.

Kahn, L. (1978)   *Hermès Passe: ou les ambiguités de la communication*, Paris.

Karl, G. (1995)   *George Eliot: A Biography*, London.

Kay-Shuttleworth, J. (1862)   *Four Periods of Public Education as Reviewed in 1832-39-46-62*, London.

   (1868)   *Memorandum on Popular Education*, London.

Keen, R. ed. (1988)   *A Melanchthon Reader*, New York.

Kersey, S. (1981)   *Classics and the Education of Girls and Women*, Metuchen and London.

King, H. (1998)   *Hippocrates' Woman: Reading the Female Body in Ancient Greece*, London.

Kingsley, C. (1868)   *The Heroes*, London. (1st edn 1855)

Klawiter, R. (1977)   *The Polemics of Erasmus and Ulrich von Hutten*, Notre Dame and London.

Klienberger, H. R. (1985)   'Hofmannsthal and Leopold Andrian' *MLR* 80: 619–36.

König, J. (2000)   'Athletic Training and Athletic Festivals in the Greek Literature of the Roman Empire', PhD, Cambridge.

Konstantikovic, I. (1989)   *Montaigne et Plutarque*, Geneva.

Kristeller, P. (1961)   *Renaissance Thought: the Classic, Scholastic and Humanist Strains*, New York.

Lambropoulos, V. (1993)   *The Rise of Eurocentrism. Anatomy of Interpretation*, Princeton.

Lane Fox, R. (1986)   *Pagans and Christians*, London.

Larmour, D. (1992)   'Making Parallels: *Synkrisis* and Pluarch's *Themistocles* and *Camillus*', *ANRW* II. 33.6: 4154–200.

Larrabee, S. (1943)   *English Bards and Grecian Marbles*, New York.

Larson, V. (1999)   'Classics and the Acquisition and Validation of Power in Britain's "Imperial Century" (1815–1914)', *International Journal of the Classical Tradition* 6.2: 185–225.

Lauvergnat-Gagnière, C. (1988)   *Lucien de Samosate et le Lucianisme en France au XVIe siècle: athéisme et polémique*, Geneva.

LaValley, A. J. (1968)   *Carlyle and the Idea of the Modern*, New Haven.

Leask, N. (1992)   *British Romantic Writers and the East*, Cambridge.

Lee, R. (1967)   *Ut Pictura Poiesis: the Humanistic Theory of Painting*, New York.

Leopold, J. (1980)   *Culture in Comparative and Evolutionary Perspective: E. B. Tylor and the Making of Primitive Culture*, Berlin.

Leoussi, A. (1998)   *Nationalism and Classicism: the Classical Body as National Symbol in Nineteenth-Century England and France*, Basingstoke and London.

Le Quesne, A. (1982)   *Carlyle*, London.

Le Rider, J. (1993)   *Culture and Society in Fin-de-Siècle Vienna*, trans. A. Marks, Cambridge.

Lesire, F. (1980)   *Igor Stravinsky: Le Sacre du Printemps: Dossier de Presse*, Geneva.

Levine, G. and Knoepflmacher, U. eds. (1979)   *The Endurance of 'Frankenstein'*, Berkeley.

Levinson, M. (1988)   *Keats' Life of Allegory: the Origin of a Style*, Oxford.

Lincoln, B. (1999) *Theorizing Myth: Narrative, Ideology and Scholarship*, Chicago.

Livshin, R. (1990) 'The Acculturation of the Children of Immigrant Jews in Manchester, 1890–1930', in Ceserani ed. (1990).

Lloyd. A. (1990) 'Herodotus on Egyptians and Libyans', in *Fondation Hardt* (1990): 215–44.

Lloyd Jones, G. (1983) *The Discovery of Hebrew in Tudor England: a Third Language*, Manchester.

Lloyd-Jones, H. (1991) 'The Two Electras: Hofmannsthal's *Elektra* as a Goethean drama', in *Greek in a Cold Climate*, London.

Lloyd-Jones, K. (1995) 'Erasmus and Dolet on the Ethics of Imitation and the Hermeneutic Imperative', *International Journal of the Classical Tradition* 2.1: 27–43.

(1999) 'Valeur classique ou valeur humaniste: qu'est-ce que la rhétorique pour Dolet?', *International Journal of the Classical Tradition* 6.1: 21–9.

Lowe, R. (1867) 'Primary and Classical Education', Edinburgh.

Lowell, A. (1924) *John Keats*, 2 vols., London.

Lowell, J. (1904) *The Complete Writings of James Russell Lowell*, 15 vols., Boston and New York.

Ludwig, W. (1998) *Hellas in Deutschland: Darstellungen der Gräzistik im deutschprachigen Raum aus dem 16. und 17 Jahrhundert*, Hamburg.

Luther, M. (1908) *Letters*, ed. M. Currie, London.

McAlmon, R. (1997) *Being Geniuses Together*, revised and supplemented by Kay Boyle, Baltimore. (Originally published, New York, 1938; revised first 1968, New York.)

McBride, M. (1988) 'Matthew Arnold and Andrew Carnegie: the Religion of Culture and the Gospel of Wealth', in MacHann and Burt eds. (1988).

McConica, J. (1965) *English Humanists and Reformation Politics under Henry VIII and Edward VI*, Oxford.

MacHann, C. and Burt, F. eds. (1988) *Matthew Arnold in His Time and Ours: Centenary Essays*, Charlottesville.

Mackintosh, F. (1995) 'Under the blue pencil: Greek Tragedy and the British Censor', *Dialogos* 2 (1995) 54–70.

(1997) 'Tragedy in Performance: nineteenth- and twentieth-century productions', in Easterling ed. (1997).

(2000) 'Medea Transposed: Burlesque and Gender on the mid-Victorian Stage', in Hall, Mackintosh and Taplin eds. (2000).

MacMullen, R. (1984) *Christianizing the Roman Empire*, New Haven.

(1990) *Changes in the Roman Empire*, Princeton.

McMullen, S. (1985) 'From the Armchair to the Stage: Hofmannsthal's *Elektra* in its theatrical context', *MLR* 80: 637–51.

Mack, P. (1984) 'The Dialogue in English Education of the Sixteenth Century', in Jones-Davies ed. (1984).

Magriel, P. ed. (1977) *Nijinsky, Pavlova, Duncan: Three Lives in Dance*, New York.

Mahaffy, J. (1890) *The Greek World Under Roman Sway*, London.

Makdishi, S. (1998) *Romantic Imperialism: Universal Empire and the Culture of Modernity*, Cambridge.

Manley, F. and Sylvester, R. eds. (1967) *De Fructu qui ex Doctrina Percipitur by Richard Pace*, New York.

Mann, W. (1964) *Richard Strauss: A Critical Study of the Operas*, London.

Marc'hadour, G. and Lawler, T. (1981) 'Scripture in the Dialogue', in *CWM* VI. ii.

Margolin, J-C. (1990) 'The Epistle to the Romans (Chapter 11) according to the versions and/or commentaries of Valla, Colet, Lefèvre and Erasmus', in Steinmetz ed. (1990).

Marius, R. (1984) *Thomas More: a Biography*, London.

Marryat, F. (1872) *The Life and Letters of Captain Marryat*, 2 vols., London.

Marsh, D. (1998) *Lucian and the Latins*, Ann Arbor.

Martens, L. (1987) 'The Theme of Repressed Memory in Hofmannsthal's *Elektra*', *GQ* 60: 38–51.

Martin, Patchett, A. (1893) *Life and Letters of the Right Honourable Robert Lowe, Viscount Sherbrooke, G.C.B., D.C.L.*, 2 vols., London.

Mason, H. (1959) *Humanism and Poetry in the Early Tudor Period*, London.

Massing, J-M. (1990) *Du Text à l'Image: Le Calumni d'Apelle*, Strasburg.

(1995) *Erasmian Wit and Proverbial Wisdom*, London.

Mattioli, E. (1980) *Luciano e l'Umanismo*, Naples.

May, G. (1964) *De Jean-Jacques Rousseau à Madame Roland: Essai sur la sensibilité préromantique et révolutionaire*, Geneva.

(1970) *Madame Roland and the Age of Revolution*, New York.

Mayer, C-A., (1984) *Lucien de Samosate et la Renaissance France*, Geneva.

Mazzeno, L., and Lefcowitz, A. (1988) 'Arnold and Bryce: the Problem of American Democracy and Culture', in MacHann and Burt eds. (1988).

Meyer, M. (1971) *Ibsen*, London.

Micale, M. (1995) *Approaching Hysteria: Disease and its Interpretations*, Princeton.

Mill, J. S. (1867) 'Inaugural', St Andrew's; reprinted in Cavenagh ed. (1931).

Millar, F. (1993) *The Roman Near East 31 BC – AD 337*, Cambridge, Mass.

Miller, C. (1978) 'Proverbs in Erasmus' *Praise of Folly*, in DeMolen ed. (1978).

Miller, P. C. (1994) *Dreams in Late Antiquity*, Princeton.

Mitchell, S. (1995) *The New Girl: Girls' Culture in England, 1880–1915*, New York.

Momigliano, A. (1975) *Alien Wisdom: the Limits of Hellenization*, Cambridge.

Montgomery, M. (1923) *Friedrich Hölderlin and the German Neo-Hellenic Movement*, Oxford.

Monti, J. (1997) *The King's Good Servant, but God's First: the life and writing of St Thomas More*, San Fransisco.

Morgan, T. (1998) *Literate Education in the Hellenistic and Roman Worlds*, Cambridge.

Morrison, J. (1994) *Winckelmann and the Notion of Aesthetic Education*, Oxford.

Mosse, G. (1964) *The Crisis of German Ideology. Intellectual Origins of the Third Reich*, Wisconsin.

Mossman, J. ed. (1997) *Plutarch and His Intellectual World*, London.

Moxon, I., Smart, J. and Woodman, T. eds. (1986) *Past Perspectives. Studies in Greek and Roman Historical Writing*, Cambridge.

Mugglestone, L. (1995) *'Talking Proper': The Rise of Accent as Social Symbol*, Oxford.

Muller, J. (1926) *Stephen Gardiner and the Tudor Reaction*, London.

Müller, K. O. (1858) *A History of the Literature of Ancient Greece*, 3 vols., trans. J. W. Donaldson, London.

Murray, G. (1917) *Ancient Greek Literature*, London.

Murray, K. M. E. (1977) *Caught in the Web of Words: James Murray and the Oxford English Dictionary*, New Haven.

Murray, N. (1996) *A Life of Matthew Arnold*, London.

Nagy, G. (1987) 'Herodotus the *Logios*', *Arethusa* 20: 175–84.

(1990) *Greek Mythology and Poetics*, Ithaca.

Naiditch, P. (1996) 'The Slashing Style Which All Know and Few Applaud: the Invective of A. E. Housman', in Jocelyn ed. (1996).

Nauert, C. (1973) 'The Clash of Humanists and Scholastics: an approach to pre-Reformation controversies', *Sixteenth-Century Journal* 4: 1–18.

Naumann, F. (1967) *Hofmannsthal: der jüngste deutsche Klassiker*, Darmstadt.

Nead, L. (1988) *Myths of Sexuality: Representations of Women in Victorian Britain*, Oxford.

Nehamas, A. (1998) *The Art of Living*, Princeton.

Nehring, W. (1991) '*Elektra* und *Ödipus*: Hofmannsthals "Erneuerung der Antike" für das Theater Max Reinhardts', in Renner and Schmid eds. (1991).

Nelson, E. (2001) 'Greek Nonsense in More's Utopia', *The Historical Journal* 44.

Nesselrath, H.-G. (1985) *Lukians Parasitendialog*, Berlin.

Newiger, H.-J. (1969) 'Hofmannsthals *Elektra* und die griechische Tragödie', *Arcadia* 4: 138–63.

Newman, E. (1895) *Gluck and the Opera: a Study in Musical History*, London.

(1962) *Testament of Music*, ed. H. van Thal, London.

Newman, V. (1963) *Ernest Newman: a Memoir by his Wife*, London.

Nicholson, N. ed. (1975) *The Flight of the Mind: the Letters of Virginia Woolf 1888–1912*, London.

Noble, G. B. (1970) *Christian Herter*, New York.

Nochlin, L. and Garb, T. eds. (1995) *The Jew in the Text: Modernity and the Construction of Identity*, London.

Norman, F. ed. (1963) *Hofmannsthal: Studies in Commemoration*, London.

Nussbaum, M. (1994) *The Therapy of Desire*, Princeton.

Nutton, V. (1972) 'Galen and Medical Autobiography', *PCPS* 198: 50–62.

Oakesmith, J. (1902) *The Religion of Plutarch: a Pagan Creed of Apostolic Times*, London.

O'Donell, A. (1981) *Erasmus: Enchiridion Militis Christiani*, Oxford.

Olender, M. (1989) *Les Langues du Paradis: Aryens et Sémites: un couple providentiel*, Paris.

Olin, J. (1979) 'Erasmus and St Jerome', *Thought* 54: 313–21.

Olin, J. ed. (1975) *Christian Humanism and the Reformation*, New York.

Oliver, J. (1953) *The Ruling Power*, Philadelphia.

Oppenheim, J. (1991)   *'Shattered Nerves': Doctors, Patients and Depression in Victorian Britain*, New York.

Paine, T. (1794)   *The Age of Reason.*

Palmer-Sikelianos, E. (1993)   *Upward Panic: the Autobiography of Eva Palmer-Sikelianos*, ed. J. P. Anton, Tampa.

Parker, C. (1867)   'On the History of Classical Education', in Farrar ed. (1867).

Pelling, C. (1986a)   'Plutarch on Roman Politics', in Moxon, Smart and Woodman eds., reprinted in Scardigli ed. (1995).

  (1986b)   'Synkrisis in Plutarch's Lives', in Brenk and Gallo eds. (1986).

  (1989)   'Plutarch: Roman Heroes and Greek Culture', in M. Griffin and J. Barnes eds. *Philosophia Togata*, Oxford.

Pelling, C. ed. (1990)   *Characterization and Individuality in Greek Literature*, Oxford.

Perrin, B. (1901)   *Plutarch's Themistocles and Aristides*, London and New York.

Phillips, M. (1975)   'The mystery of the Metsys portrait', *Erasmus in English* 7: 18–21.

Pick, D. (1989)   *The Faces of Degeneration: A European Disorder 1848–1918*, Cambridge.

Pocock, T. (2000)   *Captain Marryat*, London.

Politzer, H. (1973)   'Hugo von Hofmannsthal's *Elektra*: Geburt der Tragödie aus dem Geiste der Psychopathologie', *DVLG* 47: 95–119.

Poovey. M. (1998)   *A History of the Modern Fact: Problems of Knowledge in the Sciences of Wealth and Society*, Chicago.

Porter, H. (1958)   *Reformation and Reaction in Tudor Cambridge*, Cambridge.

Potter, R. (1976)   *Zwingli*, Cambridge.

Potts, A. (1999)   'Walter Pater's unsettling of the Apollonian ideal', in Wyke and Biddiss eds. (1999).

Pratt, J. C. and Neufeldt, V. (1979)   *George Eliot's 'Middlemarch' Notebooks*, Berkeley.

Pratt, M. L. (1992)   *Imperial Eyes: Travel Writing and Transculturation*, London.

Praz, M. (1970)   *Mnemosyne: the Parallel between Literature and the Visual Arts*, Washington.

Preston, R. (2001)   'Roman Questions, Greek Answers: Plutarch and the Construction of Identity', in Goldhill ed. (2001).

Prins, Y. (1999)   *Victorian Sappho*, Princeton.

Puffett, D. ed. (1989)   *Richard Strauss. Elektra*, Cambridge.

Radford, J. (1998)   'The Woman and the Jew: Sex and Modernity', in Cheyette and Marcus eds. (1998).

Rajak, T. (1999)   'Jews and Greeks: the invention and exploitation of polarities in the nineteenth century', in Wyke and Biddiss eds. (1999).

Raleigh, J. (1961)   *Matthew Arnold and American Culture*, Berkeley.

Raphaely, J. (1999)   'Nothing but Gibberish and Shibboleths?: the Compulsory Greek Debates, 1870–1919', in Stray ed. (1999).

Ratcliff, A. (1928)   *Five Lives from Plutarch*, London.

Rather, L. (1976)   *Lovely Isadora*, London.

Reardon, B. (1971) *Courants littéraires grecs des IIe et IIIe siècles après J.-C.*, Paris.

Redesdale, Lord (1909) '*Die Grundlagen des Neunzehnten Jahrhunderts*: by Houston Stewart Chamberlain. An Appreciation by Lord Redesdale, G.C.V.O., K.C.B.' privately printed, London.

(1921) Introduction to Chamberlain (1921).

Redfield, J. (1985) 'Herodotus the Tourist', *CP* 80: 97–118.

Reinhold, M. (1976) 'Survey of Scholarship on Classical Tradition in Early America', in Eade ed. (1976).

(1984) *Classica Americana: The Greek and Roman Heritage in the United States*, Detroit.

Reith, J. (1924) *Broadcast Over Britain*, London.

Renner, U. and Schmid, G. B. eds. (1991) *Hugo von Hofmannsthal. Freundschaft und Begegnungen mit deutschen Zeitgenossen*, Würzburg.

Rey, W. (1962) *Weltenzweiung und Weltversöhnung in Hofmannsthal's griechischer Dramen*, Philadelphia.

Reynolds, E. (1953) *Saint Thomas More*, London.

Rice, E. (1985) *Saint Jerome in the Renaissance*, Baltimore and London.

Ringer, F. (1969) *The Decline of the German Mandarins: the German Academic Community: 1890–1933*, Cambridge, Mass.

(1979) *Education and Society in Modern Europe*, Bloomington and London.

Ritter, F. (1967) *Hugo von Hofmannsthal und Österreich*, Heidelberg.

Roach, J. (1991) *A History of Secondary Education in England 1870–1902*, London.

Roatcap, A. S. (1991) *Raymond Duncan: Printer . . . Expatriate . . . Eccentric Artist*, San Francisco.

Robertson, R. (1986) '"Ich habe ihm das Beil nicht geben können": the heroine's failure in Hofmannsthal's *Elektra*', *OL* 41: 312–31.

(1998) 'Historicizing Weininger: the nineteenth-century image of the feminized Jew', in Cheyette and Marcus eds. (1998).

(1999) *The 'Jewish Question' and German Literature 1749–1939: Emancipation and its Discontents*, Oxford.

Robinson, C. (1979) *Lucian and his Influence in Europe*, London.

Robinson, M. (1992) 'Acting Women: the Performing Self and the Late Nineteenth Century', *Comparative Criticism* 14: 3–24.

Rogers, E. ed. (1961) *St Thomas More: Selected Letters*, New Haven.

Rohde, E. (1925) *Psyche*, trans. W. Hillis, New York.

Roland, Madame (1989) *The Memoirs of Madame Roland*, trans. and ed. E. Shuckburgh, London.

Romm, J. (1990) 'Wax, Stone and Promethean Clay: Lucian as Plastic Artist', *CA* 9: 74–98.

Rose, P. L. (1990) *Revolutionary Anti-Semitism in Germany from Kant to Wagner*, Princeton.

Rosenberg, A. (1927) *Houston Stewart Chamberlain als Verkünder und Begründer einer deutschen Zukunft*, Munich.

Rosenberg, J. (1985) *Carlyle and the Burden of History*, Oxford.

Rothblatt, S. (1968) *The Revolution of the Dons: Cambridge and Society in Victorian Britain*, Cambridge.

(1976) *Tradition and Change in English Liberal Education: an Essay in History and Culture*, London.

Rousseau, J.-J. (1995) *Confessions* eds. C. Kelly, R. Masters, P. Stillman, Hanover and London [vol. 5 of *Collected Works*].

Rudolph, H. (1971) *Kulturkritik und Konservative Revolution: zum kulturell-politischen Denken Hofmannsthals und seinem problemgeschichtlichen Kontext*, Tübingen.

Rummel, E. (1981) *Erasmus' Annotationes on the New Testament: from Philologist to Theologian*, Toronto.

(1985) *Erasmus as a Translator of the Classics*, Toronto.

(1989) *Erasmus and his Catholic Critics. I. 1515–1522*, Nieuwkoop.

(1992) '"Et cum theologo poeta bella gerit": the conflict between humanists and scholastics revisited', *Sixteenth-Century Journal* 23: 713–26.

(1993) *Scheming Papists and Lutheran Fools*, New York.

Rupp, E. (1949) *Studies in the Making of the English Protestant Tradition*, Cambridge.

Russell, D. (1973) *Plutarch*, London.

Rutherford, R. (1989) *The Meditations of Marcus Aurelius: a Study*, Oxford.

Ryan, L. (1963) *Roger Ascham*, London.

Saïd, S. (1993) 'Le "je" de Lucien', in Baslez, Hoffman and Pernot eds. (1993).

Saladin, J.-C. (2000) *La Bataille du Grec à la Renaissance*, Paris.

Sampson, G. (1921) *English for the English*, London.

Scardigli, B. ed. (1995) *Essays on Plutarch's Lives*, Oxford.

Scattergood, J. ed. (1983) *John Skelton: the Complete English Poems*, Harmondsworth.

Schadewaldt, W. (1999) 'Richard Wagner and the Greeks', trans. D. Durst, *Dialogos* 6: 109–32.

Schama, S. (1995) *Landscape and Memory*, London.

Schlegel, A. W. (1846) *A Course of Lectures on Dramatic Art and Literature*, trans. J. Black, London.

Schmid, W. (1940) *Geschichte der griechische Literatur III*, Munich.

Schorske, K. (1980) *Fin-de-Siècle Vienna: Politics and Culture*, New York.

Schwartz, J. (1965) *Biographie de Lucien de Samosate*, Brussels.

Schwartz, S. (2001a) 'The Rabbi in Aphrodite's Bath: Palestinian Society and Jewish Identity in the High Roman Empire', in Goldhill ed. (2001).

(2001b) *Imperialism and Jewish Society 200 BCE–640 CE*, Princeton.

Schwarz, W. (1955) *Principles and Problems of Biblical Translation: Some Reformation Controversies and their Background*, Cambridge.

Scott, I. (1910) *Controversies over the Imitation of Cicero as a Model for Style and Some Phases of their Influence on the Schools of the Renaissance*, New York.

Screech, M. (1980) *Ecstasy and the Praise of Folly*, London.

Sellar, W. Y. (1967) 'Theories of Classical Education: Lecture Delivered in Opening the Third Humanity Class, Friday November 8th, 1867', Edinburgh.

Sessa, A. (1979) *Richard Wagner and the English*, London.

Seymour, M. (2000)   *Mary Shelley*, London.

Shapin, S. and Schaffer, S. (1985)   *Leviathan and the Air-Pump: Hobbes, Boyle and the Experimental Life*, Princeton.

Shaw, G. B. (1908)   *The Sanity of Art: An Exposure of the Current Nonsense about Artists being Degenerate*, London.

(1911)   Review of Chamberlain 1910, *Fabian News* 22.7: 52–3.

(1960)   *How to Be a Music Critic*, London.

Shelley, Mary Wollstonecraft (1974)   *Frankenstein, or the Modern Prometheus*, ed. James Rieger, Chicago.

Showalter, E. (1985)   *The Female Malady: Women, Madness and English Culture 1830–1980*, New York.

Shuger, D. (1994)   *The Renaissance Bible: Scholarship, Sacrifice and Subjectivity*, New York.

Shuttleworth, S. (1984)   *George Eliot and Nineteenth-Century Science*, Cambridge.

Sidgwick, H. (1867)   'The Theory of Classical Education', in Farrar ed. (1867).

Silk, M. and Stern, P. (1981)   *Nietzsche on Tragedy*, Cambridge.

Skrine, J. (1889)   *A Memory of Edward Thring*, London and New York.

Simon, B. (1974)   *The Two Nations and the Educational Structure 1780–1870*, London.

Simon, J. (1966)   *Education and Society in Tudor England*, Cambridge.

Smith, L. P. (1931)   'Robert Bridges: recollections', *Society for Pure English*, Tract 35, Oxford.

Smith, O. (1984)   *The Politics of Language 1791–1819*, Oxford.

Spencer, H. (1861)   *Education. Intellectual, Moral and Physical*, London and Edinburgh.

Spencer, T. (1954)   *Fair Greece, Sad Relic: Literary Philhellenism from Shakespeare to Byron*.

(1959)   'Byron and the Greek Tradition', *Byron Foundation Lecture*, University of Nottingham.

Spender, H. (1924)   *Byron and Greece*, London.

St Clair, W. (1972)   *That Greece Might Still Be Free*, Oxford.

(1977)   *Trelawny: the Incurable Romancer*, London.

(1996)   *Lord Elgin and the Marbles*, 3rd edn, Oxford.

Stanhope, P. (1932)   *The Letters of Philip Dormer Stanhope, 4th Earl of Chesterfield*, ed. B. Dobrée, 5 vols., London.

Stein, G. (1933)   *The Autobiography of Alice B. Toklas*,

Steiner, D. (forthcoming)   *Images in Mind: Statues in Archaic and Classical Greek Literature and Thought*, Princeton.

Steingruber, E. (1956)   *Hugo von Hofmannsthal's Sophokleische Dramen*, Winterthur.

Steinmetz, D. ed. (1990)   *The Bible in the Sixteenth Century*, Durham.

Stephen, J. K. (1891)   *The Living Languages: A Defence of the Compulsory Study Of Greek at Cambridge*, Cambridge.

Stern, F. (1961)   *The Politics of Cultural Despair: A Study in the Rise of German Ideology*, Berkeley.

Sterner, D. (1999) *Priests of Culture: a Study of Matthew Arnold and Henry Tanner*, New York.

Sterrenberg, L. (1979) 'Mary Shelley's Monster: Politics and Psyche in *Franken-stein*', in Levine and Knoepflmacher eds. (1979).

Steyn, J. (1995) 'Charles Dickens' *Oliver Twist*: Fagin as sign', in Nochlin and Garb eds. (1995).

Stocking, G. (1987) *Victorian Anthropology*, London.

Strauss, R. and Hofmannsthal, H. von (1961) *The Correspondence between Richard Strauss and Hugo von Hofmannsthal*, trans. H. Hammelmann and E. Osers, London.

Stray, C. (1998) *Classics Transformed: Schools, Universities, and Society in England, 1830–1960*, Oxford.

Stray, C. ed. (1998) *Classics in 19th and 20th Century Cambridge: Curriculum, Culture, and Community*, PCPS Supplement 24.

Strohmaier, G. (1976) 'Übersehenes zur Biographie Lukians', *Philologus* 120: 117–22.

Strype, J. (1821) *The Life of the Learned John Cheke Kt*, 2nd edn, Oxford.

Styan, J. L. (1982) *Max Reinhardt*, Cambridge.

Sutcliffe, E. (1948) 'The Council of Trent on the *authentica* of the Vulgate' *Journal of Theological Studies* 49: 35–42.

Svenbro, J. (1976) *La Parole et le marbre*, Lund.

Swain, S. (1988) 'Plutarch's *Philopoimên and Flamininus*', *ICS* 13: 257–74.
  (1990a) 'Cultural Interchange in Plutarch's *Antony*', *QUCC* 34: 151–7.
  (1990b) 'Hellenic Culture and the Roman Heroes of Plutarch', *JHS* 110: 126–45.
  (1996) *Hellenism and Empire: Language, Classicism and Power in The Greek World AD 50–250*, Oxford.

Sylvester, D. (1974) *Robert Lowe on Education*, Cambridge.

Symonds, R. (1986) *Oxford and Empire: the Last Lost Cause?*, Basingstoke and London.

Tatum, J. (1989) *Xenophon's Imperial Fiction*, Princeton.

Thompson, C. (1937) 'Lucian and Lucianism in the English Renaissance: an introductory study', diss., Princeton.
  (1940) *The Translations of Lucian by Erasmus and St Thomas More*, Ithaca.

Thompson, J. and Porter, H. (1963) *Erasmus at Cambridge*, London.

Thompson, Sister J. (1973) *Under Pretext of Praise: Satiric Mode in Erasmus' Fiction*, Toronto.

Thring, E. (1864) *Education and School*, Cambridge and London.

Tilley, H. (1938) 'Greek Studies in England in the Early Sixteenth Century', *English Historical Review* 53: 221–39; 438–56.

Titelmans, F. (1529) *Collationes quinque super epistolam ad Romanos beati Pauli Apostoli . . .*, Antwerp.

Tóibín, C. (2001) 'Love in a Dark Time', *London Review of Books* 23.8: 11.

Too, Y. L. ed. (forthcoming) *Education in Antiquity*, London.

Tottenham, H. (1895) *Cluvenius His Thoughts*, Cambridge.

Tracy, J. (1972) *Erasmus: the Growth of a Mind*, Geneva.
 (1980) '*Against the Barbarians*: the young Erasmus and his Humanist contemporaries', *Sixteenth-Century Journal* 11: 3–32.
 (1996) *Erasmus of the Low Countries*, Berkeley.
Traubel, H. (1906–64) *With Walt Whitman in Camden*, 5 vols., Boston.
Travis, R. (1999) 'From "Shattered Mummies" to "An Epic Life": Casaubon's Key to All Mythologies and Dorothea's Mythic Renewal in George Eliot's *Middlemarch*', *International Journal of the Classical Tradition* 5.3: 367–83.
Tree, V. (1926) *Castles in the Air: the Story of my Singing Career*, London.
Trench, R. (1873) *Plutarch: his Life, his Lives, his Morals*, London.
Trevelyan, H. (1934) *The Popular Background to Goethe's Hellenism*, London.
Trewin, J. (1960) *Benson and the Bensonites*, London.
Trilling, L. (1962) *Matthew Arnold*, Oxford.
Tucker, T. (1903) 'Tucker's *Choephoroi* of Aeschylus: a reply', *Classical Review* 18: 125–8.
Tunberg, T. (1997) 'Ciceronian Latin: Longolius and others', *Humanistica Louvaniensia* 46: 13–61.
Turner, F. (1981) *The Greek Heritage in Victorian Britain*, New Haven.
Urban, B. (1978) *Hofmannsthal, Freud und die Psychoanalyse: Quellenkundliche Untersuchungen*, Frankfurt am Main.
Van Thal, H. ed. (1955) *Fanfare for Ernest Newman*, London.
Van Vechlen, C. (1977) 'Duncan Concerts in New York', in Magriel ed. (1977).
Varcl, L. and Willetts, J. F. eds. (1963) ΓΕΡΑΣ: *Studies Presented to George Thompson on the Occasion of his Sixtieth Birthday*, Prague.
Verrall, A. (1892) *On Editing Aeschylus: A Reply*, London.
Versnel, H. (1990) 'Myth and Ritual', in Edmunds ed. (1990).
Vidal-Naquet, P. (1981) *Le Chasseur noir: formes de pensée et formes de société dans le monde grec*, Paris.
Villey, P. (1908) *Les Sources de l'Evolution des Essais de Montaigne*, 2 vols., Paris.
Vocht, H. de (1934) *Monumenta Humanistica Lovaniensa*, Louvain.
 (1951–5) *History of the Collegium Trilingue Louvaniense*, 5 vols., Louvain.
Voigt, J. H. (1976) *Max Müller: the Man and his Ideas*, Calcutta.
Volkov, S. (1978) 'Anti-Semitism as a Cultural Code: Reflections on the history and historiography of anti-Semitism in Imperial Germany', *Leo Baeck Institute Yearbook* 23: 25–46.
Vout, C. (2000) 'Objects of Desire: Eroticized Political Discourse in Imperial Rome', PhD, Cambridge.
Vrettos, A. (1995) *Somatic Fictions: Imagining Illness in Victorian Culture*, Stanford.
Wagner, R. (1911) *My Life*, London.
 (1912–29) *Richard Wagner's Prose Works*, trans. W. Ashton Ellis, London.
Walcott, F. (1970) *The Origins of Culture and Anarchy*, Toronto.
Walker, G. (1988) *John Skelton and the Politics of the 1520s*, Cambridge.
Wallace, J. (1997) *Shelley and Greece: Rethinking Romantic Hellenism*, London.
Wallace, R. (1850) *Antitrinitarian Biography*, 3 vols., London.
Walter, H. ed. (1850) *William Tyndale: An Answer to Sir Thomas More's Dialogue; the Supper of the Lord; and Wm. Tray's Testament Explained*, Cambridge.

Walton, J. ed. (1987)   *Living Greek Theatre*, New York, Westpoint, London.

Waquet, F. (2000)   *Latin or the Empire of a Sign: from the Sixteenth to the Twentieth Century*, trans. J. Howe, London.

Warner, O. (1953)   *Captain Marryat: a Rediscovery*, London.

Watson, F. (1913)   *Vives: on Education*, Cambridge.

Webb, T. (1993)   'Romantic Hellenism', in Curran ed. (1993).

Webb, T. ed. (1982)   *English Romantic Hellenism 1700–1824*, Manchester.

Webster, J. and Cooper, N. eds. (1996)   *Roman Imperialism: Post-Colonial Perspectives*, Leicester.

Wechssler, E. (1947)   *Hellas im Evangelium*, Hamburg. (1st edn, 1936.)

Wecklein, N. (1893)   Review of Headlam (1891a), *Berliner philologische Wochenschrift* 13.2: 37–8.

Weiner, M. (1995)   *Richard Wagner and the Anti-Semitic Imagination*, Lincoln and London.

Weiss, A. (1977)   *Medieval and Renaissance Greek*, Padua.

Weston, W. (1911?)   *Plutarch's Lives for Boys and Girls*, Edinburgh.

Whitman, W. (1964)   *Prose Works 1892* vol. 1, ed. F. Stoval, New York.

Whitmarsh, T. (2001)   '"Greece is the World": Exile and Identity in the Second Sophisitic', in Goldhill. ed. (2001).

(forthcoming)   *Symboulos: Philosophy, Power and Culture in the Literature of Roman Greece*, Oxford.

Wilamowitz-Moellendorf, U. von (1924)   *Die griechische und lateinische Literatur und Sprache*, 2nd ed., Berlin. (1st edn, 1905).

Wilde, O. (1966)   *The First Collected Edition*, ed. R. Ross, 15 vols. (facs.), London.

Wilhelm, K. (1984)   *Richard Strauss: persönlich*, Munich.

(1989)   *Richard Strauss: an Intimate Portrait*, trans. M. Whittall, London.

Wilkins, C. (1959)   'The English Reputation of Matthew Arnold 1840–1877', PhD Urbana, Illinois.

Wilkinson, L. P. (1980)   *A Century of King's*, Cambridge.

Willinsky, J. (1994)   *Empire of Words: The Reign of the OED*, Princeton.

Wilson, J. D. (1969)   *Milestones on the Dover Road*, London.

Winter, J. (1976)   *Robert Lowe*, Toronto and Buffalo.

Wohlleben, J. (1992)   'Germany 1750–1832', in Dover ed. (1992).

Woolf, G. (1994)   'Becoming Greek, Staying Roman: Culture, Identity, and the Civilizing Process in the Roman East', *PCPS* 40: 116–43.

(1999)   *Becoming Roman: The Origins of Provincial Civilization In Gaul*, Cambridge.

Woolf, V. (1925)   *The Common Reader*, first series, London.

(1950)   *The Captain's Death Bed and Other Essays*, London.

Worbs, M. (1983)   *Nervenkunst: Literatur und Psychoanalyse im Wien der Jahrhundertwende*, Frankfurt am Main.

Wunberg, G. (1972)   *Hofmannsthal im Urteil seiner Kritiker*, Frankfurt.

Wyke, M. and Biddiss, M. eds. (1999)   *The Uses and Abuses of Antiquity*, Bern.

Yates, W. (1992)   *Schnitzler, Hofmannsthal and the Austrian Theater*, New Haven.

Young, R. (1990)   *White Mythologies*, London.

(1995)   *Colonial Desire: Hybridity in Theory, Culture, and Race*, London.

Zweig, S. (1961)   *The World of Yesterday*, trans. C. and E. Paul, New York.

Index

326 *Index*

Trinity College, Cambridge   40, 232–43
Trojans, the   39–40
Tucker, T.   239–40
Tyndale, William   32, 48
type, Greek   29, 44, 51

universiies and Greek   28–30, 193–5, 200–13,
    232–43

Verrall, A. W   8, 111, 194, 232–43
Vives, Juan Luis   45
Volk, das   149–50, 164, 165
Voltaire, François   49
Vulgate   4, 23–4, 24–43

Wagner, R.   94, 95, 98, 99, 115, 160–6, 242,
    291–2, 299
Walker, Edyth   131–3
walking   83–4, 89, 201
Warham, Archbishop William   21
Wechssler, E.   98

Wedgwood, Col.   100
Whitman, W.   115, 230
Wilamowitz, U.   97–8, 194, 284
Wilde, Oscar   118, 120, 166, 172, 213, 230
Wilhelm, Kaiser   94, 193
Winckelmann, Johann   164–5, 192, 225
Wolf, M.   222
Wolsey, Cardinal Thomas   27, 30
women, and Greek study   8, 56, 129,
    220, 234
women and psychology   151–3
Woolf, Greg   75
Woolf, Virginia   234, 249–50
Wordsworth, William   178, 180, 183

Xenocrates   272
Xenophon   68, 86, 288–9

Yiddish   99–100

Zweig, S.   141, 142